THE AUTHORS

FRANCES LOMAS FELDMAN is Associate Professor at the School of Social Work of the University of Southern California. She has also been a caseworker, supervisor, administrator, and researcher, has conducted workshops and institutes throughout the United States, and has served as consultant to numerous social welfare organizations and committees, among them the Governor's Commission on the Los Angeles riots and the Governor's Advisory Committee on Mental Health. Professor Feldman is the author of *The Family in a Money World* and has contributed widely to professional and scholarly books and journals.

FRANCES H. SCHERZ is Director of Casework of the Chicago Jewish Family and Community Service. Mrs. Scherz has directed seminars, workshops, and institutes for, among others, the Child Welfare League of America, Chapters of the National Association of Social Work, and the Family Service Association of America. At present she is also directing graduate seminars at the Smith College School for Social Work and the University of Chicago School of Social Service Administration. A frequent contributor to professional publications, Mrs. Scherz has also edited and contributed to the *Casebook on Family Diagnosis and Treatment* and the recent *Casebook on Families with Adolescents*.

FAMILY SOCIAL WELFARE
Helping Troubled Families

FAMILY SOCIAL WELFARE

Helping Troubled Families

FRANCES LOMAS FELDMAN
and FRANCES H. SCHERZ

ATHERTON PRESS
NEW YORK · 1968

INTRODUCTION

WE ARE ENTERING a new socioeconomic system. Its requirements are as different from those at the inception of the industrial revolution as those of the emerging industrial revolution were different from agrarian life in feudal times. During the age of feudalism human skills were combined with human and animal power in a system that provided a minimal standard of living for the vast majority of the people. In the developing industrial revolution, human skills were combined with machine power to provide great wealth for a few, a reasonable standard of living for a large proportion of the population, and abject poverty for those unable to find a place within the productive system.

The new socioeconomic system is, in large measure, the response to the acceleration of the technology of automation and mechanization—an acceleration paralleling increased legal and social emphasis on the civil rights of millions of citizens whose economic and educational attainments pin their employment opportunities to a rapidly obsolescing socioeconomic order. And like the upwardly mobile householder who, in moving from one dwelling to a better one, suddenly discovers that his old furniture is either too unsteady to withstand the move or too shabby to be placed among the new and modern household appliances and appurtenances marking his growing affluence and social status, socioeconomic crisis in the United States becomes more apparent as the nation stands on the threshold of a changed socioeconomic system.

The manifestations of this crisis are paradoxical: millions of Americans living in poverty and deprivation in the midst of general prosperity enjoyed by the majority of citizens; a relatively high level of unemployment while many jobs go unfilled; social unrest derived from the social and economic disadvantage which is the lot of large segments of population in a democratic nation founded upon principles of liberty, equality, and opportunity.

Perhaps the greatest paradox is this: Although people on the whole are benefiting from technological and scientific progress, they also are increasingly alienated from each other in the human sense because technological advancement reduces the necessity for people to rely on each other for goods, services, and human relationships. Yet the basic need for human relationships continues to exist. Somehow a bridge must be found, a balance must be struck between a mechanized and a human world.

It is the purpose of this volume to describe the place of the family in this world, to identify the family's tasks, its common human needs and problems, and the resources essential to help families meet common and uncommon difficulties.

Because human needs outstrip facilities, programs, and personnel with specific knowledge and skills to provide the help required to meet these needs, this volume also intends to make available, in pragmatic and usable form, knowledge about human behavior and ways of dealing with it that many "helpers" with diverse educational and experiential backgrounds, knowledge, and skills will find useful in the performance of their respective tasks.

The focus in this volume is upon understanding the family, and work with the family (or segments of families), regardless of the institutional or agency setting in which such work is carried on—a focus growing from the fact that "people are people" whether their troubles have come to the attention of a school, a family agency, or a medical clinic.

This focus recognizes the family as the core unit in American society, with each family group and its members maintaining a reciprocal relationship with society that is essential to the well-being not only of the individual *family* but also of the *community* and of the *nation* as a whole. It recognizes that the adequate social functioning of the family members in our modern world requires a family climate conducive to appropriate psychological and physical development of the individual members. And it recognizes that such development is influenced by environmental and cultural factors surrounding and impinging upon family life—that the real world in which family members must function contains stresses with which they need to cope: competition in the labor market, fluctuations in the availability and costs of goods and services, war-related tensions, changing societal attitudes and demands in many forms.

Accordingly, the focus upon understanding the family, the individual and intra-family behavior, and the relationship of such behavior to coping with the continuing and changing socioeconomic conditions or circumstances of today's society, takes into account that not all families are able to cope equally or adequately with the stresses that originate either internally (that is, within the family or within a family member) or in the external world. Also it takes into account the fact that, regardless of the kind of agency or setting in which the family members are encountered, certain understandings must be brought to the work with the family and its members to enable them to gain mastery of their affairs: a mastery satisfactory to themselves and acceptable to the community at large.

The "think" pieces comprising this volume emerge from the experiences, observations, research, and thinking of the authors. Their intent is to provide, in relatively nontechnical fashion, information about human behavior that is "normal" or that, in response to various forms of stress, is deviant. Some guides, or steps, are suggested whereby those in helping positions may move constructively toward the alleviation or resolution of family problems: motivating or encouraging the troubled family (or the family that is untroubled but creating trouble for the community) to work toward the attainment of goals that seem desirable to the family and the surrounding community, and helping the family to use internal and external strengths and resources in achieving sub-goals en route to the major one.

No effort has been made to be comprehensive in the scope of any single chapter or in the scope of the chapters in the aggregate. Rather, selectivity was exercised with the aim of offering useful knowledge that has general as well as specific application in the practice of those in helping capacities.

While information is directed primarily to social workers (designated generically as "he" for the sake of simplicity and not because of discrimination against women), the authors hope it will also be of practical use to persons in any helping position: teachers, ministers, nurses, attorneys, and so on.

The approach employed throughout this book is predicated upon the validity of several principles, among them the following:

Movement toward goals that represent an improved level of socioeconomic functioning cannot be effectively accomplished without the family's (greater or lesser) *awareness* of, and *interest* in, attaining the goals;

Involvement of the individual family members is essential for goal-attainment, and such involvement requires that the client have opportunity to express his own wishes and aspirations, whether or not these have a high degree of reality;

The social worker (or other person in a helping capacity) must be interested in *being* a helping person and be one who, when listening, *hears* what the client is saying;

Even when the weak or soft spots in the client's personality or community situation seemingly overshadow all other considerations, it is through the *strengths*, few or weak as these may seem, possessed by the family or its members, that movement can proceed toward the goals.

The chapters are divided into five parts. Part One is an introductory overview of the family in a changing world. It sketches an idealized image of the American family; it describes certain factors in our society that serve to propel families toward or away from this dominant ideal; and it offers a picture of what the American family really is like as a consequence of the modifying factors. Part One then presents a view of the arrangements developed by our society, in the form of social welfare agencies, to help troubled families to deal with stresses and crises that arise in a changing world. Part Two is addressed to consideration of the life tasks in the cycle of family life: the developmental tasks that are relevant in the stages of marriage, child rearing, and the later years. Because special problems arise with some frequency to affect, in various ways, the conduct of the life tasks in various stages of the family life cycle, Part Three is devoted to a delineation of certain of the more common ones; namely, families broken by death, divorce, desertion, or the failure of the mother to marry; placement tasks involving children or adults; and physical or mental illness.

Part Four focuses on requisites for social functioning, identifying the essential ingredients and discussing in more detail the meaning and management of trust, self-esteem, identity, and communication. The application of knowledge about these requisites to the helping of troubled families is incorporated in Part Five. While previous chapters presented the helping role of the social worker, Part Five considers the social worker's helping tasks in a more intensive fashion. Particular attention is given to application and intake as a helping process, to continuing work with families, to money counseling in work with families, and to the use of social resources in work with families.

The case material used throughout the book, in brief form, for illustrative purposes, is drawn from various social welfare agencies. In general, the cases were chosen because each has applicability to the work of different kinds of social agencies. Selected reading suggestions have been compiled with respect to each section for the reader interested in enlarging his knowledge about human behavior, our society, and the giving of help to troubled families and individuals. These reading suggestions include not only relevant nonfiction, but also fiction—old and new—that offers valuable insights into certain behaviors and circumstances of troubled individuals and families.

Finally, readily evident to the perceptive reader may be the authors' optimistic convictions about the worth of humans and about the value of helping those in trouble—convictions reflected in an old Yugoslav proverb: "People are made for happiness as birds are made for flying."

CONTENTS

PART ONE

The Family in a Changing World

THE IDEALIZED FAMILY

A FAMILY *is a unit composed not only of children, but of men, women, an occasional animal, and a common cold.* This Ogden Nash definition conjures up an idealized image of the American family. It is an image repeatedly reflected in motion picture and television portrayals of family life; it is an image which, with the exception of the gratuitous common cold, is perceived as the inspirational and aspirational standard for many segments of American society. It depicts a comfortably middle-class family, its likeness reasonably within the reach of most families who are part of a democratic nation.

In the idealized model the father, whether proprietor of his own business or employee—the executive or sub-executive or (at the very least) supervisory level—in someone else's business, supports his family by means of work for which he is equipped by education, experience, and temperament. His work holds seemingly endless opportunities for advancement in status and income; and it is employment which he chooses, motivated by qualities of industry, enterprise, and self-fulfillment, and by acceptance of his role as family provider and protector.

The mother fulfills her maternal role and her role as marital partner with wisdom and equanimity: she operates her household smoothly and efficiently; she chauffeurs moderately well-behaved children to orthodontists, Scout meetings, dancing and piano lessons; she shares with composure and encouragement the large and small problems confronting husband or children or household; and she carries out with aplomb her responsibilities to the community as an active participant in PTA, church and welfare functions, civic affairs, and so on.

Whether this model family occupies a suburban single dwelling —for which mortgage payments are made painlessly and promptly— or lives either in an urban apartment building with central heating and automatic elevators or in a modest family neighborhood in the heart of the city, the home contains relatively modern conveniences and, above all, arrangements for the privacy to which any family member might wish to have access. The family possesses at least one car of recent vintage; the younger children have skates and bicycles, the older ones probably have some kind of "jalopy." When confronted with an occasional crisis, this family draws on resources— savings or some form of insurance or other negotiable asset—planfully accumulated to protect the family members against a range of possible emergencies. Or it turns for help to willingly cooperative relatives possessing similar familial characteristics. Under *all* circumstances the members of the idealized family are industrious, ambitious, thrifty, socially and emotionally well adjusted in their inter- and intra-personal relationships—and happy and independent.

Some of the details in the picture evoked by the Nash definition may be altered by highly personalized and cultural experiences, wishes, values, and expectations: to her other roles the mother may add that of being a member of the professional or other vocational sector of the labor force, contentedly performing employment tasks from which she derives a sense of fulfillment and contribution to society while concurrently and effectively meeting the needs and demands of family and household. To his other responsibilities the father may add serious participation in civic affairs; or—even *and*— he may be a Little League or Indian Guide father, devoting a substantial portion of his "free" time to these and other parenting tasks.

Some families may place special emphasis on the educational achievement of their members. Others may stress early financial independence above continued education. Some households may continuously or periodically include a grandparent or other relative (ideally as *guests* who have independent means). In other situations there may be grandparents who are financially, emotionally, and geographically independent of the family, but whose warmth and wisdom are readily accessible in time of family need or for celebration of holidays, birthdays, and other special events that lend themselves to a little "spoiling" of children without their actually being "spoiled." But the matrix of the idealized family generally comprises a married couple with children—a family unit socially and economically productive, its members emotionally secure within themselves and with each other.

SOCIETY'S EXPECTATIONS

This idealized image of the American family is the receptacle in which are stored essential values prevalent in our democratic, affluent, industrialized society. We value the qualities of loving and working that are expressed in the paternal role of family provider and protector, in the maternal role that assures continuity of relationships, and in the attachment of father and mother to each other and to their children. It is in the climate created around these qualities that the family is held together as a group in which the children progress from their early dependencies to mature adults who themselves will fulfill the idealized paternal or maternal roles.

In the United States, we value the qualities expressed in independence and self-reliance, in ambition for increasingly higher levels of family living (more education, good jobs, utilization of economic goods and services, good health), and in resourcefulness that translates these ambitions into achievements.

We recognize clearly defined societal barriers and expectations with regard to family life; we confidently believe that the majority of families in fact *do* fulfill these expectations. Accordingly, we ascribe various functions to the family: meeting of survival needs—food, shelter, and clothing; providing for the care, protection, education, and rearing of children; creating a physical, emotional, social, and economic setting that nurtures the development of the individual members within the family, provides for an affectional bond among them, and helps each member to become a contributing member of

the family as well as of the wider community. It also is to the family
that we turn for social control of the individual's behavior—a task
which the idealized family unquestioningly performs.

THE FAMILY'S EXPECTATIONS

This idealized family, in turn, holds some fairly clearly
defined expectations of society. It expects to be able to avail itself
of opportunities to educate its children. It expects police and fire
protection and other community services—libraries, public parks,
public health protection against the spread of communicable diseases, emergency hospital or other medical services, etc. It expects
the market economy to make available opportunities for jobs and job
advancement as well as goods and services designed to enhance the
conditions and comforts of daily life. It expects to be able to participate in the election to public office of persons whose political
opinions and integrity the family respects, and to have a voice in the
direction and content of local, state, and national government. And
it expects that needed community arrangements will be established
to aid the family to carry on its assigned and inherent tasks and
obligations as a family unit.

IMAGERY OR REALITY?

But in actuality, how prevalent is the pattern of this traditional ideal of the American family? What in our society reinforces
this pattern? At what point does imagery give way to reality? Or
congruence cease between the characteristics imputed to the idealized
family and the qualities typical of the family in the community at
large?

Does the idealized image reflect the goal legislators envision when
they enact laws that specify objectives "to strengthen family life"?
When ministers, publishers of newspapers and periodicals, citizens
in general demand that schools, legislators, social agencies, police,
and others "*do* something," is it because they measure shortcomings
among the poor, the actual or potential juvenile or adult delinquent,
the "disturbing" elements, and others, against a standard inherent
in this image?

And when social workers define as their objectives in working with troubled families the protection and strengthening of family life and the enhancement of the social functioning of various family members, what criteria for adequate functioning do they derive from this image?

The dominant ideal of the American family differs conspicuously from the facts. There is no single "good" model. In the American population there are many patterns of family life and composition. The "goodness" of the respective models, though less than ideal, may be unrelated to the wide variations in family composition. There are many families with only one parent in the home; one or both parents have remarried and children live intermittently with one set of parents, then the other; children often live with relatives other than their own parents; several generations live in some households. There are, furthermore, differences in ethnic origin and social class—differences that have a decided impact on the roles and relationships of the parents and children, and affect the quality and content of family life. There are major disparities in economic, social, and psychological functioning—disparities shaped by societal attitudes and environmental conditions, singly or in combination with each other and with individual physical or psychological ingredients.

These variations not only deviate in substantial ways from the idealized image of the American family; they do not blend into an "average" family. Nevertheless, they frequently are consistent with what is "normal" and, therefore, do contribute to a broader standard than that represented by the single conception that a proper family is middle-class, its contentedly and continuously married parents providing their several children with comforts and a reasonable degree of luxuries and "advantages" consistent with their favorable social status and economic standing in a stable, well-established community.

The idealized version of the American family, then, is more representative of the strivings than of the prevailing pattern. Many families have only the vaguest of notions as to how to move closer to the achievement of the idealized model. Indeed, many families, particularly in the lower echelons of our society, do not know what it is they are striving toward—if striving they are. Increasingly, however, altered modes of communication, television for example, have been bringing the idealized version closer to people even in the most remote geographic and social situations in our nation. People with severely limited kinds of resources are becoming more and more aware of what is portrayed via television as the resources and opportunities and experiences of the so-called model version of the American family. They may see only the materialistic comforts that appear to be the measure of achievement of middle-class life, but the portrayal of these kinds of achievements stimulates a desire on the part of poorer families for the same kinds of material possessions. And it is because of such yearning among troubled and poorer families that we are able to reach families in order to help them acquire a higher level of social competence.

THE HELPING GOALS

In a real and changing world, families who are troubled —or who trouble the community—can truly be helped only if the goals for improvement of their social, economic, and psychological competence are *realistically* rather than *idealistically* conceived as acceptable both to the family and to the wider community. The setting of intermediate and of long-range goals requires that those in helping capacities be alert to the many "normal" variations on the theme of the idealized image of the American family and on the different aspects of the idealized pattern that various families in our society are motivated to emulate. This awareness, in turn, places upon those in helping capacities the responsibility for taking cognizance of factors that fashion the variations and that impel families and individuals toward or away from the dominant ideal. With such cognizance to arm him, the counselor—be he social worker, teacher, minister, or representative of another helping profession—is better able to assess the impact and interaction of external and personal elements that may interfere with the family's attainment of a reasonably comfortable level of functioning. He is also better prepared to mobilize these elements in assisting the family members to reach a less troubled state. In accordance with this assessment he can aid the family—perhaps, if indicated, by enlisting the help of the community—to move closer to the dominant ideal.

It is the aim of the following chapters to paint the backdrop against which the assessment of family problems and the implementation of plans for their mitigation or resolution can be conducted. They acknowledge the wide array of variations that exists among American families with respect to their composition and the way they fulfill the major functions attributed to them in our modern Western society. They recognize some of the societal attitudes and environmental conditions that make it possible for some families to move closer to the idealized model, yet contribute to the problems of others to the extent that they are either impeded or prevented from also emulating the model—or are not at all motivated to match it. And then they call attention to the arrangements our society has created for the purpose of aiding troubled families to deal with problems that confront them. These community social welfare arrangements provide the setting in which the social worker carries out his helping role either directly with the family or in conjunction with some other social institution such as the school or church. It is under the auspices and with the support of these community social welfare arrangements, public and voluntary, that the social worker endeavors to help the family master the problems that contribute to its discomfort or dysfunctioning or unhappiness and impede their attaining a closer approximation of the appropriate and desirable aspects of the idealized family image.

2

THE MODIFIERS

She walked inside, ran her hands across the new stove, inspected the sink with faucets, bounded up and down a couple of times on one of the four beds in the spacious 21 x 17-foot room, and sat in the one straight-backed chair next to the only other piece of furniture, a small table.

"First time I've ever been inside a new house, leastwise ever stayed in one myself," said the young woman. "It'er be the fanciest place I've ever stayed in."

Los Angeles Times, March 3, 1966

THE SIGLEY FAMILY featured in this news article—a twenty-four-year-old itinerant farm worker, his pregnant twenty-one-year-old wife, and their two children under four years of age—in most respects is not typical of American families. In a number of ways, however, they do represent a sizable segment of this nation's families. Except for the "occasional animal" the Sigleys fit the Nash definition (even to the "common cold"), as well as the more general dictionary definitions, of a family as "the group of parents and their children." This young father *expects* to support his family by his labor, and has sought to do so by following the crops, as he has done since leaving school in the eighth grade. His vocational mobility has been facilitated by his ownership of a car which, though dilapidated, has served as a means of transportation as well as a shelter for his family. His earning power has been limited by lack of education and by his attachment to a form of work that, in our economy, is characterized by low and seasonal wage levels and by work opportunities steadily lessening by encroaching technological advances. But his motivation to be "independent" and to provide for his family through "steady work" is high. His motivation to emulate the dominant ideal of the American family also is high.

"All my life I've worked hard and steady and earned a good living," Don Anderson bitterly told the employment interviewer. "I've been deacon in the church; I've been payin' off my mortgage regularly. I made my children finish high school, which I couldn't do, having to get out and hustle for a living; my neighbors had respect for me, and so did my kids. How do I explain to my family and to my neighbors that I *want* to work, that I *need* to work, that I'm young and strong enough to do almost anything, but I can't find a fellow to take me on?"

Here, too, is recognition of the role assigned by a society that places high premium on independence evidenced in the fact of work and in the management of one's financial affairs. But here too is a sense of helplessness in mastering environmental elements that interfere with Mr. Anderson's fulfillment of this role. For at the age of forty-seven, Mr. Anderson is in his second year of unemployment following twenty-four years during which he progressed from common laborer to steel puddler, only to be "retired": the steel mill no longer needed his skills, and the judgments that he was too old and lacked a basic education precluded occupational retraining. A few years earlier, Mr. Anderson and his family of four children had resembled closely the idealized image of the American family; now they are alike only to the extent that the Andersons are a nuclear family.

The Andersons' and the Sigleys' modes of living differ, but their attitudes and their aspirations have much in common. Moreover, both have been caught up in the whirlwind of change. This whirlwind has revolutionized our economy: it has influenced family life; it has exposed to bolder focus the consequences of stress and dysfunction with respect to family life; and it has revealed both the positive and the negative impact on American families of the benefits brought by the changes. It has, for example, made available goods and services not even dreamed of a decade ago, and has put many of these within the reach of most families—for the Sigleys, improved housing; for the Andersons, home ownership and education. At the same time, it has altered the job market in terms of both kinds of work available and kinds of preparation required to secure this work.

The family today is affected by a wide range of external factors which intimately affect the family's social functioning in so many ways that it is not always easy to distinguish the external from the personal or intra-familial factors. Some of these external factors reflect changing conditions in the nation and in the world: technological innovation, increases in population size and mobility, rapid industrialization and urbanization, recessions, inflation, wars, and so on. Other external factors are rooted in tradition and culture, societal values and attitudes that are carriers of expectations about individual and family behavior. And not infrequently, today's family is buffeted by the conflict and inconsistencies that swirl between those attitudes and expectations that are traditional and those that are evolving from current circumstances.

The problem verbalized by Mr. Anderson has given rise to a paradox in our contemporary society: traditional attitudes and values define the acceptability of individual and family behavior with regard to work, thrift, independence. At the same time, the fundamental and radical changes taking place in Western society over the last two or three centuries have created some conditions inconsistent with these attitudes, producing some new attitudes and values that are the concomitants of the aforementioned expanding technology, industrialization, and urbanization.

Traditional societal attitudes have combined with a contemporary standard of living to form the idealized image of the American family. Measures of a family's adequacy in the fulfillment of its prescribed functions are rooted in traditional societal attitudes about work, self-reliance, and morality. The criteria of adequacy, however, are not always applied against or consistent with the backdrop of environmental factors that are important modifiers of family and community life—factors that affect differently individual families with their disparate intellectual and emotional capacities. Nor do the criteria generally tend to acknowledge variations related to ethnic or nationality influences. Yet all of these—societal attitudes, environmental factors, cultural and personal endowments—have a marked impact on the manner in which families deal with the tasks that confront them in each stage of the cycle of family life. Awareness of the nature and force of this impact, with its potential for improving or retarding the quality of a troubled family's functioning, adds a vital dimension to the understanding necessary for helping troubled families in a dynamic society.

SOCIETAL ATTITUDES

The Puritan ethic has made work the cornerstone of virtue and leisure fraught with anxiety. It has made thrift a pillar of lofty character and independence the foundation of worthiness. These values, along with a rigid sexual code, have continued to influence modern social and economic life. A political tradition has developed concurrently, rooted in Yankee Protestant middle-class life, expressing a common feeling that government should in some ways control the lives of individuals. These two concepts—government's role in morality, and the impact of economic life on individual character—emerged largely from rural America, predating industrialization and urbanization of the country.

The rise of industry, however, brought some contrast—indeed, a conflict. The mass migration of peasants, chiefly from the southern and eastern parts of Europe, injected a different kind of tradition. They were unfamiliar with independent political action; they were familiar with compliance with authority. They had urgent needs growing out of their migration, and they took for granted that the political life of the individual would arise out of family needs; that personal obligations and personal loyalties would be placed above allegiance to abstract codes of laws or morals; that political action and the laws themselves would be bent to personal and family needs. The champions of these needs emerged in the persons of political bosses whose power derived in large measure from the personalized relationships they maintained with their constituents.

The two systems of values—that of highly moral leaders of social reform on the one hand and the political machine and bosses on the other—have merged in American tradition. Social justice as a matter of morality is protected in the law, which also places restrictions on the limiting of individual opportunity. With the advance of industrialization, laws could result from movements against monopolies and special political and economic privileges (first against those of "big business," then against those of "big unions"). With the onset of devastating national economic upheaval, laws could be enacted to insure a greater degree of general economic stability as well as to deal with specific needs of individuals. With the increased social awareness stimulated by air travel, television, and other technological advances facilitating visual and aural communication, laws once advocating protection against social distinctions could be broadened to prohibit abridgement of individual civil rights. With an elevated national standard of living, laws could move against particularly troubling social conditions which denied opportunities to specific segments of the general population identified as "the poor."

The separate threads of the two value systems are discernible today. It also is evident that there is continuing conflict between the two systems, with important social consequences. A dramatic example was the Volstead Act's moral public policy position about alcohol consumption and the far-reaching impact of this legislation on the nation. The persistence of the conflict to the current moment is evident in the 1966 decision of the Iowa Supreme Court denying Harold Painter the custody of the son he had left in the temporary care of the child's maternal grandparents the previous year, when the boy's mother and sister died in an automobile accident. The court held that seven-year-old Mark would be better off in the "stable, dependable, conventional, middle-class midwestern (grandparents') home" than with his "exciting and challenging but romantic, impractical and unstable" father, who had remarried and sought the return of his son. The court had not declared Mr. Painter to be an unfit father. Rather, it appeared to look askance at the nature of his work (writing for an acknowledged conservative newspaper: "arty!" and his subsequent job as a commercial photographer: "bohemian"), his reading ("intellectually stimulating"), and his $9,000 income in the preceding year ("negligible," although it was above the national median family income).

The Court's statements pinpoint some of the societal issues that are our heritage from the different philosophic and cultural contributions to the American social system: conformity versus individualism; an *assured* income from a respectable and steady nine-to-five type of work versus *adequate* income from work performed on some other time basis; equating deviance from a rigid standardized breadwinning role with weak moral fiber, personal inadequacy, and social incompetence. Furthermore, the Court's statements illustrate that within the over-all pattern of the prevailing American culture there are infinite variations in the way certain values in the social structure are shared and perceived. A unique system of beliefs, attitudes, values, and customs with regard to social roles, the importance of work, material possessions, health, formal or informal education, and other determinants of behavior has grown up in each of the subgroups in our social system: class, occupational, professional, religious, regional, urban, rural, ethnic, and others.

Nonetheless, despite differences in origin and traditions as well as of philosophic and social contributions to our current society by immigrants who have become part of this nation's population during the last several centuries, and despite the means they may utilize to express variation, certain prevailing values generally have been accorded high importance both by majority and minority groups. Concomitants of these similar values have been criteria, also fairly similar, for assessing adequacy of individual performance, or achievement, or of individual morality. These values are implicitly and explicitly summarized in the Iowa Court decision: adequacy and morality are two sides of a single coin, its worth assayable in these terms: *work*—as evidence of independence and reliability; *thrift*—as evidence of good management and self-discipline, particularly with regard to money and resources; physical and emotional *health and stability*—as reflective of strength of character, and competence in coping with the stresses and vicissitudes in life. The decision appears to make no allowance for variants that derive from cultural attitudes, personal endowment and development, and environmental factors that may affect individual capacities, opportunities, and values in fulfilling of life tasks in accordance with the expectations of the broader society; nor does it appear to take into account whether these variants enrich or only draw from the wider community.

Measures of Adequacy

An individual's (and often, therefore, his family's) adequacy in functioning in accordance with the expectations of society are measured by many socially-developed criteria in addition to those contained in the above judgment. The most common, however, probably because they are the most readily identifiable by their presence or absence, are work, thrift, and health—in that order. They have a major impact on the quality of a family's functioning; consequently, their particular meaning to society and the family needs to be understood if the troubled family in our changing society is to be helped effectively. Only two of society's measures of personal adequacy will be discussed here: work and thrift.

Work in some form and to some degree has been essential to man's survival from his earliest beginnings, and this has been no less true since the arrival of the first settlers on this continent. Thus, the sheer necessity to insure the group's survival required that every colonist among the early Pilgrims invest what efforts and energies he could muster in productive activity; undoubtedly this necessity was instrumental in reinforcing the existing Calvinistic orientation to the morality of hard work. Certainly, it is not uncommon today to speak in almost a single breath of the work ethic and the Puritan ethic. Yet later European immigrants likewise were dedicated to the idea of work. They may have perceived it less as a requirement for demonstration of strength of character than as a means, first, for meeting survival needs and, then, as a bridge to the well-publicized gold-paved streets. And immigrants from other parts of the world—Orientals, for example, who long had been accustomed to equating grueling work with survival—continued to accept work as the way of life.

While there may have been differences within various waves of immigrants in the motivational underpinnings for work—survival, religious conviction, philosophical attitudes, or combinations of these and others—the work ethic has become deeply ingrained in our American culture. The concept implies that work is an essential component of strength of character, that such strength and independence are synonymous, that an individual's independence and capacity for self-maintenance are demonstrated through work, and that independence is reflected by the twin facts of employment and self-support and, therefore, symbolizes social competence and morality.

The continued high value placed on work in today's society is manifest in a variety of ways. The common accolade that a person is "worth his salt" attests to the prevalent regard for the one who earns his way, especially if he "pulled himself up by the bootstraps." This idea of being worth one's salt is not related to the valuable and indispensable one per cent suspended in human plasma. It stems from ancient forms of payment for service in salt because other money forms were scarce. In antiquity, salt possessed a religious symbolism closely analogous to that of the early coin metals and was believed to possess magical qualities. We have long tended to forget the original import of being worth one's salt, but we have retained a certain respect for work that yields payment—in a more modern money form that today is also viewed by many as having magical qualities.

The still-common expression "poor but honest" likewise encompasses value judgments about the place of work in American life. Less than a century ago it still was the popular view that poverty was the natural punishment for idleness; wealth and prosperity were the natural reward for industry and intelligence. To be considered both poor *and* honest emphasized the probability that only the singular individual was impoverished because of forces beyond his control rather than because he made little or no effort to work and to maintain himself and his dependents by "honest labor."

Periods of severe economic depression, particularly that of the 1930's, contributed to some modification of the attitude that poverty is the consequence of indifference to honest labor: far too many people who had always labored hard and prudently saved for their advancing years were unable to find work and, at the same time, suddenly deprived of their carefully accumulated financial reserves. Nevertheless, at the end of 1964, the American Institute of Public Opinion reported a poll disclosing that 30 per cent of those surveyed considered the major cause of poverty to be "lack of individual effort"; 34 per cent blamed "circumstances beyond the individual's control"; and another 30 per cent attributed poverty both to lack of individual effort and to circumstances beyond the individual's control. When the first and third groups are viewed together, it is eminently clear that a substantial portion of today's American society seems to retain the Puritan attitude of a reciprocal relationship among poverty, failure to work, and worthlessness.

Over the years the ancient and deeply entrenched respect in our society for work *per se* and for the products that testify to the success of that work has come to hold special import in each stage of the cycle of family life and, in one form or another,[1] to play a vital part in preparation for, and effectiveness in, the carrying out of life tasks.

Boys, by and large, grow up with the expectation that they will become the earners, that on their shoulders will rest the responsibility for their own support and for that of their dependents. In the American culture, the parents are expected to instill in their children, particularly boys, the expectation that they will make vocational choices that in later years will enable them to fulfill these tasks of support and self-support. The importance of education is perceived less as an opportunity for broadening intellectual, emotional, and personal horizons than as a passport into an adult world wherein remunerative employment generally symbolizes maturity, responsibility, independence, and those other qualities reflective of competence in the fulfillment of adult—especially male—roles.

High commendation, on the other hand, is directed toward the boy who works while completing his education, whether or not work resulted from financial necessity—and especially if it did *not*. But the ambitious, persistent, generally self-disciplined boy or girl who overcomes the odds of poverty, environment, or early responsibility for the care of other family members to procure the education essential for productive and financially successful work, is additionally admired for his—or her—strength of character.

A first pay check in a permanent and full-time job is a merit badge of achievement by the young man or woman: successful entrance into an adult world. Even the person whose schooling or vocational training was possible only because of his concurrent earnings generally is not inclined to feel that those wages have afforded him the self-supporting independent status now irrefutably evidenced by the full-time and steady employment central to self-maintenance.

For the man, throughout his life, special meaning is attached

---

[1] For learning as work, see Chapters 14 and 16.

in our American culture to the fact that he works and earns. It influences his role as husband and father: whether or not his wife is employed, the community—and often his wife and children as well—perceives the fulfillment of his masculine role in terms of the effectiveness with which he functions as earner and provider; the degree of his success in this capacity bears directly both on how others actually perceive him and on how he perceives and respects himself.

Shifts in the general national economic situation and in the employment market may diminish or terminate his chances for continuing in the work force regardless of the amount of his education, the kinds and quality of his skills, the intensity of his motivation to work, the basic or peripheral nature of his needs and aspirations, or his investment of effort and ingenuity in remaining productively attached to the world of work. He and those who observe his efforts may readily recognize the presence of circumstances that are beyond his control. Yet, as in the case of Mr. Anderson and many others, rational explanations do not entirely dispel the sense of failure and diminished self-esteem that are the products of societal attitudes that equate work and adequacy.

The man approaching the retirement period is affected in special ways by community attitudes about work.[2] He may be well prepared financially for this stage of the family life cycle; he may acknowledge the expressed envy of his friends and associates that his "new life" requires "no clock punching" or "clock watching." He may recognize the reality of his diminishing physical energies, or that legal or other compelling requirements governing his work remain inexorable. Nevertheless, the actuality of retirement may serve to lessen his conviction that he is an adequate member of society because he no longer is "earning his own way," and his growing doubts about himself are reinforced as he notes the reduced interest of the younger generation in his opinions on matters of their common interests.

The traditional societal attitudes that connect work with mature independence and self-reliance, that view the attainment of individual comfortable levels of living as a result primarily of individual work efforts, that consider the enjoyment of free time as possible only if it is a "reward" for work continue to be dominant in spite of certain countervailing trends emerging from our steady industrialization, mechanization, and automation. For men like Mr. Anderson— or others whose "retirement" is not connected to their vocational

[2] For elaboration of impact on personality in the later years, see Chapter 8.

preparation or marketable skills—their sense of well-being is assaulted by both their failure to work and their failure to prove their continued industry and productivity through being able to display material results of their efforts. In fact, even though the retirement age is set considerably lower, our public policy encourages the continuation of work by rewarding with full "Social Security" retirement benefits those who are still employed after they reach seventy-two years of age.

Women in recent years have begun to feel the force not only of societal attitudes about work but also of the divergent views about women in gainful employment. While the adult life of the male in our society in large measure is anchored to a vocational choice through which he will maintain himself and his dependents, it has not always been expected that girls too will make vocational choices. However, as longevity is extended, as conditions in the home free them to undertake activities outside the family, as standards of living move upward and the levels of living for individual families also rise, girls increasingly have also been expected to make vocational choices. If they do not, they generally are not censured, for girls, after all, have their "work cut out for them": they are expected eventually to assume the roles of wife, homemaker, and mother. Nor is the unmarried or older woman of independent means criticized if she prefers to use her time in community affairs rather than in paid employment; after all, she thus is productively engaged. However, the unmarried, unemployed woman is less and less invulnerable to criticism if no compelling family circumstances like illness of a family member or supervision of siblings require her presence regularly in the home, and if the family's economic position is not strong enough to permit her to choose volunteer over salaried work.

On the other hand, even though they constitute a substantial proportion of the labor force, employed wives with children yet in the home continue to be the object of considerable community criticism and to be subject to much guilt-provoked anxiety. But if the mother, as head of her family, elects to maintain her household fully or partially through paid employment, she is accorded a high degree of respect. She may fulfill her homemaking as well as her employment roles superbly; she may perform either or both faultily. Nevertheless, her manifest striving for independence through work, and her modeling of a pattern that implies to her children that work is more desirable than other means that might be utilized for meeting the family's basic physical needs, assure her recognition and esteem as an adequate and enterprising parent.

The employment of mothers whose children are still in the home is not a new phenomenon. For centuries many have added work tasks to their household activities in order to have "pin money" or increase the family's income of money or goods. Prior to the last several decades, however, unless the family was *very* poor, the mother's employment was not viewed by the broader community as essential. Indeed, public policy was against it for the "poor widow" and evidenced this by enacting the early Mothers' Pension programs, sporadic as they were.

Nevertheless, from time to time, as special economic or war conditions developed, the emphasis that woman's place (at least *some* women's places) was in the home underwent modification. Thus, in the eighteenth century, Alexander Hamilton could issue a policy statement that women and children were an untapped source of labor in our growing nation and simultaneously encourage their entrance into a labor market in need of their services and open a way for some families to sustain themselves. During the first and second world wars it was deemed the patriotic duty of women to work in essential industry; their guilt rose if they did not "do their bit," and, if they *did* work, was kept elevated by their ingrained acceptance of the societal attitude that women should be at home to care for their families.

Other circumstances also have had an effect on the attitudes of and toward working mothers, and these have had particular import for social welfare. In one way, the relationship of women and the work ethic had a marked bearing on child-care developments following the Civil War. The influx of immigrants from various parts of Europe at that time included many whose earning power was sharply limited by the industrial society in which they found themselves; in order to maintain the family, it often was necessary for the mother as well as the father to obtain work. The fact that the women worked, however, was viewed as acceptable because it was certainly better that they earn than starve. But it also was "well known" that these foreign people were "inferior"—this was apparent from their "different" behavior and language—and it could therefore be assumed that they were inferior parents, whose children might be better off if the mother's work took her out of the home and the community took steps to provide for the care of the child during the day. It might be speculated that this arrangement offered an opportunity to "brainwash" children while their "inferior" mothers worked. Certainly, there is little doubt that this attitude toward immigrant mothers contributed to the inspiration of Charles Loring Brace to send children to foster homes in the West where they would be better off in the homes of hard-working strangers than in the urban slums where the ways of people were "different." (In some respects, Brace's attitude resembled the Iowa court's 1966 decision that Mark Painter remain in the home of his "middle-class midwestern" grandparents.)

The vacillating societal attitudes about women working have significance not only for voluntary family and children's agencies and a range of private and public child-care services; they have special relevance for public assistance programs that today are geared to financially aiding women with children for many reasons in addition to widowhood. There have been, for example, periodic shifts in policies reflecting community attitudes and questions as to whether mothers should or should not be required to work instead of receiving aid, whether they should be required to remain in the home and supervise their children—either because children *should* have their mothers with them, or because otherwise the children might engage in delinquent behavior. Recipients of public assistance —men as well as women—are recipients also of society's uncertainty and uneasiness about the inviolability of the work ethic in a time when the economic climate offers new opportunities, restricts or eliminates others, and requires some new responses in the family's fulfillment of its intertwined economic and socialization functions.

Clarity with regard to the pragmatic advisability of encouraging dependent mothers to work is obscured by the question of motives that may underscore the policy decision: Is the purpose of urging mothers to work chiefly to save public money? Is work seen, instead, as a device for building self-esteem in the mother? In the children? But the question of whether mothers should or should not be encouraged to prepare for, and seek to obtain, employment now also has to be evaluated against other societal responses to the employment of women, the circumstances under which it is condoned, the circumstances under which it is deplored.

For today, the sheer numbers in the labor force of married women with children, as well as women heads of families, place in sharp perspective the changing attitudes about the employment of women. Moreover, while a substantial proportion of those who work do so because of financial reasons—either to meet basic economic needs or to provide the family with more of the goods and services (including education) available in the American economy, many work for other reasons and, thereby, add a dimension to the quality of feeling about women in employment outside the home. They may take employment, full or part time on a regular or occasional basis, when their time is no longer completely absorbed by tasks of family and household management. Many services are now performed outside (laundry, cleaning, etc.), modern household appliances and conveniences (including convenience foods) release time and energy for other activities, the availability of school facilities that begin with the nursery years require less constant supervision of children. Such release of time may be a factor in mothers going to work. The work ethic holds that people in our society should be "busy"; if household management does not keep them so, a paid job will.

They may be gainfully (but not always financially profitably) employed because of the opportunity for self-fulfillment or to make a contribution that is acknowledged by a profession or the community or the general economy as meaningful and important enough to be compensated by wages. And the lamentable shortage at any given time of womanpower in nursing, teaching, medicine, social work, and other fields, provides incentive to many women to work, to feel they are filling a need that society recognizes as important.

A growing number of married women work today for other reasons as well, such as escape from a difficult situation at home. Marital discord, low tolerance for daily day-long demands of children, controlling behavior of an extended family member living in the household, or the desirability of channeling depression or other troubling feelings into constructive activity not possible in the home —these and other circumstances, familial and personal, can often be handled with greater equanimity by the mother who gains some release from these pressures while in a work situation. She not infrequently is able, then, to return to the home to confront the troubling situations without too devastating effects on herself or those around her, knowing she will have further release the following day. This kind of reason for working often is of tremendous value in keeping the family equilibrium on a positive level, and in its contribution to the mental health of the mother and the other family members.

Regardless of which reasons impel the mother to work, the fact of her working often brings upon her the expressed or covert censure of neighbors, friends, and relatives. They wonder *how* she manages to keep her several jobs (in and out of the home) in efficient balance. Unless she and her husband and her children are clear about why she works and reasonably comfortable in her doing so, she frequently responds to such wondering with feelings of guilt and anxiety.

The essential fact is that societal attitudes toward women in employment have been undergoing marked transition in the last thirty years. They persist, however, to be critical and sometimes even scathing unless a reason for work seems apparent: financial need, free time, or self-fulfillment in a job that is needed in our economy. The attitude that a woman—especially a mother and especially if a husband is in the picture—should not work grows out of conflicting and, sometimes, archaic beliefs and the circumstances which gave rise to these. Not only is maternal employment disapproved in principle by many persons, but this disapproval may be highly distressing to the working mother or her family and, in a variety of ways, affect policy and program of agencies concerned with family social welfare.

Closely related to work as a measure of adequacy is the criterion of thrift, a euphemism for appropriate management of one's economic resources. This criterion, like attitude about work, is inherent in the Puritan ethic, which equated postponement of gratification with strength of character, identified prosperity with work, and held financial independence to be a natural concomitant of self-supporting work. In a sense, the Puritan ethic was a prosperity ethic; it was essential to the accumulation of the capital resources necessary for the development of an expanding economy in the newly emerging industrialized society. However, the virtue of thrift as evidence of mature management of one's income remained an overriding attitude spanning several centuries.

From the beginning of colonization, American families took seriously Poor Richard's advice to "Never a borrower be" and "A penny saved is a penny earned." It is noteworthy, however, that Benjamin Franklin actually developed these maxims on the basis of his own experiences. Of himself he had said: "It is necessary for me to be extremely frugal for some time, till I have paid what I owe."[3] It may be speculated that the pragmatic Pilgrims out of necessity placed as much emphasis as they did on postponement of gratification. They certainly were the first Americans to "go now, pay later," but the negotiation and renegotiation of the loan that enabled them to sail from Holland to the New World obligated them financially for so many years that it is not entirely unlikely that the Puritan ethic of thrift was reinforced by the necessity to be frugal.

Well into the present century, thrift was associated with hard work, goodness with being rich, and poverty with wrongdoing. The semblance of thrift warranted the respect of one's neighbors—or

[3] *Autobiography*, footnote to "The Art of Virtue," in *The Works of Benjamin Franklin*, Jared Sparks, Ed. (Boston, 1844), vol. I, p. 105.

at least deflected censure. As longevity increased, it became more and more necessary for people to plan for more extensive periods in which they would need to maintain themselves without the prospect of earnings, thus adding a sense of urgency to the then prevailing emphasis on the value of thrift. It undoubtedly was further reinforced by the widespread advertising by insurance companies in the 'twenties urging that people plan for the "sunset years of life" although this was, to be sure, an effort to increase the sale of annuities.

A common thread runs through the beliefs and behavior of the Pilgrims and of Benjamin Franklin and of the people in the 'twenties faced with longer lives requiring resources for maintenance. Thrift and saving were matters of necessity.

Some movement away from complete acceptance of this dominant attitude in our society became apparent also in the 'twenties, with the development of more credit devices during years having only a façade of prosperity and influenced by persuasive urging to "buy on time." The rebellion against the concept of saving in order to buy for cash was briefly halted during the Great Depression, but as goods and services became more plentiful—and governmental regulations for control of credit arrangements became more general—certain inconsistencies became more evident between traditional attitudes and changing economic conditions affecting the majority of American families. The inconsistencies were discernible in the question as to the degree of security and risk possible for the economic safety of families in a highly industrialized nation in which all individuals desire a high degree of security and an equal degree of comfortable living.

This wish for security and comfort is paralleled by the dual necessity, in the interests of the nation's economy, to continue to produce goods and offer services that will maintain production at a relatively high level, and at the same time to keep funds in circulation. This essential requirement in an industrialized national economy contributes to a need for potential consumers to continue to purchase, for without the demands created by purchasers, the level of production declines and the circular effect may be under way of reduction in employment by producers, reduction in capacity to buy goods, and further reduction in production.

How does the family with limited income and relatively unlimited desires for the goods and services being produced continue to be thrifty, yet have the material accoutrements of comfort for the family members? Our society urges families to bolster the economy by going into debt (although it does *not* urge them to assume more debt than they can reasonably handle), and contributes to their sense of guilt and anxiety because they are not thrifty, as witness the fact that they are in debt.

The Puritan, and still common, idea of frugality as a paramount quality of character requires some re-examination in the light of current social and economic conditions and how thrift—saving—is exercised today. This is not to say that it is undesirable to be saving, planful, and solvent; rather, the standards have changed along with perceptions of needs and ways in which these are now met. For example, the increased longevity and the health hazards associated with aging have not reduced the necessity for people in our culture to plan for their maintenance during the later years. Today's social insurance arrangements, however, *require* individuals to invest, by means of Old-age, Survivors, and Disability Insurance Benefits contributions, in retirement and medical plans that will in large measure meet the basic economic and medical needs of those later years; the voluntary effort is no longer as compelling as in the past. Today, thrift has become a joint endeavor of individual families and the nation, with the latter providing some social controls as well as economic devices for assuring that, whether a family wishes to or not, it does actually save for the future.

Even though some pressures are being relieved in the sense that there is some mandatory financial planning for the future of the majority of American families, the fairly general use of installment and similar methods of handling purchases in every-day living causes many to look askance at the debtors because they *are* in debt whether or not their solvency is threatened. At the same time, two other conditions obtain. One is that the installment-payer has access to the material items that permit a higher and higher level of living, which, in many instances, he undoubtedly could not afford were he required to use his financial resources without the flexibility possible via credit arrangements. The other is that the outward evidences of his high level of living also appear to constitute evidence of both competence in earning and good management of income, thereby inducing respect even among those who question the indebtedness. For it is an incontrovertible fact that, anxiety-producing though it may be for many, the level of living is often measured by material goods owned. Most people are able to manage reasonably well the reality of handling debts appropriately, maintaining a safe balance between meeting needs for security and maintaining an optimum level of consumption. Whether the procurement of goods and services is managed by cash or with the help of devices for consumer credit, whether the management is good or moderately passable or poor, whether an individual family is envied or envious, there persists in our society today considerable ambivalence about the virtue of thrift. Society's persistent use of thrift as a measure of adequacy continues to have some impact on the family members in their performance of the developmental tasks essential in the cycle of family life.

The societal attitudes about thrift, and its implications for abstinence and security, are intimately associated with attitudes about money *per se*. These attitudes actually grow out of concepts of work and thrift as virtues, but they take on a kind of life of their own and they have special import in marital and family equilibrium and in personality development. The way the individual family and its members respond to the possession or absence of money and the way they can use it, as well as the way our society responds to meeting the needs of troubled families, is shaped by prevailing attitudes about the meanings, sources, and uses of money.[4]

Measures of Morality

Morality and adequacy, in the minds of many people, are practically synonymous. Some people in our culture, for example, question the morality of the Sigleys and their nomadic life, the influence of the standards and aspirations of these young parents on the development of their children. Because their pattern of life is different from the *majority* of American families, the actual measures of adequacy—working, managing, loving—are given scant attention.

Differences in family and behavioral patterns, whether minor or grossly deviant, often are viewed with mixed suspicion and anxiety, the former because we tend neither to trust nor to tolerate what is not entirely understood, and anxiety because differences threaten the established accepted patterns. These differences are most frequently related to cultural or vocational factors, or regional or ethnic patterns. The way, for example, Appalachian mountaineers settle (or fail to settle) their differences by feuds prolonged over many generations is viewed by the wider society as deviant, yet this is customary and normal behavior as far as these people are concerned.

Another measure of morality that affects not only the way a family perceives itself but also the specifics of public policy with regard to social welfare is the assumption of responsibility of relatives for each other in terms of economic, social, or emotional sup-

[4] See Chapter 20 on money counseling.

port. Legislation in many states and within jurisdictions in a state offers either guidelines or mandates for the legalizing of this moral matter, and sets forth who is responsible for whom, under what circumstances, and to what extent. Yet for many centuries, in many parts of the world, it was simply expected that relatives would care for one another as need dictated. India is noted for its extended family system; other Asian and Middle Eastern countries place great store by the fact that even a relative of obscure degree may properly demand care from the head of a household.

Nor is this an unknown pattern in Western civilization. Who has not heard about the dependent aunts and cousins who are part of English—and often also New England—households? It is a common practice among Negro families and families of Mexican background to care for stray relatives even though the nuclear family may barely be able to maintain itself. The efforts to legislate morality and responsibility of relatives, however, while purporting to keep to a minimum the state's responsibility for aiding needy people by requiring the relatives to do so, was actually a device to insure the continuance of a family system in the face of relatively rapid industrialization and its concomitant displacement and mobility of a work force drawn from the agrarian community that earlier had been able to accommodate dependent relatives.

Throughout our society, there is considerable cultural lag between social attitudes and practice with regard to divorce. While divorce is widely practiced today, our laws and our moral judgments still reflect vestiges of previous disapproving attitudes. This cultural lag is further complicated by special attitudes held by certain religious groups that divorce is immoral. The impact of this social ambivalence is reflected in the feelings of members of many families in which a divorce has occurred, these feelings being expressed in the form of a sense of inadequacy, guilt, or shame.

Similarly, many people hold that remarriages also signify immorality, especially if there is more than one. Such attitudes rarely seem to take into account that while multiple (consecutive) marriages may sometimes be symptomatic of personal disturbance they also inevitably reflect the acceptance by the oft-married person that marriage is an appropriate arrangement in our society to which he is seeking to conform.

Probably the least acceptable family pattern in our society, and one which since antiquity has been stigmatized as immoral, is that of unmarried parenthood.[5] In general, the stigma attaches less to

[5] For a discussion of unmarried parenthood, see Chapter 9.

the father than to the mother and the child. The community censure rises in geometric proportion to the number of children a family contains and the number of different men who have fathered them.

ENVIRONMENTAL FACTORS

A second category of elements having a significant impact upon family life and the effectiveness with which family members are able to fulfill the functions expected of them includes environmental factors such as employment opportunities, educational facilities and opportunities, housing and medical care arrangements, and other institutional aspects of community life. Each of these in and of itself is important. They may spell opportunity for a family to improve its general level of living, its economic status, its mental and physical health. Or environmental factors may be such as to oppress the family by limiting or denying opportunities for advancement. Thus, environmental factors may enable some families to move close enough to touch the idealized version of the American family; other families may be impelled further away from the ideal.

Consideration of some of these environmental factors in the context of societal attitudes and expectations adds a dimension of special value to the understanding of the problems and conditions that trouble families and individuals in our society. For the conflicts that trouble many families because of their more or less conscious recognition of societal attitudes and the greater or lesser degree of anxiety they may feel about compliance or noncompliance with these attitudes, contribute to family malfunctioning in many ways and in various stages of the family life cycle. These conflicts and feelings may be exacerbated by societal attitudes that have not altered even though massive changes have occurred among environmental factors.

The current press and literature report with frequent regularity the conditions in today's world that vitally affect family functioning: the changing labor market, the number of school dropouts, the growing pressure and opportunities for education, and so on. Attention will be directed in the following pages only to a few aspects of selected environmental factors, with the primary purpose of illustrating the manner in which environmental elements and societal attitudes, in apposition, can contribute to family distress and impede achievement of the idealized version of the American family.

Employment Opportunities

The prevalent expectation in our culture that the rational man will maintain himself and his dependents by means of his work must be assessed against an industrial society in which rapid mechanization and automation have reduced the number of employment opportunities available to undereducated or uneducated individuals, and to those lacking either actual or potential skills for reasons that either are personal or originate in the labor market. This expectation may contribute to deep anxiety on the part of the older man who, like Mr. Anderson, has always been hard working and self-supporting but who, for a variety of reasons, is now unable to find a place in a changing labor market. It may cause the man who has entered the retirement period to feel "worthless" because he no longer has at hand the evidence with which to demonstrate to the world his usefulness as a man: his wages. The self-esteem of the young, inexperienced person with capacity too limited for more than minimal education may be so damaged by failure to meet these societal expectations that he lapses into behavior characterized by dependency on others or antisocial activity.

Freud has said that "work is the chief means of binding the individual to reality." Certainly, work is the major source of income for most American families in the foreseeable future. Whether the individual's need for work derives from emotional factors, economic factors, the Puritan work ethic, or any combination of these, the availability of work that he can perform holds significance that extends far beyond the individual's own mental health. It also has important implications for the discharge of family functions and the competence with which the family carries out the various life tasks. Other implications affect social welfare organizations, for dysfunctioning will persist to trouble families and the community when a primary means of "binding the individual to reality" is inaccessible. The help of a social worker or member of some other helping profession cannot alone be instrumental in assisting all families to improve social functioning. For many, such help can be minimal only. Arrangements have to be developed whereby those who cannot fit into the work possibilities contained in the general economy can have access to public-supported employment that, through wages, enables the individual to retain or regain the self-esteem essential for competent social functioning.

Education

To function competently in today's climate requires that at least the minimal education be available to equip individuals, women as well as men, for gainful employment. Increasingly, some form of certification is necessary for almost any kind of job—at least completion of high school, if not more. A substantial number of people who are now, or will be in the not too distant future, endeavoring to establish themselves in employment, lack this basic education. This may be due to lack of motivation, to lack of opportunity or accessibility of facilities, or to intellectual or physical handicaps. Whether the need for a high-school diploma is always realistic in terms of what is required on the job itself is of less moment than the fact that job opportunities are fewer and fewer for the person who does not have this evidence of achievement.

Mobility

Our industrial society requires considerable geographic as well as vocational mobility and, indeed, many segments of the economy depend in large measure on flexibility of this kind. Mr. Sigley, for example, is part of the necessary mobile work force in the agricultural industry—despite accelerated mechanization in this industry, hand and back labor still are requisites in many aspects of agriculture. Construction, engineering, sales, and other kinds of work also depend often on employee mobility. That this need for a mobile working population is met is evidenced in the fact that a high proportion of American families move during each year. Yet knowledge about behavioral development points to the importance of consistency in physical as well as in emotional environment. Unlike the idealized image of the American family that has deep roots in a community where the family owns its home and the children grow up happily among other stable families, the requirements for geographic mobility mean that many parents and children move voluntarily or otherwise from house to house, community to community, school to school, peer group to peer group. Mobility, then, that is work-connected—or is the concomitant of a family's search for better living opportunities—may serve in many respects also to move the family away from the dominant ideal of the American family and to complicate the developmental tasks that face the family.

Economic Factors

A variety of economic factors may serve, individually or in combination, as modifiers of the idealized version of the American family. These may be directly related to the work situation. There may be economic need because the family has no working member, or there is underemployment because of lack of steady work or failure to earn an adequate wage at a full-time job. Or economic need may be a factor in the mother as well as the father going out to work, even though other circumstances indicate this to be inadvisable, or it may influence the father to moonlight even though the physical and emotional toll and his protracted hours away from home are a disadvantage to the family's well-being. In some families, economic need leads to younger family members going to work at the expense of their appropriate educational or emotional development.

The necessity of managing on limited income—limited in relation to a particular family's aspirations, achievements, and level of living—may influence some families to overextend themselves financially to procure desired consumer goods, or it may lead some to constricting certain aspects of living in undesirable ways, depriving the whole family or some members. Housing arrangements, for example, may be unsatisfactory: there may be crowding or doubling up of families. There may be sharing of housing with relatives or others. The housing facilities may be physically below standard; they may be part of a housing development that has special disadvantages for some family members.

Whether or not a family's income appears to be adequate to meet normal needs, the family's economic behavior and adequacy may be markedly affected by steadily rising costs of living, by inability to resist increasingly available and appealing consumer goods and services, and by other blandishments in the environment.

Many families are dependent upon public or voluntary sources for income with which to meet economic needs because there is no person in the family who works or can work. This economic dependence on sources outside the family may veer the family sharply away from the ideal. If the amount of income the family has available falls short of what is required for reasonably adequate maintenance, further deviation from the ideal may be expected. For these families, as well as for those who have income from underemployment—which does not lend itself to increased earnings—our society needs to consider providing sufficient resources so they can function at an adequate level and be helped to the extent possible ultimately to be tied "to reality" through work.

Disadvantageousness

The last several years have brought sharply into focus a variety of factors which disadvantage families, thus precluding their congruence with the idealized image of the American nuclear family. These disadvantages may be in relation to job, or housing, or educational opportunities which are either or both unavailable or inaccessible. Similarly, medical and other necessary services may be lacking or insufficient, thereby contributing to the disadvantaged conditions. Discrimination may be directed toward ethnic or cultural or regional or religious differences and it may be active or passive. It may be in regard to factors of age or sex—or any combination of these with ethnic or regional or cultural factors.

Negro families, for example, in many communities, in spite of an accelerated civil rights movement, still have little opportunity for appropriate or adequate jobs. Some population segments, through their isolation geographically and culturally, have fewer opportunities than other groups either for employment or for exposing their children to other ways of living more consistent with the prevailing culture. Puerto Rican women in New York often become the family breadwinners because it is easier for them to find employment in a labor market that discriminates against Puerto Rican men. In other places women may experience considerable difficulty in becoming part of the work force; or, in some communities, interaction of women with others than their own family members may not be accepted within the social framework of the given community. Age *per se* may serve as a basis for discrimination: the individual may be "too old" or "too young."

In many instances, rural families have little, if any, chance to emulate the idealized version of the American family because they are subject to forces of isolation that preclude their having opportunities for education, for material advantages requisite to comfortable living in our American culture, or even to medical care that may be needed for the maintenance of health. Housing conditions in rural areas on the average are considerably inferior to those in urban centers. However, the rural families do not feel so sharp an impact from their deteriorated housing arrangements as do families doubled and tripled in small, substandard tenement dwellings in crowded urban centers. For at least the rural family living in inferior housing—even housing devoid of inside plumbing—has greater possibilities for privacy for some of its family members.

PERSONAL FACTORS

Families have different degrees of susceptibility to influences of environmental factors and societal attitudes. Some families are far more vulnerable than others to elements that propel them away from the direction of the dominant ideal of the American family.[6] The reasons may derive from limited intellectual endowment or from personality factors that reduce or deny them the opportunity to function more effectively in our society. They may be physically handicapped by illness or disability so that their functioning in our society is limited. Some families are more vulnerable to the impact of environmental factors and societal attitudes because they are broken families, generally with only one parent in the home.[7]

The modality of a family's functioning is influenced by a constellation of factors. Some are the products of a changing society, represented largely in environmental conditions: employment, education, disadvantageousness, and others. Some are societal attitudes that were shaped long ago, often reflecting the conditions of the times in which they evolved, and because of this lag contribute to standards and expectations that are unrealistic in the world in which the family lives and works today. And the quality of the family's responsiveness to these environmental and attitudinal modifiers is shaped by the physical, emotional, and intellectual capacity and readiness of its members to cope with society's standards and expectations in a changing world. The consequences of the impact of these modifiers are evident in the extent to which American families resemble, or begin to approach, or move away from, the idealized image of the American family in our democratic society. What some of the variations and similarities may be are described in the following chapter.

[6] See Chapter 12.
[7] See Chapters 5 and 9.

3

THE REALITY:
TODAY'S FAMILY

*A*LL HAPPY *families resemble each other; each unhappy family is unhappy in its own way.* These words uttered by Anna Karenina in another age and in another land might have been used to describe today's American family. For although American families possess many characteristics that are similar, and although most of the families are exposed to common environmental factors and societal attitudes, the particular constellation of elements that may trouble a family (or the community with regard to a specific family) differs from one family to another. Although the disturbing constellations also may contain similarities in ingredients and in patterning, certain aspects nevertheless are unique to each family. This uniqueness requires identification if the individual family is to be helped to master the problems that interfere with its competence in social functioning.

This uniqueness may affect or be affected by the family's composition. The uniqueness—and the composition of the family—may closely resemble that of the image of the idealized family. They may be alike only in part, or they may appear not to resemble each other at all. The uniqueness may influence or be influenced by the way the family fulfills the major functions and carries out the various tasks specific to these functions—a way congruent with the idealized model's, or differing moderately or sharply from it. The characteristics of the dominant idealized model of the American family were sketched in Chapter 1. Some of the societal, environmental, and personal factors that enable some families to emulate that model or propel them away from it, or preclude their movement toward it, were touched on in Chapter 2. The intent of this chapter is to offer, albeit briefly, a broad view of today's families in terms of family composition and some of their economic and social characteristics. It will include also a categorization of troubled families in today's American culture. The objective of this presentation is to facilitate identification of the uniqueness in a particular troubled family so that required help can be extended in a fashion appropriate to the individual family's needs and the welfare of the larger community. The specifics for understanding of the family's functioning with respect to its accomplishment of the developmental tasks in the respective stages of the cycle of family life are contained in subsequent chapters.[1]

TODAY'S FAMILY IN PROFILE

Family Composition

Neither the idealized image portrayed earlier nor the harsh reality of the Sigleys typifies the composition of today's family. In actuality, only slightly more than half of the families in the nation contain both father and mother as well as children who have not yet attained adulthood (a nuclear family) with the father the family group's chief provider. This in no way implies that the gloomy head-shaking of those anxious about an accelerated process of family breakdown is based on valid facts. For one thing, in many of the nuclear families which constitute the primary source of social and psychological support of the family members, the chil-

[1] For elaboration on life tasks and the cycle of family life, especially, see Part Two.

dren are over eighteen years old.[2] They still may be in the parental home, or, married or not, living elsewhere—although it is not uncommon for some children to remain in the parental home long after marriage.

Nor can these forebodings about family disunity be properly attributed to the continued high rates of divorce, for although the high rates persist, there has in fact been a steady upward trend in the number of households in our nation with complete nuclear family groups, and a considerable increase in the proportion of husbands and wives living together. Indeed, the evidence shows that the use of the divorce court does not automatically turn people away from marriage as an undesirable state: a high proportion of divorced persons remarry, and these new marriages are enduring.

Despite the continued popularity of the concept of marriage (three-fourths of all men and two-thirds of all women eighteen years of age or over are married and live with their spouses), one out of ten families is headed by a mother with no husband in the home. She either is divorced, widowed, separated (by agreement, by desertion, or by the institutionalization of the husband), or she has never married. Approximately 3 per cent of the families in the United States are headed by a father with no spouse present, generally because of divorce, widowhood, separation, or institutionalization of the wife. In nearly half of all of these one-parent families there is at least one child under the age of eighteen; about a fifth of these family units has at least three young children. It is obvious that such families have greater susceptibility to various personal and external problems than the majority of intact family groups and, furthermore, that the division of responsibility for the conduct of the major functions and the developmental tasks must differ in essential ways from the dominant model.

It is not only the one-parent family or the family whose children are no longer under eighteen which do not coincide with the idealized image of the American family. The latter usually connotes parents and their biological or, sometimes, adopted offspring. But one of every nine children in this country is a stepchild. Either or both parents may have remarried, sometimes more than once; the child may live with a parent and a stepparent, with siblings, step-siblings, or half-siblings, or with one or more of each. Even if a person rationally remains unaffected by a heritage of fairy tales re-

[2] For definition of nuclear family, see Chapter 5. It should be noted that the nuclear family is sometimes also designated as "family of orientation," "conjugal family," "the normal family group," or "family of procreation."

plete with the wickedness of stepparents and their children, it is readily recognizable that the completion of developmental tasks may encounter some extra barriers in these kinds of family arrangements. Certainly, it is not uncommon for the child of remarried parents to belong to more than one family group and to be shuttled back and forth between households maintained by each remarried parent.

Significantly different from the idealized version of the American family is the unit of mother and one or more children born out of wedlock. Chapter 9 considers this kind of situation with regard to its status as a "broken" family. Nevertheless, some comments are in order here in light of the estimates indicating a steady rise in the number of such births (it exceeded a quarter of a million in 1964).[3] In reality, the *rate* of illegitimacy appears to have been fairly steady over a period of several years, both among white and nonwhite women. More than half of the children born out of wedlock are Negro, although the nonwhite population is approximately 12 per cent of the total population. But these data have to be scrutinized and interpreted with caution: for one thing, it is not known how many out of wedlock pregnancies occur among white (or nonwhite) mothers whose economic and social status enable them to take measures that preclude a vital statistic notation that implies illegitimacy. Nor is it known how many of those children who are designated as illegitimate are the products of fairly stable relationships not blessed by a legal marriage. The implications for the family's social functioning are not necessarily altered by awareness of these and other cautionary points, but they do need to be taken into account by the social worker or other helping person who wishes to avoid the pitfalls of stereotyping.

The Cycle of Family Life

The family has been affected over the last several decades by significant changes with regard to age at marriage, to spacing of child bearing, and to longevity. Thus, couples are marrying earlier (the average for girls is twenty years, for boys about twenty-two years); they are compressing the child-bearing period so that the American mother, on the average, is twenty-six years old when her last child is born—and she has more children than her mother had (an average of three). *These* children are marrying young, so that the

---

[3] No accurate statistical data are available because out-of-wedlock births are not recorded as such in all states and no national, uniform, or centralized reporting system exists.

marital partners are still fairly youthful when the last child has left the home and each parent still has many years ahead to complete the life span (on the average, approximately seventy-three years). And, when the later years arrive, the now usually childless-again couples—or the widowed parent (more often the wife)—continues to maintain residence separate from the adult children. These changes in the family contribute in many respects to some alterations in the way families fulfill their functions in a changing world and complete the developmental tasks discussed in later chapters.

Some Economic and Social Characteristics

Over the long history of man, changes have occurred both as to the *means* employed by the family to fulfill its obligations to its members and the broader community, and as to the *perceptions* of the family and the community regarding what these obligations are. Marriage and parenthood have long been anchored to certain expectations and obligations, both legal and informal, which are not discretionary with the individuals concerned. Accordingly, the family has been the locus of the meeting of the survival needs of the members, and it has been the primary agency for the psychological and social development of children—what sociologists now term "socialization."

The idealized version of the American family achieves these social objectives with relative ease and, seemingly, with a minimum of pain. Although the achievement often is the result of considerably more effort and may be characterized by wonderment about the outcomes, the vast majority of American families, even those who may not conform precisely with the idealized model, are successful in their economic role: providing the food, shelter, and other necessities for physical survival and security of the family members. They are also successful in carrying out the socialization tasks. Their children are loved and learn also to love; they obtain high-school and often college education; they learn to make and implement vocational choices; they, in turn, enter into stable and loving marriages, have children of their own around whom they center economic and socialization functions; they participate in the civic and social life of the community. In each generation, these families move steadily through the cycle of family life, taking in flexible stride the different psychological, social, and economic requirements and the different demands on emotional and physical energies and economic resources that characterize the successive stages of the cycle through which children progress from infancy to adulthood.

The manner and the success with which a family executes its economic function affect the fashion and adequacy with which it deals with its social roles. At the same time, the family's perception of its socialization functions influences its view and handling of its economic functions.

The idealized image of the American family clearly grows out of the widely held expectation in this country that the husband and father in the family supplies the family members with the income required to meet their needs at a comfortable, if not always affluent, level. We generally view the father as the primary breadwinner, even though the wife or some other member of the family may be employed. It is the *father* who is expected to provide the funds for daily living and to provide for future income protection. It is the *father* who is expected to deal with the costs of medical care, either through a prepaid health plan or on an "as needed" basis. It is the *father* who is expected to protect the family against the common financial hazards associated with disability, unemployment, retirement, or death. It is not only through his work in a social insurance-covered job that he is expected to arrange for such protection. As magazine and television advertisements regularly remind American fathers (and their wives and children), a father's continuous and planful investment in commercial insurance or other savings plans during his working life will secure the day-by-day economic future of those who continue to be dependent upon him; and farsighted investment will safeguard Jimmy's or Mary's opportunities for a college education, whether or not their father still is around to see them don cap and gown. It is far from unusual for the employed mother to be the family's primary breadwinner; however, there is not the same high degree of expectation that she provide both for the present and for the future of those she supports.

In reality, although most American families depend on earnings as the primary source of their income, there are marked differences in the earnings of breadwinning fathers and breadwinning mothers, and these differences are further affected by ethnic, cultural, educational, or regional variables. Thus, while one out of every four families had entered the $10,000-and-up bracket in the mid-'sixties and the median family income had reached $6,600 (before taxes), the median income for the fully employed breadwinning mother was less than half the latter figure, pointing to the greater vulnerability of such families to the impacts of poverty. Among Negro families, three-fifths of whom contained both parents, both husband and wife had to work in more than half of these families—and the median income still was only slightly more than half that of white families. And Negro breadwinning mothers earned about half that of white breadwinning mothers. Similar differences exist among other minority groups in the population, and these differences from the median for white families are sharper in all groups when the educational achievement is low, when the family lives in a rural area, or in certain regions in the country. The net income may be further reduced for some —mothers, for example—who often have extra costs like child care to consider against earnings.

The adequacy of income cannot be measured merely in dollar amounts; nor is income the only factor that determines if a family is living in comfort, affluence, or poverty, or if the future economic security of the family members is being protected. A major real test of the adequacy of income is how far it must be stretched to meet the needs of all the persons dependent upon it. Other factors of importance include the size of the family, the ages of the children, the living costs in the locality, the "normal" expectations of the family with regard to matters such as levels of education and planning for income continuity during future periods when income from work will have decreased or ceased, and how wisely income is spent.

A family of five in a small town with $5,000 a year income may be better off than a five-person family living on an annual income of $5,000 in a large urban center where rents are higher, there are greater costs for transportation to enable the breadwinner to reach his work, and where there may be more opportunities to spend money for cultural, recreational, or other purposes. But the urban family may be able to manage better in other ways. It may, for example, feel less the pinch for education or medical care because it generally has access to more facilities and, therefore, more choice exists for dealing with educational aspirations or medical needs. In any setting—rural or urban—a planful and careful family might successfully handle its survival needs, procure some symbols of affluence—a car (nearly 60 per cent of all families own *two* cars), color or "plain" television (more than 90 per cent of all families own at least one television), and others—and even acquire some other assets in the form of savings or equity in a home (62 per cent of all families are home owners). A family like the Sigleys, however, with their average weekly earnings of $33, is unlikely to be able to stretch this amount to procure even the minimal requirements to maintain life at a physically and psychologically healthy level. And, for reasons quite different from sheer lack of sufficient financial means, some families with an income well above the median level also fail to meet such minimal requirements.

Winton McCormick has earned an average annual net sum of $89,000 for each of the last five years in his automobile insurance business. Three of his eight children regularly report to school without bringing either lunch or the money with which to buy it; all are thought by the school nurse to be malnourished and her reports to the mother elicit only complaints about how hard it is to feed so many children on the small household allowance the father gives her. The family lives in a sizable mansion; each of the six older children has a television set and a horse; three expensive cars stand in the six-car garage; and the father has his $300 suits tailored to order. Mrs. McCormick and the children wear clothes passed on to them by relatives. She has a cleaning woman to help her one day each week—and she carefully saves trading stamps with which to procure "necessities" such as toasters, coffeemakers, and the like.

Clearly, the Sigleys and the McCormicks are poles apart, not only with respect to the source and amount of their income, but especially in the matter of the degree and nature of choice as to how and for what they will use the funds they have.

The criteria by which the success of the socialization functions is assessed obtain largely from middle-class values and expectations. The way the social roles are filled varies from family to family and in different cultural, economic, and social class groups. There are often differences as to social goals of the family, as to the economic and social values and aspirations to be transmitted to the family members, and as to the manner, if at all, in which the socialization functions are performed. Wealthy Mrs. Jones leaves the care of her young children to a nursemaid, giving them only a prescribed amount of time each day from her busy social life; her equally wealthy cousin devotes most of her time to being with her two young children, taking them to and from school, supervising their meals and recreation. Mrs. Smith leaves her young child in the care of a foster day-care facility during the ten or twelve hours she spends daily in reaching and working on her job as a domestic servant. Mr. Johnson, an affluent businessman who "worked my way up to the top" requires his adolescent son to earn enough to pay the insurance on his car; Mr. Thompson, whose earnings are below the national median and limited by regretted lack of education, requires his son to maintain a high scholastic level as a condition of having a jalopy. The Glass boy, whose father is only intermittently in the home, has three times helped himself to cars left unattended by their owners. Not all of these are intact nuclear families; not all have parents (living at home or not) who offer the children care, protection, and love. But all are judged by the same standards that reflect middle-class values, although they are not all middle-income families.

The degree of adequacy with which a substantial number of American families perform their social roles falls far short of the standard inherent in the idealized image. Either the cause or the consequence may be that the family is broken; there may be serious mental or physical impairment or incapacity in the family, or adult behavior just neurotic enough to tilt the family's equilibrium. There may be insufficient money not just because the income is low or a key family member is unable or unmotivated to find a better—or any—place in the work force, but because the income is dispensed unwisely or unhealthily. The quality of socialization may be further impaired by problems of alcoholism, by adult or juvenile delinquency, by sheer disregard or defiance of responsibility. And the complexity of any of these may be compounded by factors of ethnicity, social class, religion, regional or cultural beliefs which cause families to perceive differently or to discharge differently their socialization functions.

THE TROUBLED FAMILIES

The presence or absence of income, of education, of a good standard of housing, do not in and of themselves guarantee that a family either can or will competently or happily pursue the developmental tasks required in life. With a few exceptions like the McCormicks or Hetty Green (who, though one of the richest women in the world, wore stockings mended until they disintegrated) or John D. Rockefeller or other persons of great wealth who have become the subjects of published biographies, relatively little data are available about the way families in the highest income brackets deal with the everyday tasks inherent in the fulfillment of family functions. Clearly, their problems about financial functions are of an order other than its availability. But social and behavioral scientists have not focused on the family patterns of the rich as they have on other groups in this nation and, although there are limited supporting data, it is generally accepted that their values do not differ markedly from middle-class values.

There has, however, been a growing body of literature that ascribes to social class differences and problems the way that families generally perceive and exercise their social role—that attitudes and behavior of the "poor," for example, derive from the "culture of poverty." There are some who hold that certain non-middle-class behavior patterns have an ethnic or regionally limited cultural base as in the instances of the high proportion of Negro families headed by a woman, or the Appalachian family's contentment with work that is long enough to assure that the winter's needs are met, but not so long as to interfere with the pleasures of hunting and fishing.

Yet, while the social worker or other helping person needs to know and recognize socialization patterns that prevail in poverty culture and that can be categorized by social class, the objective of understanding and working with a family toward a mutually acceptable goal focused on the development or attainment of social competence requires that any one family be distinguished from all others. It requires awareness of the fact that in our society criteria for adequate social performance derive from middle-class values; that—without extolling these—the poor subscribe at least partially to middle-class culture, which they adapt to their own situation; that, by and large, they want the greater social and economic rewards that characterize middle-class rather than poverty life; and that efforts to help poor families to be less troubled involve helping them to move closer to the middle-class ideal.

Furthermore, it is important to recognize that the culture of poverty is not homogeneous; the characteristics and values of the poor are not standardized and unalterably alienated from middle-class standards and values. The Sigleys, wintering with three hundred other farm workers in a squatter's camp, cooking over a mesquite fire, using candles for light, and hauling their water in jugs from a park fountain twenty miles away, long to have the housing and other material items that characterize middle-class standards; they already have the drive for self-support and independence. The Negro family living in Watts wants a life more like that observable in the daily television programs and in the communities around this ghetto-like neighborhood.

It is evident that families who are troubled cannot be stereotyped and that, as was noted earlier, myriad elements assign to each family a uniqueness that governs the family's over-all performance *as* a family and the performance of its individual members as family members and members of the broader society. They may be reasonably congruent with the idealized model of the family in some respects and not in others; there may be a wide gap between the reality and the model because of ignorance, indifference, choice, or paucity of opportunity.

Troubles Categorized

The problems that may develop within a family fall into four broad categories, with some families experiencing problems that cut across several categories. One category contains problems centering around the need for money. Some families, perhaps because of physical or mental or intellectual limits, do not have enough money to meet basic survival needs. Some have insufficient funds from earnings or other income sources because there is no employable person in the family, or there is unemployment or underemployment, or because the insufficiency of money is in relation not to meeting of survival needs but to managing to provide family members with items required for living either at a more comfortable or at a luxury level.

A second category includes problems that relate to the need for one or more members of the family to be away from home for a short or a long period. A child, for example, may have to be in a foster family home or in institutional care; an adult may require medical care in a facility outside the family home, or may be institutionalized for health or correctional reasons.

Comprising a third category are problems revolving around deviance from the norm in social or psychological behavior, to the extent that one or more family members simply cannot get along with others: other family members, a marital partner, the law, or society in general. These situations wherein the individual is unable to form *any* meaningful and substantial relationship with others, are exemplified by isolates, persons who remain lonely whether or not they are with other persons. Many people can form relationships with others in the family and outside, but their relationships are problematic to them because such individuals are inconsistent, uncertain, fearful. For example, marital partners afraid of closeness and intimacy with each other may fight constantly: this is their life pattern. The fighting keeps them emotionally apart at the same time that it provides an avenue for some intimacy. Should such a couple discontinue their quarreling, they would be bereft unless some better element could first begin to emerge in their relationship.

A fourth problem group includes situations of social and vocational disadvantage related to social, physical, or mental handicaps. For example, the Mexican American who is unable to find a job for which he has been trained may be at a disadvantage not because there is a job shortage, but because he has not located an employer willing to hire a Mexican American for that particular job. A person who is blind may be decidedly limited as to the tasks he can learn to do and which are suitable for gainful employment. A man who has been discharged from a state mental hospital as recovered may encounter considerable difficulty in procuring work because potential employers view his health history with unrealistic alarm. Similarly, the person who has been imprisoned is confronted with serious hurdles in procuring work and being accepted back into the community.

All of these problem situations reflect stress with which families deal on an individual and differential basis. The stress may be of long duration, and its very chronicity may enable the family to tolerate it. Crisis, on the other hand, disturbs the family's usual pattern of functioning. Crisis may be the result of sudden unemployment or other shifts in the family's economic status. It may be due to illness or to the death of a family member. The crisis may be precipitated by a social or economic condition in society, or by a situation within the family, or within an individual member of the family.

The family with an adequate capacity for social functioning may temporarily find its pattern disrupted by the crisis. Help may be needed from some source for a short period or even for a fairly lengthy period of time until the family's equilibrium is regained, and the family again is able to manage the situation. Both the amount of help that a family requires and the duration of this help depend upon the severity of the crisis, the capacity of the individual family members to cope with problems as they arise in their day-to-day life, and the capacity of the family *as* a family to rise to the situation. The need for care of children during a mother's hospitalization during a time-limited illness or the birth of a new child ordinarily will require less assistance than the family's gaining mastery of the situation in which the wife is suffering from a post-partum psychosis.

When Mrs. Jensen found that she was going into labor earlier than had been anticipated, she was able to arrange quickly to have someone come into the home to care for the children and, upset as they were by her impending absence, she was able to prepare them for her departure. She handled this sudden crisis, which occurred while her husband was out of the city on a business trip, with relative ease and in not too different an emotional fashion than the crises that had confronted the family from time to time around sudden illnesses, a serious automobile accident in which the husband had been injured, unexpected shortages of money when bills were due, and so on. Her ability to act in this fashion was evidence of the family's adequacy, its ability to adapt flexibly and, therefore, the need for help only in implementing the appropriate arrangements.

Arrangements had been made by the Thomas family for the care of the children during Mrs. Thomas' hospitalization for the birth of her fourth child. The plan developed was the same as that followed for other confinements. Mrs. Thomas' mother was to come to the family home to care for her grandchildren, and arrangements were made for the help of a practical nurse for the several days following Mrs. Thomas' return to the home. This plan was put into effect. However, two days after her return to the home, Mrs. Thomas' behavior became hallucinatory and threatening, so that she had to be placed quickly in a protected hospital situation. The anxiety created by the nature of the illness and her sudden departure caused havoc in the household. The practical nurse, with whom no arrangements had been made for continued stay, carried the infant to the home of the grandmother. The father accompanied Mrs. Thomas in the ambulance, in his anxiety barely waving to the children, who were left in the home with the eight-year-old girl to care for the two younger siblings. Mr. Thomas' reaction to the crisis and the reaction of his mother-in-law were similar. They saw nothing beyond the crisis situation itself and the person central to it. The children felt abandoned and helpless.

During the night the grandmother remembered that three children had been left in the home and she rushed to the Thomas home. She discovered that the neighbors already had reported the "abandonment" of the children to the police, and the children were in a detention home. Mr. Thomas had gone out to drown his sorrows in the same fashion in which he had met other crises in the couple's married life.

Crisis, in this instance, confronted a family already less able to deal with it, and the consequences for them in handling such situations were more difficult to bring under control than would be true of the normal, adequately functioning family. The Thomas children illustrate a situation of far-reaching import when there is limited capacity of adults close to them to cope adequately with a crisis.

Mrs. Jensen also suffered a post-partum psychosis and, approximately a week after her return home, required hospitalization. There was no break in the continuity of the children's care, their father explaining to them, in the same fashion as had been done previously, the mother's absence as a temporary measure.

The stressful situation that constitutes a crisis ordinarily is a situation beyond the usual coping resources of the family. The problems of lack of income and resources may be precipitated by unemployment, by illness, by disability, or by the death or absence of the breadwinner. A crisis such as the death of the breadwinner may bring on the problem, but these situations tend to persist beyond the crisis state and often require help of a more enduring nature, such as providing assistance and other services until a child is grown and able to care for himself.

The problems that are related to personal functioning and intra-family relationships may be manifest in marital disharmony, strained parent-child relationships, difficulties in work adjustments or in retaining a job, money management, and so on. Neurotic or psychotic behavior may be evidenced in problems such as neglected children, alcoholism, desertion, delinquency, chronic overindebtedness, and the like. These disturbances in personal functioning may create economic need so that the family requires financial assistance as well as help with emotional and social problems.

The manner of some families in dealing with a crisis or with stress may be governed by lack of knowledge or experience. In such instances, education is all that the family requires in order to be prepared to cope with subsequent stressful encounters. In some families, where limited intellectual or emotional endowments seriously curtail the family's capacity to deal with the problems, help of another kind may be required to bring such families safely through a critical or stressful experience.

Any of the aforementioned kinds of problems may confront almost any family in our American culture. The help which they can use in ameliorating or alleviating these problems must be geared to the structure and capacity of the family to handle the daily tasks of living. The kind of family and the specific problem it experiences will determine the nature of help that should be offered or could be utilized.

The Adequate Family

This family generally has made reasonably mature adaptations to the various life tasks confronting all families. It is a family likely to come to the attention of a social agency when some externally-created problem presents aspects that are more severe or disturbing than the family's usual coping ability can handle. The events that precipitate the unmanageable problems commonly are the death of the mother or of the breadwinner father, an acute serious illness, a chronic illness that depletes the family's economic and emotional resources, loss of work through circumstances over which the family has no control, problems of old age, retirement with inadequate income, and the like. The family or the family members may be temporarily immobilized by shock or show temporary regressive feelings or behavior. For example, the mother may go into a temporary reactive depression. The sudden and generally unexpected crisis may throw out of balance the habitual problem-solving patterns of the family and call for a solution that is new for the individual or for the family in relation to its life experiences. But the reasonably adequate family will find reasonably effective new ways for bringing the stress situation under control, and a new equilibrium of some sort will be achieved. They may turn to friends or relatives—or even the recently popularized "helping" bartender— to develop healthy new adaptations; or they may turn to a social welfare agency and, because they are reasonably mature, will perceive the worker as a neutrally empathetic person who is in the agency to give them assistance. These families are able, with a minimum of intervention by the worker, to mobilize themselves and their resources, and regain or establish a new adequate level of independent social functioning.

The Chaotic Family

Some families, often both socially and psychologically disorganized, appear to operate as though they were a family of siblings. There is little or no differentiation between the roles of the parents and between the parents and the children. There is confusion in marital and child-rearing roles. No one knows who is to do what, or which bed to sleep in. Often there are concomitant problems in the marriage such as delinquency or alcoholism. The parents give orders and rescind them whimsically; they assign responsibilities to children that are inappropriate for their ages; the parents fight with the children *like* children; and they feel helpless or overwhelmed by tasks that have to be carried out. These are families who have basic troubles with trust, self-control, and other aspects of identity.[4] These kinds of persons generally have very serious characterological problems.

The main function of the social worker, after developing some trust (as will be described in Chapter 13), is trying to help the family establish and develop some capacity in role performance.

The Burns family was bewildered by the school's complaint about ten-year-old Tommy who seemed to have little notion of how to behave in the classroom. He roamed at will, played while the other

[4] See Chapter 15.

children were working. The parents saw no problem. Exploration revealed much disorganization in the family. No one in the Burns family knew who was who, and who was responsible for what, including the parents and two younger children. Beds were slept in at random by whoever reached them first. Food was prepared according to the likes and dislikes of each member, and at whatever time it was demanded. The family was constantly in debt, in part because they fell prey to every credit buying plan they encountered. If one child was "bad," all were punished indiscriminately. Although the parents loved the children in an immature, protective way, the children were out of control; the parents felt helpless. Mrs. Burns had never made a decision by herself. Every day she called or saw her mother who made all the decisions for the family.

The Neurotic Family

There are many variations and degrees of neuroticism in this category of families. All, however, display symptoms of anxiety which is not necessarily so severe that it blocks all areas of functioning. Nevertheless, it is deep enough to create unhappiness and uneasiness. The family may perform many tasks well but have difficulty with one major one. It may manage tasks reasonably well in one stage of the family life cycle and not in another. The nature and severity of the problem depends on the sources in the earlier life situations, on what residual problems are reactivated by the new life tasks, and how benign or malignant the social milieu of the family is at the time a particular and troubling task emerges.

The Goldbergs managed most tasks reasonably well except that from time to time Mr. Goldberg went on a gambling binge that distressed the family economically and emotionally. It became apparent that Mr. Goldberg gambled when his wife withdrew dependency gratification from him at times such as when a child was born or when her mother became seriously ill.

The Martin parents did a nice job of child rearing until each child was ready to enter school. Both Mr. and Mrs. Martin had been reared in an orphanage. They could not tolerate the emotional separation requisite for the child's comfortable entrance into school. Panic would ensue and the children, one after another, reacted with such phobic symptoms as vomiting each morning. Old unresolved residual conflicts in the parents came to the fore when a special task, school entrance, had to be undertaken. They needed help to recognize the source of the difficulty before they could manage the daily task.

In the Petree family all went reasonably well until Joan was ready for college. This, too, might have proceeded smoothly except that shortly before she was to leave home, her father had a coronary attack. Separation had always been hard in this family, but it had been accomplished. Now it became a crisis that was out of control because an external factor intruded at the same time that a separation task had to be undertaken.

The Psychotic Family

The psychotic family also may present social and psychological disorganization, but it is different from the chaotic family that is primitive or has character difficulties. The latter often is described as having severe characterological problems because of difficulties or fixations in early development that, though severe, are less malignant than in the psychotic family. The backgrounds may be similar, but for reasons that often are unknown, differences are manifest. One family develops a clinically psychotic member. Another family operates in bizarre ways. Or there may be a psychotic core; that is, the family evidences psychotic symptoms in some respects but in others is able to function and adapt to life tasks. The worker's task often is to enable understanding and reduce fear, guilt, and hostility toward the sick member by helping both the sick person and the other family members to express, as much as they can, their feelings of conflict, anger, and fear by pointing out discrepancies and distortions with respect to confusions between outer and inner needs and wishes. Mrs. Peters, for example, insisted that she wanted nine-year-old Judy to be well again; Judy had not uttered a word since she was four years old. Judy was being used as a scapegoat for the parents, who fought over her in order not to fight more directly with each other about their marital relationship. Judy's illness thus served the purpose of holding the marital balance in check. As the parents began to be aware of how they were using the child, they began to direct their attention to the marital conflict. In many families with a psychotic orientation to life, the struggle of the individual for adjustment to confusing and contradictory severe internal or external stresses causes the family member to resort to utilizing even more severe overt or covert behavior into withdrawal from reality. Mrs. Peters began to see the nonrealistic way in which Judy served as an excuse to avoid open quarreling with the husband about the parents' own marital relationships, that it was irrational for them to quarrel about why Judy was ill, and what had caused it, and to keep their quarreling focused only on this point. At the same time,

Mr. Peters competently held a responsible job and both parents managed the older children somewhat better than Judy.

The problems that arise to trouble families, the myriad internal and external factors that lead to their creation or exacerbation, the differences in family capacity or readiness to cope with the problems —all require separate yet interrelated assessment if the family wishing help is to be assisted in gaining or regaining a level of social functioning acceptable both to the family and to the community. Our society has established various arrangements to carry out such objectives. What these are and how they purport to help unhappy families to master the troubling aspects of their lives, is the subject of the next chapter.

4

SOCIAL WELFARE AGENCIES AND THE SOCIAL WORKER

Troubled FAMILIES are not unique to modern civilization. The form and depth of some of the troubles have differed with time, geography, external conditions, and factors of a purely personal (and personality) nature. Generally, however, everywhere people have been confronted with troubles of two kinds: those related to *survival*—food, shelter, clothing; and *socialization*—the social and psychological roles of individuals and families with regard to themselves, each other, and the community at large.

SOCIAL WELFARE OBJECTIVES

Most societies provide some culturally-determined methods for dealing with these problems. Usually the family group—the nuclear family and, often, the extended family also—constitute the primary source for meeting both survival and socialization needs. Typically, the family serves as a producing and consuming unit, shaping its effort in a fashion that will assure support to all of the members for which the unit is responsible in accordance with the pattern of the society of which it is a part. India, for example, commonly follows the practice of having kin care for older relatives. Begging also is a common practice there, and the results of this endeavor are shared with the extended family members as well as those in the nuclear family unit. The United States does not accept begging as an appropriate means for attacking a problem of survival; instead, we have developed an extensive system of public assistance and social insurance, of private pensions and services of voluntary welfare agencies—all of which form a part of our income-maintenance system.

In most societies it also is expected that the family group—the immediate or extended family—will rear the children and prepare them for assimilation into adulthood. Likewise, the care of the sick and those handicapped by age or other factors, and the meeting of many other subjective needs associated with social or personal functioning, is left to the family. In turn, these family activities are supported by religious and cultural values and practices that revolve around enabling people to assume the expected roles within the family and in the community. In our rapidly changing world, however, the modifications in traditional roles of each generation, the disruption of family cohesion as members gravitate to industrialized urban centers, the shifting of various tasks from the household to the community as technology and industrialization have advanced— all have led to a narrowing of the family's functioning and increasingly have called for the establishment of specialized institutional arrangements to aid the family in performing its various tasks. Thus, schools supplement learning conducted within the family; clinics, hospitals, rest homes, and other facilities provide health care; foster care is available for children and adults who cannot be provided with needed care at home; family counseling is extended when marital discord or parent-child relationships indicate a need for the intervention of an outside authority; juvenile courts and correctional institutions assist with severe problems needing control.

Regardless, however, of the extent to which community arrangements are developed to aid the family in the discharge of its survival and socialization functions, the nuclear family remains central to the performance of these functions. There are, of course, circumstances which result in the family relinquishing or drastically reducing its responsibilities in these two areas: death or mental or physical incapacity may effectively alter the family's ability or capacity to meet these needs. When this occurs, the interests of the family and of society require that there be measures that can either substitute for the family or augment what can be done by the family. The point at which augmentation ends and substitution begins depends upon the ability of the individual family to make constructive adaptation to necessary change.

The measures developed in a community, then, to strengthen the family as the basic social institution through which survival and socialization needs are met, and to strengthen the individual's capacity to cope with the tasks related to meeting these needs, are designated as social welfare. This term, social welfare, denotes a wide array of organized voluntary and governmental activities that seek to solve, or prevent, or alleviate social problems, or to improve the well-being of individuals, families, groups, or communities. The programs undertaken under the auspices of social welfare agencies utilize the services of many specialists with technical and professional skills: teachers, physicians, ministers, anthropologists, nurses, social workers, and others.

Within this social welfare system, the role of the social worker with the troubled family may be to support, to strengthen, or to supplement the family in fulfilling its economic and socialization obligations; it may be to arrange for a substitution for the family in order to aid the victims of broken families or untenable family situations. It is through the organized system of social welfare that the social worker's and the agency's activities are directed toward aiding families and individuals to attain a level of economic, social, and emotional functioning that is satisfying to them and in harmony with the community.[1] In recent years, social workers and the agencies under whose auspices they conduct their work have recognized that achievement of maximum competence in social functioning requires that in addition to meeting needs related to survival and socialization, a third objective is in order: *self-realization* or self-fulfillment.

THE EVOLUTION OF SOCIAL WELFARE

Recognition of Social Need

The arrangements that have evolved in the United States for helping families with problems of survival, socialization, or self-realization cannot be separated from the mainstream of the nation's economic, social, political and cultural history. For just as the individ-

---

[1] See Chapter 17 for the major functions of the social worker.

ual family's functioning is related to the impact of societal attitudes and environmental factors on the personalities of the family members, so are today's social welfare arrangements the product of societal attitudes (past and present) and environmental factors (past and present).

At every point in our national development, social welfare problems have been met with social welfare answers that emerged from the times and the then-existing social-economic-political climate. These answers—the social welfare programs and services—were shaped by the readiness of our society first to *recognize* the *existence* of a social problem: not just the trouble experienced from time to time by an occasional family or even by some families; rather, to become aware that a particular problem was making a negative impact on family after family and, consequently, the health of the community.

The recognition of a social problem, however, depends on several dynamics. For one thing, there has to be a readiness on the part of some leaders, if not of the community at large, to acknowledge the problem's presence before any measures can be considered for dealing with it, let alone undertaken. Then there must be readiness to act in accordance with the technical knowledge and financial and other resources available to be utilized in moving toward resolution of the problem. And the answers have to be consistent with the prevailing beliefs. Thus, when the long and arduous trip from Europe to the New World brought death to many parents unable to withstand the rigors of the long journey to the colonies, arrangements of some kind had to be devised to meet the needs of the sizable number of widows (even then many women appeared hardy enough to survive their husbands!) and orphans who survived the trip. When advancing technology resulted in frequent and often dramatic industrial accidents that deprived families of the breadwinner, there was growing awareness that some provision had to be made for their survivors. When epidemics of contagious diseases decimated large segments of population, it was apparent that some means had to be provided to protect society against continuing ravages by disease. When the depression of the 'thirties brought unemployment and havoc into the lives of millions of heretofore hard-working Americans, unprecedented steps had to be taken to make financial relief available throughout the nation and to develop mechanisms to prevent recurrence of such tragedy.

Mobilization of Resources

Recognition, therefore, led to *mobilization* of available resources with which to attack the problems, whether the resources consisted of tax funds or voluntary financial contributions as well as the volunteer services of community-minded citizens. Spurred by the leaders who had come forward to insist that measures be undertaken to control the problem and mitigate its consequences, specific programs were developed that would deploy these financial and service resources toward resolution of the social problems that had been identified. In this manner, there emerged aid for widowed mothers, workmen's compensation for industrial casualties, public health measures for the control of contagious diseases, institutions for the delinquent or wayward child, placement of children in foster family homes, protective services for children, family services ". . . to strengthen family ties . . . ,"[2] unemployment insurance benefits, and other social welfare answers to social needs and problems.

Compatibility with Conscience

The specific objective, the form, the scope, and the direction of evolving social welfare programs inevitably are shaped by the prevailing attitudes in society at the point that a social welfare problem is identified. Accordingly, the Puritan measures of adequacy and morality described in Chapter 2—particularly the work ethic and the virtue of thrift—have continued to be a dominant influence in social welfare with regard not only to economic need but also to socialization. The children orphaned by the death of parents en route to the colonies on the Atlantic Seaboard were apprenticed: thus they were placed in "good" homes, but they also learned early the virtue of hard work. The widowed mother was not required to take employment, for the place of women was in the home; she might be given a cow by the townspeople, or supplied with firewood or some other necessity to help the family survive. When the children were grown (not infrequently by the age of ten years), they were expected to work and to assume responsibility for the family's maintenance. This was not inhumane, judged by the standards of the day—schooling was not expected for all children, work for many children began long before the age of ten, knowledge about essentials for physical and emotional development was not applied differently to the children of the poor than to children of the more affluent.

Well into the nineteenth century needy persons who did not accept work generally were considered defective and various measures were adopted to be sure that dependency was not encouraged. Thus,

---

[2] Rev. R. E. Thompson, *Manual for Visitors Among the Poor*, published by the Philadelphia Society for Organizing Charitable Relief and Repressing Mendicancy (Philadelphia: Lippincott Co., 1879) p. 18.

they might be placed in almshouses or work farms or other settings where work was mandatory. The strength of feeling in this regard is illustrated by the "confidential" instructions issued by the New York Association for the Improvement of the Conditions of the Poor[3] after the middle of the last century to its volunteer visitors (usually men). It reminded them that, while almshouse relief was a "legal" charity to provide for those who might perish if neglected, the voluntary charity was based on the social and economical wants of the community and could choose to aid only those it could "physically and morally elevate." Similar attitudes among vocal community interests have led to the insistence in more recent years, in many jurisdictions, that employable unemployed men work at any kind of job in preference to relief for themselves or their families, that aid in programs not governed by federal standards not be enough to encourage a family to be dependent in preference to taking work at whatever wages or under whatever conditions it might be available, and so forth. Out of these earlier but persistent attitudes about morality have come requirements in public assistance with regard to the legal responsibility of relatives for certain kin, observance of residence, means tests, and other requirements as conditions for the receipt of public assistance, and, sometimes, a massive quantity of requirements and documents designed to assure that only those who are "worthy" are aided at public expense.

Devices for Meeting Need

In essence, social welfare in this nation has been deeply influenced by seventeenth-century English Poor Laws, with their emphasis on localism, less eligibility, work tests for employable persons, legal responsibility of relatives, and other elements intended to deal with changing economic and social conditions in a plague-ridden agrarian society feeling the first thrust of an industrial revolution. These poor law principles fitted the needs of the colonists whose Puritan attitudes and agrarian society could readily adapt them as the answer to the social welfare problems they saw. While programs and services over the years have been modified, expanded, and refined, the Puritan values, though mellowed in many respects, have continued to affect the formulation of policy and the implementation of policy governing a variety of social welfare activities.

Nevertheless, the evolution of social welfare has been characterized by shifts from concern only with the protection of society

[3] This organization in 1938 merged with the New York Charity Organization Society to form the Community Service Society of New York.

against the "worthlessness" of those not caring for themselves in a land of rugged individualists for whom all kinds of opportunities abound, to the rehabilitation of those having some potential for self-care and self-maintenance for the sake of the family and the family members as well as in the interests of having productive communities and a strong and healthy nation.

Social welfare, voluntary and public, has thus moved from stages concerned primarily with *survival* needs (food, shelter, clothing— and, increasingly, medical care), to *socialization* of the family and family members (dealing with deviant emotional, social, or economic behavior for the purpose of enabling the family and its members to function in our society as a reasonably self-maintaining and socially adequate unit of the community), to *self-realization* or self-fulfillment, whereby individuals and families can function more nearly at their maximum capacity and lead lives that are both personally satisfying and socially productive and constructive.

SOCIAL WELFARE TODAY

Today's social welfare programs, then, in general are the distillate of three and a half centuries of ways of coping with the major social problems that are ever present in a dynamic and changing industrial democracy. New arrangements have evolved, along with new techniques, for dealing on a large scale with many kinds of problems—either before they emerge or after they have made an appearance. Thus, the social insurances (Old-age, Survivors, and Disability Insurance Benefits, Unemployment Insurance Benefits, Temporary Disability Insurance Benefits—in the four states where these are available—Workman's Compensation, and the latest addition, Medicare) *assume* the likelihood of economic need if wages of the breadwinner stop because of death, disability, work-related injury or illness, retirement because of advancing age, loss of employment. In accordance with state and federal laws, taxes paid by the wage earner, or by his employer, or by both, provide certain protections against these common hazards. Public health departments, with the protective aims of preventing ill health and controlling contagion of disease, provide a variety of health services to children, to mothers, and to other adults. Deviant behavior that is disturbing to an individual or his family and inimical to the interests of the community may receive attention from public or voluntary in-patient or out-patient mental health facilities, or from local or state or federal correction agencies. Adults or children, families or individuals, generally have available a range of generalized or specialized counseling and helping services, sectarian or nonsectarian, voluntary or public: family agencies, children's agencies, group work services agencies, medical services, vocational guidance, school guidance, psychiatric clinics and care, settlement houses, and so on.

Financial assistance may be extended to needy families by voluntary or public agencies—for maintenance of the family, for board and care payment for an adult or child in placement, for vocational training or retraining, to meet a special need like a homemaker (as in the case of the Kovacs family in Chapter 21) or some other special purpose (as was requested by Mr. Link in Chapter 18).

The providing of income for maintenance may be part of a total plan in which rehabilitative or other services are being extended to a needy family in relation to the family's particular problems and potentials for making some constructive use of the help. On the other hand, the assistance may be the sole goal because, given income for meeting its ongoing needs, the family is adequate to the tasks with which it needs to cope. Ordinarily, economic assistance is viewed as the responsibility of the public assistance agencies, with their federally aided (and financed in part with state or state and county monies) programs for the aged, the blind, the totally disabled, families with dependent children; sometimes these agencies also offer general relief services (which are not funded from federal sources) to needy families who do not qualify for one of the previously mentioned federally aided programs, which have their origins in the Social Security Act.

Social welfare programs may differ in the specific focus of their function; they may be based in law and financed from tax sources (the public social services) or governed by policy established by a voluntary board and financed by a united way or community chest or a church or other private source (the private or voluntary social agency). But they have certain characteristics in common. All are working with families or segments of families, and they have the common theme of family unhappiness and the common goal of increasing the effectiveness of the social functioning of various family members as well as for the family as a whole.

They differ in an essential way from the program added in recent years to the total social welfare structure: the War on Poverty (Economic Opportunity Acts of 1964 and 1965). This addition reflects the dynamics noted earlier with regard to social welfare problems: the need has been recognized and accepted by national leaders who, imbued with the importance of attacking the problem, have striven to make resources available to implement the attack. The Social Security programs are designed to help *individuals* and *individual families* whose problems stem from stressful factors in the community or from personal or developmental problems: These programs, consistent with their reason for being, do not aim to correct the broad social problems that arise in the community or in the nation; their effort is focused primarily on individual needs, and any inroads on the broad social problems constitute a bonus. The War on Poverty, on the other hand, was planned to tackle basic social problems—poverty *per se*, disadvantageousness, factors that feed poverty. While many parts of the "War" focus on services to individuals and families, these are secondary to the primary objectives of the program.

But whether the objective of social welfare is to modify or correct a wider social problem or to meet the problems of an individual, the personnel engaged in carrying out the social welfare functions, the basic knowledge and skill that have to be brought to the execution of the function, are the same: an interest in helping troubled people and knowledge about basic human behavior that facilitates extending constructive help to troubled families. For whether the objective is to modify the troubling community problem or to help the troubled family, *people* are involved and have to be understood so that they are aided directly or indirectly to function competently in our society. Information fundamental to this understanding and how this information may be applied to helping troubled families are presented in the chapters that follow.

Developmental Tasks in the Cycle of Family Life

5

THE TASKS

THE FAMILY

THE SIMPLE WORD "family" undoubtedly is known to everyone, everywhere. Yet it conveys meanings that may differ sharply from country to country, and it evokes feelings that vary from individual to individual. That generally accepted authority, Webster's Dictionary, describes the family in a variety of ways: "The body of persons who live in one house, and under one head; a household. . . . Those descended from a common progenitor; a tribe, clan, or race; kindred. . . . One's children collectively. . . . A group of closely related individuals or groups. . . . A group comprising immediate kindred; (especially) the group formed of parents and children."

Each statement in this definition is correct in itself; taken alone, no single one is sufficient to define today's family. The parts must be put into a whole—and perhaps expressed in somewhat different terminology to advance an adequate definition of the family in our American culture, in today's world. For today the family generally is viewed as a biological unit, that is, its members constituting a family through birth; as a social unit, its members comprising the household; as a psychological unit, its members bound together by emotional relatedness. And these three units intermesh. The intermeshing can be described in still other terms: as an interpersonal system. The family, then, is a network, a system of interpersonal relationships. In this context, the total family group contains a network of forces and roles which directly influence the uniqueness of each family's functional goals of living. The family network also can be perceived as a series of subsystems containing two-, three-, and more person relationships: marriage partners, parents, parents and children, and siblings. The family may be seen as a collection of individuals who have separate and joint goals and problems and whose individual identity is maintained but also develops as an integral part of the family. All these are valid ways of looking at the family system for the purpose of understanding how to work with people. The main emphasis, however, is on viewing the family as an interpersonal system, the smallest but most important system in our human society.

Nuclear and Extended Families

The term "nuclear family" has come to mean the family members who live together as a unit in one household. In our culture these generally are the parents and their children. The term "extended family" refers to the relatives who have close emotional or blood ties with the nuclear family but who do not necessarily live in the same household with the nuclear family. The use of both terms, nuclear and extended, has grown in importance as changes have been wrought in our culture by increasing urbanization and its related pattern of smaller dwelling units than can accommodate extra relatives; by increasing mobility of population not only from farm to city but from one part of the country to another as industrialization and automation escalate; by increasing employment opportunities for women, and so on.

Families in some subcultural groups still live in units that are more inclusive than just parents and their children. However, the trend away from the extended family and toward the nuclear family is very strong. This is not to say that the ties between nuclear and extended families are not close. The extended family still is seen as an important resource for social, financial, and emotional support, especially in the event of a crisis. In the United States today by and large there is not the same interdependence of nuclear and extended families as when this was more of an agrarian nation and major aspects of education, economic productivity, and other functions were carried on in the home itself. Yet, even though relatives may live many hundreds of miles apart, it is evident that they still are very much involved with the nuclear family from the standpoint of economic, social, and emotional interactions. The healthy family, though emotionally and economically independent, maintains and retains strong ties with the extended family on an equalitarian basis. This is a relationship in which services are offered and accepted without destroying the independence of the nuclear family. In an unhealthy family situation, the nuclear family may be isolated or maintain the kind of relationship with the extended family in which there is a financial and social or even an emotional dependence. Thus, a young couple, instead of beginning to rely on its own inner and external resources, may continually turn to the extended family for economic assistance or for advice about a variety of matters of social or emotional nature.

The modern emphasis on the nuclear family and the sloughing off to the wider culture of some of the functions that the family had in the past, however, have not altered the importance of the family as the basic unit in our society. No real substitute for the family has been found to develop the physical, social, and emotional well-being and productivity of the family's members. Character is formed in the family; and no alternate device has been discovered for the development of the capacity of the family member to love and to harness aggression toward personal and social benefit. The work of Dr. René Spitz and others, for example, shows dramatically that even the best of institutional care of infants does not produce children who thrive either physically or emotionally. They seem particularly liable to physical illness, to serious delays in development, to intellectual retardation, and to emotional apathy.

The Family Arena

An individual's basic preparation for the tasks of life evolves within the family. The family setting is an arena of utmost importance in the individual's day-to-day living; it is here that he is a participant, giver, receiver, and collaborator in a network of interpersonal experiences which cannot be isolated from the family system, and which echo through the family system. Individuality is a matter of achieving identity. Identity, as will be described in Chapter 15, refers to one's view of oneself. This can be achieved only by learning that one is both similar to and different from others in the family and the outside world. It is through relationships established primarily in the family that a person achieves identity: his maturity as an individual with respect to sexual identity (relationship to the opposite sex); parenting identity (relationship to children); work identity (tasks and work relationships); self-esteem (self in comparison to others); and self-responsibility (control and management of aggression). In other words, the capacity to love and the capacity to work, the two basic ingredients for sound personality development, are germinated within the family. Although the development of personality continues through life experiences outside the family, and growth potential exists at all stages of individual life, what is instilled within the individual in his early years in the family remains the most potent force in his life.

Not long ago it was generally believed that personality development was largely a matter between mother and child. More recent developments in ego psychology, however, indicate that personality is shaped by the total family—not only by its membership at any given time but also by what is going on at any given time. It is recognized that a child needs both parents for sound development. The child absorbs much from the family atmosphere, which includes the relationship between the two parents, their standards, the patterns of their behavior, and the models they offer him. These, then, contribute to the formation of his own personality. The child both knowingly and unknowingly takes in his parents as persons; he observes them in their relationships to each other and to him, separately and together; and he observes their relationships, separately and together, to the other children. He imitates them and later he identifies with them. He incorporates into his own life their values, standards, ways of behaving and feeling. If conflict between the parents is not resolved satisfactorily, the child senses or knows this and is affected by it. The child's maturational process may be delayed or impaired because of the parents' inability to meet his needs at the appropriate time if there are serious problems in the family such as illness, financial difficulties, death, undue preoccupation with the extended family by either or both parents.

Character formation may show serious defects if there are problems such as alcoholism, perversions, delinquencies, family values that are contrary to those considered socially acceptable. The child may become the recipient of attitudes and behavior that distort his development if one or both parents carry too many unresolved personal problems from their own pasts into the present family.

This is not to say that the child is an empty slate on which his parents write. His native endowment, physically and psychologically, has considerable bearing on how his parents relate to him. An active or passive infant, for example, may stir positive or negative or ambivalent feelings in the parents, much depending on the emotional state of each. As the child becomes observant, he responds not only to what he senses the parents want from him and how he can please them but also to what will bring him gratification. For example, if a child learns that he can stoke the fires of marital conflict by his provocative behavior in playing one parent against the other, and feels that he gains advantages by doing this, he will develop a manipulative character trait that will carry over to other life experiences. In other words, the child elects to behave in certain ways that afford gratification to himself and, if he wishes, to his parents. In this sense, the child has self-responsibility for his own development as well as for some of what transpires in the family. Accordingly, the constant dynamic interchanges between the parents and children are forces that shape individual development.

Roles of Family Members

The family operates through roles that shift and alter during the course of the family's life. Roles can be explicit or instrumental; they can be implicit or emotional. In the division of responsibilities, explicit or instrumental roles are discharged through the management of tasks such as those connected with breadwinning, parenting, father-son or mother-daughter or husband-wife relationships. Implicit or emotional roles encompass the feelings, attitudes, beliefs that go into the family relationships and affect the ways in which explicit roles are discharged.

The healthy family carries out explicit and implicit roles appropriately according to age, competence, and needs during all the different stages of family life. The disturbed family experiences serious difficulties in the management of roles. This can be illustrated by the parents who are uncertain or confused with regard to the parenting function and so abdicate needed roles; they simply may not know how to behave as parents. Thus a family is created where there is role confusion or role diffusion, with each member unclear as to who he is or the nature of his responsibilities, and with attendant problems in the development of identity. Or role reversal may result, with the parent behaving like a child and the child behaving like a parent. In marriage there often is conflict when the marital partners are confused about their respective roles. This conflict contributes to the formation of poor models of identification for the children if the woman, for example, assumes masculine attitudes and responsibilities and the man takes on feminine attitudes.

Role performance should be clear, appropriate to our culture's expectations and requirements, and to each unique family. It should be flexible as tasks change in the family. This does not mean that there may be no overlapping of roles between family members, as, for instance, the husband and wife. Many men in our culture perform household tasks, but this need not disturb the essential masculine quality of their relationship to wife and children. Many women work, but this need not obscure their feminine qualities. When children understand the reason for divisions of responsibility in the home, and the parents are clear about role performance, the children can develop proper identity.

Individual families may differ in their perceptions of the tasks connected with the acceptance of responsibility and appropriate role performance. They may view differently how the tasks they perceive are to be discharged. Nevertheless, the basic tasks are universal for all families in all cultures and, just as it long has been recognized that an *individual* has a cycle of development tasks that are universal, the *family* also has development tasks that are universal.

THE COMMON TASKS

What are these tasks? They fall into four broad areas: the provision for security and physical survival; the provision for emotional and social functioning; the provision for sexual differentiation and the training of children; and the provision for support of growth of individual family members. These are the common ones, whether the family copes with them well or poorly. They can be condensed into the universal tasks of loving and working, two separate yet interrelated and interdependent tasks with which every family must struggle from its inception as a family.

Security and Physical Survival

All families are concerned with managing to survive in a literal sense. Somehow the basic necessities for life must be procured.

In our dominant American culture the emphasis is on obtaining these by money from work, and a high premium is placed on work. Certainly there are variations, family by family and in different cultural groups, as to the meaning of work and money. For many middle-class families security means achievement in the form of education, savings, home ownership, and similar items. For many families security means reliance on income-maintenance programs: the social insurances or public assistances or veterans' allowances. For many it means any kind of a job that will produce enough to hold body and soul together.

Similarly, along cultural lines, security to an Appalachian family may compel only the amount of work sufficient to assure food and fuel for the winter, when pleasurable fishing and hunting are limited. This kind of family does not easily understand the urban employer who demands steady appearance on the job. Security to some Negro families means "desertion" by the unemployed father so that his wife and children can obtain public assistance more readily. Security for the Puerto Rican family often means the wife's working because she is less subject to discrimination in the job market and better able than her husband to get and hold jobs. Whatever form the search for security and physical survival may take, it is shaped by a compelling urge. In our culture this urge not only is felt by the individual, it also encompasses the family. It is taken for granted that parents are responsible for the physical survival and security of the children. Great moral censure and serious legal measures are the fate of those parents who abandon or fail this charge. Many states hold adult children legally and morally obliged to provide for parents in need. Apart from the legal, moral, and cultural implications, there generally is something within the human animal that makes him want to provide for the security and physical survival of his family.

Emotional and Social Functioning

Despite previously described changes taking place in society that result in delegating to it some of the tasks formerly retained by the family, such as primary education and certain work chores, the basic task of the family continues to be viewed as the establishment and maintenance of a climate in which sound emotional development can take place, and in which the groundwork is laid for the family members to be able to function in a wider world. The family is held responsible for providing an atmosphere of love, of protection of its young from emotional turmoil, of good values and standards, of moral and ethical attitudes that will enable the individual to manage himself in the outer world of school, work, and relationships with others than the family members. The family is held responsible for initiating work habits that will enable the individual to meet the reality demands of the external world.

The family, too, recognizes its obligations to provide this necessary climate and strives to fulfill it in spite of weaknesses and problems within the family, cultural factors related to behavioral and attitudinal differences toward love and work, and the changes occurring in society. It is rare to find a family that does not want its children to have a better life than that the parents had experienced. Families may err in this approach to providing love, habits, and standards; they may be myopic or even blind in specific application. But most families yearn to provide their children with a climate of love that is basic to good emotional development, and most families want their children to do well in the outside world.

Sexual Differentiation and Training of Children

Every family, no matter what its culture and uniqueness, has the task of helping children know who they are and to train, or socialize, them. In its own way, each family recognizes that tasks differ for boys and girls, that one of the main functions of the family is to aid in the differential development of masculine and feminine identity in the children and to help them to use such identity productively. The family achieves this goal by assigning to each child the different kinds of tasks that are appropriate to the child as a boy or a girl, and by each parent behaving as a model for the child of the same sex. At the same time, in his or her relationship with the marital partner, each parent models how the children of different sexes are to manage in relation to each other.

Each family has the task of training or socializing children in habits of self-control and control in relation to others: to develop ability to get along with others who may be in or outside the family; to respect the needs, values, and standards of others; to learn to work with others; to learn to *learn* from others; to manage aggression so that it is socially useful; to master sexual impulses so that they are not harmful either to themselves or to society. Each family has to come to terms between its own way of socializing children and the demands of the larger community. How successful they will be depends on their need to cling to cultural standards that may deviate from the requirements of the dominant society, and on the family's ability to compromise in the interests of permitting the children to meet the demands of the prevailing culture while remaining stead-fast in those areas it considers basic to its own cultural orientation.

Support of Growth of Individual Family Members

In its own way, every family is confronted with the basic conflict between wanting to allow each individual member to estab-lish his own identity and wanting him to remain an undifferentiated part of the family. This old and universal situation may be ex-pressed in these terms: the conflict between holding on to children and letting them go. Thus, at every stage of the individual's life, each family simultaneously must struggle with giving him permission to separate emotionally and physically, yet provide him with the support that creates and maintains healthy continuity and inter-dependence within the family. Each family must struggle with the conflicting desires that its members remain dependent on the family and that they ultimately develop mature independence. Each family has to figure out when individual members are ready to undertake the new and increasingly mature tasks requisite for emotional growth, and how to help each child assume the tasks without either holding him back or pushing him forward unduly. Each family has to recog-nize individual differences and support the right of each member to be different, to have different interests, to want different things. At the same time, it is the family's task to keep these differences within the bounds of the family's and society's best interests.

THE CYCLE OF FAMILY LIFE

The universal life tasks are intimately bound up with the universal cycle of family life. In the usual meaning of the term "family" the cycle comprises marriage, child rearing, the middle years—when children usually leave—and the later years. The tasks that were described as general become specific in relation to the various stages of the cycle of family life as well as of the individual's life cycle. Every family has unique strengths and vulnerabilities in each part of the cycle of family life and in all of the tasks attached to each part. In a broad sense, the family's capacities or strengths to meet the tasks of each developmental stage, as well as the family's vulnerabilities, weaknesses, and failures, depend on how successfully the family has mastered tasks in previous stages of the family life cycle; on the unique strengths and vulnerabilities accruing to each family member because of his own past life experience; on how the coping capacity of the family has been affected by such external factors as death, ill health, loss of work, and the like; on how the meeting of the tasks has been disturbed by such internal stresses within the family as marital discord, emotional breakdown, and other difficulties; and on how social conditions affect the family's capacity to manage.

Family strength and vulnerability must always be viewed as uniquely different for each family. The particular current stress must be identified and seen in its place in relation to a specific life task and to the specific phase of family development. One family may be more vulnerable during the early child-rearing years, another during their offspring's adolescence. One family may be more susceptible when external factors coincide with a particularly difficult phase of the cycle of family life as, for instance, if a father loses his job when his adolescent son is having absolutely no trouble finding work.

Families do not meet with equal ease and competence all the tasks in the several stages of the family life cycle. All families find that in the transition from one stage to another of the cycle of family life the attendant tasks merge and blur into each other. At the same time, each change provides striking new features that require shifts from accustomed ways of living.

Normal stress, then, is to be expected as each new task emerges in each new stage of the cycle of family life. Normal stress requires that the family strike a balance between accustomed ways of meeting tasks and new ways of meeting the demands that change with the arrival of successive stages of the cycle of family life. Understanding of the nature and the extent of deviance from normal devices for coping with tasks relevant to particular stages of the family life cycle requires a base of knowledge about healthy and usual ways of dealing with tasks. The succeeding chapters consider some of the healthy coping methods as well as those ways that deviate from the wide range of normalcy.

6

MARRIAGE

ALL FAMILIES in our American culture are expected to start with a marriage. To this marriage each partner brings his individual heritage, earlier family experiences, cultural expectations and values—the sum of the personal qualities that constitute his individuality. The strength the marital partners put into the marriage structure in the beginning stage of the family cycle is a major determinant for the effectiveness of each succeeding stage.

In a society that long has foregone the formality of arranged marriages, what brings the man and woman together to continue unbroken the flow of life from birth through childhood, adolescence, adulthood, and old age, with each of the adult children and his adult children initiating his own cycle of family life? For centuries poets have offered answers containing a core of agreement. Heywood coupled weddings and hangings as destiny. A century later Robert Burton qualified this pessimistic view by adding that *matches* are made in heaven and this was subsequently skeptically qualified by Southerne's declaration that "if marriages are made in Heaven, they should be happier." But when two more centuries had passed, Tennyson encapsulated the optimism of his time with a flat "marriages are made in Heaven." Pragmatic Benjamin Franklin, however, with his profound faith in common sense and in the efficacy of reason for the solution of human problems and the advancement of human welfare, proposed: "Keep your eyes wide open before marriage and half-shut afterwards."

Today, without depreciating either the forces of destiny or man's ability to reason and to act accordingly, considerable knowledge is available about some of the elements that bring two people together and that enable them to maintain a healthy marriage or an unhealthy one—or, indeed, to dissolve the marriage in a healthy or unhealthy fashion.

Today's marriages are based on the needs, wishes, and hopes of each marriage partner. Some of these needs, wishes, and hopes are more or less readily apparent. The partners are conscious of similarities and differences in interests—religion, education, sports; in needs —love, sympathy, complaints; in wishes and goals—economic comfort, social status, educational achievement, colored television. But not so apparent are needs, hopes, and goals about which they are relatively or completely unaware. For example, a person whose childhood was emotionally deprived will tend to find a partner with similar needs, each hoping that somehow the other will meet the dependent needs that stem from his earlier emotional deprivation. Such factors, generally lying below the surface of consciousness, are of even greater importance than those about which the couple is cognizant. The oft-used analogy of the iceberg is relevant here—not, however, with respect to temperature, although coldness is not unknown in many marriages. The visible upper section of the iceberg represents the qualities of which the marital partners are aware; submerged below the water surface lurks the larger and often more critical part of the iceberg, out of sight and generally out of consciousness.

COMPLEMENTARITY

The meshing of the couple's conscious and unconscious needs and wishes is termed "complementarity of need." The manner and the success with which the meshing process occurs—how, and the degree to which the couple's conflicts are resolved or prevented from interfering with the performance of tasks that are part of a healthy marriage—constitute a barometer for the development of the family members. Complementarity also is expressed in terms of marital equilibrium, a dynamic balance of stability and change characterizing the marriage on an even and stable course, recognizing that each new task emerging during the cycle of family life brings changes in the marriage and in the family.

An important current theory holds that people find each other in relation to similarities in their personality development. Thus, two people who feel they were abandoned by their own parents will, like orphans in a storm, tend to find each other and seek to obtain satisfaction from each other as abandoned human beings. In this sense their personality development is similar and it follows, therefore, that their efforts to work out the usual conflicts in marriage would yield similar results such as defending themselves as well as each other against feelings of abandonment. For example, the wife may feel her husband is losing interest in her because his job takes him away from home so much, or the husband may view the amount of time his wife spends with the children as evidence of her loss of interest in him. Each partner's now ingrained feeling of being abandoned increases, and he may defend himself by placing all the blame for this situation on his spouse or by a reinstated sense of being completely worthless—for, after all, the marital partner is abandoning him in the same way that his parents did; they also thought him worthless.

The level of maturity of the partners in an unhealthy marriage generally is identical. Although each may express his feelings by different forms of behavior, the underlying personality of each partner is similar. Both marital partners, for example, may be seeking the same thing: each to have the other meet his basic dependency needs. Yet one expresses the need by aggressive demands and the other by passive demands. One may complain about a lack of closeness for which the other denies a need. However, scrutiny reveals that both, though expressing it differently, fear closeness or are ambivalent about it. The wife may demand that her husband pay much more attention to her than he appears able to do. The husband may display exactly the same need but mask it by accusing his wife not of failing to give him what he wants but of not paying sufficient attention to the children's needs. This expression of concern for the children enables him to disguise from himself as well as from his wife his wish for the same thing she desires.

Dynamics of Healthy Complementarity

The future of a marriage is determined by the dynamics of complementarity throughout the marriage. The influence of the extended families, the intensity of mutual dependence of marital partners on each other, the ability of each to allow the other to be an individual in his own right, the effects of external factors such as money, health, changes in the family structure with the arrival and departure of the children—all are dynamic operational factors that affect complementarity and, therefore, marital equilibrium. The operational course of marriage and family is affected by the point at which the marriage is fixed, its basic complementarity as, for example, in the marriage of two affection-hungry childlike people or in the marriage built on adolescent rebellion.

The course of the marriage and each stage of the family cycle also are influenced by the pattern of regression that each marital partner follows. People under stress not uncommonly tend to regress to previous ways of doing things in their effort to manage the stress. Once the stress is lifted, they generally give up their clinging to these older, known and perhaps more comfortable, ways of behaving; they again pursue the usual course of life in an expected and accepted manner. Normal regression occurs when an ill person who is hospitalized permits himself to accept all the services that the hospital provides in order that he become well; this is only common sense, but it requires the patient to behave in a somewhat childlike fashion. On the other hand, under stress, people who have not matured sufficiently in themselves and in the marriage will revert to older ways of behaving for longer periods, or even permanently. Such a person may turn to his own parents in such a way that the parents seriously interfere with the tasks of marriage and, consequently, this fact becomes a problem in the marriage itself.

Whether the marriage partners during stress mobilize their energies so that they deal with the stress *together* or they withdraw from each other likewise is a significant determinant of the course of the marriage. Some partners can accept and tolerate the fact that when stress is present the spouse may need to withdraw into himself or that he may need to have periods of being alone; this is not really a withdrawal *from* the other partner, nor is it an attack on either the partner or the marriage. This manner of responding to stress may differ from the partner's, but understanding and accepting the differences reflect a capacity to support each other in day-to-day living and in crises, the flexibility necessary for appropriate and satisfactory compromises, and the ability to work out conflicts in ways that are growth-producing or adaptive.

To the healthy marriage the partners bring certain qualities from past life experiences. One is the previously noted ability to tolerate separateness and difference as illustrated above. Another is the ability to free the energy necessary so that they can engage in the tasks of marriage. These partners are reasonably mature. They are able to come to decisions such as how to manage their money, with an economy of emotional expenditures, and learn to divide the responsibilities for household tasks so that these become routine and, therefore, leave both with the time as well as the energy to pursue the tasks of learning to live with each other and to manage children when they begin to arrive on the scene. Still another quality they possess is the ability to communicate with each other without undue recriminations, to face the facts and reasons for disagreement without either rushing "home to mother" or resorting to silent sulking or childish tantrums. Important to the healthy marriage also is respect brought by each partner for individual and joint decisions; such respect requires the presence of a reasonable degree of self-esteem coupled with an ability to be appropriately concerned about the partner.

To maintain the health of the marriage requires the partners to work, separately and together, on each phase of the marriage as it proceeds through the cycle of family life. A healthy marriage may be described, in broad terms, as including these essential ingredients: the couple should have a clear awareness and mutuality of goals that are relatively realistic, and that are stable yet appropriately flexible to accommodate changing circumstances. There should be reasonable compatability in emotional, social, sexual, economic, and parental spheres. Although some conflict inevitably is a part of marriage, it should derive from realistic differences rather than irrational needs; nor should the conflict be so excessive that it cannot be kept under reasonable control. Pleasure, responsibility, and authority should be shared in fulfillment of the goals of the marital relationship and of each partner. Existing differences that are reasonable should be accepted by each as a stimulus for growth. And fundamental in a healthy marriage is tolerance for difference in the partner and tolerance for residual immaturities in the partner.

The marital partners in a healthy family are able to talk directly and openly with each other about their feelings, their wishes, their needs.[1] They blame each other once in a while, not persistently. If

[1] For the meaning of communication, see Chapter 16.

one is hurt by something the partner has done, there is only an occasional withdrawal into the kind of silence that disturbs the marital partner, or an occasional talking about problems with parents instead of with the spouse. The fairly frequent occurrence of such regressive behavior, in which neither partner is a totally mature human being and under stress reverts to more childish ways of behaving, is in contrast to the normal kind of regression referred to earlier. The partner in a healthy marriage recognizes that such immaturities will emerge from time to time in the heat of conflict, that they are not serious, and that each partner can bear them in the other.

Implicit in this description of a healthy marriage is the concept that marriage is a series of tasks and is more than the union of two individuals. Through the dynamic interplay of needs, wishes, and goals, it becomes a new family unit and comprises different phases in each of which tasks and functions both overlap and are different. Marriage, therefore, can be viewed as a series of transitional normal crises in terms of stages of the family life cycle.

The Tasks in Healthy Marriage

During the early years of marriage, the partners' tasks and functions are to loosen their bonds from their families of origin and to reorient themselves from the status of two completely separate individuals to a newly married couple engaging themselves in the building of a unique family life. They have to learn to understand and deal with each other sexually. They have to learn how to divide and jointly manage economic and household responsibilities. They have to learn how to be wives or husbands in terms of the different roles that must be assumed at different times and under different circumstances, to understand and respect individual freedom and difference, and to manage as a married couple in the outside world.

When children come, the partners face new transitional normal crises. There may be temporary regression of each or both partners to eralier modes of operating until common feelings and attitudes can be worked out about this new stage of marriage. It is not uncommon, for example, to find that a husband becomes jealous during his wife's pregnancy when her interest necessarily is turned in on the coming baby or upon the baby's arrival when she is preoccupied with the infant. Since our culture does not find it acceptable to stress jealousy, the young husband may resort to various subtle devices for hiding this feeling—devices characterized by childish behavior.

In the healthy marriage these regressive aspects of behavior are nonpathological; they are temporary, persisting only until a new marital equilibrium is attained and common interest in the children comes to the fore. A new and compatible division of labor in the home is worked out that is unique in each marriage. The marital pair learn how to become parents and they see and deal with the children as children, not as tools or weapons of the parents. The parents may have differences regarding some details about child rearing, but they support each other in such major points as freedom for the children to develop individual identity through appropriate permissions and limits, and the establishment of sound values and standards of behavior.

As the children grow and prepare to leave the home, new normal tasks arise for the married couple. Again, some regression may take place because of the process of separation from the children. Recognition of the temporariness of regressive needs enables each partner to support the other and to acknowledge freedom to engage in regressive behavior. The parents support each other in permitting the children to leave the parental home and supervision. The division of labor in the home again becomes different. The parents who thus far in the marriage, or in the greater part of it, had focused on the child-rearing aspects, now have to find new ways of living and communicating with each other. Thus is established a new kind of equilibrium, in which the partners turn to each other. As so often is the case, if these changes come at the same time that the climacteric is taking place, the pair support and protect each other against undue regression, anxiety, and depression.

With the children's final departure from the home a new orientation takes place between the parents. Often each has to accord the other increased permission to satisfy regressive needs. The amount of support each requires of the other may become greater because of the various losses the marital partners sustain: loss related to the departure of the children from the home or to the death of other meaningful figures; physical loss stemming from illness or infirmity and leading to reduced physical energy and ability to manage the home or to cook, or to retain a job, or to maintain various relationships in or outside the home.

Growth and development are stimulated by the crises of transition natural to each phase of the marriage. Failure to manage reasonably well these tasks connected with the discharge of essential functions tends to obtain from the fact that the marriage itself did not develop appropriately in relation to the changing demands of life, and, therefore, complementarity. From the beginning of the marriage the elasticity required for initial adjustment was absent or too limited to allow for the flexibility required to deal with the new tasks that confronted the marital partners with the arrival of each stage in the family life cycle and with each phase within the respective stages.

It is important to note that although the healthy marriage requires a high degree of maturity on the part of each spouse, the designation "healthy" is nevertheless a relative term, for health and illness are viewed not as separate and distinct entities having fixed parameters or clear beginnings and precise points of termination, but rather as a continuous range with many shadings and overlappings. When the complementarity of needs is gratifying and is active, a reasonably healthy marriage can result even though individuals bring to the marriage many unresolved problems from the past. A somewhat disturbed marriage, therefore, does not necessarily mean that the children it produces will be disturbed. However, the disturbed child is almost always an indication of disturbance in the marriage. Similarly, when no legal marriage has existed or the marriage is broken by death, desertion, or divorce, the barriers in child rearing are more difficult to hurdle than is true in the intact sound marriage. Nevertheless, these barriers need not be insurmountable or necessarily seriously destructive to good personality development in the children.

TYPES OF MARITAL EQUILIBRIUM

Work on marriage problems must take into account the malleable aspects of the personality of each partner, their respective ability to deal realistically with their problems of conflict, their wish to strive for better adaptation, the positive qualities in the marital relationship and in the family life, and the motivation for change to counterbalance rigid tendencies or tendencies to regress to more youthful modes of behavior. In essence, the psychological principles that govern the behavior of an individual and those that govern the behavior in a marital relationship are not the same. The marital relationship adds a new dimension to each individual by creating a new life situation that is uniquely interpersonal for each couple and that changes their adaptations to life.

Marital equilibrium is basic to total family operation but it is not always in a good state of health. In addition to the healthy forms described above there are many that verge on but do not achieve health, and there are some forms that fall at the negative end of a continuum of marital equilibrium. Several kinds of marital equilibrium are brought to the attention of various kinds of social agencies; some of the more common ones are briefly presented here.

Mutual Dependence

Some marriages are complementary on intense mutual dependence that does not allow for separateness or difference and, therefore, for healthy individual growth. It is as though the identities of the marital pair were fused, leaving little room for growth in the marriage and in the children. The equilibrium is based on interlocking pervasive and overpowering dependent needs for which each partner seeks to obtain infantile gratification from the other. When these needs mesh, the marriage may gratify each partner as each one takes a turn in the process of supplying gratification to the other. If the marital pair can sustain the supplying process when children come, the marriage will remain in balance. Their children are likely to develop the same personalities as the parents and may have some difficulties in performing tasks in the outside world. These parents often are loving but unable to promote proper growth patterns in their children because they are themselves so childlike.

However, because of the intense mutual dependence the needs and demands on the partners often are so great that they cannot gratify each other. But at the same time the intensity of their needs keeps them bound to each other. These marriages generally remain intact even though serious marital difficulties are evidenced by continual complaining, conflicts, and outright battling. Sometimes the marriage remains in balance until there are children. At that point—and this is common—either or both parents may withdraw dependency supplies from each other and redirect their needs and supplies toward the children. In such instances the children are likely to become tools of the parents. A mother may focus completely on a child, withdrawing from the husband. In retaliation, he may also withdraw completely, offering the child and his wife nothing emotionally. Or, when the next child comes along, he may act toward that child as though it were his alone. It is not uncommon to find in such a family that one child belongs totally to the mother and one belongs totally to the father. The third child is left out altogether. Of course this not only impedes the development of each of the children but also increases the risk to the marriage itself.

"Parent-Child" Marriages

This kind of marriage is based on the need to rescue or protect. A marital partner, as a child, may have felt abandoned emotionally in his own life situation, or he may in reality have been abandoned by a deserting parent. He may seek and find a partner with a similar experience. He assumes a completely protective role toward the partner, thereby deterring growth in the marriage both for himself or for the partner. These marriages sometimes are described as parent-child, or, more specifically, father-daughter, mother-son marriages. These can be highly successful marriages and remain so after the children are born, provided the protecting partner can spread the umbrella of his benignancy to cover the other spouse and the children as well.

In some marriages the element of rescue takes a different form; each partner uses the other to bind anxiety. Some of this goes on in all marriages: marital partners allay each other's anxiety and buttress each other's defenses. One spouse may have paranoid ideas of which he is not aware but which he nevertheless fears; it is, however, his partner who may really express the paranoid ideas and thereby rescue the other from having to do so. Both husband and wife in this kind of marriage may have some paranoid qualities, but the man may discharge his paranoid feelings in his work situation. Mr. Mallon, for instance, believes his employer "exploits" him and he quarrels constantly with his fellow-employees because they "take advantage" of him. Mrs. Mallon is sure her neighbors slight her and the tradesmen cheat her. But neither Mr. nor Mrs. Mallon exhibits these ideas in the home. Neither needs to express or act out his paranoid ideas and feelings toward the other in the marriage. Thus they bind each other's anxiety, making the marriage relatively successful. The marriage is in a reasonably healthy balance, and children develop reasonable personality structures. In such cases, however, it is not surprising to find that many years later the wife's paranoid ideas have come forth forcibly following the death of the husband whose protection no longer is available to her.

If the anxiety of one or both partners gets out of hand, marital difficulty may appear. It is likely in such situations to preserve the equilibrium in the marriage by using a child as a scapegoat. The symptom then is displaced on the child who is seen by the parent as the source of trouble. This can be illustrated by the situations in which the anxiety of the parent or parents becomes unduly exaggerated when a child is working out sexual identity problems with the parent of the opposite sex, or when a child is working out control tasks; the anxiety is related directly to similar problems that were not adequately resolved during the growing-up years of either or both of the child's parents. These parents are likely to be unaware that there is a marital problem and to deny the existence of such difficulty. The marital equilibrium is stable because the child is used for the discharge of excessive anxieties that the marital pair cannot support with each other.

Projective Identification

Some marriages are based on complementarity in which one partner seeks to project on the other the wishes, ideals, and hopes that he cannot successfully achieve as an individual. Such partners look to the spouse to fulfill needs of self-esteem and of values that they wish they possessed and hope the partner possesses. Or they rely on the spouse, for example, to discharge aggression that they themselves fear to release. These partners express through each other what they want for themselves but cannot openly permit. For instance, both may feel intense anger. One of the marital team will openly castigate the other for exposing the anger while at the same time covertly stimulate him to express it. Or one partner may appear to be meek and mild yet enjoy tremendously the fact that the spouse fights openly. One partner may admire, envy, and complain about the social outgoing qualities of the other. This may represent his ideal, but because he is ambivalent about his inability to behave similarly, he frustrates the other even as he competes with him. Many marriages are successful on the basis of this positive use of projective identification. Others flare into acute marital difficulties when ambivalence about the projective identification is high, or when one partner becomes too successful and the other cannot tolerate the fact that his ideal appears to be completely out of his grasp.

The Detached Marriage

The "detached" marriage maintains its equilibrium by emotional distance. Healthy closeness is feared. Often there are intellectual and social interests, general compatability, and physical sexual compatibility, but little emotional warmth. Difficulties are likely to occur when children present demands for affection that neither parent can offer. The parent feels overwhelmed and begins to make demands on the partner who also cannot tolerate them and so withdraws further. The complaint is frequently phrased as an unwillingness to share responsibility. Difficulties also may occur when intellectual and social interests begin to change or wane, leading to incompatability and feelings of emptiness in the marriage. Some of these marriages remain intact because the partners agree to find their separate ways through outside interests, but to remain married. But many of these marriages dissolve when the children leave home, causing considerable consternation among children, relatives, and friends who "would have sworn" the twenty- or twenty-five-year-old marriage was "happy" and "would have gone on forever." Some of these situations also evoke surprise when either the man or the woman deserts after twenty or even thirty years of living together.

Immature Marriages

Several kinds of marriages may be categorized as immature. One is the marriage based on a mutual need that is specific, such as the marriage in which one marital partner is strongly impelled to find a lost parent or someone who has a particular behavioral trait like infidelity or gambling. If the person's particular problem—such as seeking to replace a lost parent—is resolved either through some form of help or through life experience itself, this marriage also may dissolve, often each partner going on to a different kind of marriage. In many instances, the satisfactory resolution of the problem leads to a more successful second marriage.

Another form of immature marriage is that made by acting-out adolescents. This marriage is based on an extreme of the rebelliousness that characterizes the adolescent phase of an individual's development. This particular kind of immature marriage often does not continue as a lifelong venture. When the need to rebel no longer exists, the marriage itself often breaks up. Often as a result of social work or other help—pastoral counseling, psychiatry, psychology— the partners will seek new marriages that are more mature. If the adolescent's rebellion is temporary, the marriage will dissolve unless both partners develop other needs that complement each other's. In other words, these kinds of marriages are likely to terminate because they represent only partial involvement of the partners in each other rather than full involvement with each other's needs.

Dominance-Submission

A kind of marriage particularly well known to social agencies is that based on dominance and submission. One partner has an overwhelming need to dominate; his goal, of which he generally is not aware, is power and the degradation of the other partner. Somehow he succeeds in finding someone who needs to submit to such domination. In spite of the fact that the submissive partner frequently complains about the other, especially when the problems are outwardly reflected in physical attacks, because the needs of the two intermesh, it is rare that the marriage breaks up: one needs to degrade and the other needs to submit to the degradation. A common illustration is the wife who has her husband arrested because he has beaten her, then she refuses to press charges against him because she is sure he will reform or she is sure he "needs" her. This generally is also termed a sado-masochistic marriage.

Symbiosis

Finally, there is the symbiotic marriage in which the two partners are as peas in a pod, not only completely like each other but totally unable to see or permit any differences whatsoever in each other or in their children. These marriages often produce psychosis. Sometimes one partner is openly psychotic and the other latently so. Sometimes they take turns in the latent or open psychosis. Frequently when symbiosis is present, with both partners having a paranoid orientation to life, it is extremely difficult actually to identify both as paranoid; at any particular time, one may be better able to conceal it than the other and, therefore, it sometimes is assumed that only one partner is ill while the other is healthy. It should be noted that marriages based on symbiosis do not necessarily include such illnesses as post-partum psychosis, reactive depression, and involutional states. Symbiosis refers to the marriage that on scrutiny shows a psychotic personality base or core from the *outset* of the marriage.

MARRIAGE TASKS AND
THE SOCIAL WORKER

It must be emphasized that the foregoing marital descriptions are not offered with the intent to designate specific diagnostic classifications or categories; the purpose is only to offer some broad guidelines for the understanding of how marriage takes place and what contributes both to healthy and to problematic marriages. The adaptive aspects of the marriage also are influenced by benign external factors. The positive complementarity in few marriages is so completely destroyed that nothing can change for the better. Most people have some adaptive capacities and some abilities that can be fostered, strengthened, and developed either by life itself or with the assistance of a social worker. Changes and crises in the family in relation to tasks and stages of development often disturb the marital equilibrium but they also provide an impetus to growth and development of the marriage, either spontaneously or with the aid of counseling. These descriptions have been formulated with the intent of providing a broad base from which the social worker can begin at least to assess the nature of the equilibrium and to arrive at some determination about the possible loosening, shifting, or altering of the equilibrium in the interest of a better marriage and better family life.

Presentation of the Problem

The social worker in working with families often finds that the marital difficulty is either the overt problem or the problem that underlies other complaints—about children, about money, about "in-laws," and so on. People may come to social agencies with a general or specific complaint about a marriage. The complaint may be expressed about children ("they're always nagging for something!") and not about the marriage. Or the request to the public assistance agency may be for funds to meet survival needs without the applicant voicing the fright and anxiety she feels because of her husband's failure to retain jobs not only for the reason that he lacks vocational skill, but more specifically for the reason that his rising "irritability" provokes anger in employers who quickly dismiss him as a "troublemaker"—and then he beats her or the children.

The social worker should be aware of the possibility that the serious underlying problem may be a marital one, consider what it may involve, but address himself to the request that is presented. Whatever the complaint, whether it be in the area of money, alcoholism, aggressive behavior, sexual behavior, withdrawal, or some other, the social worker needs to take note of the nature of the marital equilibrium. The complaint about the children of course, justifies the worker's immediate attention; the request for financial assistance must be met with appropriate help.

The Exploratory Process

But if underlying causative problems are to be tackled and controlled so that more competent social functioning may ensue, the worker must keep in the back of his mind—but not *too* far back—some questions about the nature of the disturbance in the marriage itself and at what point, and in what fashion, an exploratory approach should be made in the direction of improving this condition. When the complaint is about the marriage itself, certain specific areas for exploration are indicated. Not all of the answers might be procured at once: the exploratory process at some points might take the form of direct activity; at other points it might be contemplative only. The spacing, timing, and intensity of the exploratory process must be geared to fit each individual situation.

What is the particular event that brought the marital problem to a head? What is the nature of the equilibrium (the kind of complementariness that exists)? What disturbed the equilibrium to the point that assistance is now sought or that has brought the matter to the attention of a social agency? How do social, cultural, economic, and health factors influence the marriage in its adaptive and maladaptive aspects? How do the marital partners function as parents? How has the couple dealt with conflicts, in what way and with what success have they resolved these? What areas in the marriage are adaptive, which conflict? What are the communication patterns? What compatability exists in goals, values, standards, and interests? How does the couple manage in day-to-day living? Is this a new crisis? Is it a chronic one? What has already been tried by or on behalf of the family, and *what do the marital partners want to try now?*

These explorative areas are designed to provide answers to questions for the purpose of understanding the nature of the problem and identifying in what way the social worker can be helpful directly and by drawing on other social resources.[2] Is the problem largely situational, brought about or exacerbated by external factors such as lack of money or health difficulties? Is it largely interpersonal, that is, in the couple's operations with each other that show failure in complementariness so that there are disturbances in empathy and identification resulting in defects in communication? Is the problem largely centered in one partner because of internal distress that is chronic or that erupts, critically overflowing into the marriage? Is the problem fixed because of external events that cannot be altered, or because the husband and wife, though they complain, need each other the way they are? Is it flexible with regard to external factors that can be alleviated or altered or shifted in relation to the wish to find a better balance?

[2] For the use of social resources in helping families, see Chapters 17 and 21.

Choosing the Counseling Method for Use

When a disturbance in equilibrium seems to be the fundamental trouble in the marriage, it is obvious that effective alleviation or modification will require that both partners be seen by the social worker. Also, when a problem involves misperceptions in communication, it is clear that the couple should be seen together in order to enhance the worker's understanding of the interpersonal aspects of the marriage. Thus it is becoming increasingly common to request that the husband and wife meet together with the worker either initially or very early in the exploratory process. A marriage partner can talk about himself, about his own feelings and perceptions, but he cannot describe the marital difficulty with objective clarity and accuracy. He is too hurt, too angry, too preoccupied with what the spouse has done to him to be able to perceive the areas of unreality and invalidity in his behavior or in the partner's actions or reactions.

The social worker may choose to see the partners separately and in this way learn a good deal about each one, including how each feels about the other; but the social worker will miss vital data if the couple is not seen together. There would be no opportunity to observe the communication modes that Chapter 16 presents as a source of significant data. The importance of such data is clearly evident in the Brooks interview during which Mrs. Brooks looked as though she smelled something bad whenever her husband made a remark. The worker observed that Mr. Brooks consistently reacted to this facial expression by withdrawing into silence and also by pushing his chair back almost into the wall. As soon as he did this, Mrs. Brooks would launch into a tirade, its theme centering on the point that his withdrawal into silence was exactly what she could not stand! The tirade was countered by further withdrawal by Mr. Brooks. The worker called this piece of circular, escalating behavior to the astonished couple's attention. For the first time, they became aware of the part each played in the marital difficulty.

The worker may miss significant subtleties of role aspect, of satisfying interdependence in areas a couple is unable to put into words because of their hurt, their anger, or their fear. Neither Mr. nor Mrs. Lee was aware of the change in voice and the exchange of warm looks when they talked about the child who was doing well, yet this was the very area the worker could point to that indicated their marriage was not so completely on the rocks as they thought.

Without both spouses present in the interview, the worker has no access to important clues; furthermore, he is not free to use with both spouses material that he has obtained from one in a separate interview. Moreover, seeing both partners together reduces the likelihood that the worker will overidentify with one or the other; the requisite empathic neutrality is more apt to be preserved. In most instances, the worker who is convinced that understanding of the marital difficulty necessitates interviewing both partners together will be able to deal effectively with the resistance that may be evidenced in a variety of ways. Exploration, then, is best undertaken by one worker who, on the basis of experience with each and/or both marital partners can develop at least a tentative plan for the approach to the couple's marriage problems.

The choice of the form of interview to be used—whether joint, individual, or family—to see how the children affect and are affected by the marital discord, depends on clues that are discernible in the interview process. Whether combinations of methods are to be used and, if so, the most desirable sequence for their use, can be determined in the initial interviews. Some of the clues pointing to use of different types of interviews are related to questions posed earlier: whether the problem seems to be largely interpersonal (induced by external or interactional stresses), or whether it is one partner's intrapersonal problem. Most situations appear to require a combination of kinds of interviews in order to answer questions and it is not uncommon to revise the original plan from time to time as emerging data and feelings point to the advisability of a change in course.

The decision reached by the worker and the marital pair that ongoing intervention is needed can be implemented by any or several of the variety of methods briefly described here.

Conjoint Method. This method engages both partners in interviews through the helping period. It appears to be particularly useful when both partners are convinced, or at least partially so, that they wish and need to work on the marriage relationship and that they have the strength to tolerate the exposure of fears, hostilities, wish for closeness, and emotional wear and tear that is entailed. Clues to the advisability for employing this helping method are found in at least a minimal wish and ability to hear and perceive each other's needs, some capacity for closeness, some underlying warmth toward each other, and some signs that support can be available to the more openly anxious and upset member. It may take some time during exploration to discern and clarify these clues because the first picture offered the worker may be one of explosive anger or fear that presumably would contra-indicate conjoint work. The validity of conjoint treatment is evidenced when the initial anger or fear dissipates with reasonable rapidity.

The usefulness of the conjoint method has been effectively demonstrated in a variety of marital problem situations. A common one is the marital crisis that is based on or related to situational, or external, stresses: the illness of one spouse becomes chronic, or a job change or job loss occurs. Another grows out of crises brought about by such transitional developments as the coming of children, adolescence, the departure of children from the home, and others. For example, an older adolescent is ready to leave the family but the parents find it extremely difficult to permit the separation. The separation itself may constitute a crisis or may lead to other problems: between the parents and the adolescent, or between the parents. Crises may be due to delays in maturation such as occur in the early stage of marriage as the parents are finding their way in a major new task. For example, the joint management of money may provoke discord as the young couple attempts to decide how to manage their income and the priorities in using it for their separate or joint interests.

Some marriages, which are consistently unhealthy but in which the married partners are able to cope reasonably well, experience periodic crises which tip the balance to the negative side. The crisis may be precipitated by an external factor such as illness or loss of employment or the coming of a new child. The couple is not able without help to tolerate the change required to meet these needs; the conjoint method facilitates their effective use of the proffered help.

The conjoint method can be particularly effective also in situations containing a partner who can support the more distressed one. Partners in a psychotic marriage (symbiotic) often can be helped more by the conjoint method than by the one-to-one relationship which may be excessively threatening to each partner.

The goal in the conjoint method is to change the perception of the self and of the partner and to modify ways of manifesting faults, feelings, and behavior: to loosen, shift, or change the marital equilibrium. As has been stated previously, all marital couples have a great need both to cling to accustomed ways of thinking and behaving and to meet the challenges of new tasks. The major technique is modification of the nature of communication through working on discrepancies in role function and on those developmental matters that were not accomplished in the families of origin; developing proper congruency in communication; helping the partners both to accept difference and to compromise. The worker's communication draws on the specific evidence revealed in the interviews and the communication should serve as a model of clarity and directness.

Individual Work with One Marital Partner. In one sense, a question might be raised as to whether work on a marital situation can proceed effectively when understanding of the marriage is necessarily restricted or incomplete because in effect work can proceed with only one member of the pair. Sometimes, however, one partner absolutely refuses to become involved in the helping process. In other instances the decision may be to work with one member because the problem presented is an intrapersonal one. Nevertheless, the social worker's skill still may touch the marital problem because of those aspects of personality disturbance that overflow into and interfere with the marriage. With regard to these, there always is the hope—often realized—that as intrapersonal difficulties are minimized, clarified, and relieved, the marriage itself will be benefited.

But if only one partner is in treatment the other often feels threatened by the idea that treatment will result in dissolution of the marriage. The consequence not infrequently is that the threatened spouse is influential in one way or another in preventing his partner from continuing in the counseling relationship. There may be active sabotage of the helping process. On the whole, the marriage is far more important to the marital couple than is the treatment and the disturbed partner is likely to respond to the threatened spouse by withdrawing from the counseling relationship with the social worker. It is not unusual for the wife of an alcoholic husband to make every effort to keep her husband out of treatment even while she pleads for help. She requests help at a point of acute anxiety or distress; when this feeling is alleviated, she withdraws from the agency until the next crisis occurs. Or she makes sure that her husband behaves in such a way that she has an excuse for not continuing to see the worker. She assures the worker that the husband will not come or that he is so alcoholic he cannot conceivably change. Yet the reality frequently is that there is no real wish to alter the marriage in spite of the fact that life is made difficult by the alcoholic husband.

Of course it is not always possible to arrange for the simultaneous presence of both husband and wife for any of a number of reasons. One spouse may flatly refuse to be a participant or otherwise remain unresponsive either to the worker or to the spouse's pleading. Or the partner who willingly or unwillingly sought agency help may be unable to mobilize early courage or the requisite directness in communication to involve the partner in the interviews with the worker.

The father who no longer is in the home—or, occasionally, the mother who has left the home—may simply be living apart from the family, or may have married. If he still is emotionally involved with the children or if this involvement presumably is limited to child-care payments, the interests of the children point to the advisability of the worker endeavoring to reach the father and to involve him in working on the problems of the children, either individually or together with the mother of the children. If the father is not physically available or is no longer emotionally engaged with the family, there often seems little use in bringing him into the consideration of the family problems requiring attention. There may be a legal requirement for his continued financial relationship with the family and this may indicate the advisability of continued contact with him and, in fact, may be a way of reaching him for the purpose of giving the children something besides money—if he does give that. But the problems in such instances no longer are problems in marriage: they are problems specific to one-parent families.

Collaborative Method. Each marital partner may work with a different social worker. By agreement with the marital partners, the workers then collaborate through frequent conferences. As the conjoint method has become increasingly prominent, the collaborative method has been less in the ascendancy. Collaboration requires a high degree of capability on the part of both workers to respect each other and work well together, each supporting his own viewpoint but hearing and weighing the viewpoint of the other.

The collaborative method can be especially useful in dealing with particular marital problems—as when two workers of different sexes are required, or the marital pair refuse to share one worker. It can correct distortions of reality that each partner brings to his own worker. It can help correct possible overidentification of the worker with his client. And it may serve to keep the marriage in better balance while each partner is working on his own intrapersonal problems.

Generally speaking, the sex of the social worker has no significance in work with marital problems. If at an especially critical time in a person's life a particular model is needed, then a worker of the same sex may be required. Thus, in the Bennett case, a severe loss of masculine self-esteem at a given time showed the need for a male worker for Mr. Bennett until some self-esteem was restored.

Mr. and Mrs. Bennett separated after twenty-two years of marriage. When Mr. Bennett's business failed, Mrs. Bennett went to work to support the family. The blow to Mr. Bennett's self-esteem was so severe that, although both Mr. and Mrs. Bennett desperately wanted to be reunited, he could not tolerate even being in the same room with his wife and the woman social worker—both of whom would "surely" penetrate to his "inadequacy" as a husband. It was evident that some of the effects of the blow to Mr. Bennett's self-esteem had to be counteracted early. Therefore he was seen by a male worker until he had recovered sufficiently so that he and his wife could begin talking together about their problems.

Concurrent Method. One worker may be engaged in working with both partners, but separately rather than together. As in the collaborative method, the concurrent method is undertaken when the partners are unable to involve themselves together in a conjoint arrangement because their self-centered needs or wounded self-esteem interfere with even minimal perception of each other's needs; or because each needs privacy to express certain feelings, thoughts, or behavior; or because the focus of treatment should be on personal introspection.

In contrast with the collaborative method, there is a disadvantage in the concurrent method: one person may develop the kind of relationship with the worker that makes it very difficult for that partner then to permit the other partner to enter into a working relationship with the worker. If this occurs, the marital situation may deteriorate, with each partner fighting for a position of favoritism with the worker; or each partner may become unduly suspicious of the influence of the worker on the other partner, or may use interview time to try to find out what is going on with the partner. The advantage is that there is no "middle man" through whom to channel communications and, therefore, there is possible reduction of misinterpretation and misperception by the worker. Also, the worker can actively and directly use communications from one partner with the other and thereby clarify distortions, projections, and reality much more quickly. A disadvantage, in contrast to the conjoint method, lies again in the possibility that one partner develops the kind of relationship with the worker that makes it very difficult for that partner then to permit the spouse to become involved in the helping process.

The partners in concurrent work need to be able to tolerate the tensions created by working with one worker. The goal is to change the personal resources of each spouse so that the marriage will improve. The techniques are the established ones of individual treatment: support, guidance, reflection, clarification, confrontation, with the additional direct use of communication conveyed by each partner. The worker must be careful in deciding which communications are privileged, which can be shared, which can be shared only with permission, which the worker must insist on sharing in the interests of the marriage.

. *Combined Work.* This method is prevalent in many agencies today. Various types of interviews are used flexibly, with one worker taking responsibility for selecting the type that appears appropriate to a given situation at a given time. As new diagnostic material emerges in the course of work with the family and the objectives in each case situation alter as there is progress which contributes to some change in the situation, the method utilized may be altered. Frequently both conjoint and individual interviews are undertaken at the outset of work with the couple if there is indication that changes in communication patterns via the conjoint method should proceed with introspection to be encouraged in individual interviews. The same pattern may be followed when the partners are able to tolerate only limited closeness to each other in conjoint interviews or limited closeness to the worker in individual interviews, or when one or both partners feel the need to express feelings, thoughts, or material from the past or present that they consider too private to disclose in the presence of each other. Sometimes this particular method is used to obtain the support of the less distressed partner so that the tensions created in the other by one-to-one work with the social worker are lessened. If there is considerable competitiveness between the partners because of strong individual dependency needs, or when the partners cannot tolerate separation because of intense mutual interdependence, conjoint and individual methods may be the choice—dealing with these factors in conjoint interviews, while the separate interviews are used to foster separateness of identity or reduce competitiveness.

In some situations, work may begin on an individual basis, then move to the combined method. This may be appropriate when the husband and wife both lack capacity to hear and perceive the other's needs; or when one partner regularly overwhelms the other by explosive hostility or acting-out behavior; or when the severe hurt to the self-esteem cannot be borne in the sight of the partner; or when self-centered or narcissistic needs are overriding. Until these elements can be dealt with to some extent, it may not be possible to utilize the conjoint method.

The opposite may occur. Work may begin with both partners conjointly, then move to individual or combined interviews. This situation arises more frequently when the marital equilibrium has been improved to the partners' satisfaction and one or both now express the need for individual examination of personal problems.

If an impasse is reached in any type of ongoing interview, the worker may move to other methods to stimulate further involvement of one or both spouses. Similarly, this may be done when the worker senses that tensions are so high that some relief or change in pace is indicated. Experience shows that it is easier to begin with the conjoint or combined (conjoint and individual) method than to begin with the individual method and then shift; individual relationship factors are likely to become more intense if work is begun with one partner alone and maintained that way for a period of time before the other partner is brought into the treatment situation.

Combined work is carried on with the collaborative method (two workers) in some agencies when this seems a way to open channels of communication between the partners, to clarify distortions directly, to deal with impasses, or to accelerate the rate of progress.

Group Method. Work with marital couples is also undertaken in groups—either just in groups, or combined with any of the methods described above. Two primary types of groups, to some degree overlapping, exist in social welfare agencies: the educational group and the counseling group.[3]

The educational group is used largely with people who need knowledge about what goes into marriage, what is meant by role performance, what the tasks are, how to manage them, and so forth. These groups often are homogeneous by economic class, religion, race, or cultural status. They serve a purpose both in conveying knowledge about marriage and, sometimes, in enabling marital couples to work out problems on their own or to seek appropriate professional help. The direction by the leader and the support of the group, the technique of universalization of marriage conflicts and resolutions, can open new vistas in marital tasks.

The counseling groups are particularly useful for couples with trouble in marriage who cannot tolerate individual, conjoint, or combined counseling methods. Explosive hostility, fear of retaliation, fear of exposure, need for emotional distance—all are clues to the feasibility of using this method. The support of the group, the universality and commonness of problems, the safety in numbers, make this kind of arena a more tolerable one for many couples trying to alleviate problems. The leader uses the same techniques that apply

---

[3] For some elaboration about types of groups, see Chapter 21.

in conjoint or combined work. He and the group counteract inappropriate use of defenses such as denial and projection; concealed interpersonal problems are brought into active interaction; hidden intrapersonal aspects directly affecting the marriage are brought into the interpersonal sphere; reality testing is encouraged by the group members. Sometimes counseling groups are combined with individual work to stimulate movement or to reach areas that cannot be touched by one method alone. Sometimes one method will be the forerunner, or it will follow another. A couple may be able to respond to conjoint or individual methods after experience with the group method.

Whatever the method used, the goal is to help the marital couple retain or acquire the kind of equilibrium that provides proper satisfactions in the present and prepares for future marital and family satisfactions. This goal is consistent with the aims of social welfare generally. Regardless of the agency setting in which service is given or the fact that the nuclear family or a segment of one is the immediate concern of the agency, the social worker who is aware of the nature and variety of marital problems and alert to different methods for working toward their amelioration, in effect will be helping to avert or reduce family troubles in the succeeding stages of the cycle of family life.

7

CHILD REARING

THE PROPER TIME to influence the character
of a child, according to William Inge, is about one hundred years
before he is born. This, no doubt, is true. The development of children is substantially affected by the character of their parents, whose
development likewise was affected by *their* parents and the times in
which they lived. Even with the increase in our population of more
and more generations that overlap, literal implementation of this
Anglican prelate's admonition is not practical in the cycle of family
life as we know it today. However, the nature of marital equilibrium
established and maintained by the married partners and the forces
that influence the marital equilibrium have a marked impact on
the *family* equilibrium which both affects and is affected by the
children. Indeed, the marital equilibrium in large measure determines

the children's emotional security, their capacity to trust and to learn self-control, their development of proper sex identity, and their competence in functioning socially, economically, and psychologically in a dynamic, changing society.

The forces that combine to steady or ruffle family equilibrium (the balance of stability and change throughout the family's life) require the same attention as those influencing marital equilibrium.[1] The arena in which the forces operate, however, is a broader one because it must encompass children as well as marital partners. And the family equilibrium is affected and altered with the coming of the children and with their progression through the various growth stages from birth to departure from the paternal home.

Because of both positive and negative identification with their parents, most married people want to have children. Some hope to rear them as well as their parents; some wish to improve on what was done by their own parents; others desire to undo what their parents did. Whatever the individual motivation, certain functions in relation to child rearing—the socialization of children—are expected to be carried out by the family along with other tasks that support the growth of the individual family members.

THE FAMILY RULES

Accordingly, every family has a complex set of rules to be rigidly or flexibly followed. Some of the rules are formed deliberately; some are developed intuitively; and some may exist with or without the conscious awareness of the family. Each family's rules are permeated with the family's unique cultural values and standards which the family needs and wishes to retain; at the same time, family members may have to operate within the rules adopted by the wider society.

Children especially may have family rules to observe, yet they have to be able to conform to rules established within their school situation. Illustrative is the situation in which a child is permitted to use certain words at home and the family has to help the child understand that these are words he may not use in the outside world although he does not have to give them up at home. There also are the many instances in which the rules of a somewhat disorganized family may permit the child to do much as he pleases about going to bed, eating, keeping himself clean; this family has to establish

[1] See Chapter 6 for marital equilibrium.

for the child the fact that what is permissible in the home may not be in the school.

Some families striving to move into the middle class establish more stringent rules for behavior of the child outside the home than might be found in the family that already has achieved middle-class status. Thus Mrs. Larson, an upwardly mobile Negro mother, insists that each of her two children report to her immediately upon termination of classes in school. They are not allowed to remain for supervised play on the school grounds because she wants "to know where they are every minute. They won't get into trouble like some of the other children" living in the same disadvantaged neighborhood who are allowed to "run wild at school" and therefore "show no respect for their elders." Likewise, many mothers dependent on Aid to Families with Dependent Children are much more punitive with regard to the child's infractions of the rules both in and out of the home; it is not uncommon for these mothers to possess lower tolerance for some kinds of behavior than is evident among families who feel more secure in the community.

The rules shift as the structure of the family alters because new members are added and others depart, either temporarily or permanently. Rules undergo modification also with each phase of development and its concomitant tasks; and rules may be changed with changes in environmental factors that affect the family. The rules are designed to meet family life tasks as economically as possible. Certain rules generally are worked out between parents when the children arrive; as they develop, additional rules are formed by the parents or by the parents with the children, depending on the stage of the child's development and on the way the parents approach their parenting tasks. Parents take primary responsibility for establishing the rules about division of responsibility between them for the physical care of the children, discipline, specific tasks to be assigned each child in accordance with his age and competence.

The child takes a part in establishing rules in relation to his wish to please his parents and to please himself. The rules that develop without the family members' conscious effort stem from the meshing of the complementary needs originally in the marriage;[2] they change as the children arrive and grow. How the parents feel toward each other in relation to the children, how each child develops and in his development affords gratification and satisfaction to either or both parents, what feelings are transferred from the parents to the children in terms of the parents' own past life experiences, all contribute

[2] See Chapter 6 for "complementarity of need."

significantly to the formation of the family rules. In his own way, a first child, then a middle one, and then a last one shapes and is shaped by the rules in the family structure. It is common to hear parents exclaim that, because of all the mistakes made with the first child, the second one should have been born first.

These rules, unique to each family and shifting in concert with changing tasks and stages of family development, form the basis for the unique pattern of conflict and resolution to be found in all families. Conflict and resolution always exist in relation to tasks. In fact, they provide the stimuli to growth and development. Little development would take place without some conflict between parents about different points of view in child rearing and without conflict in the child in relation to satisfying his own growth needs at the same time that he is pleasing his parents. The resolution of conflicts determines the health or illness or delay in development. Parents need not be in total agreement about all aspects of child rearing, provided they do have basic agreement on vital matters such as transmission of values and permission for each child to develop separateness (identity) according to his stage of development. When the parents are in total agreement about everything, the child has difficulty in distinguishing between what is masculine and what is feminine; it is difficult for him to test the meanings of differences in behavior and feelings so that he can learn to make appropriate judgments. For example, when both parents are in fundamental agreement about continued infantilization of a child, he has little room or wish to grow. When both parents transmit corrupt or deviant values, this becomes a way of life for the child. Similarly, pervasive disagreements between the parents in areas about which they may be aware or unaware inhibit the child's possibilities for developing strong identifications with either of his parents. He is likely to be pulled continually between the two as he attempts to please one or the other or to play one off against the other—and he is apt to carry this kind of pattern into later life relationships.

It is now generally recognized that no parents are equally "good" parents in all of the child-rearing stages. Parents who manage well during the early phases of nurturing through feeding may have difficulties with the child's toilet training. Parents who manage comfortably during the adolescence of their children may have had a troubling experience during the latency period. Parents who manage jealousy among children may not be able to manage themselves or the children when it is time for the children to separate from the family. Thus it can be said that all families have unique strengths and unique vulnerabilities with respect to child rearing. The nature of the unique strengths and the unique vulnerabilities is indicative of the individual patterns of conflict and the manner in which such conflict is resolved, both in day-to-day living and in times of crisis. The resolution of conflicts and the means by which the resolution is achieved are indicative of the capacity of the various personalities in the family to make appropriate adaptations when the need arises.

The rules, then, are governed by the family's patterns of conflict and resolution. It is a continual intermeshing of rules and patterns of conflict that creates family equilibrium. In the healthy family the forces of stability and change that contribute to family equilibrium are in adaptive balance; namely, even while tasks are changing and conflicts are being resolved, the stimulation of the growth of individual members must continue. To facilitate carrying out of tasks that will permit such stimulation of growth, the rules have to be applied with some flexibility; nevertheless, the basic rules are maintained. The family's day-to-day operations are discharged through appropriate communication of the rules among the family members. As will be evident in Chapter 16, the communication may be in both verbal and nonverbal forms.

The healthy family may be somewhat vulnerable at some points but manages alone or with some professional assistance to overcome problems associated with a particular task and to move on to the next task. Because of such stress points or personality difficulties, some families maintain adaptive equilibrium in some respects but not in others. And the equilibrium of some families is largely maladaptive in all respects and in all phases of the family's life.

Each nuclear family has special tasks related not only to the development of each individual child but also to the larger phases of family development. The family is confronted with transitional crises. The successful resolution of these crises is essential to insure that the individual's development will lead him to become a well-adjusted family member with competence for moving on to the next developmental stage and achieving success there also. Each stage of development is a prelude to each succeeding stage so that successful childhood rests on successful development in infancy, adolescence on childhood, young adulthood on adolescence, and so on through to the older years and the close of the individual's life cycle and the cycle of family life. Failure to accomplish adequately the developmental tasks of any one stage hampers the individual in achieving success in a later one. The family equilibrium is the thread that ties the success in development in one stage to success in another. The strength of the thread is established in the first stage of the cycle of family life: the marriage. In the second stage, when children are present, the strength of the thread is constantly tested, the pulls and tugs varying as children move from the earlier phase into adolescence.

THE EARLY YEARS

The early child-rearing phase in the family's life covers roughly the first twelve years of each child's life—until the onset of adolescence. The objectives of the major child-rearing functions in this phase are the development of healthy trust, self-control, healthy love capacity, and the ability to learn.[3] The child is in continual transitional conflict between his inner needs to satisfy himself in all ways and the outer tasks imposed by the reality represented first by his parents and later by school and friends. The parents have to steer a continuous and flexible course between permitting the child to express inner needs and frustrating these needs in the socialization process. Only the parents—and the child needs both parents—can know when a child is ready for new responsibilities, when his impulses and wishes should be curbed, when he should be stimulated to try new ways, and when he has to be held back. It is in the management of these tasks that the child develops his own identity as well as the requisite healthy interdependence in the nuclear family and healthy relationships outside the family. Child rearing is a continuous learning task for the parents and for the child, partly intuitive and partly consciously learned. It has two main features: the development of healthy separateness or individuation and healthy interdependence. These can emerge only from a sound process of conflict and resolution between the parents and the child.

The Parents' Tasks

In these early years of the child-rearing process the parents generally have other tasks they must perform concurrently. These are usually the years when the man is endeavoring to establish himself vocationally and financially as the family provider. Our increasingly competitive economy and culture often cause him to be so preoccupied with work and money—especially in establishing a vocational base—that most of his energy goes in this direction

[3] See Part Four for requisites for social functioning, especially Chapters 13 and 16.

and he tends to leave child rearing largely to the mother. This often is a source of conflict between the parents. The mother feels depleted, too much responsible for discipline and too much with the children. The father feels he wants peace and quiet at home. If he is moonlighting or otherwise works long hours, he becomes guilty over the many hours of absence from the family as well as over what may appear to be a wish to withdraw; he may compensate for this feeling by engaging in activity with the children that is sporadic and at times overstimulating. The mother thinks she is viewed as the ogre in the family while the father, because he is at home less, is perceived as "the giving one." This may create an overt marital problem or, if the partners cannot express their feelings to each other directly, the result may be a misplacement of the problems on the children: they become the recipients of the parents' problems. The mother may turn to the children for love, binding them too closely to her and withdrawing them from the father; both parents may battle for the love of the children; the mother may handle her frustrations by hostility to the children who seem to be separating her from her husband's attention; the father may over-give materially to atone for his realistic or irrational guilt. The problem often is compounded when the mother takes gainful work for realistic reasons or solely to meet her own emotional needs. Unless she and the father are in agreement that she work, and unless she is comfortable about working and providing an adequate substitute to care for the children, the children are likely to suffer developmental difficulties.

Difficulties often are compounded if the marriage has not yet jelled for either of two reasons: the couple might not have been ready for parenthood in a marriage which they entered without sufficient maturity; or the children might have come so soon after the marriage that the spouses had insufficient time to establish a reasonably sound marital equilibrium. It is not uncommon in such situations to find that either parent, and more frequently the father, is unduly jealous of the children, or that the mother is deeply resentful toward the children because she feels she has lost her freedom too soon or has lost her husband's love—to the children or elsewhere.

In addition to the parental tasks of establishing an equilibrium in the marriage that permits the parents to be ready for children and to fulfill normal economic functions as parents, they have the task of defining the division of responsibilities for household management and for specific child-rearing tasks. Each family approaches these responsibilities in ways that suit them and that make the household run as efficiently and economically as they find possible. It is not significant whether the father in one family bathes the children and the father in another does not. What is important is that the mother and father reach some agreements and support each other emotionally in carrying out the necessary tasks. This means, for example, that when a child's departure for nursery school or kindergarten provokes normal ambivalence in the mother about separation from the child, the father has to understand the regressive side of the mother's ambivalence that wants the child to remain a baby, and he has to support the other side that wants the child to grow. If the father is preoccupied at home with thoughts about his work, the mother has to understand that this is not tantamount to emotional withdrawal from her and the children. Such recognition will help her to discuss the implications of the preoccupation reasonably instead of irrationally. In dividing the responsibilities for child rearing, both parents are compelled to adopt compromises with the realization that neither can really take the place of the other. In other words, the quality of the parents' relationship with each other and with the children in regard to the division of responsibilities is far more important than the quantity of functions assumed by or assigned to each. The amount of actual time a father spends with his children is far less significant than what he does with the available time and how he feels toward the children.

The parents also have the task of establishing and changing their sexual relationship during these early years of child rearing. The arrival of the children requires a different kind of privacy in intimate sexual demonstrations, and in exposing of the body and body functions. Parents and children must learn the meaning of privacy in the use of clothing, body functions, and intimate sexual functions, The tensions of child rearing may necessitate the creation of new patterns of sexual intercourse. The husband and wife have to see and adapt to these requirements for change realistically rather than viewing them as manifestations of a loss of interest in the sexual sphere. They should not view the necessity for adaptation as threatening them with loss of their marriage in family life.

Undoubtedly conditions of housing influence the child-rearing process in the matter of sexual relations. When families are crowded into an inadequate number of rooms, or room assignments are made without due consideration to the ages and sex of those expected to share the sleeping quarters, the young child's appropriate development is handicapped by exposure and sexual stimulation. By and large such circumstances tend to be related to sheer poverty or cultural deprivation. They also are commonly present among families who are not necessarily at or below the poverty level but who by choice or necessity reside in the disadvantaged enclaves of low-income public housing projects or blighted or slum areas, or who live in relatively primitive communities like some of those in Appalachia or the deep South.

As successive children appear, each brings a repetition of the parents' first-child adjustment, although with each child the situation changes for everyone. The parents need to learn the particular developmental needs and capacities of each child and to gear tasks accordingly. Each child differs from the others with respect to his intellectual and physical endowment; how he develops physically at his own pace in size and coordination; how health and sickness affect his physical, intellectual, and emotional development. The tasks should always be related to what the child seems ready to undertake and achieve with some success, and they also should be geared to something that requires effort, a little stretching beyond his present capacity—though not more than he can accomplish. The parents have to be alert to signs of readiness, then gently push the child to try himself. For example, readiness for toilet training can be tested when the child is able to sit comfortably with minimal support. He may be ready but he may not necessarily like the new task. With emotional support, patience, and pleasure expressed by the parent, he will continue to exert some effort and will be pleased with success. If he expresses intense and continued fear, the parent would be well advised to wait for several weeks or even months before essaying this test again. And so it is with other tasks. No child is completely and finally ready for a particular undertaking at a prescribed, designated time. He wants to achieve, but he also is afraid and only the parents can discern when he appears to have sufficient readiness to be propelled toward the new task.

Gross developmental norms are useful only as broad guides. Each child has its own timing and rhythm for learning and achieving success in developmental tasks. It is only when the child's development falls far short of the gross developmental norms demonstrated in Gesell[4] that parents need to be concerned. Nor does development usually proceed in a straight line. Some children develop more rapidly in one respect than another: one may talk early but begin to walk some time after others of his age are doing so; some children develop more quickly physically than intellectually. It also appears to be

[4] Arnold Gesell and Frances L. Ilg, *The Child from Five to Ten* (New York: Harper, 1946).

in the nature of development that some regression takes place as each new major developmental phase approaches. Thus children who are toilet trained may regress when school is in the offing or when a new sibling is born; regression also may be evidenced following an illness or while parents are under particular stress. Such manifestations of regression are not significant if they are temporary, sporadically transient, or related to an identifiable reality experience. They need not become a problem if the parents recognize and accept the regressive need and at the same time encourage the child to have pleasure in the new task. Nor do parents need to view each child as utterly fragile; if some regression follows encouragement for performance of a task before the child is completely ready, there generally is opportunity for the parents and the child to make a new beginning and reach a successful completion of the task.

A major developmental task for parents and for children, particularly during the first five years, is that of separation: physical separation and emotional separateness. It is normal for parents as well as children to feel ambivalent in the wish to grow and the wish to remain young. The child who is beginning to walk often shows his fear of separation and separateness either by clinging to the mother or by nightmares and temper tantrums. Later, when he is engaged in the task of forming sexual identity, nightmares, fear of animals, wanting to get into bed with the parents are common. These manifestations of separation fears subside and become a stimulus to further growth if the child's parents are together in their sympathy for the child, in supporting each other with respect to their relative regressive feelings about separation from the child, and in kind firmness with the child.

The Child's Mastery of Tasks

Healthy nurturing during the first eighteen months or so of the child's life should result in developing self-trust in him and therefore trust in relation to his parents and later to the outside world. The groundwork is laid for a capacity to test reality, his readiness to challenge as well as to trust, his sense of self-esteem and his potential for self-control as this is evidenced by his ability to wait for gratification. In this critical period of the baby's development, social and emotional factors are on a continuum with biological factors, and growth comes about through proper feeding and through proper stimulation of the child to feed himself when he is ready, through parental relaxation about his individual eating habits, and through gentle encouragement to try new foods and new ways of eating. Emotional giving and emotional limiting underpin these tasks.

During the next phase, approximately from eighteen months to three years, our culture expects weaning to cleanliness. This is largely achieved by proper toilet training. The child's readiness when he can sit and the parents' readiness, patience, and willingness to permit the child to test himself are important. In one sense this task is the first one about which the child can exercise his own control. With regard to feeding he must rely on the giving or withholding by the parents. But on the toilet the child is the master—no one can force him to give up or to withhold. It is therefore crucial that an acute contest of wills between himself and his parents be avoided at a time when the child is testing his self-autonomy. He must be led gently to experiment, neither too early nor too late. It is out of this experience that the child acquires the capacity for self-control that is so essential to learning and acquiring of knowledge. If the contest is acute, the child may emerge as the controller of the parents, or he may develop control as a consequence of fear rather than as an internal process. In true self-control the child need not fight the parents continually or be blindly obedient. In later years he will not have to carry the same patterns into the outside world. He will be able to learn and he will be able to work because the true acceptance of self-control means the acceptance of outer boundaries, and the acceptance of limits in relation to others.

The child-rearing task in the next phase—the four- five- and six-year-olds—is to socialize the child through teaching him to cope with both parents as love objects. In order to retain the love of both parents, the child must learn to give up his infantile wishes for the exclusive love of one parent. He shows curiosity about his parents, he wants to know about birth and sex, he tests how much each parent loves him versus their love for each other, and he often is jealous of their love for each other. Parents who are united as parents and in their affection for each other can accept the child's curiosity and diversionary tactics. They do not permit him to play one parent against the other; neither parent responds to the seductive expressions of the child. They answer sexual questions directly, accurately and without undue elaboration. The major task, then, for parents and child is to permit the development of curiosity about the world —a curiosity that triggers the capacity for initiative. At the same time, the parents have to set proper limits: permitting the child to find out what he wants to know but not at the expense of others; helping the child to control himself in the finding-out process. The mastery of this conflict—the exercise of initiative within limits—produces an appropriate balance of proper curiosity and initiative, the development of conscience, and the capacity to identify.[5] The child who has mastered this phase of development learns through identification with the teacher and at the same time has the internal resources to resist identification so that the learning becomes an active process. The child whose curiosity is inhibited, for example, has greater difficulty in learning to read and cannot reach into the world outside the family with ease and comfort.

During the latency years, approximately six to twelve, the parents must allow the child to separate from them by giving him permission to roam, to experiment in various ways in the larger environment, and to test himself in school and with peers. If the child has mastered the earlier conflicts, he now is really industrious. He can learn readily and he can make friends without suffering from a belief that he is inferior. Such a feeling of inferiority inhibits learning, and when it is present the child reacts by withdrawal or difficult acting-out behavior. All phases of development are overlapping, all involve conflict for parents and child, and each phase sets in motion new mechanisms of defense and adaptation that influence the total development. The more successfully each phase is mastered, the better the child can review his actions, correct what he did wrong, and make decisions about how to do things differently. He is able to undertake corrective ways of performing because the pleasure of mastery of tasks performed has also given him a sense of freedom to experiment further. Again parents need to realize that learning readiness differs with each child and that each child also has different readiness for learning different subjects.

The child has to develop an equilibrium between his internal needs and the tasks that are required of him. The parents have to develop an equilibrium between their own needs and those of the child, and between their understanding of the child's readiness for each task and the right amount of push to help him move on to each new task. Normal anxiety and normal conflict exist; in healthy families these are resolved.

The Child of Disadvantaged Parents

In families that are disturbed because of marital disequilibrium or personal difficulties of the parents, or because of external or disadvantaging stresses that are unmanageable, difficulties result

---

[5] See Chapter 15 for meaning of identity.

for the child: there are defects or delays in development. The consequences often are reflected in learning difficulties, behavior disorders,
phobias of neurotic origin, limited ability to perform on a job, and
other evidences of less than adequate social functioning.

There is considerable evidence to support the fact that such consequences in large measure are connected with child-rearing practices
and family life and living patterns within segments of the population
that differ markedly from that reflected by the idealized image of the
American family—or its "runner-up," the American middle-class
family. Middle-class parents place strong value on permissiveness and
gentleness. These are qualities that middle-class parents (literally)
can afford: they have enough room in their homes; there generally
are few children, carefully spaced; they live in "good" neighborhoods
with established middle-class standards and values. Television appears to be one of the major devices likely to narrow class differences
in child rearing. To aspiring families with less opportunity in our
social organization it shows families who are "successful" and socially
and economically comfortable. Nevertheless, a combination of environmental conditions, cultural patterns, and the personality development of the parents conspire to perpetuate child-rearing practices that are not conducive to sound transformation of healthy
young children into healthy adolescents and into healthy adults.

Loving though parents in many disadvantaged families may be
toward their children—and all too frequently the quality of their own
personality development has affected their capacity to love—their
marital equilibrium and family equilibrium are characterized by
qualities that fail to permit the children to realize their potentials.
The parents, their own self-esteem and trust severely limited or
nonexistent, foster in their children an alienating distrustful approach to the society outside the family. These children have low
self-esteem; they develop little belief in their own coping capacity;
they respond to inconsistent, harsh physical punishment by reduced
curiosity, initiative, and learning interest. If the family is one that
falls into the characteristic neurotic or psychotic categories, the
parenting behavior and the children's developmental responses to it
hold additional negative implications.

Of significance for social workers is the kind of performance and
parental roles the environment—physical and emotional *and* cultural
—permits. The mother whose energies are invested in coping with
physical crowding and continuous exposure, or (often *and*) who lacks
a marital partner, requires a different approach than parents with
sufficient internal resources to enable them to be creative and attentive to their parenting tasks. Not infrequently early intervention by

the social worker needs to be in terms of aiding a disadvantaged family to develop different living arrangements, provided opportunities and motivation exist. Given sufficient economic and housing resources (and the social worker may have a special responsibility in encouraging the community to develop these) and an approach that is not condemnatory or moralistic or judgmental, an important step can be taken toward change. The worker may need to acknowledge with the parents the reality problems they face: the ghetto-like isolation from the wider community that public-housing residents often feel; their need always to keep shades drawn so that, as happens in some low-cost housing projects, some privacy may be experienced and some protection to possessions assured because this "hinders" mischief-bent individuals from breaking in ("they won't know if someone is here"); the exposure of the children to the overt "week-end carousing" common in some such enclaves. The worker has to be aware in such instances that often the demeaning impact on the parents of such living arrangements and the realistic necessity for being distrustful are not designed to enable the parents to instill in their young children either trust or self-esteem or the beginning self-control essential to healthy personality formation. And the worker has to be patiently aware that the distrust is extended to the worker as part of the "oppressing" wider community, and that this distrust will not readily be reduced or dispelled.[6]

THE ADOLESCENT YEARS

By the time the parents are in their middle or late thirties —or even earlier if they married young—their family life changes almost abruptly. The second transitional crisis is upon them: the child is giving way to the adolescent whose interests appear to change overnight as he enters an entirely new world and feels the impact of new familial and societal expectations. This stage—adolescence—encompasses the years that begin around the thirteenth year and often continues to the advent of adulthood: years fraught with anxiety for the children and insecurity for the parents.

The fact is that many young people manage to grow up without running into special difficulties; the vagaries and the erratic aspects of behavior so characteristic of adolescence are taken in stride by most parents, uneasy though they may be. This is simpler to do if

[6] See Chapter 13 for management of trust.

the child-rearing tasks in the earlier years have been relatively smooth. Regardless of what has gone before, adolescence is a time of life that requires considerable understanding; in every family at one point or another there is apt to be a troublesome spot. Some families, however, have more such spots than others; in many instances the numerous spots blend into a continuum from the inception of this stage to its termination—which for some appears never to come.

The adolescent, though preoccupied with his own development, is peculiarly sensitive to the world about him, its expectations of him as a future adult, and his family's responses to the world. The rapidity with which changes have occurred in our society in the years since the adolescent's parents were themselves adolescents have contributed to some problems between them: the parents tend not to have had certain experiences on which to draw in their modeling for their children—major scientific and social changes have been too recent. As a consequence, there is some unsureness and uncertainty that is unsettling to their children—parents cannot call on their own experiences to reply to the challenging "How do you know?" Nor can they readily know, as did past generations, what expectations they realistically can hold before their growing children.

This kind of break in generational experience, an experience containing stabilizing properties, in and of itself contributes to uncertainty of children and parents alike. This uncertainty has been compounded by the addition of external factors, including economic and social disadvantage, declared and undeclared wars, changes in general social and economic conditions.

Adolescence in our American culture is becoming prolonged as school requirements are extended and technology advances. Among middle-class families, with college attendance becoming commonplace and postgraduate study increasingly undertaken, the adolescent's financial dependence on the family is protracted and as a result adult emotional maturity often is delayed. Although emotional maturity does not necessarily derive from financial independence, there often is a relationship between the two. Some of the increased rebelliousness occurring in universities today among older adolescents who chronologically are adults can be attributed to the delayed conflict between dependence and independence.

Among families in the lower economic classes, learning difficulties brought about by family predicaments, personal difficulties, financial insecurity, and poor educational facilities, in the aggregate or singly, create special problems. The adolescent has little incentive to remain in school, and consequences of "dropping out" are serious for him and for the community. Increasingly, steady or reasonably well-paying jobs are unavailable for the unprepared adolescent; often he can procure no job of *any* kind. His frustration mounts while society suffers from the defiant behavior in which many of this group engage because of lack of education, jobs, or any constructive gratification.

There is some difference of opinion as to whether the statistical increase in crime is a real increase in the crime rate or is more reflective of the numerically larger adolescent population. However, there is statistical evidence of an increase in crimes of violence that occur in the adolescent years. Some violence of a minor nature can be productive if its expression is appropriately related to social causes; violence that is antisocial and self-destructive to the adolescent always is unproductive. Many adolescents are confused by a world in which open aggression in wars is condoned and competitiveness in work is fostered while personal aggression taking other forms is frowned upon.

Recent years have seen a growing recognition that the adolescent needs his family as much as the younger child but in ways that are different. Instead of the adolescent's task being viewed as a straight line from early childhood toward independence or emancipation from the family, the task must be perceived as the establishment of a workable relationship with the family if the adolescent is to gain the independence of a mature adult. His maturation is a consequence of appropriate resolution of his conflicts within the family. Whether the process of working out these conflicts is achieved with relative ease or with great difficulty—or *not* achieved—depends both on the parents and on the adolescent. Therefore it is not enough for a social worker or other helping person to focus only on the troubled adolescent. His family, to whatever extent this is possible, needs to be understood and involved.

The Parents' Tasks

Both the adolescent and his parents face unique maturational tasks during this phase of life. The adolescent is confronted with a host of tasks at one time. Because of this, and the intensity of emotion involved in working on the tasks, the period of adolescence is known as the "identity crisis." This is the time when the adolescent seeks to establish who he is, what he is, and what he will be in the future. He struggles with the crucial tasks of establishing sexual identity, of achieving and learning and defining and implementing vocational goals, of developing responsibility and self-reliance, of making a place for himself outside the family, of finding a new place in the family and experimenting with values that differ from the accustomed ones within the family. At the same time the parents frequently also are struggling with their own maturational tasks, thereby adding some pain and trouble at a time that in any event would be difficult for them. The father generally is settled vocationally and probably is at his peak earning level—a peak which may be far lower than either he wishes or the family's needs require. He has to come to terms with the fact that his work with its satisfactions and dissatisfactions, and his earning capacity in most instances, are not likely to alter very much in the future. If he is an unskilled or semiskilled worker, the middle years of life bring him face to face with worry about obtaining and retaining jobs. If he is steadily employed for a large organization, or even a small one, he is not really free to effect changes in his employment because of his vested interest in pensions or other benefits. The unskilled adolescent, at the outset of his vocational activity, may earn more than the father and stir resentment and competitiveness in the father. If the adolescent is not employed, the father is faced with a long-term drain on income because of rising costs of education, in addition to the extended time required today for education and increasing demands during the prolonged period of adolescence for money to meet expanding social needs.

Many mothers consider child rearing the most important function in life; when the last child reaches adolescence, the mother may feel lost and depressed. At the same time the climacteric may bring additional problems which affect the sexual relationship with her husband. Thus she may feel doubly at loose ends, that her life no longer has a specific purpose.

As longevity increases, parents in their middle years more and more face problems with their own aged parents for whom they may have to take both economic and emotional responsibility if the aged parents are poor, or ill, or one dies.

When the adolescents leave home for college or marriage, or to live alone, the parents for the first time in many years need to turn to each other: to support each other, to find new interests, and, if possible, effect new divisions of responsibilities within the home. Some parents deeply fear this separation and its consequences, and they try to cling to the older adolescents, making undue demands upon them. Each of the marital partners may experience some normal regression and have to seek understanding and support from the other. In some families the child-rearing needs have held a poor marriage in check. When the last child leaves, the marriage disintegrates and divorce follows. In others, as was described in the last chapter, a new balance takes place.

In any event, the middle years for the parents contain as much of a transitional identity crisis as do the adolescent years for their children. The adolescent's tasks continually intermesh with the family's as a whole and with the parental tasks. The adolescent's tasks in the areas of sexual maturation, of establishing his independence, of educational and vocational achievement, of incorporating a set of values and standards, and of forming relationships with peers will be examined in the light of this intermeshing.

Sexual Identity

The emergence of biological sexual development during adolescence and the accompanying emotional aspects are crucial to the adolescent's total development. Every adolescent struggles to understand the needs of his physical impulses, how to manage them, and how to find proper expression for these needs. At the same time parents are likely to be struggling with similar conflicts expressed in different ways. The burgeoning sexuality of the adolescent arouses in nearly all parents remnants of old, unresolved sexual conflicts. This is evidenced in competitiveness between father and son or mother and daughter. In the healthy family, the parents support each other so that sexual competitiveness does not move out of control. They are careful not to permit the normal increased seductiveness of the adolescent toward the parent of the opposite sex to form a wedge between them. The division of labor between the parents becomes different in the sense that the father, while retaining interest in his daughter, begins to detach himself from much physical contact with her, refers her to her mother for "female" talk, and avoids acting seductively toward her by sexually tinged remarks or behavior. The mother behaves in a similar manner with the son. When the parents are clear about their roles in the sexual sphere, behave accordingly, and support each other in appropriate behavior, the adolescent feels supported and is not likely to discharge sexual tensions in undesirable ways.

In troubled families, where old sexual problems in the parents may become accentuated as the child enters adolescence, or where the parents cannot support each other and make the necessary role changes, the adolescent may encounter severe difficulties. If the parents are too repressive and deny the existence of sexuality in themselves and in the adolescent, he may become either severely inhibited or overly preoccupied with sexual fantasies and thus be unable to attain success in other tasks; or he may act out impulsively and self-destructively. If the parents are overtly or covertly seductive, the adolescent may never free himself from the parent of the opposite sex, and he may move into a deviant homosexual adjustment; or, in an effort to free himself, he may act-out sexually. It is not uncommon, for example, for unmarried motherhood in adolescence to occur because the father—who may or may not be oblivious to this cause-and-effect situation—is sexually overstimulating to the girl and she is unprotected by the mother; or the mother, out of sexual competitiveness and jealousy—of which she likewise is unaware—pushes the girl to sexual acting-out. Overcrowding, close quarters, or lack of privacy for other reasons constitute factors that are conducive to the paternal overstimulation and the maternal jealousy that sometimes lead to the unwed parenthood of the young girl. There is a somewhat general community readiness to stereotype these out-of-wedlock pregnancies, to hold factors of culture, poverty, and others like these to be primary contributors to the behavior leading to the unmarried motherhood. Important though these may be, however, the tasks that adolescents face—including that of forming sexual identity—really must be examined by the social worker from the point of view of the dynamic factors, the growth factors in the adolescent, the relationship between the adolescent and the parents, and the adolescent's relationship with the outside world.

A common phenomenon in social agencies is the parent who is deeply hurt by the sexual acting-out of a girl or boy at the same time that the parent unconsciously stimulates this. These may be parents who leave teenaged youngsters unchaperoned at parties, or do not set limits on when they are expected to return home, or simply do not know where they are, or who have promulgated no clear family rules with regard to sexual behavior. Further, the family arrangements may provide for insufficient privacy for individuals within the family. The young and middle adolescents need to have limits established for them for protection, even though they fight against the limits and the parents for setting them. The parents, then, need to be in accord about their values concerning sex. The difficult task is to permit freedom and, at the same time, to set limits: the adolescent needs privacy rather than parental obtrusiveness as he works toward resolution of his sexual identity conflict; he also needs a sympathetic, protective ear when he wants to discuss these matters. He needs to be free to experiment in dating, but he also wants his parents to set some limits on this. Otherwise, he becomes frightened and reacts to his fear by withdrawal or by acting-out.

The older adolescent in the healthy family generally is one who is past eighteen years of age, accepts his sexuality and the sexuality of his parents as completely private matters. His basic values are identified with the values of his parents. His sexual expression will be directed toward a true love object, whether in or out of marriage.

Dependence and Independence

The resolution of this task is inextricably intertwined among the adolescent and the family members. The healthy adolescent simultaneously feels a compelling push toward growth and independence and fears the loss of his dependence on the parents. The parents are caught in a similar conflict. They want the adolescent to grow, to become more self-responsible; at the same time it is difficult for them to let him go, to permit separateness and separation. This aspect of development takes a difficult course. The feelings of the adolescent as well as of his parents vacillate and the management of these feelings is not always resolute.

Rebelliousness is a major means utilized by the adolescent to express his struggle to be independent even as he clings to dependence. He rebels against time limits, choice of clothing, the values of his parents—including their religion and standards of behavior. He ridicules his parents, their knowledge, their ways of doing things, their manner of speech; at the same time he wants them to be models of propriety and models of conformity to community standards. He knows more than they do. He argues about everything. Rebelliousness is a necessary mechanism employed by the adolescent to sort out his own confusions, feelings, and ideas and to effect gradual separateness and separation. This is his way of establishing his own identity.

This is an exceedingly difficult period for the parents. They need to walk a fine line in permitting the rebellious behavior without letting it swing out of control. The greatest asset the adolescent possesses during this time is the support that the parents give to each other. When the parents stand together and do not permit the adolescent to place them in competition with each other, he feels their support. He may rail against it, but without necessarily being aware of it he is grateful for it. When the parents can give way in such matters as clothing and hair styles, no matter how distasteful they feel them to be, they are likely to find that the adolescent will be less rebellious with regard to more important issues such as school performance or selection of friends among his peers.

A second major aspect of the dependence-independence conflict is the adolescent's regressive behavior. In his efforts to achieve identity, he swings between adult behavior and childlike behavior. For example, the adolescent typically goes through alternating periods of slovenliness and cleanliness in his person and in his belongings. The dirtiness, a regression to an earlier phase of development, casts the parents into despair. They also despair of the characteristic disorganization among the adolescent's personal belongings. In contrast to skills the adolescent had displayed in earlier stages, he now appears to be handicapped by an unusual number of thumbs. Regression and spurts of development are characteristic of this phase. Although they are hard to live with, they need cause no real concern unless the regressive features become fixed ways of operating. Again, the parents have to recognize that such behavior is a manifestation of the struggle for independence versus dependence. Perhaps the best advice that can be given to parents is that they try to ignore the adolescent's regressive behavior. For example, if the parents can bring themselves to do so, it is better that they close the door on a messy room than either clean it up themselves or nag the adolescent to clean it. Eventually he will get to this job.

The troubled adolescent who is part of a disturbed family will have great difficulty in achieving independence. If the parents try to stamp out the rebelliousness, the adolescent may conform to their demands because he is afraid not to and he may remain too closely tied to the parents to leave them for a good adjustment in education, in employment, or in marriage. Or the adolescent may rebel violently, resorting to socially or personally destructive behavior. A girl may rebel by sexual acting-out and, motivated by anger and guilt, bring the baby home to be reared by the parents. A boy may rebel by engaging in antisocial behavior in which he manages to be caught and is then punished. This kind of situation is illustrated by Jim Evans, a brilliant nineteen-year-old who was expelled from medical school at the end of his first year because of several instances of cheating. The cheating was flagrant and self-destructive, each time managed in a way calculated to insure detection. As is often true, particularly in middle-class families, this boy's every wish had been indulged in earlier adolescence by parents who endeavored to protect him from any troubling experience. The father, a physician, had high hopes that Jim some day would join him in medical practice. Jim had never protested against this expectation, nor had he been anything but compliant and conforming with his demanding father and equally controlling mother. His expulsion was at once a defiance of his father and an effort to handle the conflicts reflecting his delayed maturity.

The parents of disturbed adolescents often have difficulty with their own unresolved problems about dependence and independence. These problems may come sharply to the fore when provoked into prominence by the adolescent's dependence-independence conflicts. These parents generally fail to give the adolescent the support he needs, then not infrequently regress to childlike behavior, fighting with each other and with the adolescent as though they were all siblings together. A marital problem, previously submerged, may rise acutely to the surface. The parents may resort to former kinds of activity, for example trying to reinstate family outings appropriate to younger children.

Educational and Vocational Achievement

The adolescent is confronted with making tentative or final vocational plans and directing much of his learning toward this objective. He often has to undertake this task at the same time that the father has successfully attained his vocational goal and is well settled in his chosen work. The mother's major task of caring for children (often *her* work) is drawing to a close. In the healthy family there generally is a wish that the children achieve more than the parents did. But as the adolescent begins to tackle the task of making educational and vocational decisions, the parents tend to become more aware of their own failures or unfulfilled achievement dreams. Even in the normal family they may place too much urgency on the adolescent's achieving in this area, not realizing that learning in adolescence is uneven in the same way as is the performance with respect to other tasks that the adolescent must undertake. They may insist that he go to college although he may have neither interest nor capacity nor vocational need for such education.

Parents do not always realize that entrance into high school or college is both desired and feared by the adolescent because each of these events brings to a close a particular era of dependence. It is important for the parents to encourage the adolescent to strive without placing heavy pressure on him to achieve. The adolescent often belittles his learning achievement; he may not admit he is doing as well as he really is, or he may hide failures. Parents have to learn to live with the kind of normal anxiety this arouses in them. They have to learn to refrain from prying or expressing pleasure exuberantly or disappointment bitterly when the adolescent does inform them of his achievements or of his failures to achieve. Their attitude should be one of expecting self-responsibility by the adolescent for his attainments.

In the disturbed family, competition for achievement may arise between father and son or between mother and daughter. Such competitiveness may place stumbling blocks in the path of the adolescent's development. If the adolescent boy is fearful about competing with an envious father, the boy may need to fail. He will fear success; he will feel he cannot equal or surpass the father's educational or work achievement. The girl also may retreat by declining to compete with the mother in womanly achievements. Such a girl may permit herself education or work achievement but not feminine gratification. Her fear of competition with the mother may lead her to marry an inadequate man. The achievement gap for both girl and boy may become greater when the parents encourage the adolescents too strenuously to make up for the parents' failures or under-achievements; or the parents may not encourage or stimulate sufficiently if they cannot tolerate the possibility of being outdone by their children.

The problems take on different forms of severity for the adolescents whose families are poor or have only one parent in the home, or whose cultural or emotional patterns offer the adolescent no incentive for vocational or educational achievement. The economically disadvantaged family may find it necessary to insist that the adolescent boy or girl find gainful work, "make his own way," before he is ready to do so. This adolescent is thrown into a kind of pseudo-independence that affects his development. The forcible entrance into a "self-supporting" status deprives him of an opportunity to work out the normal conflicts related to his and society's expectations of the vocational role of an educated person in our broader culture. The failure adequately to resolve conflicts about vocational choices prohibits the appropriate development of self-esteem and is commonly found among school drop-outs who were forced into emancipation—by virtue of pressure from the family, an external economic situation, or the adolescent's own uneasy indecision about continuing in school.

If there is only one parent in the home—the mother—and income is limited, the adolescent may be impelled to interrupt his education to take whatever work might be available in order to augment the family's income. Again, he may have to assume this responsibility before he is either emotionally or educationally ready to do so. It may lead him to take on the role of family provider too soon and thereby shoulder heavy financial and emotional responsibilities which his inadequate preparation probably will not permit him to continue productively throughout his adult life. Or he may escape by leaving the family home to be "on his own." If the father either is out of the home or, being in it, is unemployed, the adolescent may see no value in working; he may hopelessly emulate the model he perceives: a weak and submissive male figure.

In the disadvantaged family, particularly one from a low income culture, the characteristic tendency to think only about the present and not plan for a future that is invisible discourages the adolescent from aiming his sights toward education or training which he has little hope of ever achieving.

Standards and Values

The adolescent's problems in establishing standards and values are related both to the family and to the broader societal and environmental influences that affect the family. The upward mobility of many into the middle-income levels of our society has been accompanied by a tendency to shed older values without replacing them with identifiable new ones. As the gap between the middle class and the culturally deprived becomes more apparent, the resentment of the latter group about inadequate and insufficient resources creates problems in values for the adolescent. Social values in relation to material matters and in behavior regarding sexual matters are shifting so rapidly that parents are at a loss because, as was stated earlier, their own experiences and those of their peers offer no definitive answers. This creates an identity crisis for the parents too. There are confusions about money values—giving, earning, saving, spending; about sexual activity—dating, premarital relations, very early marriage; about aggression in work—what is corrupt and what is not. For example, a father may boast at home about a profit made in the course of his work by exploiting someone, or by manipulating tax reports in his favor, or by outright, overt connivance and cheating. He often is not at all aware that he provides his son with the model for cheating in school examinations. His horrified reaction to such behavior is not connected in his mind with his own work behavior. On the other hand, his son may react with anger at his father's performance, the father then feeling himself to be the victim of his son's "unreasonable" attitudes.

Adolescents expect parents to identify limits for them. If the parents do not or the youth finds himself at variance with these limits, he looks to outside influences such as schools, employers, or other social institutions to set the needed limits and to represent the authority that either he has not accepted from his parents or that they in their confusion and uncertainty have not provided.

This is indeed a difficult time in which to rear children, especially adolescents. It is trying for parents to stand up against the prevailing values in their own segment of the world or in the broader culture. It is not possible to provide them with specific guidelines, but parents should realize that adolescents want rules for standards, even if they rebel against the rules. They want the parents to stand together on what the parents conceive as right and wrong; they need parents who are themselves not corrupt even in small ways; they need and want parents who will represent values without ambivalence—without vacillating and changing their minds in such a manner that the adolescent does not know what the parents think is right or think is wrong. The adolescent's preference and requirement are that the parents lean on the side of strictness rather than permissiveness with regard to values.

Relationships with Peers

Many of the adolescent's identity problems are worked through with his peers, but to do this he needs the overt and covert permission of his parents. He experiments with many different kinds of friends drawn from both sexes, often from a wide range of economic groups, religions, and social backgrounds. He imitates the behavior, speech, and dress of the peer groups encompassed in his experiments. He can discuss with them intimate sexual ideas and fantasies which are not appropriate for discussion with his family. He works with his peers on conflicts about achievement, values, and life goals.

Sometimes parents are inclined to become overly anxious about the choice of friends and their influence, particularly when the adolescent flirts with fringe antisocial behavior or moves out of his class, ethnic culture, or religious group in his experiments. Certainly there is cause for concern when the fringe activities over a period of time are repetitious or truly antisocial. At the same time, one piece of antisocial behavior does not necessarily betoken a serious problem. Similarly, experimentation with a variety of peers, unless the adolescent consistently seeks friends who are inadequate or in trouble, is not a basis for worry.

The Onset of Adulthood

As the identity crisis for parents and adolescents is successfully worked through during the long span between the thirteenth and the twenty-first year, the adolescent in the healthy family emerges as a mature adult on an equalitarian basis. He has his own identity; he loves his parents without being dependent on them; he has his own set of values which also reflect the values of his family; he respects the opinions of his parents without necessarily subscribing to them; he is vocationally established or at least on the way toward his goal; he is ready for mature, heterosexual relationships. The parents have effected separateness and separation from the children; they have given each other emotional support during this process and they continue to support each other following the emancipation, agreeing consciously or otherwise to new divisions of household and family responsibilities and seeking new interests.

The adolescent and his parents in the healthy family have to work together—often along parallel lines, occasionally converging but generally remaining separate—on the goal of identity formation and decision-making about what to do with his adult life. The adolescent needs to have the freedom, initiative, and curiosity to experiment with choices, but not be compelled to commit himself too early to a specific choice. Although this process may produce anxiety, anger, and envy in parents, they have to be cognizant of his need for a variety of identity models and tolerate his switching of models. They should know that a major outcome of the identity struggle is the mature capacity to make sound choices.

The parents in a healthy family will recognize that the older adolescent struggles with problems of intimacy, that is, with the problem of whether he can love and whether he is lovable. In his striving for independence he wants to leave the family, yet in his wish to retain his dependence relationship within the family he fears independence. He wants to love but he also fears the commitment that goes with love. He wants to learn and to work for himself and for those who depend on him. Again, the parents must be emotionally ready to grant him genuine permission to separate from them and to love someone outside the family. The healthy outcome is learning, working, and loving with a purpose and goal in life.

CHILD-REARING TASKS AND THE SOCIAL WORKER

Troubled families with young children may voluntarily turn to a social agency for assistance because of problems that seem unrelated to the children's needs, or for help to the parents specifically with regard to the children. The problem apparent to the family may be marital difficulty or financial assistance; it may be clear to them that the problem is the child's or about the child. Other families may approach a social welfare agency only because of referral from a school, or a court, or some other legal or quasi-legal organization. Later chapters focus upon the ways in which help can be given, some of the specific tasks of the social worker, and some of the devices for extending help. Brief attention, however, will be addressed here to the role of the worker in connection with problems in child rearing, regardless of whether the family is culturally or economically advantaged or disadvantaged.

Work with Parents of Young Children

When a family with a young child is in need of help, the work of the social worker characteristically is with the parents—or parent—in behalf of the child. Most of the work undertaken is in guiding or educating or helping the parents to work on the amelioration of their own problems that affect the child and, consequently, to improve their relationship with him. Some parents, particularly in very disorganized families, require a considerable amount of direct education to learn to understand what responsibilities a child should and can have at certain ages, what tasks he must perform, how he should behave in various settings, and how the parents should behave in relation to him. In other words, they need to learn how to differentiate their roles from those of the child, to distinguish their responsibilities and tasks from his.

Less chaotic families often present the problems of the young children to the agency in terms of school phobias, underachievement, hyperactivity, or undue aggressive behavior. Many times these are reflective of marital difficulties or problems that are personal within one or both parents. In these kinds of situations it is most common to undertake to help the parents in working out their own problems —those that relate to their past life experiences and are contributing to the child's difficulties, the problems in the marriage itself, or their feelings about the particular child. Such activity on the part of the worker frequently entails helping the school to understand the nature of the problem that is being attacked and distinguishing between the school's educational function with respect to the child and the agency's function in counseling with the parent.

Direct Work with the Young Child

In some instances it appears advisable to work concurrently with the child and with the parents. This plan generally obtains if the parents have little capacity or energy to deal indirectly with the child's problems by working directly on their own problems; or the child's growth problems may be so severe that work with the parent will not suffice to enable the child to handle the growth tasks appropriately. The decision to work directly with the child should be based on a careful assessment as to the nature of the treatment, the frequency, who is to provide it, and under what auspices it is to be extended. Professional assessment may indicate that the child's treatment should be extended by the same worker who is engaged with the parents in tackling their problems, or by another worker in the same agency, or by a social worker in another agency, or by someone in another helping discipline—a psychiatrist or psychologist, for example. In any event, irrespective of the person or auspices providing the direct service to the child, work with the parents must proceed simultaneously.

The Young Child in a One-Parent Family

It is not unusual that a child in a family requires not intensive treatment but a relationship with a male adult. This need commonly arises if the father of a boy is completely or frequently out of the home or has never been a part of the household and, therefore, has not established himself as a model for the child. A male social worker may serve as such a model: the warm relationship provided by the worker enables the youngster to know how to handle himself, how to behave as a boy both within the family and in the community beyond the doorstep.

The Adolescent

Problems posed in relation to adolescents contain features somewhat different from those in regard to the young child. It was pointed out earlier that there is important intermeshing between the problems of the adolescent and those of his parents. Where once it was thought sound to have separate workers, one for the parents and one for the adolescent, experience has demonstrated that because of the interrelatedness of the problems of the parents and of their adolescent offspring, the involvement of the same worker with both the parents and the adolescent is a more effective approach. When both parents can be available, for example, it is imperative that they be included together in the interviews because of the importance to the adolescent of knowing that both parents, though they may be having serious marital difficulties, nevertheless can still stand together on certain issues regarding him and share an interest in his welfare.

It is often possible to engage the adolescent and the parents in jointly working out such problems as competitiveness, obstacles to achievement of learning, self-responsibility, and self-esteem. In such instances, the family members can tackle together questions and disagreements concerning values or behavior standards in order to effect compromises necessary to free the adolescent to move ahead in completing his developmental tasks.

In some situations the desirable approach is to work with both the parents and the adolescent as a family group, and also to afford some individual interviews to the adolescent as well as to the parents. This approach can be illustrated by Jerry Rhodes who, together with his parents, has been seen by the social worker with reference to his underachievement in school. There are also separate counseling sessions with Jerry. These are designed to underscore the need for his accepting some responsibility for achievement, but their purpose is also to give him an opportunity to express his sexual longings and fantasies and discuss his experimentations in other areas in an atmosphere that is not as charged as when his parents are present. His parents have a low threshold of tolerance with regard to both conflicts around sexual identity and Jerry's strivings toward the independence he wants to acquire "like the other fellows."

The matter of separation and separateness of the adolescent frequently lends itself to effective resolution by means of family counseling sessions in which both parents and the adolescent can test out the work on the data manifesting the adolescent's two-pronged wish: to remain dependent upon his parents and, at the same time, to move on to more adult behavior. Together, also, they can understand and deal with the parents' suffering from their wish to hold on to their child while letting him mature into adulthood.

Sometimes it is advisable to work separately with one or both parents in addition to the work with the family group. There may be special vulnerability which a parent simply cannot expose to the adolescent. Mr. Walker, for example, was facing the prospect of being released from the bank job he had held for eighteen years; the manual tasks he was performing were henceforth to be machine-operated and no other place had been found for him. The monthly take-home pay from his seventeen-year-old son's summer job was nearly the same as Mr. Walker was bringing home after eighteen years of steady work. He was deeply troubled by his son's antagonism; he was more troubled about letting his son know what a "failure" he had for a father. Mr. Walker's battered self-esteem obscured his perception of the boy's maturational problems and of his own real strengths that could effectively be mobilized to deal with his employment and other problems. The worker met with the parents and the boy separately until the father's increased self-esteem permitted him to discuss problems of achievement directly with his son.

The same kind of approach may be indicated when a girl and her mother are "at each other all the time!" The mother, on the "downgoing" path, is competitive with her attractive daughter and requires some help for herself before she can tolerate the daughter's presence at a discussion that might be too revealing.

The one-parent situation may call for similar approaches. It is possible, for example, to work with an adolescent boy and his mother, or an adolescent girl and her mother. At the same time, however, the absence of one parent—usually the parent of the sex opposite to the adolescent's—frequently means that in addition to interviews that include the remaining parent, the adolescent needs individual help, either alone or in a group of his peers. The family atmosphere in broken families often is so highly charged, especially when the adolescent and the parent in the home are of opposite sexes, that it may not be possible or practical for the worker to attempt to attack many problems with the mother and son together; each may have to have individual work as well as some help in groups.

The fact is, of course, that many different combinations are possible and a prescription cannot be written for *the* one that is most likely to be productive. The choice can be made only on the basis of assessing the special areas of vulnerability and strength within a given family and the factors that facilitate or retard the adolescent's progress through the adolescent years into mature and productive adulthood.

8

THE LATER YEARS

T HAT A PERSON is as old as he feels is a commonly heard observation. It contains considerable truth, for certainly the mere tally of years is a poor measure of aging: although it cannot be arrested, aging can be delayed or accelerated. Moreover, the rate at which physiological and psychological aging takes place varies widely among different individuals and from stage to stage in the individual's cycle of life. And this rate has a marked impact on the competence with which older persons handle their life tasks in their later years; likewise, it has marked impact on the extent to which their adult children will feel and accept responsibilities connected with their parents' aging as they themselves approach the later stages of their family life cycle.

The observation also contains considerable apprehension: most of us anticipate our own aging process with a mixture of anxiety and reassurance to others and, therefore, ourselves, that the magic qualities of youth and vigor and self-sufficiency can be retained by "feelings" that ward off the aging process. Are the poets who write of "the beauty of an aged face" motivated only by esthetics? Or do they also acknowledge the trembling of those who sight their first gray hair or the faint hint of the first facial wrinkle?

There is ample evidence of the fact that not many people truly welcome the arrival of their later years. This youthful nation still holds the expectation that people will "carry their own weight" even though our national affluence and advanced medical, scientific, and social technology make more and more liberal obeisance in the direction of "happy retirement." The wisdom that presumably grows with the years—with the exception of an occasional park-bench Baruch—is not accorded the same degree of respect by younger generations in our culture as is true in some others. In his own eyes, the man who is beyond the productive years—chiefly regarded as those in which he works and earns—often feels a sense of loss of self-esteem and adequacy; even though her household operation tasks may remain essentially unchanged, his wife may share the sense of loss as the children more and more turn their attention to the life tasks of their own nuclear families. The diminishing health and sexual energy so often presumed to be natural concomitants of the later years not infrequently enhance the sense of loss.

What, then, is the point of onset of the often anxiety-provoking older years?

Aging is, of course, a natural process continuing throughout life and, in this context, we are growing old before we are born. (Indeed, the Chinese, traditional venerators of old age, for centuries began the count of an individual's years in the year that preceded the actual birth.) Perhaps it is this continuity from conception that was in the mind of Browning when he wrote:

> Grow old along with me
> The best is yet to be.

But the fact that a particular chronological age has been reached in and of itself is not a criterion for the identification of the older years. At the age of forty, aside from their young children's perceptions of them as old, some men may feel old because they can no longer find a place in the labor force; others feel—and are—productive even though the calendar reminds their employers that the conventional retirement age, be it sixty or sixty-five or sixty-eight or older, has inexorably arrived. Some women view the beginning of menopause as the corridor to old age; the productive energy of others resembles that of a Grandma Moses long after they attain the biblical age of three score and ten.

Vigor, health, emotional state, family relationships, community attitudes—these are variables in identifying the older population; neither singly nor in combination do they offer a precise or practical definition of old age. Similarly, there is no clear-cut line of demarcation in the cycle of family life between the middle years and the later years. However, the focus of this chapter, with reference to life tasks that fall in the last stage of the cycle of family life, will be upon those family members who have reached and passed the sixtieth year. This age has been arbitrarily chosen: it heralds the time increasingly defined in public social policy (for purposes of social insurance retirement benefits and pension plans of other kinds) as the retirement age; and, experientially, it reflects the point at which the troubled individual or his family begins to feel stress sufficiently to seek help in various forms from social welfare agencies, voluntary and tax-supported.

The focus also will be largely upon older individuals who are part of the nuclear family (comprising parents and their children) or the family of origin (the family of the adult children who have established their own nuclear family). Some attention will be directed to the life tasks of elderly persons who, either living alone or in a group setting of some type, are isolated without family or other relatives or close friends. The primary consideration, however, will be to that generally more neglected area requiring help to troubled families: their older members in the final stage of the cycle of family life.

FAMILY PATTERNS IN THE LATER YEARS

A substantial number of nuclear families with adolescent or younger children are headed by parents past their middle years, the father often being more than sixty-five years old. Other nuclear families with elderly parents contain unmarried adult children, frequently self-sufficient and self-maintaining, who remain in the parental home largely as a matter of convenience—although many remain because neither they nor the parents have successfully completed the tasks essential for emancipation. Some adult children remain in the parental home because severe retardation or other handicap requires the parents' continued care of the adult child. Either or both the parents in any of these kinds of situations may display the symptoms associated with aging that are considered in this chapter, or their particular problems may be those discussed in the chapters on placement care or on physical or emotional illness. The life tasks in these families are of two orders: the developmental tasks already discussed with regard to child rearing and the tasks specific to the later years of life.

By and large, however, with the exceptions noted, persons who have reached the later years do not continue to have children as part of the nuclear family. This is not to say that children are not in the home. A married child with offspring may live in the parental home, the married child's family of origin. Or the older persons—either one or both parents—may reside in the home of a married child's nuclear family. But the developmental tasks of the grandchildren under these circumstances are the responsibility of the grandchildren's own parents, not the older people who now constitute the "extended" aspect of the family group. These patterns of "doubling" family groups—whether the married child returns to the household of the family of origin or whether the older parents join the household of the younger nuclear family—are less and less common in the United States although still in evidence in certain regional or cultural settings or in instances of economic or other stress felt by either of the family units.

Increasing longevity has contributed to the presence of another kind of family arrangement involving older people. It is now not unusual to find three generations living in the same household with all of the members in their later years. There are some households with as many as five generations living together, with the older three in their sixties or beyond. Among such families the problems specific to mastery of tasks of the elderly may arise among any of the three older units.

For example, widowed Mrs. Briggs, aged sixty-two, is maintained on a widow's allowance from "social security" sources. Her mother and father make their home with her. This couple, the Thomases, are in their eighties. Mr. Thomas has a small income as a veteran and this is supplemented by old age assistance. His father also lives in the home and is reputed to be a hundred and ten years old, but according to Mr. Thomas, no one really knows. The older Mr. Thomas spends his day reading and complaining about the noise that Mrs. Briggs' grandchildren make (two of these under age ten have lived in the home since the death of their father and the long-term hospitalization of their mother). The younger Mr. Thomas is showing marked signs of senility, and his wife has been complaining about the fact that she no longer can "put up with him" and that Mrs.

Briggs will have to "get rid of him somehow." The social worker is in the process of helping Mrs. Briggs and Mrs. Thomas to consider what plans should be developed with regard to the younger Mr. Thomas as well as to deal with Mrs. Briggs' anxiety about what will happen to her grandchildren when she herself "passes on."

Many elderly couples, or individuals who are widowed or alone for other reasons, maintain their own homes: a house, an apartment, or a housekeeping room. This independence in living has increasingly been possible as this society's expanding development of income maintenance (the "Social Security" or Old-age, Survivors, and Disability Insurance and Old Age Assistance) has made such arrangements financially feasible and as advances in science and technology have contributed medical knowledge and labor-saving devices that permit the older person to maintain a reasonable level of health and to conserve his physical energies in the performance of everyday chores and activities. While a large number of these elderly persons are healthy and productive, relatively few continue to work in industry, although some organizations do permit older people to stay on the job under special conditions.

But a substantial number, generally self-sufficient and active though they are, feel useless, unneeded, and disregarded by their children and by society. Certainly the extent and depth of such feelings vary and the prevalence with which they derive from a rational base differs among families as well as among cultural groups. Nevertheless, in many instances the older person no longer appears to himself or to his family to be a dynamic person unless his economic productivity can be evidenced by a salary check or the goods he produces; even service as the family gardener or babysitter usually does not heighten his sense of self-esteem.

Some family members who are in their older years are unable to continue to live in a home of their own because of health or other reasons; for any of a number of reasons they may be unable to reside in the home of children or other relatives. Such elderly persons may require a congregate living arrangement of some kind, possibly a foster family group or a large or small institutional setting. Still other aged individuals, or couples, persist in living in an accustomed abode long after their relatives or the community believe this is advisable.

A wide range of factors contributes to the decision of an elderly couple or individual—or of the family or the concerned community when a family member cannot be brought into the picture—to continue or to change the pattern of living in the later years of the cycle of family life. The unavailability of income of course is an important element in the decision about the kind of housing arrangements the older person can utilize. But the availability of reasonably good housing facilities or special living arrangements in a given community likewise is important for this population group. A community's provisions for recreation and work opportunities for engaging the leisure and energy of the elderly persons is also of considerable moment. There has been a significant expansion of medical services available to the elderly in many communities. Nevertheless, the gamut of their needs, if physical and emotional health is to be maintained, requires not only a more accessible and wider range of medical services but also supportive services like housekeeper and homemaker services that can facilitate the continued healthful stay of the person in his own home. Undoubtedly, however, the factor that is of paramount importance is the availability and accessibility of people who care about the older person as he deals with the tasks that occur in the later years.

Many families tend to isolate the older person who is a member of either the nuclear or extended family until a crisis develops that requires intervention. The family's sense of guilt is then compounded because of previous "neglect." At the same time, many older people in our culture are reluctant to burden the younger generation and, consequently, often do not make known to the younger members their needs and distress. For example, the laws governing public assistance in some states require that adult children contribute financially to the extent of their ability (with ability sometimes defined by the law rather than by assessment of the individual's circumstances) to the care of their elderly parents who are applicants for or recipients of old age assistance. It is not uncommon for the parent to refuse to divulge information about the whereabouts or the financial circumstances of the children even at the risk of being denied assistance. They cannot expose their rational or irrational hurt, they cannot bring themselves to be dependent upon their children or to deprive their children of funds that the elderly parent believes may be needed for other purposes.

It also is not uncommon, when the agency has made a determination of the financial liability of the adult child and arranged for contributions, that the recipient of assistance "protects" the adult child by declaring that contributions are being regularly received even though they are not, and by endeavoring to maintain himself on considerably less income than he actually needs. On the other hand, many adult children who have no legal responsibility in the eyes of the law for contributing to the support of their parents do so nevertheless, often to the disadvantage of their own nuclear families.

THE TASKS

It has already been emphasized that the adequacy with which an elderly person adjusts to life in the last stage of the family life cycle in large measure grows out of the competence he displayed in his social functioning during the preceding stage in his own life cycle as well as in the cycle of family life. A number of new tasks, however, and some variations of old ones confront him in his older years. These tasks have several dimensions: physical, emotional, and social—including economic. The social worker has to understand some of the specific implications, not only for the individual but also for the family, of certain components of the several dimensions that influence the social functioning of the elderly person—and often influence also the social competence of the nuclear or extended family.

The Physiology of Aging

Certain manifestations and consequences of the aging process can be disturbing to the elderly person and unsettling to the family. If he is to be helpful to the person and the family, the social worker should possess some knowledge about the normal aspects of aging in order both to recognize the possible presence of some abnormality that requires expert attention and to assist the family to channel its anxiety in a manner appropriate to the particular situation. This help can be effective when the worker is aware that the aging process may be viewed as secular aging—that is, normal aging, accelerated aging, and pathological aging.

Secular aging is normal aging. The body organs age differently, not all at the same rate or in the same way. Provided they have enough metabolic supplies to stay alive, all organs age normally within their life spans. Otherwise, the entire growing, maturing, and aging process of the organ may be accelerated or become pathological.

The life spans of different organs fall into three general patterns. One is that of the temporary organs. The teeth, for example, secularly age in childhood and are replaced by permanent teeth; the thymus gland ages and dies when the individual is between twelve and sixteen years old. The second is that of the autumnal organs: eyes, ligaments, elastic tissues, prostate, and ovaries begin to change around the fortieth year of life. The third pattern is illustrated by the diminishing functions and beginning involution that appear around the sixtieth year in the permanent organs: the heart, lungs, eyes, etc.

As secular aging proceeds, body fat increases and connective tissues and muscles atrophy. There is decreased use of oxygen; alteration in the amount of blood pumped by the heart; change in excretion of hormones, acuity of vision, strength of muscles, elasticity of tissues, and cells of the total body. This results in shrinkage of body frame and increasing poverty of total body movement. The neurological reflexes are diminished. Tremor may be expected, but unless it is exaggerated, it is not pathological.

With advancing age "chronic brain syndrome" appears with greater frequency. The term now is being used as a global category to replace terms of narrower meaning such as senile, psychosis, and cerebral arteriosclerosis. Because this condition is encountered relatively often by social workers, it is important for them to be aware of some of the facts about this particular illness. It is not easy medically to sort out what is organic and what is functional in this syndrome. The organic aspects reveal difficulties in thinking, faulty orientation to time and place, and memory defects. In mild cases there may be a certain vagueness; however, the individual can name dates and places, and he is able to recognize family members and friends. In moderate cases, the elderly individual can only identify persons; he has marked trouble with dates and places. In severe cases, the aged person is confused, disoriented, and has no dependable memory function.

Although medical diagnosis is essential, the social worker can make some gross differentials between chronic brain syndrome and depression—differentials that offer clues for further investigation. Some confusion may exist with depression, but the confusion lifts readily as the depression lessens. Depression may be combined with organic disturbances, but if the depression is lessened the individual can function adequately even though there is a considerable degree of organic impairment.

Accelerated aging refers to the process of aging of the body or of certain organs earlier than is ordinarily the case. *Pathological aging* is the serious breakdown in specific organs as occurs in the instance of a severe chronic brain syndrome, or the serious breakdown in organs of the total body.

The normal and pathological aging are not sharply demarcated; nor is there a clear demarcation between organic and functional. Furthermore, what is normal in aging must be evaluated in light of the individual's family, his environment, and his culture.

Psychological Aging

In one way or another, normal aging is common to young, middle-aged, and old. Consequently, it is difficult to pinpoint normal psychological aging. The young and those who function effectively in middle age often are unaware of the phenomenon of aging in themselves. Very old people are likely to ascribe differences in their functioning to physical rather than emotional changes, to failing vision, for example. Although specific tests are not readily available, certain clues can be used to ascertain whether the aging has psychological aspects. Thus, how the aged person meets social situations can be assessed in the light of his current life situation, his physical condition, his intelligence, the circumstances of his rearing, his contacts with family and others, and his economic situation. Older people react strongly to their environment, so that the attitudes of others toward them and, in turn, their reactions to others offer clues to the state of psychological aging. The lifetime pattern of meeting crises is a particularly important clue. For example, an older person may view his unemployment as a consequence of a physical inability to engage in any work; actually, his unemployment may be due not to the aging process but to his lifetime pattern of reacting to stress.

Psychological aging often is accelerated when the older person loses a spouse or some other important figures in his life, or feels unwanted by his children, or when he retires and feels—or in reality is—isolated. These lossses of people close to him or of self-esteem associated with rejection by children or termination of a job often lead to depression in an older person.

The losses may lead to what appear to be paranoid feelings, particularly in the deaf aged, who feel very cut off from communication with others. It is important to discover whether these are truly paranoid ideas, or whether they result from physical and emotional losses and, therefore, are used as defenses. Delusions in later years, if circumscribed or paranoid ideas, may not be harmful to the aged person or others. Just the fact of their existence does not indicate that the aged person needs to be hospitalized.

When the social worker and the family understand certain normal aspects of psychological aging, the result can be a reduction in anxiety and less precipitate planning by the worker and the family with regard to handling of the problem the elderly person faces. Thus, understanding would lead them to expect changes in the following areas: decrease in alertness; narrowing of interest span; lack of spontaneous recall or, conversely, an effort to tell *everything* in order to cover up a memory defect; nocturnal restlessness; and alterations in body organs that often are accompanied by withdrawal of interest in the outer world and heightened awareness of internal organs.

There may be a tendency to hoard. The older person is losing a lot in a variety of areas; hence, he wants to keep what he has. He also may have periods of confusion about time or place or people. Because he feels isolated and alone, he may possess ideas of persecution. Or the older person may manifest a magnified sexual interest, often expressed in peeping or touching or pinching. Unless there is severe deterioration evidenced by bizarre sexual behavior such as molesting strangers or exposing the genital organ, this is not necessarily serious.

Bizarre swings in making decisions or conversation often point to impaired judgment. Before an alarm is sounded because of this, consideration should be given to the person's competence in handling everyday living.

A quality of conservatism generally becomes prominent among these older persons. For example, as is shown in the case of Miss Rose that appears below, they resist any kind of change around the house. It is important for the worker and the family to ascertain how intense the individual's feeling is about this.

The total appraisal with regard to psychological aging requires testing of other functions, including hearing, vision, motor ability, manual skill, and intelligence. When such an appraisal is undertaken in connection with the changes and symptoms described above, anxiety of relatives as well as of the worker often is alleviated and permits the undertaking of better planning.

There is an inextricable relationship between psychological and physiological factors. Failing powers may tend to produce "invalid reactions" in some people and initiate an onslaught of physical illness. The same factors may push others toward overcompensation and lead the individual to deny the existence of illness. Sometimes healthy persons react to injuries to their self-esteem by developing severe physical symptoms. An emotional blow may, in some, produce rapid deterioration in the form of severe personality changes. Many times there are discrepancies between the degree of the personality changes and the trauma or shocks that produced them. For example, there seems to be no direct relationship between arteriosclerosis of the brain and the degree of mental capacity or impairment of the individual. Some people function very well in spite of severe brain arteriosclerosis; others with less organic impairment are more confused and disorganized. The basic personality structure determines how the individual musters his reserve and reconstructive ability.

How the person has met his problems in the past will help in evaluating his present functioning. When there is chronic illness, an impairment of health over a protracted period of time, an assessment of the aged person's reaction to his illness is significant. The person who can come to terms with chronic illness by investing in interests outside his own illness is apt to live longer than others who are unable to accept the fact and nature of the chronic illness. Conversely, the use of all of his energies to fight the illness may in fact contribute to shortening his life.

Emotional Factors in Aging

It is an incontrovertible fact that the aged person is being asked by life to make adjustments at a time when he is most vulnerable. He may simultaneously experience the normal physiological and psychological changes associated with aging and suffer acute or chronic physical conditions that impair health. He also may be undergoing psychological changes in reacting to physical changes: loss of fertility and physical attractiveness as well as changes due to normal or accelerated physiological aging.

Current industrial practices may have denied the older person opportunities for useful and gainful employment and may have forced retirement before he was either physically or emotionally ready for it. Tendencies prevail in our culture to equate success and personal worth with economic achievement and with producing rather than receiving; these frequently arouse feelings of uselessness and guilt in the older person, often influencing his position in the family and his integration in the community. Since most people are work-centered, the loss of the job leaves a void and overthrows the structure around which daily life is built. This is a serious problem for younger people; it is sometimes intensified for the older person who realistically knows of the unlikelihood that he will have much of a future in which to seek and hold work again.

The aging person may be sustaining one or a series of losses through the death of the spouse or relatives or others—losses that are a normal hazard in later life but that, nevertheless, remove sustaining relationships at a time when they are most needed and may produce feelings of isolation and arouse fears of one's own destruction. And he may lack close and satisfying relationships with members of a younger generation.

Erikson describes this stage of life as the phase of "integrity."[1] In this stage the older person should become an ideal, the "wise elder statesman," to his family and society. He should set examples and be the one who "gives" to younger people. But relatively few people in our culture achieve this status. Instead, many aged people in our American culture are expected to adjust to tremendous life changes

[1] Erik H. Erikson, "Identity and the Life Cycle," *Psychological Issues* (New York: International Universities Press, 1959) pp. 98-99.

at a time when their capacity to master new adaptations is declining.

This is not to say that older people do not continue to adapt or that they cannot be helped to adapt and be rehabilitated. However, emotional problems have to be understood if the aged person is to be helped to adapt.

Adaptation problems of the aged person can be contrasted with those of the infant. The infant's survival needs require only vegetative functions and only later is self-initiated mastery necessary; although the aged person still has a task of survival, he is losing his self-sufficiency and becoming helpless. Aging can be described as a period of declining mastery, declining self-respect, and declining security. The infant's helplessness is met by people around him who do everything for him, give him love, complete protection, and complete help. On the other hand, the aged person's increasing helplessness is augmented by a decreasing sense of security from the outside. In infancy the adaptive powers are helped by increasing internal powers; in aging, the opposite is true: the internal powers are diminishing.

Decreasing learning power occasions emotional stress for some of the aged, but the wisdom and experience of later maturity more than suffice to enable most individuals to make up for the decreasing ability to learn quickly. In this respect old age can be viewed as a period in which there is an overlapping of the waning power of maturity with a helplessness of "second childhood."

The capacity for adaptation is lessened in the older person because of physical and psychological changes. Character formation occurs mostly in childhood and in adolescence, and may be defined as a summation of the habitual outlook on life, attitude toward oneself, moral and ethical values, and methods of dealing with basic impulses. Although character in part is determined constitutionally, the far greater part is determined by the individual's life experiences and the significant people in his life. The ways in which people learn to handle anxiety are a measure of how successful they will be in relationships with other people. Conservatism in old age is symptomatic of the normal anxiety about the new or untried; changes become too much of a burden when powers are failing. As the older person senses the ever-increasing decline within himself, powers of adaptation acquire definite limits.

In order to gauge the adaptive capacity of older people, it is important to endeavor to determine the proportion of the person's total energy that is invested in a single symptom or in an illness. If the proportion is small and does not interfere with the total conduct of the person's activities, no effort should be made to take the symptom away. For example, if it does not absorb the total character, some paranoid ideation may help the aged person to channel his anger over losses he has sustained. Similarly, rigidities in ways of doing things are to be expected and respected.

One of the first threatening symptoms of aging appears in the form of memory difficulties. Memory generally is intact with respect to past events but recent memory is dulled. This is not due only to organic changes; it is indicative of a turning away from the unpleasantness of a present in which independent powers are decreasing. Even when the memories of the distant past are painfully unpleasant, the aged person derives some satisfaction that he survived these troubles; there is an implication that even those unrewarding experiences were superior to the current difficulties. It is not unusual for the elaboration and exaggeration of past events to provide the elderly person with a point of security.

The domineering, self-assertive personality of many older people is an expression of compensation for loss of self-esteem or current inferiority. The older woman may become even more "boss of her own kitchen" than before. Moderate depression frequently is observed in the older person and the anxiety and loneliness accompanying it resemble the "separation anxiety" found in abandoned children: they present similar symptoms of fear and dejection. When these feelings are extreme, there is increased sensitivity that borders on paranoia.

Often there is much self-exploratory behavior, and unbounded anxiety is expressed as somatic symptoms in susceptible organs. Through the medium of such an illness the older person can derive personal satisfaction from contacts with and attention from the physician, the social worker, or an interested relative. The adaptive process reveals itself psychologically in the older person's reaction to physical illness. A cardiac patient may find it impossible to conform to regulations and limitations because permitting himself to be cared for "like a child" is emotionally threatening. If his own feeling of status and self-confidence is assaulted by this sudden dependency, he may be unable to relinquish this previous point of security. Conversely, there may be unwarranted invalidism in a slight illness, with intense regression to complete dependency. This reaction may occur in those older individuals who in the past have been only outwardly self-responsible. The façade disappears under stress to reveal the underlying tendencies.

Regression in old age may be a common, normal, or pathological phenomenon. Sometimes old people lose or loosen previous standards of morality, ethics, and personal cleanliness. Emotional energy and creativity are introverted into earlier levels and expressions as, for example, in childish interest in the body and sex. There is a desire to recapture or re-establish an earlier situation. In older women this may take the form of bizarre dress, or display and exhibitionism. The threat of impotence in the older man is very great, and may bring about psychotic episodes in which he may act out sexually in order to prove his invulnerability.

Whether their life experiences together have been satisfying or not, elderly couples need to stay together. Often there has been a synchronization of their personality structures so that in effect their personalities have become fused: the death of one may precipitate or accelerate emotional or physical change in the remaining partner.

Family Factors

It is generally a crisis that brings elderly persons or their families to social agencies. The crisis may be primarily a financial one. The older person may lack economic resources and the relatives be unable to help. On the other hand, the problem may be presented as financial need because the elderly person is fearful about "using up" the resources he has or about drawing upon "rainy day" reserves for use on what appears to be only a cloudy day. The crisis may arise from the death of a spouse; or an acute or chronic illness of the spouse or the elderly person that requires a change in his living arrangements.

Often anxiety colors the family's initial presentation of the situation without these relatives being aware of the extent to which their portrayal of the problem is influenced by their fantasies, feelings, and anxieties, and how fraudulent a picture they may offer. The family may underplay or overplay the elderly person's symptoms and difficulties, depending on the kind of help they seek. For example, the social worker may find denial of severe psychosis because the family fears hospitalization; or the social worker may discern that exaggeration of memory losses is related to the family's worry about having the older person continue to reside alone. Either distortion may arise from the family's limited comprehension of the meaning of such behavior, from apprehension and fears about contamination, stigma, or physical harm—with the elderly parent the victim or the perpetrator of the harm.

The cause of anxiety is not always in the older person; it may be in the total family machinery. Its balance is upset and hence its integration is affected. There may be open conflict between the grandparents and the grandchildren because of the older person's wish to retain control over the family. The parents in the nuclear family, for example, find themselves in difficulties with their own children when the grandparents are critical—excessively or mildly, overtly or by silence—about how the grandchildren are disciplined or *not* disciplined, and so on. And the parents in the nuclear family also find themselves in conflict with *their* parents: the elderly father may still believe himself to be the titular and actual head of the household, and his wife, long accustomed to managing her own household and family, cannot bear to relinquish this role. Such elderly parents find it difficult to acknowledge their children as emancipated adults who now must head and manage their own families. For the nuclear family the trouble may be exaggerated if they live in the home of either the maternal or paternal parents.

Frequently, however, the conflict that precipitates the request for agency help is external to the older person himself. The reason for the request for help lies partially in an element of guilt prevalent in many child-parent relationships. The parents in the nuclear family generally are not conscious of this quality of guilt and, consequently, do not distinguish between guilt that is real and guilt that is not. Realistically, no child could ever do as much for them as the parents expect that he should. The process of living stimulates the adult children with reasonably good emotional health to become aware of many things they might do to please their parents or make them more comfortable. To do so is not always possible; nor do the children always want to *act* on this awareness. This commonly gives rise to reality-based guilt which may augment unconscious guilt about not fulfilling the parents' explicit or implicit expectations.

It becomes important, then, to evaluate the place of the adult children in the total family constellation. Were they formerly rejected by the parents and do they now have to prove the rejection was unjust by taking over responsibility for the parents, demonstrating that *really* they have been "good" children? Are the children behaving in an overprotective fashion or are they demanding the worker do something "immediately" because of hidden hostile guilt about wanting the parent out of the way? Do they exaggerate the parent's infirmities and demand immediate institutionalization? Do their overt and covert feelings interfere with or prevent their discussing the need for a change in living plans with the older person?

Many times adult children assure the social worker either that the older person is incapable of planning or that the older person will do whatever the children think is best. The unrealistic guilt felt by some of these adult children stems from early childhood when they had normal unconscious fantasies about their parents; the elderly person's helplessness, illness, and dependence or death revitalizes these fantasies so long dormant. This kind of guilt often is normal.

Some guilt also is stirred up by the role reversal whereby, in a sense, the adult child now becomes a parent to *his* parent and needs to take over some responsibility for him.

The situation is additionally complicated if the middle-aged child of an elderly parent has adolescent youngsters who behave toward him as he and his siblings in their adolescence behaved toward their own parents. Furthermore, the adult child who is in the midst of struggling with his own adolescents often becomes aware that his offspring's behavior is reminiscent of his behavior during his own development; he may be acutely alert to what he must have put his parents through in those past years! This increment to his sense of guilt toward his own older parent often makes him more punitive or more permissive with his adolescent children and thus possibly intensifies the conflict with the members of the impinging generations. In the confusion of feelings that results the adult child may seek to assuage his own feelings by soliciting help for the parent.

The adult children of immigrant parents or of culturally disadvantaged native-born parents may be particularly sensitive to symptoms of disturbance in their aged parents. If the growing-up years of the adult children were arduous and economically marginal, they may overreact because of remnants or of full-blown problems of self-esteem. They are unsure of their place in society, and they respond with special vigor to signs of psychological deterioration in their parents.

In the emergence of pre-senile or senile behavior in the aging parents, their middle-aged children behold the image of their own aging process thirty years hence and tend to overidentify with the parent. As a result, they often find it difficult to talk freely to the social worker about the parent because, in effect, they feel they are almost exposing themselves. Either they tend to avoid this altogether, or they essay some elusive comments. The worker may have to sit through a considerable period in which the adult child engages in defensive maneuvers before revealing the true picture. Many times these evasions are expressed as adoration of the parent. The adult child will offer an idealized version of the parent's present as well as of his past behavior because it is so painful to face the implications of deteriorating change in the parent. Also the lovely vision he proffers places the child in a better light, conveying the idea that the child is a better-integrated person than one might expect from seeing his aged parent.

Parents frequently want to retain some sort of hold on their children even though gaps have developed between the social level of the parents and the social progress of their adult children. The latter may appear as proud and aloof but, nevertheless, the parents still regard them with affection—although some hostility may be felt and expressed about the child's *spouse* being responsible for any rejection that may occur. Nonetheless, the upward social striving of adult children may often be interpreted to mean an unconscious repudiation of the parents who feel they no longer are socially acceptable to their children.

Indubitably the family in a variety of ways holds a great and continued significant place in the life of the aged relative. Some of the poor planning with regard to elderly persons results from the failure of a nuclear family to work through the normal family conflicts exacerbated when the aged person appears to be in the midst of some form of crisis.

The family and the aged person often can be helped to put the total situation in better perspective when the social worker recognizes some of the health aspects of the aging process. Many older people, for example, can adjust to new circumstances and new skills. Even though the capacity for learning new skills diminishes, the older person frequently can perform well on jobs that require patience and emotional investment. When the aged person wishes to continue work, his active interest and zest for life can be fostered through work of almost any kind, be it voluntary or salaried.

Just how the aged parents and their grown children are to relate to each other is, of course, a highly individual matter. Many situations are considerably healthier when there is a substantial physical distance between the nuclear family and the family of origin—not so great that it cannot readily be encompassed by correspondence, telephonic communication, or an occasional visit, but sufficient to permit each family to conduct its life tasks without undue imposition by the other of interference, control, or emotional demands. Others—both parents and their adult children and grandchildren—thrive in arrangements that keep them reasonably close together. From the standpoint of the older person's immediate present and his adult children's own later years, however, there is particular value in a continuity of interaction that enables each to deal adequately with current needs and reduces the prospect of the adult child's later self-castigation for real or fancied neglect of his parents.

THE SOCIAL WORKER AND THE TASKS OF LATER YEARS

Social work with the person facing the tasks of the later years generally aims to meet realistic deprivation, to bolster weakening defenses, and to help maintain and sustain emotional balance within the limits imposed by the effects of time on physical and mental abilities. Work with the families of such an older person has as its objective helping the family members, including the elderly person, to master as effectively as possible the new tasks that characterize the later years of life and of the family life cycle. Work with the older person and with his family requires a multifaceted approach and a wide range of community resources, whether the help is being extended under the auspices of a voluntary agency or a public assistance agency, or some other organization—including church or union groups, for example.

Family Relationships

Particular attention needs to be directed by the worker to the strength and nature of the family relationships. It is natural for older people to turn to their children, whether they want to or not, whether it is wise or unwise. Yet this is the period, generally, when affectional ties of children have shifted in primacy from the parents (the family of origin) to their own nuclear families or other relationships. It cannot be overemphasized that work with a family around the problems of an elderly member of the nuclear or the extended family could result in a new equilibrium in family relationships.[2] Through the work of the social worker or some other helping person, aged persons and their children sometimes gain new awareness of their normal needs for each other, or mend long-standing unhappy relationships.

In addition, however, to the impact of the worker's intervention in parent-adult child relationships, families often require considerable aid in understanding the behavior of the older person and in engaging in planning appropriate to the particular circumstances. Much of this understanding and planning realistically centers around the elderly person's physical or psychological illness.

Illness and Medical Planning

It was observed previously that an indispensable part of the worker's understanding of the problems of the older person —*his* problems as well as those of his *family*—is information about the specific limitations imposed by organic disability. This often

[2] Refer to Chapter 10 for placement of the elderly and to Chapter 11 on physical and mental illness in the later years.

necessitates procuring of precise medical information in terms of diagnoses and prognoses. How the aged person feels and functions may be related directly to his state of health. Personality changes may be the result of organic damage rather than emotional responses to the stresses of age. Frequently the grouchiness of the older person is ascribed to his age when it more properly should be attributed to illness. The organic damage may be a factor of special importance in the interviewing situation as well as in the individual's day-by-day living. For example, an older person may have been able to focus well for half an hour in the interview process, then suddenly becomes restive, fails to listen or respond. He may not be resisting the discussion; his mind may not be moving away from the present reality: he may simply have bladder impairment, with problems in retention and, for any of many reasons, he may be "ashamed" to excuse himself to seek out the nearest facilities for his relief.

Knowledge of the individual's health, or of the absence or presence of disease to account for behavior symptomatology, may be a decisive guide to assessing the modifications that should be made in his living plan and whether or not changes can be expected in his responses.

When the elderly person appears to be using his illness to secure gratification or to exercise control within the family, the worker can be helpful to him and to the family by understanding what the individual is hoping to gain by this behavior. If illness is one of the few useful mechanisms left by which the elderly family member can exercise power and authority or command attention and care to reassure himself that he still has meaning and value to the family, it may be possible to help him to meet these needs in ways that are more acceptable—and less wearing on the family. Interpretation to children or relatives or friends may be instrumental or at least may quiet their anxieties.

In work with people in their later years, medical evaluations and continued medical supervision are essential for both preventative and rehabilitative reasons. The social worker can offer important help to the family and to the older family member if they gain understanding of the need for such medical supervision and how to use the community resources available.

Protective Services

Protective services often are required for persons who are experiencing acute breakdown; for those physically incapable of managing their own planning and financial affairs; for those who are confused and unable to plan for themselves; and for those whose poor judgment results in risk to themselves, to their families, and to the community. The request for protective services may originate with the elderly person himself who, in his occasional more lucid moments, recognizes his vulnerability and danger; it may originate in the community—a landlord, neighbor, or friend, or it may be initiated by the troubled relatives. The protective services may require the combined efforts of medicine, law, and social welfare. Legal protection sometimes is needed for the aged person as well as his estate. If commitment is indicated, medical and psychiatric protection may be required. Sometimes institutionalization can be avoided by offering protection in the home through such resources as homemaker services, home medical care, visiting nurses, "meals on wheels," or someone to do marketing or household chores. But some people in their later years need the protection of a hospital, nursing home, boarding home, home for the aged, or apartment living where medical and socially stimulating activities are provided.

Economic Planning

A high proportion of elderly persons who come to the attention of social agencies require help in utilizing or augmenting income. The financial problems are common concerns regardless of either the amount of income that the older person may have or its source. There may be realistic problems in managing on grants from old age assistance or Old-age, Survivors, and Disability Insurance Benefits, or veterans' pensions, but almost as often there may be realistic reactions to the economic situation of the elderly person. These reactions commonly stem from anxiety about depleting resources that cannot be readily replenished, and from emotional meanings of money as it relates both to economic and affectional security. Although a high proportion of elderly people whose income comes from transfer payments (such as public assistance, pensions, or annuities) are able to manage their financial affairs competently, many need help in planning the use of the resources they have or in procuring, when necessary, supplementation of their limited resources. Many families need help in realistically assessing their financial resources from the standpoint of resolving—or at least alleviating—their guilt and anxiety about how much economic assistance they can or should extend to the elderly family members and the effects on the nuclear family if financial resources in a substantial or steady flow are diverted to the use of the elderly relatives.

Individual Adjustment

The participation of the aged person in planning—unless he is totally incapable because of physical or psychological reasons —often is the first step in beginning the process of restoring self-esteem and lifting depression. Engaging him in activity on his own behalf, no matter how limited or what the form of the activity may be, is generally perceived by the older person as the worker's recognition that the elderly person is "still good for something."

Certain pitfalls need to be avoided. Unless there is evidence to the contrary, the aged person should be accepted as one who is able and wishes to participate in planning, who can consider his problem realistically, and who does not require excessive protection by the family and the social worker. Many aged people have sturdy adaptive capacities that make it possible to explore anxieties, troubled feelings, and unhappy family relationships and plans. Overprotection by the social worker is sensed by the aged person, who becomes frightened or angry because his self-esteem is depreciated. The overprotecting worker also is unable to test the individual's capacity to look at his problem or to cope with it.

Aged people frequently prefer to talk about the past, often to the distress of those around them who have heard the same statements repeatedly or who feel that the aged person's references to the past reflect lack of orientation to the present. But often he speaks of the past because of hurt self-esteem in his present circumstances. He may ramble from past to present and vice versa. Many times this is an expression of his loneliness and a wish for human contact. It is an offering of evidence that he has been an adequate, competent person in the past. This rambling or dwelling on the past provides the social worker with valuable data about previous adaptive capacities. And these data may contain clues to present overt or latent adaptive ability. In these situations, the worker must have both patience and willingness to listen and maintain an attitude that is relaxed and flexible. Any troubled person reacts negatively to his listener's hurry; the older person particularly, because he may be or feel rebuffed in many areas, must be helped to recapture or increase a sense of his worth as a human being. Patience, a sharing attittude, and genuine empathy on the worker's part may inject hope in one who increasingly has been confronted with responses of irritation or overprotection. The worker's interested and unhurried listening (often hard to achieve in agencies where characteristically the caseloads are exceedingly large) can serve to dispel fears of rejection or ridicule and to bring out facts as well as important and honest feelings.

Another pitfall to be avoided is that of being pushed by the anxiety of the aged person or of his family into hasty planning. The family of the older person can be helped to understand why thorough exploration is indicated in areas such as health, money, previous life experience in marriage, parenting, work, family, and other relationships. They can be helped to understand why knowledge is needed about specific day-to-day living in terms of what the aged person can and cannot do and that the degree rather than the kind of behavior distinguishes normal from abnormal. Explanations may have to be repetitive. They should always be explicit. If a crisis requires immediate planning, at least the medical picture and a clear understanding of the specific areas of breakdown should be obtained, so that the most appropriate resources can be utilized.

Many times, because of fright, the aged person mobilizes himself for an initial interview in which he puts his best food forward, presenting himself as more adequate than he really is. The social worker may feel that the family exaggerated the symptoms. It may require several exploratory interviews to determine if the initial mobilization is real, or whether it disintegrates as the aged person really is able to express his problem.

Conversely, the aged person initially may present himself as more helpless and deteriorated than he really is. He may also deny the need for help or express considerable anger because he is not being left alone, or he may show considerable suspiciousness about the family's and the worker's intentions. The worker who recognizes these defensive maneuvers for what they are will not be misled; he will continue patiently his expression of interest.

The Isolated Person

Many older people have neither the family's interest nor interested friends. They have lived isolated lives by choice, or they have become isolated because of losses suffered. Loneliness, even when self-chosen, is disintegrating. Many times such people are hostile or suspicious. Anger is not only hostility; it often also is a device for testing the worker's acceptance of the older person. It is not uncommon that these aged people fail to go voluntarily to a social agency, even though their need for financial assistance is desperate. It is more usual that someone in the community alerts the agency to the serious problem about an aged isolated elderly person. In these circumstances, the worker must be persistent and ingenious in gaining admission to the home; he must be prepared for suspicion, hostility, unwillingness to talk, and similar evidences of loneliness, and he must reconcile feelings he may hold about invasion of privacy, about self-determination, and often even submerge them in the interests of honestly ascertaining if the elderly person is in trouble and needs to grasp even feebly at the outstretched hand.

This was the case with Miss Rose, a retired schoolteacher. She had never married, had always lived with a spinster sister. When the sister died Miss Rose continued in the apartment alone. The landlord became concerned when he was unable to gain entry after a complaint was made by another tenant about a leak from Miss Rose's apartment. It was at the landlord's request that a social worker called on Miss Rose. He knocked and called repeatedly until a window finally was opened. The worker explained who he was, and that he had come because Miss Rose seemed to be in trouble. She slammed the window. He came back repeatedly before she would admit him. Each time he came, she attacked him verbally, denying the need for help.

The worker found the apartment a dirty shambles, with hundreds of boxes piled up and spoiled bits of food lying around. Miss Rose looked starved and appeared to be groping blindly. She was exceedingly suspicious, and seemed afraid that the worker would rob her. Although he was greatly concerned about Miss Rose's physical condition, the worker saw no way of obtaining her consent for a medical examination. Unless it were to become imperative, he deemed it inadvisable to bring either the police or a doctor to her. For several weeks he called on her every other day, bringing food, even though he suspected that Miss Rose had money. She wolfed down the food, repeatedly asked who he was, and what he wanted. She denied that she needed any help, yet continued to ask when he would return again.

The worker finally persuaded Miss Rose to permit a doctor to call, who recommended hospitalization for a complete work-up. Miss Rose agreed to go only on the condition that the worker would accompany her and assure her that the apartment would be kept intact.

During the first week in the hospital, she was disoriented, then she settled down to enjoy the dependency. Cataract surgery was successfully performed in spite of her eighty years. Other conditions were discovered which contra-indicated the advisability of her continuing to live alone. However, there was reason to believe that to remove her to a nursing home might in fact destroy her. Therefore she returned home, the hospital having developed a plan to provide her with home medical service. Although the worker persuaded Miss Rose to use her money for food, nothing was attempted with regard to cleaning the apartment.

The worker visited frequently for short periods, chatting about whatever Miss Rose wished, but also gradually introducing and discussing the idea of a change in living arrangements. After several months she admitted she was increasingly "tired" and agreed to enter a nursing home. The struggle to persuade her to part with her boxes, filled with old clothes and newspapers, was tremendous. The worker went through them with her, persuading Miss Rose to discard many and to place the rest in storage. Meanwhile, as facts about money gradually emerged, it became clear that Miss Rose really could not manage without supplementation. She was helped, therefore, to obtain public assistance that would assist in defraying the cost of the nursing home care.

As it had been when she entered the hospital, so it was now: For a period of time after she entered the nursing home, Miss Rose was disoriented. Then she began to blossom physically and mentally, showing a keen interest in the outside world and in her fellow residents. She clung to the worker, but gradually accepted the visits of a volunteer who came regularly to talk with Miss Rose about a variety of matters of interest to her.

The case of Miss Rose illustrates a number of points in work not only with the isolated aged in need of protective service, but with all aged people. The importance of the immediate surroundings cannot be overstated. The threat of isolation, whether from relatives or familiar surroundings, has almost the same anxiety-provoking impact in old age as it has in early childhood. The threat of hospitalization or nursing home placement is felt by many a person to be a prelude to death. Hence, in Miss Rose's case the disorientation was evident; for other aged people death often does follow soon after a change in environment. A crisis may require immediate new living arrangements, but if this can be avoided by developing the arrangements at a pace the aged person can tolerate, the likelihood of better adjustment to the new setting is greatly enhanced.

Clinging to possessions is clinging to life itself. Possessions make the aged person feel he still has an identity, that he is not just one patient or one inmate or one resident among many. The same feeling about identity arises with regard to personal privacy. As with Miss Rose, aged people should be maintained in their usual way of living, in the community, as long as is possible. Today this may require community supports such as domestic help, home medical service, nursing, or other care. When the need arises to change the living arrangements, plans should be suited to the pace of the aged person and the transition from the old to new arrangements made as painless as possible.

Home Visiting

Home visits often are necessary because of the elderly person's physical or psychological infirmity. When the aged person resists intrusion, the worker must recognize this as a defense and patiently persist. In spite of continued protests and attacks, Miss Rose obviously welcomed the worker's visits. The visits, the seemingly aimless or desultory conversations, usually are far more important than anything that is said. It is common to find that when there is continued visiting, depressions lift, disorientation vanishes or is minimized, memory becomes better, physical health improves: the aged person has been starved for human contact that is with *him*—an individual. This points to the fact that when an agency is instrumental in placing aged persons in commercial boarding or nursing homes, some arrangements should be made for a worker or a volunteer to continue some regular contact.

Marital Adjustment

It is not uncommon for couples in the later years to experience more or less severe marital difficulties. The couple may feel the marriage has become empty when the children leave; the couple may become rivals for the love of the children and grandchildren. Marital difficulties may flare when the husband retires from work. His feelings of uselessness may lead him to interfere in established household routines at a time when his wife becomes fiercely possessive of these routines because of her need to be and feel useful. They may need to be helped to understand what is happening and to find new divisions of responsibility.

A particular trauma occurs when a spouse dies. Defenses are shattered and the bereaved partner often wants to die too, and retreats into morbid solitude. Yet this behavior signifies what the worker can do in such situations. He can help the aged person reinstitute contact with the outer world and replace, for example, delusions about the need for more money and material things with the impact of human contact and sympathy.

The Worker's Task

The worker almost always is younger than the aged person and so is likely to be viewed as, or like, one of his children. The aged person's pride about his illusory authority is sensitive and he must be listened to seriously. Again, unhurried time and patience are indicated. Work with the aged person often substitutes for the lost social contacts until the elderly person can establish new relationships, as Miss Rose did in the nursing home. Reviewing old memories over and over is restorative to the aged person; this serves to bolster his self-esteem, the most important single factor in work with older people. As with Miss Rose, the worker has to show that the aged person can adapt to new circumstances. Money matters have to be discussed with sensitivity for, whether it is realistic or not, he often feels poor; holding on to money is a way of feeling that time is not running out.

For many social workers and others in helping capacities, work with the aged is very gratifying. The older persons' obvious need for human contact, their quick response to interest displayed in them, the striking changes that take place even when the individual is very ill, afford much satisfaction to most workers. At the same time, work with the aged has its problems. Some people are skeptical about regeneration and rehabilitation when there is organic deterioration. Some workers find the anxiety, anger, and dependence of the older person hard to bear. Some workers dislike crisis intervention and the need to make quick, far-reaching decisions. And old conflicts with one's own parents can be dredged up and make it difficult for the worker to contain his anxieties and feelings.

Although all workers have positive, negative, and ambivalent reactions to different people, aged persons tend to stir up more anxiety, for their problems come close to the worker's personal attitudes developed in his own growing-up. As a consequence, some workers will be overprotective, wanting to do too much for the older person, or to rescue him from his "bad" family and "bad" life. Others will negate or deny the seriousness of a situation. Both attitudes and others that are not constructive for the older person may be rooted in the worker's feelings about older people, including his own parents. What is significant is not the fact that these feelings exist but how they are handled by the worker in dealing with the aged person.

Perhaps the most difficult factor for the worker is the unobtrusive fear of death in both worker and aged person. This may be why workers do not like to deal with older people. The worker needs to recognize his own fear of growing old and dying. He may not be able to come to terms with this, as very few people can, but the recognition itself may aid him in his work.

Given the impact of the aged person who needs help, it is important to recall that responsibility for himself and solutions to his problems lie with the aged person first, then his family, then the agency that represents the community's interest and concern, and then the social worker—in that order. If the aged person is competent, it is up to him to make a decision which then can be integrated with both the family's plan and the agency's ability to be of help through the worker. If no family exists and the elderly person is incompetent to make his own decisions, it is the agency that assumes responsibility for working out, through the worker, plans for helping the aged person in meeting the tasks of life in the later years.

Special Problems in the Cycle of Family Life

9

BROKEN FAMILIES

AT ANY POINT within the cycle of family life the nuclear family may be broken: by death, divorce, desertion, or separation of the parents.[1] The cycle itself is not fractured, but two consequences do obtain from the change in the family's structure. One is that the tasks appropriate to the family life cycle's several stages may be altered or their achievement impaired or retarded. The other is that responsibility for major family functions, otherwise shared by the parents, now rests largely with the one parent who remains with the children.

Families may be broken because of another reason, unmarried parenthood, which bypasses the initial stage of the cycle of family

---

[1] See Chapters 10 and 11 for consideration of hospitalization of a parent.

life. But these segments of families too have to adapt to the demands and tasks appropriate to the respective stages of the cycle.

Any of these broken families may become intact nuclear families: the unmarried mother might marry her baby's father; the divorced or widowed parent may remarry; the spouse absent for other reasons may return. Whether the families remain broken or subsequently are reformed into a complete nuclear family group, they are confronted with certain problems, tensions, and needs that are not characteristic of the intact nuclear family.

Many broken or "mended" families demonstrate competence in social functioning despite the complexities related to the rupture. Many of these require the help of a social welfare agency in order to master the crisis and the stresses induced by it. Such help may be of short duration or may continue for many years. Others are able to mobilize their strengths and resources independently, and proceed with the matter of living in a relatively or completely satisfactory way. A number of families are broken *because* of inappropriate or inadequate social functioning. They may voluntarily turn to a social welfare agency for help with the developmental tasks, or they may be turned to the social agency by the authority of a legal or quasi-legal community institution. Depending on a variety of factors, the result of the social worker's help may be that the family members achieve partial or full mastery of the tasks they face or may manage only to arrest further deterioration. And there are others, of course, who may or may not be known to social agencies, whose behavior continues to be socially unacceptable and whose children either as adolescents or adults begin a new generation by bypassing the first stage of the family life cycle: marriage.

What problems with reference to the successful accomplishment of developmental tasks accrue to the broken family? Literature is replete with real and fictitious characters who dramatically illustrate the relationship of personality development and the problems associated with impaired family structure. For example, Elizabeth, declared illegitimate by a royal court, could become a powerful Queen of England but was so affected by the violently emotional turmoil of a motherless (despite many stepmothers) childhood dominated by her compellingly sexual father, Henry VIII, that she developed numerous somatic ailments and could not bring herself to truly trust and love.

And who is not familiar with Little Orphan Annie—not just J. W. Riley's, but the one who for more years than span a generation has been despairingly watched in the daily comic strips by American readers as she makes her perpetual twelve-year-old's way in a cruel world, conquering the evil forces buffeting her, outwitting villains descending on her singly or en masse? Sometimes she has been forced to toil for bread in a heartless orphanage or other institution, but she always succeeds in extricating herself from these only to proceed from one misadventure to another. And she can't even rely on the "protection" of her wealthy guardian, who can sway nations and mighty business interests, but cannot provide one little orphan with continuous protective and loving care. But self-sufficient and courageous as this orphan is, she nevertheless reflects, despite her creator's efforts, retardation of the ability to cope with developmental tasks and some deficient community attitudes toward the parentless child.

The broken family in the American culture long has evoked a variety of feelings in the community: sympathy and protectiveness toward some—the orphan, the widow; retribution, scorn, and uneasiness toward some—the unmarried mother and her child; censure and anger toward some—the deserting parent; ambivalence toward others—the divorced parents (with commiseration toward the child) and the unmarried father. These attitudes are reflected in the kinds of social welfare programs that are available to meet the needs of broken families requiring help; they also, in large measure, are reflected in the responsive behavior and attitudes of the members of these families. Thus, when Glen's teacher asked that his father come to see her, he could reply with head held high that his father was dead. When the teacher asked Jim to have his father come to school, the boy looked at his toes, his shame apparent in his embarrassed silence.

The child who, like Jim, has been deserted feels unloved, unwanted, and that he was a participant in the desertion. The child whose parent has died does not necessarily carry the same sense of responsibility, although he, too, inwardly may feel that he was deserted; often, however, he can be sure he was loved, that he was "worth" the affection that one should be able to assume in a parent. Indeed, of the three primary methods for disruption of a family—divorce, desertion, and death—death generally is easier for the surviving members of the family to encompass.

DEATH IN THE FAMILY

In some ways the child's burden of loss is eased by the community's sympathetic approach to the child who has been deprived of either or both parents by death. It serves the surviving parent similarly, especially the mother. If relatives and friends rally around her in her time of crisis and then continue, along with the community, to be supportive of her in her bereavement and the additional responsibilities attendant on it, there is greater likelihood that she will more quickly become equal to assuming and maintaining her new role—a widowed mother with the task of working through her grief and supervising the reintegration of the family members following a period of mourning.

The very finality of the husband's death often makes it possible for the mother to mobilize herself to embark on a new life with her children. She can be bolstered in this effort "to be brave" by idealization of his memory and her recollection that she had been loved. Even though he may have been alcoholic or abusive, she can set aside such unpleasant memories and selectively remember—and tell her children—the positive qualities that had held them together; after all, in our society one usually "speaks only well of the dead." And the children for the most part can then cling to the thought that, had the father lived, theirs undoubtedly would have been a loving and ideal parent-child relationship.

Even the healthiest of families can experience serious problems if a parent dies. If the death of the father also led to a substantial reduction in the family's income, serious economic hardships may complicate other problems resulting as a consequence of the death. If the primary source of income now is public assistance or social insurance benefits, the low levels of these forms of income maintenance may further compound other already existing problems. The mother may prefer gainful employment as the means of providing economically for the family but be unable to work either because she lacks marketable skills or because of a dearth of facilities for the adequate supervision of her children, or because she does not have enough of both physical and emotional energy to perform all the tasks associated with rearing her children as well as working to support them.

The ages and sex of the children at the point of a parent's death can be critical factors in their development. An infant needs the mother or a mother substitute in the most basic sense but, until he begins to walk and talk and differentiate himself from the mother, he will not miss a father to any great degree. There are certain ages when children are particularly vulnerable because of a parent's death. In particular, if the death was sudden, the young child finds it difficult to understand the continued paternal absence; he expects the father to return to the house and his failure to do so creates usually unasked questions: Did the child cause the departure? Did the father choose to leave an unloved child, to abandon him? When the child is in the Oedipal phase—the four- five- and six-year-old—and resolving sexual identification conflicts, he is especially susceptible to this uneasiness.

Again during adolescence, when the same problem is reworked in the push toward adult maturation, the vulnerability is at a critical level. Both parents are models for identification, and both are needed also as models against whom to rebel. If the father dies, the mother is faced with the dilemma of trying to fill the role of father and mother, yet maintain her identity as a mother. She or society has to make provision for male identification for her sons so that they do not assume a fathering role to the other children or a husband role in relation to her—or run away from *both* roles because they fear the responsibilities attached to them. Either the assumption or the complete rejection of these roles contributes to the problems these sons are apt to experience as adult heads of their own nuclear families. If the mother is gainfully employed, there is strong temptation to make the daughter a substitute mother in the home, to overburden her with responsibilities that might cause overcompliance or destructive rebelliousness; the impact will be carried by the daughter into her own marriage tasks.

The death of the mother often gives rise to the question of whether the children should be placed in foster family or foster institutional care, or whether someone should—or can be—found to care for them in the family home. Either solution contains difficulties. In the past the decision generally leaned in the direction of placing the children and placing them quickly. Now, however, it increasingly is recognized that, unless negative conditions are so extreme that the safety of the children is threatened, they are better off at home. The solution, then, requires the availability of personal and community resources. Stable, continuing homemaker service is important for younger children, as well as for older but upset children, although good domestic service may suffice if the children are older. Such an arrangement may be temporary, following immediately on the mother's absence from the home, while consideration is directed to the best and most feasible long-range plan. But more and more, the arranging for a homemaker as the means for holding the family together is being acknowledged as a family solution that is superior to placement of the children outside the home or expecting the father himself to carry the full responsibility for the children's care and development. Sons need the maternal leavening influence of a woman in the home, and daughters should not be turned into substitute wives and mothers. In instances where homemaker services are used to keep the family together, continuing counseling service of the social worker often is necessary both to help the homemaker understand and meet her responsibilities in the socialization of the children and to encourage the father —who needs to remain emotionally close to the children—in his endeavors to work and to maintain the family home.

The death of a parent creates the same kinds of needs whether the family is rich, middle class, or poor. Money alone does not serve to meet the developmental needs of the children. But there is an added feature in the problems the poor face upon the death of a parent. They generally are completely dependent upon public resources when the death occurs, unless relatives or friends can provide some help; this, however, is rarely possible or likely when the bereaved family's financial need can be expected to continue for an extended period of time.

It is necessary for the social worker to be cognizant of the importance to the family of the mourning period and the different ways in which this may be handled by families who are part of different cultures. The survivor who is a man can return to work and to his normal roles and tasks, channeling his grief into such activities. The widow, on the other hand, generally does not have such an outlet and must utilize grief as nature's way of restoring equilibrium. The reactions will vary in intensity but they tend to follow a similar pattern for various cultural groups in this country: rejection of the fact of death; detached calm; possibly some effort at self-destruction; abandoned weeping, and so on. In fact, the traditional mourning period of a year reflects the length of time that, since antiquity, generally has been required for the restoration of family equilibrium following the death of a parent. Persistence of the widow's or the widower's undue grief beyond this period may offer a clue to personality difficulty and require some special attention from the social worker. It must be assessed not only from the standpoint of the parent's capacity to be restored to a more appropriate level of personal functioning. It also must be viewed in terms of what might be required to protect the children from the onslaught of attitudes that may instill in them a docile and hopeless acceptance of inevitability that stifles motivation and aspiration; it must be watched to note the possible impact of the mother's focusing of her fears, anxieties, and guilt on one particular child.

DIVORCE

The high hopes of the young bride and bridegroom for happiness and permanence in their marital state do not always materialize. Many factors may contribute to the dissolution of the union. Emotional immaturity or developmental problems, lack of flexibility in accepting each other's behavior or aspirations, inability to both give and take, breakdown in communication—all of these may have a vital part in the failure of the marriage. There may be external factors which, when added to the aforementioned, spur the young couple on to separation: overt or subtle parental interference in one way or another; heavy reliance of one of the marital partners on his own parents without regard for the role, needs, or availability of the marital partner; economic stress; differences in values; extramarital sexual acting out. In actuality these are symptoms rather than basic reasons for marital discord; they are instrumental in leading to final dissolution of the marriage only when, from the outset of the marriage or because of later developments, maturity, flexibility, and other ingredients basic to the personalities of the marriage partners are absent or in short supply.

Some marriages, as was discussed in Chapter 6, are dissolved after several decades, often because the departure of the children from the home frees the husband and wife of shared responsibilities that tied them together in the interests of the children, and parents find no mutually acceptable substitution.

The marriages terminating in divorce, whether or not the couple is young or older, and whether or not there are children in the home, generally have come to a fairly orderly ending. There is a loss of emotional investment of the marital partners in each other, although this does not necessarily occur without acrimony and recriminations. The process of acting in accordance with legal requirements to bring the marriage to a close, though not always with either objectivity or adequacy, requires in itself some planning, some thinking through of what is involved, and some consideration of the consequences. Some marriages also are brought to a close with some semblance of order without a divorce, particularly in situations where religious elements preclude a divorce action. Legal separation or separation by agreement without legal sanction may have been orderly and have involved some considerations of the implications and consequences for the couple and for the children.

In the press of the adult problems prior to a divorce or relatively formal decision to separate, the children may actually be forgotten and left to their own devices. This is not to say that they are not fed, clothed, kept clean, urged to go to school. But as feeling, thinking human beings, usually deeply responsive to the distress and antagonism surrounding them, they are ignored. The parent may in fact reject the child who was identified with the rejected or rejecting partner. Thirteen-year-old Mary, for example, considers herself as "belonging" to her father; they have been "great buddies." Her mother, too, feels that Mary "belongs" to her father, but she can keep Mary and control her as she could not the father, and so she is rigid and demanding in her rejection of the child. A child also may be rejected because of the presence of traits that remind the parent of the troublesome spouse. What has been feared or hated in the partner may be identified in the child—a physical characteristic or a mannerism; without the parent's awareness, the child may become the object of rejection—again in the form of unreasonable demands and expectations or by setting the child aside, his physical needs to be met, but nothing else.

In the period both preceding and following a divorce, many children learn to protect themselves to a considerable degree from the onslaught of the emotions of either or both parents. Boys may make demands for toys, money, or other tangible items which the mother urges on a harried and burdened father. The father may praise a girl's ability to cook, to sew, or to perform other tasks, his objective being to irk or depreciate the harassed mother. Usually the child takes one side. Sometimes the child who is cunning or self-protective or bright plays one parent against the other. If there are several children in the family, they may outdo each other in competing for the attention of either or both parents, in seeing what can be obtained from each. Their efforts are designed not only to exercise some control over a crumbling foundation but also to gain reassurance in tangible form that the dissension is between the *parents* and is not lack of love for the *child*.

The circumstances, then, that precede the divorce, as well as its consequences, may constitute personal or familial crises and stress. For the child of any age, the inadequate resolution of the crisis and overemotional reactions in the handling of the stress create special problems. His security is shaken. He does not know if he is loved. He does not know if he *warrants* love. He does not know whether he any longer has a place because of who he is: because he is just *himself*. The feeling of self-esteem and the sense of identity necessarily derive from the family setting, from the relationship of parents to each other, and from their relationship, separately and together, with him.

Divorce that occurs in the early years of the children's lives can be extremely hurtful to the children as well as to either or both parents, and the divorce brings special hazards to family life. In addition to the social and psychological consequences already mentioned, there are complications: With which parent should the children remain? What should be the frequency or nature of continued contact with the other parent? If either or both parents remarry, what is the role of the child with respect to both sets of parents?

Customarily mothers are granted the custody of children, especially if the children are young. Our society expects that the children are better served by being with her unless the mother is extremely promiscuous or otherwise inadequate. It is not uncommon that legal divorce occurs without psychological divorce, that is to say, that the parents remain emotionally entangled with each other. In such cases the children often are used as pawns between parents: as go-betweens, as purveyors of hostile messages in the parents' competition with each other for the child's affection, as carriers of requests for money. The children develop distorted perceptions about the parents and particularly the parent with whom they are not living.

If there is not full compliance with support arrangements, and even if there is, physical suffering may result because the inadequate amount of money that is available is insufficient for the maintenance of two households instead of the one for which the father formerly was responsible. The situation is complicated by the fact that divorce and support laws differ from state to state and there are few uniform criteria for determining the amount of support that should be allotted to children in a previous marriage. There are further complications for two families with reference to the determination of the proportion of a father's income that should be diverted from a current family to provide for children from an earlier marriage. If the father is affluent, this frequently poses no reality problem. However, if the payments are indeed small—and often even when they are not—the mother having custody of the children not infrequently cites the amount of the father's financial contribution as evidence that the father undoubtedly does not love the children or does not love them as much as those in a more recent marriage, that obviously the divorce was his fault, and that the failure to contribute more is clearly proof of his instability or inferiority as a parent and husband. The mother may be an inadequate person, but the fact that the court has placed the children in her custody rather than in the father's, plus his limited financial contributions, together comprise strong evidence that the father is "really the one" who is an inadequate, unloving, nonproviding parent.

The remarriage of the ex-husband may be offered by the mother as further proof of his lack of interest in his "own children." This attack serves to cover her distress over the fact that, bad as it was to lose him, it is unbearable that someone else has won him! Such a situation may contain jealousy, especially if it was not the mother who initiated the divorce action. It may also contain paranoia and a desire for revenge, which constitute a hazard to the second marriage and often are expressed through outrageous demands for money for the sake of the children or through other appeals on their behalf. It may contain a sense of injustice because, after all, *she* did not desert, *she* was not cruel, *she* was thrifty and economical. Yet she was discarded. If she waits sweetly and patiently for her children's father to discover that his second marriage is a mistake, she sometimes provokes guilt even over a successful remarriage.

In such situations, the children are often the scapegoats, with each parent trying to hold on to the children in the way that they may have tried to hold on to each other. The child has no champion; he is buffeted between the parents.

DESERTION

Of a different order than those created by divorce are the stresses that are the concomitants of desertion, with or without warning, by either parent. The father's desertion may be periodic and precipitated on each occasion by the same type of event in the household. It is not uncommon for the husband to desert during the wife's pregnancy, sometimes returning shortly after the birth of the child, sometimes waiting longer to return to the home, if he is going to do so at all. Such husbands are unable or too fearful to accept the responsibility of fatherhood; they require the full attention of the wife in much the same way they had required the full attention of their own mothers. The level of their maturity has remained fixed at that of the young dependent child. These fathers frequently are unable to face the competition of a child in the home and can be helped to return to the home and assume responsibility again for the family only as their own dependency needs can be modified and they are assisted in developing tolerance for the parental role. Desertions in such instances do not necessarily mean that the absent father is not continuing to provide some or all of the financial support of the family. He may be unable or unwilling to do this, but the core of the difficulty rests not with his economic functioning (indeed his financial resources may be considerable) but with the personality disturbance and the shift in marital equilibrium which are created or recreated at the point of his wife's pregnancy.

Personality factors contribute in many instances to the actuality of the desertion. However, certain problems in society also are seriously causal in the creation of broken homes. The Negro husband who is discriminated against by society with reference to jobs and education, who is depreciated by society and therefore depreciated in the home as a male figure, may desert when he cannot obtain a job or earn enough to support his family. He frequently is impelled to desert because he feels worthless in his own view as well as in that of his family and society. The desertion may be temporary or long-term; or he may be in and out of the household. In any event, it carries serious consequences for the family and the growth of the children. Socially and economically it creates insecurity and, at times, real hunger.

Desertion because of economic need of the family is not unique to the Negro father. Men of various ethnic and cultural backgrounds have resorted to this device in order to insure that their family's survival needs can be met, often through public assistance. They utilize the only way they see to assure the family of income for its maintenance. The failure of many states to grant assistance to families in which the ablebodied unemployed husband is in the home, or the severe restrictions placed by some jurisdictions on the amount of assistance that may be available to families in such circumstances, provides little incentive to the father to remain with the family at the risk of their being without sufficient funds for maintenance. In many situations of this kind, the father continues to have contact with the family, to keep in touch, even to see them.

It is not uncommon, however, for the mother to deny his presence or knowledge of his whereabouts because of her fear that revealing this kind of information will lead to a discontinuance of needed assistance. Her denial and his inability to remain a continuous part of the household create particular problems not only for the parents but also for the children, whose sense of trust both in the integrity of the parents and in the society on which they must depend for help fails to develop or is shaken. The obvious patterns of evasion and dissembling are destructive forces in the development of the children's personalities.

There are many other reasons for desertion by the father, and many consequences of such an act for the family. These may be particularly serious if his desertion is accompanied by a complete break in voluntary communication with the family; they probably are equally negative if communication is law-enforced only.

Psychologically, desertion always creates guilt and rage in the family members. The young children, particularly, are fraught with anxiety and other conflicts stemming from the parental desertion; they *especially* feel that somehow they must be responsible for the father's desertion. Children commonly try to rid themselves of their feelings of guilt either by overattachment to the mother or by aggressive behavior toward the mother and toward the father, if and when he reappears. The adolescent can perceive the father as a "free" person who lives a wonderful life because he is irresponsible; or he can perceive the father to be weak and irresponsible. In either event, the model and the adolescent's view of life are skewed. Children may attack the mother for being "weak" if she permits the father to return; or they may accuse her silently or overtly of being responsible for the father's desertion. The mother, in addition to her own complex feelings about her relationship with the father and about his actions, has the burden of providing physically and financially for the family as well as dealing with the children's disrupted lives.

It is less common for the mother to desert. Her desertion is equally serious and in some cases even more disastrous for the family than the father's desertion. Society expects the mother, especially when her children are young, to carry the major responsibility for child rearing, for their physical protection and security, and for meeting their affectional needs. Working men are unable to undertake this total responsibility; nor should they, in our culture, take over the mother's role by remaining at home. One must view with caution the temptation to place children whose mother has deserted, attempting first to find social resources for their care in their own homes and turning to placement out of the home as a last resort. Emotional deprivation for children has lasting significance when the mother deserts. The child always feels abandoned, guilty, and angry. He always wonders in what way he contributed to her leaving.

Whether it is the father or the mother who deserted, the child develops ideas about the absent parent that may have little connection with reality but generally are specific: the deserting parent is either all good or all bad. The remaining parent's attitude tends to reinforce this perception by specific allegations reflecting a personal sense of anger and rejection, or by righteous or martyred silence. Unless the parent in the home can be helped to see the effects on the child's development and can turn from his or her own preoccupation with the hurt of being deserted, the child will form fantasies about the reason for the desertion that may directly influence his mastery of developmental tasks—influences not likely to be altered since the child's severed contact with the absent parent precludes elimination or correction of the fantasies.

UNMARRIED PARENTHOOD

The Unmarried Mother

Many intact nuclear families learn with a greater or lesser degree of horror and distress of a daughter's unwed pregnancy. Families of affluence and influence not infrequently succeed in having the pregnancy terminated early or arrange for the girl's care in a secluded locale, so that the fact of her pregnancy does not become general knowledge among her peers and the family's friends. Often, if her pregnancy has come to full term, the baby is placed for adoption. Occasionally the girl turns the baby over to her own parents and leaves the home. In other instances she establishes her own household to rear her child. The unmarried mother, regardless of her age, presents a problem that is highly complex and comprises elements unique to her, although the pattern may be similar to that of many others. The problem is different if she is from a middle-class family. It is different if she is from a low-income family that adheres to Puritan values. It is different if her social and cultural background is one that condones unmarried parenthood.

The patterns vary among the younger unmarried mothers, generally those who have not deliberately entered into a continuous living arrangement that is expected to lead to marriage—or even to having a child. Such a mother turning to an agency for help in connection with her pregnancy usually expects to be censured when she confronts the worker. Unless her background is one that does condone unmarried parenthood, the unwed mother anticipates that the social worker will share the community's condemnatory attitude and so the girl feels apprehensive and guilty about this even before she arrives at the agency. With few exceptions she is emotionally isolated and terrified, especially if she has lived in a highly protected environment, has little familiarity with the process of birth, and faces it without the emotional or other support of a husband or concerned relatives. She may react in a variety of ways in mobilizing her defenses to protect herself from the anxiety caused by the overwhelming situation: extreme helplessness and a longing for dependence; overcompensation for her feeling of helplessness by an attitude of hostility; suspiciousness; or a pose of adequacy.

The behavior patterns presented by the young unwed mother most often are of three kinds. One is the anxious, frightened unmarried girl who expresses her fear and anxiety by a barrage of questions, who is unable to wait for answers to these before she puts forth other questions. The social worker may readily discover that this is a girl who had to leave home because of her pregnant state and whose fears about leaving home for the first time are heightened by the circumstances that precipitated the separation from home and family. She does not know why she became pregnant because the underlying conflict is often of an Oedipal nature; that is, a seductive father and a mother who did not offer emotional protection.

A second pattern of behavior is the overly conforming, helpless "agreeable" girl whose arrangements for interviews are made as a rule by someone else—often her mother. This girl has difficulty in communicating what she feels; she does only what her mother has told her to do. She wants the social worker to do the same thing, to tell her what to do. With such a completely helpless girl the social worker does have to take the responsibility for giving specific directions in order to avoid an increase in the girl's panic. She has to be helped over a period of time to the point where she can begin to participate in planning and can gain enough courage to make some decisions for herself and act on them. It is not uncommon for these kinds of unmarried pregnancies to occur in a household where the mother is very controlling and has been unable to meet her child's affectional needs; the child has been helpless, completely conforming, and dependent on her mother. It is this compliance which got her into her present difficulty—mistaking a casual relationship for a true love relationship. Or the compliance may mask rebelliousness, a wish to hurt the mother.

The third pattern is defensive bravado. This is expressed by the girl who is boastful, who implies that she knows her way around. Her nonchalance is tossed like a matador's cape: she is superior to the putative father whom she regards as juvenile, her attitude toward him being a maternal one. She may be glib and seemingly emotionless. Actually behind these common defenses is a girl fearful of further hurt and with so little self-esteem that she would pick up any man who would think enough of her to have her. It is in this group that are found girls not only from middle-class families but also many in economically and culturally disadvantaged families. Here often are to be seen the girls who declare that they deliberately become pregnant in order to start their own households on a public assistance grant. The pronouncement of *intent* is in effect to show they *are* better than one might think; they are "planful" and "resourceful" and, therefore, should be accorded *some* respect. Following the completion of arrangements necessary for the girl's care and the beginning of a relationship to build up some trust, work with such girls can proceed by viewing this bravado as a strength to be rechanneled into more socially acceptable ways that will bolster self-esteem and reduce the need to cover up anxious self-depreciation.

While many young unmarried mothers are girls whose vulnerability is increased by the living patterns of their families, it often is less effective in the short or the long run to endeavor to alter the overwhelmingly and deeply pervasive social problems within some severely disorganized or chaotic families in ghetto-like enclaves. The help to the young unmarried mother must be predicated on her realization that, regardless of the family's ethnicity, religion, or cultural and social situation, unmarried parenthood transgresses against social values of family life; that "acceptance" of out of wedlock births as a pattern specific to certain cultural or economic groups is self-defeating. The worker's expectation that the girl has the capacity to alter her mode of behavior will often spur the girl to think and plan—and feel and behave—differently.

It is important that the social worker be alert to the fact that in our modern society sexual experimentation is encouraged among adolescent males and that a variety of conditions in our changing world have contributed to an increasing amount of sexual experimentation on the part of girls. This fact of experimentation *per se* appears to have led to an increasing number of pregnancies among young girls, whether of middle-class or other socioeconomic levels.

Not all unmarried mothers are neurotic or severely emotionally disturbed. Some women deliberately establish living arrangements with a man with whom marriage for some reason cannot be or is not undertaken. Though pregnancy may be unplanned and unexpected, the dynamics in these situations generally are somewhat different than with the young unmarried mother who did not enter into a continuous housekeeping arrangement with the putative father.

The primary approach of the social worker to the unwed pregnant girl in dealing with her guilt and anxiety about her situation is to be matter of fact about the situation and to make it evident that the worker is not condemning, as is the community.[2] This is basic to the trust that has to be established between the unmarried mother and the worker if they are to proceed toward a constructive goal: appropriate care for the pregnant girl, appropriate planning for her future and that of the child—a future that involves the avoidance of a repetition of the illicit sexual behavior. As a rule, verbal reassur-

---

[2] It should be borne in mind that avoidance of condemnation differs from condoning of behavior.

ance to the unwed pregnant girl by itself is not helpful. If the worker really understands the situation in which the girl finds herself and really wants to be helpful to the girl, this will be communicated to the unmarried mother by tone, expression, and manner: the girl will tend to be responsive to the nonverbal communication.

The warm interest of the worker will convey to the girl that the worker accepts her as a person with value and, though the girl may at first view the worker with suspicion, she generally will begin to respond to the worker's reaching-out to her. She will be more able to discuss realistically every step that must be taken such as planning for prenatal care; facing with parents or other persons significant for her the fact of her condition; establishing paternity, with all that is involved in this process—including the consideration of marriage or of relinquishing or keeping the baby.

The Fathers

It has long been accepted that the mother of a neurotic, unmarried pregnant girl psychologically has been a major factor in the girl's behavior; this mother is too rigid, too controlling, too restricting, too promiscuous. But it is essential to be aware of the fact that fathers, too, play an important part in the development of girls and, therefore, the kind of behavior they manifest. The father influences his daughter's feelings and behavior toward men and her conception of what it means to be a woman. If the girl has grown up in a broken family, the lack of an effective father figure may be as much a contributing element to gaps in her development as her relationship with her mother.

Consequently, it is of considerable importance that the social worker's work with members in a broken family involve the absent father as much as possible so that he may remain close enough to his growing daughter that she is aware of his feelings about her as a daughter who is maturing into womanhood. Implicit in the idea of the importance of a father figure is the point, also, that the girl reared in a foster home should develop some special attitudes and feelings about the foster father and the social worker should be alert to the value of including him along with the foster mother in consideration of the problems that a girl may experience as a consequence of being out of her own family home.

The unmarried father has a special place in our society, the place in large measure being determined by his economic or social class as well as the age and economic status of the unmarried mother. If the unmarried mother is in need of financial assistance, whether or not she wishes to do so, she generally is in a position of having to take measures that are legally—and often socially—necessary to secure financial support from the child's father. If her only source of aid will be public assistance, she may have no alternative other than legal action. If she is quite young, in some circumstances, she and the father may come within the jurisdiction of a juvenile or other court, depending on how she and her parents regard the boy and her situation. In either instance, legal action might be instituted by necessity regardless of the economic and other factors specific to the putative father.

The relatives of the young unmarried father who is part of a middle-class family may be reluctant to have him shoulder the responsibilities of parenthood before he has completed his education or vocational plans and is able to maintain himself. In such instances there often is little effort made by social agencies or affected families to have the young couple consider together the meaning of the pregnancy and parenthood for each of them. The task of the social worker, however, is to involve the young father with the young mother in the planning for several reasons. If the young father is truly a troubled adolescent, or if he is immature emotionally and unready to carry the responsibilities of parenthood, joint counseling sessions will clarify this and will help the girl cut through her fantasies about marriage when she hears the father of her baby express feelings of unreadiness for family responsibility—feelings which he is unable to communicate to her alone. Joint counseling sessions also may disclose the fact that a good marriage still can come in spite of this experience, and that the relationship really is not contaminated seriously by the premarital experience.

A substantial number of girls and boys in such situations do marry with a reasonable degree of success in their marital experience, as recent studies have disclosed. In other situations it becomes evident that marriage really is not desirable and that other plans should be made regarding the baby. Of paramount value is the opportunity and experience such sessions with the social worker afford to think through the consequences of the behavior so that the girl can and does avoid repetition.

If the young unmarried father is from a low-economic group where clearly his potential for contribution to the support of the child or to the support of the girl, should they marry, is limited, there is more likely to be legal action taken to force him to support the baby. But these boys and girls too should be provided opportunity to think through what plans might be best for them. Social workers have to be cognizant of the fact that society has provided differential means of handling situations of unmarried parenthood in terms of social and economic class, and efforts need to be made to utilize the same hypothetic approach to those from low-income groups as is used with those of middle- and upper-income groups. The unmarried mother and her child then may become part of a total nuclear family in which both the father and mother proceed to share responsibility for the developmental needs of the child.

The Single Mother

The one-parent family in a household where the father has never been a continuing member of the family, or where a succession of father figures moving in and out of the household remain for longer or shorter periods, is severely criticized by our society. The blame usually is attached to the mother for continuing to bear children. Such a family often is viewed as biologically inferior. In some situations there is in fact low intelligence, but in more cases such a family represents a picture of combined personal and social breakdown. It occurs with some highly-publicized frequency among families of considerable social or economic status or who have achieved success in a vocation noted for glamour and, sometimes, "individual" behavior.

It occurs more frequently in families who have a long history of alienation from the mainstream of society because in some fashion they are "different" from the majority of society—different by reason of race or education or poverty. Also viewed as different are people who come from "inferior" places of origin often stereotyped by certain ethnic or cultural factors. These include Appalachian Caucasians who migrate to urban areas, or American Indians who are relocated from the reservation to the city, or the Negro from the South who moves to a northern or western community, or the Mexican American who leaves the protected *barrio* for life in the wider community.

It becomes difficult to sort out from among these various conditions what constitutes personal breakdown and what constitutes social breakdown. When alienation touches several generations of a family, its members tend to congregate in closed groups and to perpetuate an isolated way of life condemned by the larger community. For many years it has been thought that mothers bearing one out-of-wedlock child after another simply were following a long-established cultural pattern and were content to continue to do so. This probably was more true in isolated rural areas than in urban centers. However, the breakdown of geographic barriers, largely through urbanization and television, has probably been a strong factor in the recent and significant studies that reveal that such mothers who are recipients of public assistance feel great shame and guilt about this behavior but also feel helpless to modify it. Some express this feeling directly, sometimes in nonverbal ways. Others speak of their hope that one of the men moving in and out of their lives will settle *in*, perhaps marrying and becoming a "father" to the children. Many, however, because of their impaired early development, are unable to form a relationship with a man on a continuing basis; some are impulsive and unplanful, unable to think beyond the immediate present wish for gratification, or some escape from a desultory existence that is lonely, economically difficult, and contains few satisfactions outside sexual or maternal activities.

But many of the mothers with several children by two or more fathers express a wish that their children do better and have better things in life; however, they do not know how to go about arranging for this. They fear the larger community and because of fear and low esteem they may be harshly critical of the children for not meeting requirements in school that they themselves could not meet. They may defiantly tolerate or permit the children's bad behavior, or when the children grow older and get into trouble shield them against the community or reject them.

Some of these mothers need and can productively use both individual counseling and group education in child-rearing practices. Their children also can be reached and should be when they are old enough to go to a nursery school—or even a day nursery. The impact on child and parent of such counseling and such community facilities is illustrated by the mother who described how she became aware for the first time of how little communication existed between her and her child. He had been enrolled in an Operation Head Start center. On his return one day from the center he said: "Look at me and talk to me like they do in school." She realized that she never had looked at him before. Such mothers and children need access not only to the help of a social worker but also to better schools and special schools which can be instrumental in effectively breaking into this kind of family life pattern.

Also required are opportunities for those families where income is low and pressures are high to provide through existing public assistance and related agencies an adequate level of income for maintenance of good standards of nutrition that will make it possible to provide children with the physical requirements that will facilitate their learning. Some fatherless families—or families with a succession of fathers—cannot be reached by individual social work methods or by the provision of resources. Apathy and anger are too entrenched and too extensive. New ways need to be found through social organization approaches that do not function as a single or separate operation but are part of coordinated effort. Individual families of this kind often have to be reached first through groups with common interests and problems, through better housing, through the provision of better facilities of various kinds; but they must be reached before their hopelessness and despair become so pervasive that no chink in their defensive armor is penetrable. It is entirely possible that what has appeared to be individual pathology in reality may respond to efforts to change social environment through changes in social organization.

The social worker must be alert to the fact that family groups that contain no husband because the mother is not or never has been married are not unique to any segment or region or ethnic sector of our society. While there are some historical reasons attributed to the fact that among low-income Negro families there is a higher proportion of unmarried mothers, this phenomenon exists among low-income families of other orientations also—white families in the Kentucky area, Puerto Ricans in New York, Mexican families in the Southwest, Caucasian families in Chicago, New York, Los Angeles, and other major metropolitan areas. The fact is that their failure to marry does not generally derive from cultural factors, although attributed to them, but rather from combinations of social and economic circumstances. Experience has demonstrated that when a social worker has time and inclination, help to these mothers is effective at least to the extent that their children begin to see another way of life for themselves.

It is not unusual among families where the mother is not currently married that a man—often the father of one or more of the children, and as often not—may be a long-time member of the household and assume the role of spouse and parent. He may provide the children with affection, discipline, some financial support if his means make this possible. For many children, particularly in Negro families at the lowest income levels and where the matriarchal figure has been the dominant and controlling one, this male figure provides the only opportunity for the children to develop identities appropriate to their sex. He offers at least some model of differentiation between the masculine and feminine roles, including that of the man's role as worker and provider. This contribution, unaware though the man may be that he is making it, sometimes offers the only pattern to the growing Negro boy regarding the place of the male in the family. And, often, this man's presence offers the child, especially the adolescent, a "parental" relationship through which the youngster can constructively work out independence, identity, and other developmental tasks that are resolved through conflict.

On the other hand, he may, because of the quality of his behavior and relationships, constitute more of a negative force than anything else. The worker then needs to give careful consideration to the meaning of his presence to the mother as an individual, and to the impact of his presence, and relationship with the mother, on the development of the children. Again, if the mother's own development was so seriously impaired that she can think—if she thinks at all —about her own needs only, and cannot really fulfill a parenting role even at the minimal level, such work as is done with this family probably will have to be on a protective basis, the focus being on the welfare of the children and the prospect of giving them the opportunity to develop some of the strengths required for more acceptable social functioning than that of the mother and the "invisible" father.

10

PLACEMENT

EVEN THE MOST loving families may be faced from time to time with the necessity for placing one or more members of the family in a hospital, in a foster home, or in an institutional setting. The family who requires help with placement may represent a cross section of all those previously described: the adequate family, the chaotic family, the neurotic family, or the psychotic one.

The placement need may grow out of psychological or social factors, separately or in combination. The need may be created by events external to the person requiring the placement. For example, the death or hospitalization of a parent may result in children having to go into the care of a foster family or of an institution because no home care or extended family care arrangements seem possible or advisable. Physical or emotional changes in an adult member may necessitate placement. Thus, a father may experience a psychotic episode during which he can best be cared for in a hospital setting, or the grandmother who has been an integral part of the household may have suffered a stroke that requires constant care of a kind the family is unable to provide through its own devices. The placement of an elderly family member may be socially advisable because of the negative impact of this person's senile behavior upon children in the household. And placement needs may result from such problem factors in the family as the severe neglect or the physical abuse of children.

CHILDREN

The most common reasons for the placement of a child out of its own home are marital difficulties of an order so severe that they seriously affect the child; a family broken by death or desertion, and some additional problem which interferes with the ability or opportunity of the remaining parent to keep the family members as an intact unit; the neglect or abuse of the child, resulting in a court order for the placement; the mental or physical illness of either a parent or the child which creates special stress in the household; and a temporary emergency which precludes the child being adequately cared for in the family home while parents are dealing with the other crises that have arisen. Regardless of the reason for the placement, it brings about the most radical change in the total structure of the child's experience, and the long-range effect on him may be negative or positive. The quality of the consequences depends to a considerable degree on what has gone into the decision that a placement should be made; how the decision has been carried out in relation to the child, to the family, and to the placement resources; and the nature of the communication that is maintained between the various parties to the placement: the child, the family, the placement facility, and the social worker arranging the placement.

Foster Family Home Placement

It presently is increasingly recognized that when long-term placement of a child is indicated it is essential that, to the extent possible, he should become an integrated member of the new family. In effect this means that he must develop allegiance to two families, his natural family and the foster family. This task is a difficult one, posing many problems. Yet, unless it is achieved, the child may remain placed physically but not emotionally—that is to say, he continues to remain a part of his natural family and an alien in the foster family.

Failure to achieve emotional placement can contribute markedly to the retardation of personality development. When five-year-old Betty was moved into the Reynolds' home because her own mother was hospitalized and in shock as a consequence of the father's accidental death, the Reynolds family treated her as a guest rather than as one of their own children. She remained emotionally distant from them. As it became clear that she would continue to be with this family for a considerable period of time, Mrs. Reynolds began to try to help Betty to feel a part of the family, to assume some of the same little responsibilities that the other children in the family carried, to reach out to her in a mothering way. But Betty was now increasingly aloof and withdrawn into herself by the blow from being abandoned by her own parents. She could not trust herself to trust Mrs. Reynolds; she might also abandon Betty suddenly.

It would have been better for Betty to struggle with attachments that might be broken on her return to her family home than not to form the attachments. The most important task with respect to the placed child is to help him to develop the capacity to form relationships, to trust, and then to grieve if these relationships are interrupted. If the natural parents are available, the child also must have sufficient connection with them so that, as soon as is realistically possible, he can understand and assess the reality of his situation. Otherwise, he is likely to develop fantasies about his parents that lead to idealization, or to mounting hate and anger, or to a kind of ambivalence so consuming that it seriously interferes with learning and with the development of new relationships.

The possibility that ability to develop new relationships is impaired generally is evident early in the placement situation, for the movement into a new physical setting means that the child perforce is exposed to a range of unfamiliar people and situations. He begins, for example, to participate in living with a new group, the family with whom he is placed. He is in a new setting, and this generally means he will attend a different school, that different people will be around him, that his environment will contain new peers. The child must make adaptations of many kinds, and these are social, emotional, and physical in nature. The elements that interfere with his effective adaptation to the placement situation will recur in later life to interfere with the establishment of relationships in other situations.

The importance of the development of trust and communication points to the necessity for observing certain concepts about working with children in placement, with their parents, and with the foster parents. It still is common to work with foster parents about the practical matters that concern the child, or when a crisis arises, to work with them alone or with the child alone. However, a deliberate effort should be made to work with foster parents and child together on everyday living matters on a regular basis with the intent of promoting proper communication and an adequate level of trust. If the child has emotional problems, as often is the case when a placement has been made, it may be advisable to work on these problems with foster parents and child together rather than separately. The child may be in regular treatment with the worker, or in treatment arranged by the worker with another resource—a clinic, for example, or a psychiatrist in private practice. Nevertheless, while the child is in concurrent individual treatment, the worker often has the task of working with the foster parents and the child together. In actuality, unless individual treatment is absolutely indicated because of psychosis, for example, it is almost always better for the child to work out his problems in the family than in an individual treatment situation. If ongoing work with the foster parents and the child together can proceed regularly, there is less likelihood that the kind of crisis situation will develop that impels the foster parents to request the removal of the child from the foster home.

When work is undertaken with foster parents and the child together right from the beginning of the placement, the foster parents are immediately in a better position to know how to deal with the child than when the child simply is described to the foster parents by the worker. Thus, had the worker talked with Mr. and Mrs. Reynolds and Betty as soon as the child entered the home, the foster parents as well as the child would have been clear about why the child was there and would have settled into being a family, since this is what they would have known was expected of them. Betty, particularly, though she certainly had never liked the idea, would more quickly have accepted the reality of her stay in this home and responded in a different way to the foster family's overtures. The simple clarification of why she was there, how she would manage, and how the Reynolds would manage, would have been a basis for establishing the kind of confidence the child needed to have in their continuing interest in her. Furthermore, it would have been a basis for the trust so essential to her growth and development.

The importance of beginning the placement with such three-way communication that includes the worker, the child, and the foster parents is evident in a somewhat different kind of situation. Ronnie, at ten years of age, had already been in five foster homes. An abandoned child, he was not considered to be realistically adoptable because of severe orthopedic problems from infancy and because of an insufficiency of Negro adoptive homes. It was fortunate that his first eighteen months of life had been spent with loving foster parents, but, although his initial placement had been a good one, the foster mother had died. Ronnie's emotional problems were severe. Under stress he would run away, and four sets of foster parents had given him up because of his behavior.

Before Ronnie was placed in the sixth home, the worker brought Ronnie and the prospective foster parents together to consider whether they might suit each other. The interview was a painful one. Ronnie communicated with the potential foster parents but not verbally. He cried, screamed, hid in a closet, kicked furniture, and tried to run out of the room. His behavior in this meeting left no doubt as to the severity of his problems. The foster parents were bewildered by the behavior and ambivalent about taking him into their home. The worker repetitiously interpreted the meaning of Ronnie's behavior and what it would take to live with him. Love would not be enough; hard work would have to be invested in helping him. The foster parents began to identify with Ronnie's hurt, with his feelings of abandonment, and they also began to recognize what it would mean to live with him. The knowledge they had acquired by their observation and by the worker's interpretation of what they had seen enabled them to decide to take the boy, knowing that they would need to work closely with the worker. Ronnie had been in individual treatment up to this point, but now it was decided to discontinue this for the time being in order to promote his integration into the family by permitting him to focus his emotional energies on this task. Ronnie had demonstrated his worst, and he wanted to be with the foster parents. The agreement was reached that they would all work together regularly.

When a child's natural parents are accessible, channels of regular communication need to be opened and kept open between the child and both sets of parents—the foster parents and the natural parents. This is not dissimilar to the situation of the child of divorced parents who have remarried, so that the child in effect has two sets of parents. Again, difficult as this may be, it is better for the child to struggle with the reality of his situation than to develop fantasies that interfere with his development and contribute to the creation of more serious problems. It is the social worker's task to keep the communication channels open between the child and the respective sets of parents.

Placement in an Institution

The placement of a child in an institutional setting also requires that channels of communication be kept open between the child, his own parents, and the worker who continues to have the responsibility for the ultimate return of the child to his natural family. Generally, the institutional placement injects other elements into the relationship situation. Instead of a single family of which the child becomes a part, there are apt to be house parents, custodial personnel, administrative personnel, specialists in group work, in psychology, in social casework. The demands on the child in an institution simultaneously are both more and less than on the child in a foster family home. There are more people with whom he necessarily has contact, and yet, in a sense, he can be and feel more isolated because there are so many. The child who has difficulty in forming close relationships and who cannot really tolerate living in an intimate family group may be able to adapt himself to an institutional setting more readily; hopefully, if he has a family home to which he ultimately can return, the transition to his own home can be preceded by his intermediate placement in a foster family home.

Some children who need to be placed out of their own homes can *only* be put into an institutional setting—not because this is what the *child* needs, but because the parents cannot tolerate the idea of the personalized and intimate relationship that the child might form with the foster family. Such parents, faced with the necessary task of placement, may be more tolerant of the institutional setting. Sometimes this is rationalized by them as "a school," but usually they are unable to explain why an institutional placement is more acceptable to them than a foster family home.

The child in an institution should be in a therapeutic milieu in which the institutional personnel, regardless of their specific job classifications and assignments, contribute to keeping the communication channels open with the child. The institution's social worker often is the bridge from the child to the institutional personnel, interpreting the needs of the resident children and working with groups of personnel to further their understanding of the effect of their roles upon the individual child. The social worker also is the bridge to the personnel from the residents, working with them singly and in groups with regard to their individual problems, and interpreting to them the institution's policies and procedures. The social worker's responsibility, in addition, extends to the institution's administrative staff to interpret changing *needs* as well as indications for policy or procedural changes. Either through the administrator or directly, the social worker reaches the board of directors of the institution and the wider community in which it is located.

The need for and the actuality of placement of the child, whether in foster family care or in an institutional setting, evoke special feelings in parents, not the least of which are guilt and anxiety. There are of course some parents who feel relief when a "troublesome" child has been placed. Such parents generally are more concerned with their own feelings than with the child's feelings and the child's development. Not uncommonly, it is this lack of concern or even overt hostility on the part of the parents that precipitates the behavior in the child that eventuates in placement. But most parents wish to retain contact with the child and look toward the time when the child will be returned to his own family.

Parents handle differently their continuing relationships with the placed child. Some interfere constantly with the foster parents out of a variety of motives; others avoid contact with the foster parents and, sometimes, with the child. In either kind of situation, the social worker has an important function in striking a balance in the kind of relationship the natural parent needs to maintain not only with the child but also with the foster parents. This task may be the more difficult when the placed child's parent is an unmarried mother who either overcompensates for her guilt by being too giving or too restrictive, or handles her feelings about the total situation by having as little as possible to do with the child.

Many placements are required because a crisis confronts the family and the child needs to have care while the parents deal with the situation which appears overwhelming. The severe illness—physical or mental—of a parent or a sibling may require that one child be in placement in order that the time and energy of the parent or parents can be directed toward the resolution of the family problem or bringing it sufficiently under control so that the placed child can return to his own family. For the child who needs to be placed, traumatic as is the situation which takes him from his own home, the negative impact of the placement can be reduced by immediately interpreting to him clearly and honestly the reason for the placement and the expectation of his return to his family. If the placement of the child is because he is retarded or in some other way handicapped, the fact of placement may stimulate deep anxiety and guilt on the part of the parents.

Other Facilities for Care

A variety of facilities have been developed in recent years which serve to meet the placement needs of children with different kinds of problems. There are, for example, halfway houses for the care of the older child who needs to have intermediate steps in his return from a correctional institution to the family home. There are group homes which also are designed for older children, particularly adolescents, and may be larger than a family foster home but smaller than an institution. These group homes may be residence clubs in which the young person may live while going to school or beginning his first job; they may be enlarged foster homes operated under the supervision of an agency. In addition to these various kinds of living-in arrangements which supplement the foster family and institutional facilities, day treatment centers also are used for the care of children who cannot be provided for in their own homes during the day but who can be in the family home during the night. The day treatment centers may serve particularly as a resource for the severely disturbed or retarded child who requires a therapeutic setting for a good part of the twenty-four-hour day.

THE ADULT

A variety of circumstances will contribute to the necessity for the placement of an adult family member in institutional or foster family care. Such placement may be precipitated by factors of physical disability, mental retardation, or mental illness—including conditions of alcoholism or narcotic addiction. Many of the considerations relevant to the placement of a younger adult family member are pertinent also to the placement of the elderly relative.

The placement of an adult family member in a correctional institution and, often, in an institution for the mentally ill, generally is beyond the control of the nuclear family. The decision is made by a court and the task of the family is to accept the reality of the decision, making the adjustment appropriate to it. But other kinds of placements may need to be initiated by the family either because the care required is more intense or complex than the family itself can offer, or because the family member requiring placement creates problems for the balance of the family who must decide whether to retain the person in the home or to place him out of the home.

Whatever the reason for the family's decision that the placement is to be effected, it is usually attended by considerable anxiety. At the same time, the person being placed may feel some resentment about the need to leave the family home. The interest of the social worker can be of particular importance to the family in weighing the merits and demerits of the decision for placement, in helping to explore the kinds of placement facilities that are appropriate and available, and in accepting the validity of the decision that has been reached.

Several kinds of facilities may be available. They may be institutions that are operated by federal or state or local organizations for meeting special needs—problems of addiction or tuberculosis, for example. Or they may be government organizations serving a specific segment of the population, such as the Veterans' Administration. They may be small facilities offering group care under the supervision of voluntary family agencies, or they may be proprietary facilities. In most states such facilities are licensed by the state or by an appropriate agency of government in order to assure that adequate physical and medical standards are maintained.

A recent trend has been the use of foster family care for adults. Such foster homes increasingly are being used for the care and supervision of adults who no longer need custodial supervision *per se* but who are not able or ready to be a part of the nuclear family home. Such foster family homes—or family-care homes, as they are known in some places—are used in much the same way as foster family home placement facilities for children. It is the social worker who works with the operator of the home for the purpose of enhancing the latter's understanding of the current and potential behavior of the placed adult; and it is the social worker who endeavors to work with the placed adult in adapting to living in the intimate situation that such a family facility offers.

The kind of help that the worker can provide the operator and, therefore, the placed adult is apparent in the situation of John Townsend. For four years he had been in a state hospital for the mentally ill and, although it was no longer necessary that he remain in such an institution, it appeared undesirable that he return to his family until he had been able to master certain aspects of his own behavior. Mr. Townsend was a recipient of Aid to the Totally Disabled, a grant from which he was expected to meet his own needs and to pay for his board and care. The operator of the home complained to the worker that although Mr. Townsend received his monthly check with prompt regularity, she experienced some difficulty in convincing him to pay for his board and care. She repeatedly had to ask him for payment. He would listen, reply he would "get around to it," and then ignore the request. The payment that was due on the first of the month she generally managed to receive by the middle of the month. She knew that he was not spending the money for other purposes since he was seclusive, did not leave the house, and had no opportunity to spend.

As the operator became aware through the interpretations of the social worker that never before in his life had Mr. Townsend had an opportunity to control his own affairs (he had had both controlling parents and a domineering wife) and that being asked for the money and having the control over the decision to pay or not gave him certain satisfactions, she was able to ask him for the money knowing that it was pleasing to him, and to make the request without impatience. Her tolerance of the situation, and her recognition of Mr. Townsend's right and capacity to make decisions, to give as well as take, were of inestimable value in his improvement. After a few months there was decreasing need for her to repeat her requests, and ultimately, without any reminder on her part, Mr. Townsend began to pay for his room and board on the day he received his check. His success in managing the board payment enabled Mr. Townsend, with the worker's guidance, to begin to view differently other aspects of his living, to move gradually toward taking a part-time job as a preliminary step to returning to full-time work and then to his family.

In recent years also there has been a trend toward family or home-care placements of adults with health problems requiring special care not available or advisable in their own homes. This is not actually a completely new idea, for the disabled or the mentally retarded or the disturbed persons whose families could not care for them came under public vendue in the early Colonial days when the problems of constructing institutional facilities led to innovative ways of handling situations in urgent need of care. Under that system such persons were "auctioned off" to those willing to provide them with care at the lowest cost to the townspeople. In exchange for keeping him, the "buyer" could exact whatever work the individual was capable of performing. But today, with facilities generally licensed by public organizations, the objective is different. Such placements aim to keep the individual as close as possible to the mainstream of family life while he receives the medical or other care that his family home cannot provide. Placements of this type may be for short- or long-term care.

As in the placement of children, the decision to place an adult member of the family may be reached only after considerable debate, and at great emotional cost to the family as well as to the person to be placed. In many ways, however, the placement of the adult is easier since need for care may be more obvious to everyone, especially if the reason is physical illness. Parents may have cared for a mentally retarded son or daughter from childhood into adulthood, but as the parents' physical resources begin to diminish they start to wonder how the defective child will be cared for when they die.

Their anxiety deepens steadily as it becomes apparent that planning for this adult child cannot be too long delayed. The imminence of placement in such situations may awaken long-dormant feelings of guilt and apprehension about the defective adult child and require that the social worker help the parents move without delay to implement the placement plan.

If the reason for the adult's placement is illness, the family of the patient may be clear about the need for the placement. The social worker, however, needs to be aware that the actual placement may lead the patient to feel rejected, a burden, even though he had participated in the planning.

Many of these placements are easier than the placement of the elderly person because so often there is little prospect that the latter will ever be able to return to the home. However, if the illness promises to be lengthy and involves steady debilitation, or if it is progressive, the patient may become so despondent and hopeless that he is unable adequately to involve himself in the use of medical care. In such an instance, the social worker's task is to help the patient and the family to understand what the placement involves for the other, and to encourage them to talk openly with each other about it. The social worker's task also is to interpret to the hospital personnel or the personnel in whatever facility the patient is placed his needs and those of his family as they affect the use of medical care. At the same time it is necessary to interpret to patient and family the meaning of the rules and regulations which may affect them.

Whether the placement is of a child or an adult, the worker must be cognizant that if it is intended to be *temporary* the years should not be permitted to drift by.

THE ELDERLY

The circumstances that give rise to a decision that an elderly person be placed outside his own home or that of a relative with whom he may have been residing are of many kinds. As was discussed in an earlier chapter with regard to the elderly person's management of his life tasks in the later years of the cycle of family life, these circumstances may be physical illness, emotional disturbance, limited family financial or other capacity or willingness to offer needed care, and others. The decision may be governed also by the kinds of facilities that are available to meet the individual's need, the costs of such care, and the nature and extent of resources that can be drawn upon to meet these costs.

The reality is, of course, that despite the increased accessibility of funds from public sources for payment of care for elderly persons who require hospitalization or other placement, the range in kind and number of available facilities continues to be limited. This factor of limited choice contributes to the problems inherent in any placement that has to be effected. If the elderly individual—or couple, since a placement plan is sometimes necessary for both an aged husband and wife—has ample financial resources, the choice of facilities is wider: medically-staffed apartments, nursing homes, boarding homes, "leisure worlds," a variety of small or larger institutions that provide an array of services.

If, however, financial supplementation has to be provided by adult children, problems may arise among them as to the apportionment of the financial load, and problems may also develop within an adult child's nuclear family. A relative may in fact make financial sacrifices to maintain the older person in "good" care; funds required for the nuclear family's daily or special needs (such as education or vacations) may be diverted to the older relative's maintenance in a placement facility. Such use of the nuclear family's financial resources may provoke a resurgence of old rivalries and conflicts that had characterized courting and early marital equilibrium when either spouse, realistically or otherwise, had resented the interfering or controlling behavior of the spouse's parents.

Conflicts within a nuclear family with respect to placement of an elderly family member are not always expressed in terms of money. The adult child—especially a daughter—may spend an inordinate amount of time in caring for the parent in an effort to forestall placement, or immediately following the placement—to the annoyance or the distress of her spouse or children. Such behavior, which is in excess of the reality needs of the elderly person, often stems from unresolved or partially resolved feelings of hostility, guilt, and the like.

The reaching of a decision to effect a placement is frequently a painful one. Even in the most "normal" of families, much guilt is aroused in the decision-making process. During this process communication between the aged person and the younger relatives frequently breaks down. The latter may wish to make the placement quickly and without the knowledge of the elderly person. They may assure the social worker that this is what the aged person wants and needs without any adequate discussion with the aged member of the family. The older person may fight placement despite his obvious need for it; or he may be apathetic and give in out of fear of the younger person. Significant is the lack of adequate communication between generations; the social worker often must undertake to open communication with the aged and the younger persons together for the purpose of bringing feelings into the open, reducing conflict and ambivalence, and effecting the placement under the best possible conditions. For the worker this may be a difficult and complex task, particularly when the family contains a number of younger relatives, each with his own feelings and ideas about what is best for the elderly person.

Whether or not the relative to be placed has been residing in the family home as part of the nuclear family, or has lived elsewhere and the nuclear family assumes, no matter how grudgingly, some responsibility for planning with or about him for his care, the social worker will find the use of a family conference an effective device for gaining understanding of the relationships and feelings, for reaching an acceptable level of cooperation among the family members involved, and for the implementation of any plan that is developed. If the result of a family conference is a decision to place the elderly person in an institution, the adjustment by the older person in the institution is likely to be less traumatic. There is another positive consequence of such family conferences; namely, that there is less likelihood that the younger people will fail to visit and maintain communication.

Many elderly people, feeling the loss of meaningful occupations in work or management of the home at the same time that they begin to experience physical changes, benefit from a congregate living arrangement offering group activities that serve to open and maintain communication with others. It is not unusual that in groups with programs designed to meet the needs of elderly persons, the aged individual begins to feel better and, despite serious physical difficulties, manages himself better. Depression commonly is present among older people; engaging such a person in meaningful communication is an effective way of lifting the depression. The elderly person may to some extent enjoy his feelings of depression, using it as a lever for attention from visiting relatives who otherwise ignore him. But the persistence of the depression contributes to both physical and mental deterioration, and it is essential that it be relieved as early and for as long periods as possible. The isolated aged person, unless isolation has been his lifelong pattern, needs to be drawn into communication with others, even if it is only to give each an opportunity to complain to the other about the ingratitude and neglect of children to whom they had given everything.

With the aged person who is alienated from his family, the social worker's task often is to effect communication. The elderly person who is isolated, as was Miss Rose, frequently is suspicious, and this impedes the worker's efforts to establish meaningful communication. It is not uncommon for the worker who persists in this effort to reach the elderly person to discover a real hunger for interaction side by side with the undue suspicion and resistance to the overtures.

The social worker who is working with an elderly person toward or during placement must constantly be cognizant of this hunger for interaction and of the emotional impact upon him of his relatively dependent position, the meaning of his withdrawal from the community, and the fact that his feelings about his placement may be complicated by his awareness of the increasing number of deaths among his peers. The worker must be prepared to have longer sessions in which slower progress is made. And the worker must recognize that while some elderly persons fear placement, others welcome it.

If an institutional placement has been arranged, the personnel of the institution need to provide a therapeutic milieu, creating proper channels of communication between themselves and the elderly resident. Again as in the instance of the placement of children in institutions, the worker is the connecting link to the residents, working with them on their individual problems and helping them to understand the institution's policies and procedures.

The social worker's task in reference to the placement of a child or a younger adult generally is directed toward the goal of aiding the placed person and his family move toward productive social functioning. The task with regard to the placement of a high proportion of aged persons, however, is to help the individual to be physically comfortable and to retain as much of a zest for living as is possible for him; a goal of almost equal importance, though often ignored, is enabling his relatives to carry out the necessary placement task realistically, with a minimum of disruption to the nuclear family, and with a sense of satisfaction rather than anxiety and guilt.

11

PHYSICAL OR
EMOTIONAL ILLNESS

ALMOST ALL FAMILIES at one time or another have problems with physical health. These tend to strike more frequently when the children are young and, again, when the family members have passed the middle years. But no stage in the family life cycle is invulnerable to illness. Nor is there a point in the cycle of family life that is not susceptible to problems with mental health, although mental illness occurs with less frequency among families in our society than does physical illness. If the physical illness is time-limited, even though severe, families generally can cope with the illness and its concomitant problems. The family may be exhausted by the illness, physically, emotionally, and financially, but— with or without help—the family members are able to renew their energies and resources and continue to function with a reasonable degree of competence. Fewer families, however, are able to tolerate either the strain of a chronic illness that consumes their income and depletes their economic resources or of a chronic illness that drains them in all areas: physically, emotionally, and financially.

The spectrum of physical and emotional illnesses is so broad and so complicated that it is not possible to present here the range in breadth or depth of ways of identifying or dealing with all the manifestations. This chapter endeavors only to suggest an approach to some of the common aspects of physical and emotional illness likely to create or exacerbate family problems. It also suggests two ways in which the social worker can be helpful to families experiencing difficulties with physical and emotional illness: working directly with the family to both understand and manage the illness, and assisting the sick member to procure and use the kind of help he needs.

PHYSICAL ILLNESS OR DISABILITY

Despite the rapid expansion both of medical knowledge and of facilities to meet problems of physical ill health, there are wide gaps in medical services in many communities throughout the nation—gaps that pose serious difficulties for many families who require care when illness strikes. The gaps range from the complete absence of any medical resources to the limited availability or accessibility of adequate facilities; and from a dearth of specialized facilities for certain illnesses, such as brain damage in children, to facilities that focus on narrowly circumscribed medical conditions of special types and which, accordingly, neither diagnose nor treat other acute or chronic illness.

Many communities lack facilities adequate for the care of senile aged persons and, consequently, families resort to placing such persons in state hospitals for the mentally ill—often to the detriment of the aged person, his family, and the facility. Numerous communities rely on inadequate commercial facilities for convalescent or nursing care for chronically incapacitated people. Such facilities as do exist may not serve all people. Thus, the low-income family dependent on public assistance or other helping sources, may fare better in procuring clinic or hospital care than the middle-income family who, ineligible to use the services in a public or voluntary clinic, may be unable to assume the costs attendant upon either an acute illness or prolonged home or hospital care.

The inaccessibility or the unavailability of community facilities may serve in different ways to render families susceptible to the impact of physical or mental illness, or to enhance their susceptibility to related problems. They also may be vulnerable because of their economic situation or because of special emotional stress factors unique to each family.

How do families react to the stress of physical illness?

The Ill Breadwinner

If the wage-earner is sick, it is obvious that problems are created for the total family, especially if it is a marginal-income family or its savings are not enough to defray both the medical costs and those for meeting the family's daily needs. Indeed the latter expenses often rise in the face of the illness, even though income from work has dropped or ceased: food types may differ and their costs increase; extra transportation needs may arise; extra sitters for children may be required while parental attention is focused on the sick spouse; little gifts may become essential for the patient or for the patient's children. Many families strain their resources to the utmost—their own and those of relatives—before seeking financial assistance from other sources. Some wait too long and become enmeshed in debts that may be impossible to manage even when the breadwinner is back at work. Under such conditions the mother often is so absorbed in nursing tasks and in struggling to juggle the financial demands that she has little energy left with which to provide necessary attention to the children; they suffer as a consequence. If she must seek gainful work, or *feels* she should, yet cannot make suitable plans for the care of the children, she as well as the children are disadvantaged by the inadequacy of the arrangements and by her related guilty or anxious concern.

If the breadwinning mother in a fatherless home becomes ill, and especially if she requires hospitalization, the problems are compounded. The family in such a situation is fortunate if there are relatives who can step in to care for the children. Some communities offer voluntary and publicly supported homemaker services to provide short-term care when the mother must be out of the home. Any crisis that takes the mother away in and of itself brings terror to children; it is of the greatest importance that their lives remain as stable as possible during the crisis, with usual day-by-day routines continued in the familiar surroundings of the home and the school. The maintenance of these routines allays the child's anxiety about his mother's return; the accustomed surroundings provide a sense of security and stability, and they offer some protection against his fears of loss and of the unknown. "Business as usual," which can be carried on only if the child remains in his own home, enables him to keep up with school tasks and thus to feel to some degree that the total situation is still under reasonable control.

The physical illness or incapacity that is of long duration or becomes chronic creates special problems for most families. If the illness attacks the father-breadwinner, there may be either a reduction in his capacity to work or a total inability to work; in either event his earnings may be curtailed or cease. In some instances, especially if the physical incapacity is not expected to continue over a long period of time, the extended family—particularly parents of the adults in the nuclear family—bridge the gap with financial help and services. There is less likelihood of such help in situations where the illness or disability is characterized by chronicity, especially if the extended family's financial and physical resources are not extensive. The alternatives that then remain to the family generally are two: to seek public assistance or to have the mother assume the breadwinner tasks.

In our culture such role reversal may hold destructive implications for the family. Whether the ill father is in or out of the home the children often turn to the mother to act both as father and as mother. Children are likely to be ashamed of a father who cannot work. Boys may reject the chronically ill father and fail to develop adequate male identification. When the mother goes out to work, the father may, if he is able, take over household chores—a course that further confuses the children as to what a father and mother are supposed to be and do. One boy of twelve, reacting to the personal and cultural conflict produced by such a situation, declared: "I won't do what my father does. He's a sissy because he scrubs the floors and washes dishes. I'll scrub the walls if my mother wants me to because that's man's work." It takes a strong couple to be able to sustain adequate masculine and feminine identification for the children whose father is chronically incapacitated and remains at home while the mother supports the family.

Role reversal also can become a problem if it is the mother who is chronically incapacitated. The father may take over the tasks of fathering and mothering. The mother who does not want to relinquish her mothering role may feel deep resentment and this may lead to marital conflict. The adolescent girl who is expected by the father to assume some of the household responsibilities, especially if the mother is not in the home, may experience considerable guilt about seeming to replace the mother. This not infrequently is the basis for sexual delinquency on the part of the girl: it is in this way that she drains off tensions created by too close a relationship with the father without the protection of the mother. Or she may become quite hostile to both parents, or place her anger primarily on one, frequently the incapacitated mother.

If the mother in a fatherless home becomes chronically incapacitated, placement of the children in foster family or institutional care may have to occur. Again, this generally is the least desirable of solutions. The mother as well as the children suffer from their separation. The mother may lose her main reason for existence and deteriorate both physically and emotionally; the children are torn from the source of their security. Such consequences point to the importance of community support like housekeeping services and home medical services to enable many chronically ill mothers to remain at home. It is no coincidence, for example, that mothers with multiple sclerosis experience more remission and maintain greater physical adaptability when they remain in the home setting where, in contrast with hospitalization, they can still manage family and household affairs from a wheelchair or bed. The availability of such appropriate community support tends to add a stabilizing element to those situations where the chronically ill mother is in and out of the home for varying lengths of time.

Physical illness is almost always accompanied by some emotional stress; in a great many instances there also is economic stress. In our American culture, a severe blow is dealt to the self-esteem of the chronically ill man whose illness precludes his fulfillment of the breadwinning role and produces financial distress. If the parent has been hospitalized, the child often behaves as though this does not matter to him; he resorts to "indifference" in order to defend himself against the anxiety the separation produces in him—an indifference the parents frequently interpret literally.

The Ill Child

Illness in a child often is less dramatic from the standpoint of its assault on the parental feelings of adequacy in fulfillment of their normal roles; yet it also carries serious consequences for the family. In most instances a family will regain its normal equilibrium upon the recovery of a child who has been acutely ill. For some families who already are vulnerable, the acute illness of a child may produce more severe and enduring consequences. All children suffer from separation anxieties when they are hospitalized. They often display this while in the hospital by refusing to eat or by regression to such former ways of behaving as toileting difficulties or temper tantrums. Children may pretend to be indifferent to the visiting parents, thus defending themselves against the inevitable separation anxiety they feel when the parents leave.

The normal child recovers from his anxiety when he returns home and the family settles down to its regular routine. Were a defect to exist in the relationship between the child and his parents, were they to feel unduly guilty or resentful about his illness, they might easily overprotect him, and in doing so contribute to developmental problems both for him and the other children who inevitably feel some resentment toward the sick but "favored" child. Some parents resent the inconvenience to them when their child is hospitalized. The demands for care and attention when the child returns home deepen this resentment. As a consequence, should the child become ill again, these parents tend to deny that *this* illness is real; they fail to provide the needed medical care—sometimes with devastating results.

The chronically ill child poses special problems for the family. It is a fact of life that parents feel both responsible and guilty when a child is born defective or chronic illness makes its appearance during the course of childhood.

Similarly, parents of a mentally retarded child—considered here to be chronically ill—tend to feel not only responsible and guilty; they often have a concomitant sense of shame. Although many parents deny that they feel guilt, it is an unavoidable component of their feelings in handling the fact of the child's illness. It accounts for the unending search so often conducted by parents who have children with chronic conditions such as brain damage or mental retardation; they go from one place to another seeking help, never quite able to accept the limitation of present medical knowledge and present social resources. Undoubtedly, the level and the quality of their social and emotional functioning are sustained by hope—vain though it may be —that *somewhere* a solution will be found. It is sustained also by channeling into the energy-absorbing activity of the search some of the sorrow and irrational belief in their culpability, and by the driving conviction that no stone should remain unturned by parents who truly care about their child! Indeed, depending upon the child's age and perception, these inexorable parental efforts may provide the child both with hope and comfort, reassuring him that they *do* care.

The Mentally Retarded Child

Parents of a mentally defective child are faced with the reality of having a lifetime in which to have to learn to live and work with this child. Many times, such parents, told their child is "mentally deficient" and to "accept this fact," are not clear as to just what it is they are being asked to do. The parents of a normal child must endure many difficulties and trials—of illness, of behavior, of conflict, and they not infrequently have moments or despair. But the parents of the retarded child in numerous instances *know* he will never become a self-sufficient adult and that there is every likelihood—even if he is somewhat educable—that they always will be burdened with the child's unrelenting demands and continued emotional and, probably, economic dependency. They *know* their despair will persist until they or the child dies. Such parents may realistically be concerned about what will happen to the child upon their death.

With few exceptions, these parents move slowly toward accepting the fact of their child's mental retardation—although they may be quite impatient with the slowness of our society in providing facilities that would help them to maximize the potential of such a child or to make institutional care available to him if this is what is indicated in accordance with medical and social assessments. Their slowness certainly is understandable. Not only is it difficult to give up hope; some of the recent remarkable advances in medical science with regard to retardation serve to buoy up hope that may be flagging. Whether their hope is reality-based or not, the social worker working with such parents must be cognizant of the elements that cause these parents to move slowly toward reconciling themselves to the fact of the child's retardation. They require more time in the counseling process than is true of many other kinds of health situations; it takes these parents longer to begin to be able to muster and maintain the strength they must have to continue to live with the tragedy of having a mentally defective child. Undoubtedly, the time required for this mobilization of internal parental resources is related to the degree of retardation and the prospects for educability. But the need of such parents to discuss the retarded child on many occasions is natural and does not necessarily reflect either undue regression or neurotic behavior.

The serious effect on family life of a normal or undue amount of parental guilt is compounded when there is a paucity of community resources for meeting the medical or social needs of the chronically ill child. The fact that placement facilities for seriously brain damaged or retarded children are relatively few in number and often not wholly adequate makes it difficult or even impossible always to place a child when the family wishes to do so. If the level of their guilt is excessive, the parents may concentrate most of their economic and emotional resources on the chronically ill child, thereby depriving other children of necessary affectional and physical care. The siblings in such a family often resent the diversion of parenting from themselves and this resentment, in turn, is guilt-producing—to the parents and, often, to the sibling.

More children are able to remain at home as resources become increasingly available. Tax-supported programs, as well as voluntary arrangements, have begun to establish comprehensive services for retarded or brain damaged children. But in addition to the medical, special nursery school and special educational facilities, there continues to be a need for some of the same kind of help noted in reference to parents of retarded children: day-care centers and home-maker and other services that can relieve the mothers with chronically ill children of some of their pressures. Additionally, many parents need counseling in order to understand the nature of the illness or of the developmental effect, to allay some of the guilt, and to be sufficiently freed from their burden so they can focus more attention on the other children—and on each other. Many parents both need and can use group discussions and family life education programs to help them to understand the facets of their problem and to learn how to cope with it in day-to-day life.

Help to Families with Illness Problems

There is little doubt that many families are ignorant about physical problems; they are not cognizant of the onset or significance of some symptoms and, consequently, it does not occur to them to seek whatever help might be available to control or remedy a health problem. Or, if they are aware of an anomaly they may assume that it does not lend itself to correction. Such assumptions are not exclusive to uneducated or geographically isolated persons. For example, twelve-year-old Jennie had transferred to her present school two years earlier when her parents, stirred by the civil rights foment, moved into a major urban center from the small rural southern community where Jennie had been born with the aid of a midwife.

A "routine" examination by a pediatrician brought to light the fact that Jennie had six fingers on each hand, that her mother put large pockets on all of the child's outer garments so that she could conceal her hands, which she had not always been succesful in doing. The object of peer ridicule, she kept aloof from the other children and was viewed by school personnel as "withdrawn." She constantly failed in school because she wrote nothing in classes although homework was well done and there was evidence that she was "quite bright."

Inquiry disclosed that it had never occurred to the parents to see what might be done about this situation; Jennie's several teachers had not considered the possibility of correction and none had referred her either to the school nurse, who attended the school regularly, or to the school social worker. Surgery successfully corrected the digital count but Jennie needed help with the emotional scars imposed by the twelve years' accumulation of despair and shame.

Other families have cultural inhibitions or emotional attitudes against the use of medical care. These families often respond to education about the meaning of illness, the need for care, how to use available medical facilities, and how to care for the sick member. Many families follow religious beliefs that proscribe the use of medical care or the following of certain medical recommendations such as surgery or transfusing of blood. It is not unusual, when the life of a child in such a family is threatened by illness that medical authorities believe can be brought under control by medical procedures not consistent with the religious beliefs of the family, for a court of law to assume guardianship of the child for medical purposes and to authorize the recommended medical action. In such an instance, the social worker must exercise considerable care in helping the parents deal with their conflict centering around their parental role and their ethical convictions. The social worker's help can most readily take the form of recognizing the parents' right to their religious beliefs and acknowledging their basic wish to have their child well again.

There is another kind of situation in which families tend to take no action in either seeking or following medical advice. It is when there is suspicion of diseases like cancer or muscular dystrophy that are strongly fear-inducing, their dramatically depressing and painful aspects highly publicized. The family's reasoning seems to be that if the feared diagnosis is not actually made, pain and death somehow will be forestalled. Such families need special interpretation about the importance of early detection for control, reassurance in confronting the reality of the absence or the presence of the dreaded disease, and, in the event of confirmation, guidance toward taking appropriate action.

One of the special problems that families face is the return to the home of a sick member who has been away for some time. Often there are natural fears about the return to the home of someone who has been seriously ill and who still may be ill. If the illness derives from a physical condition, the fears may stem from apprehension about the adequacy of the family members to provide the care necessary for the patient. They may arise from concern about the effects of the member's return on arrangements or relationships developed in the family because of the illness. They may be connected to anxiety about how the sick person will fit into a household that has established new ways of living during the patient's absence from the home. They may be related to resentment about having been left with burdens at home while the sick member was "taking it easy" in the hospital, and to guilt about feelings of resentment toward him. The interim or continued care of the patient realistically may be difficult or even impossible for the family members to handle; yet the patient may be sent home because the hospital needs the bed space.

A major service to the family may be aid in planning for nursing and other services that the returning patient will require, helping the family to understand the nature and meaning of the illness and the course the convalescence might be expected to take—including such anticipated reactions as the patient's impatience, querulousness, dependency, airs of martyrdom, and actual suffering. Many communities have services that can be called upon for such planning and implementation of the plans, among them homemaking and housekeeping services, visiting nurses from voluntary agencies, public health nurses from tax supported facilities, voluntary health agencies concerned with providing resources for such special kinds of illnesses as heart condition, cancer, and arthritis. These agencies often provide especially needed items such as dressings, hospital beds or other equipment required in the home, transportation to clinics, and others.

The patient's anticipation of his return to the home may be as distressing to him as the apprehension felt by the family. His awareness of the care he requires and the problems this may hold for the family members may cause him to resist leaving the hospital facility. He may be fearful that his dependence will be resented and prove to be burdensome to the household. But he also may find that life in the protected hospital setting is satisfying and relatively comfortable, making no demands on him to be anything but dependent; he may be unable or unwilling to find himself carrying any responsibility for decision-making, no matter how minute or infrequent.

EMOTIONAL ILLNESS

Attitudes Affecting Use of Help

The various facets of problems described in connection with physical illness and disability are equally relevant to mental illness. But emotional or mental illness frequently contains additional special and complex features that are not always associated with physical illness. In spite of extensive and intensive efforts of community mental health education programs, mental illness still is very frightening to many families. They suffer from a deep sense of shame when a family member experiences an emotional breakdown. They try as long as possible to conceal the fact of the illness and they resist necessary outpatient or hospital care, denying the presence of the illness, or insisting the person will recover by himself, or persisting in viewing the illness as a physical problem; if it is a child who is ill, he will "surely" outgrow the condition. It is true that when the disturbed member is a child it is not always easy to know when and how help is indicated unless symptoms are gross.

More often than in instances of physical illness, families feel a deep and obscure sense of guilt over being contributors to a child's illness, and they uneasily resist treatment which might expose their part in the fact of the child's illness.

The same sense of shame and guilt is likely to be present when an adult member of a family breaks down emotionally. In marriages, for example, the partner who does not become ill often feels that he has contributed in some fashion to the sickness of the spouse. He may handle his own feelings by denying the partner's illness, or he may try to put the patient out of his life by insisting on as lengthy a hospitalization as is possible "for my husband's (or wife's) own good." It is not uncommon to hear one partner say of the other, "He's not crazy; he's just mean!"

Cultural factors not infrequently have a marked effect on how a family may regard illness that is "nervous" or "crazy" or "tetched," and how the patient or his family responds to offers of help. Some groups have much greater tolerance than others for behavior that is "different." American Indians or families still close to Mexican folkways, for example, accept even bizarre behavior with equanimity and generally only when the behavior has reached a point at which it constitutes a danger is action taken to place the ill person under care—usually in an institutional setting.

Characteristically some minority groups like the Mexican Americans have made little use of outpatient mental health services. This is partly because of cultural beliefs related to the depreciating quality of exposing "weakness." It is "all right" for women to appear weak, but not for the men. The consequence is that unless a psychotic break occurs or something else that is critical comes to the fore—community complaints, for example—the mentally disturbed person tends to remain untreated in the home and the community. Such families, in which one member is seriously or moderately emotionally disturbed, are relatively common in the caseloads of public assistance and correction agencies. The task of the social worker is to help the family members to connect the patient with a mental health resource and to encourage the family to continue the treatment plan that may have been devised for a patient. A frequently used ploy that has proved to be of some success is to help the family members—and the patient, if he is able—to see this helping resource as a device for the restoration of the "strength" of the ill member.

It is particularly important in work with such cultural groups that the worker listen to the feelings below the surface description of the deviant behavior and discern the cultural motivation for acting or not acting with reference to the illness. Mr. Romero illustrates the necessity for the worker to be alert to clues of cultural import. For five years he had been in and out of a state hospital because of severe "headaches" and alcoholism. He had been unable to hold a job in this time, and his wife and four young children were dependent upon public assistance. Periodically, Mr. Romero was released from the hospital with a supply of tranquilizers and a plan for out-patient treatment. Each time, following a short stay in the community, his behavior would become violent (always when he was under the influence of alcohol) and he would be returned by the local police to the hospital. Mr. Romero insisted that the snake inside him caused the headaches, that he drank because this was his only way of forgetting about this "devil." Asked why he did not use the tranquilizers, he would reply that then he would be completely under the domination of the snake. A social worker, reasonably familiar with Mexican cultural patterns, realized that Mr. Romero's description of the snake represented a common superstition as to the source of illness and that Mr. Romero as a masculine person could not "afford" to believe he might be under the domination of the snake. Only when the worker suggested to Mr. Romero that the tranquilizers were designed to put the snake under Mr. Romero's control was he ready to follow the medical instructions. He was successful then in the control of the headache, the alcoholism—and the snake. He was able to obtain and hold sufficient work to bolster his own self-esteem and to provide for the needs of his family.

Unfortunately, even fewer facilities, adequate or inadequate, are available for the emotionally ill than exist for the care of physical illness. Many times families rightly fear that custodial care, not treatment, will be provided in large "impersonal" institutions that tend to be understaffed and overpopulated. On the positive side, there is growing recognition of the need for halfway houses for some people who need an intermediate step between the institutional stay and the return to the open community and home. There also is increasing recognition that if the family can be helped in ways similar to those used when physical illness or disability strikes, the emotionally ill member may not require full-time hospitalization or he may be able to attend a day hospital or a night hospital while retaining a place in the community and in the home.

The Patient's Return to the Home

The fairly common fear regarding mental illness often is compounded on the return to the home of a family member who, when last seen by the family, was in a violent or a withdrawn state. Certainly, bizarre behavior generally is frightening, and the apprehension is increased if the family does not know just what to expect. Either because of ignorance or because of the personal problems of the decision-making family member, some families bring the sick member home too soon. Others resist the return even when it is strongly recommended by the hospital. Such fears may obtain not only from cultural patterns and superstitions; they also may be of a personal nature. When the hospitalization has been a long one, the return home of the sick family member may disrupt the living and working adjustments that had been effected in his absence.

The return to the home of a sick or recovered family member after a long absence may be accompanied by serious problems if the family group has not been adequately prepared for the return. All too often the hospital demands that the family care for the patient without first working out with the family such real aspects of the patient's care as necessary physical arrangements, and without working through with the family their fears, questions, and anxieties. Work with the family is frequently the job of the social worker who needs to have or obtain some familiarity with the medical aspects of the particular family member's care when he is in the home, to coordinate these medical aspects with the social factors that are present, and to understand the stresses and strengths of the family. Based on this knowledge and understanding, the worker can then assist in developing realistic plans and prepare the family emotionally for the patient's homecoming.

Alcoholism

The addictions—alcohol and drugs—and the perversions are specific forms of mental illness that carry special implications for families and are encountered with considerable frequency in many social agencies, particularly the public welfare services. Alcoholism, the most widespread of these illnesses, is often both economically and emotionally the most disruptive to family life. There are many specific reasons for alcoholism: reactions to depressed feelings; reactions to specific stresses and traumas in the life situation; a particular culture that fosters drinking as manly and socially acceptable; a way of handling covert homosexual leanings, an expression of acute mental illness, and others.

Alcoholism sometimes is the route taken by a person endeavoring to forget society's discrimination against his striving for recognition, for adequate work—for some status, therefore, as a man. In these situations the worker alone, without concurrent changes in society, may be able to do only a small part in bringing the addiction under control. The worker, for example, through vocational training or rehabilitation activities, may help the person toward a better job. That action, in and of itself, may result in reducing the drinking to manageable bounds. Such activities on the part of the worker do not tackle the basic personality disturbance that underlies the alcoholism; but they do help to bring some overt control into action.

When alcoholism is a major factor in marital trouble, both partners probably have a share in the continuance of the symptom of emotional illness. One kind of alcoholic under stress resorts to the bottle much as an infant does, except that as an adult he suffers from guilt because of this action, repents, and then when again under stress, falls prey to the addiction. Many times, when this kind of alcoholism is a factor in the disturbed marital situation, the partner outwardly cannot tolerate the drinking. However, in many ways, without being aware it is being done, the partner aids and abets the drinking to keep the spouse dependent on him—or her. It is not uncommon, for example, that the partner who is trying not to drink comes home from work justifiably late; his wife will nag and taunt him with accusations that he must have stopped off "to have one" and finally, in desperation, he resumes his drinking both to assuage his own feelings and to give credence to her complaints.

Treatment of this illness is difficult. Alcoholics Anonymous has helped many; for some, psychiatric treatment has offered a possible answer. There are many situations in which family disturbance factors predominate. These situations commonly are seen in public assistance agencies, probation agencies, and voluntary family service agencies. When some of the dynamics are understood by the social worker, the worker's intervention can be effective in breaking the circle of marital and family disturbance. This kind of family treatment demands considerable skill. The social worker must constantly be aware that alcoholism is an illness, that the alcoholic is a sick person, and that, as is true with regard to other ill persons, the communicating by the worker of condemnatory or judgmental attitudes tends to reduce the alcoholic's amenability to treatment.

Narcotic Addiction

The drug addictions thus far have not been amenable to usual social work techniques. The reasons are similar to those that limit the amenability of alcoholism. The original causes of disturbance that culminate in the addiction most frequently lie early and deep in the individual's development; they need to be dealt with by a psychiatric outpatient and hospital facility. There is some hope that in certain situations of adolescent addiction, work with the adolescent and his family will yield positive results. The adolescents in disadvantaged segments of our society are more susceptible than others to narcotic addiction and, therefore, social or other work with them and their families may not suffice. The hopelessness that led to the addiction requires changes in society that will give these adolescents the kind of place in it that increases trust and self-esteem, and permits the kind of identity formation that reduces the need for obtaining satisfactions through such addictions. Of course, merely to wait for changes in society is unproductive; efforts must be continued in the search for some positive gratification for the adolescent with the hope that this will reach at least some, if not all who fall prey to narcotic addiction.

Sex Perversions

Because their roots are deep in early personality development, true sex perversions are the most complicated of emotional problems to bring under control, if not to correct. The social worker can best help the person with a true sexual perversion by getting him to the medical resource equipped to deal with it. In many instances, however, families do not know how to differentiate between age-appropriate sexual activity in a child and the activity that falls outside the range of normal development.

The worker can assist a family to know what kinds of sexual behavior are normal for different age ranges. This serves not only to allay undue anxiety but also to help the parents to understand the importance of avoiding the kind of emphasis on certain sexual behavior that may so frighten the child that his emotional development may be seriously affected. For example, some families become alarmed when a three- or four-year-old, who is exploring his body, masturbates.

Similarly, some parents become upset when a thirteen- or fourteen-year-old masturbates because he is acutely sensitive to the upsurge of sexual biological needs and does not yet know what to do about these needs. This activity is normal. It need cause no concern unless it is prolonged or excessive or is connected with other symptoms of disturbed behavior. If the behavior is age-appropriate, the worker can deal with the parents educationally and, in doing so, avoid the child's becoming overly anxious and guilty.

Likewise, it is not uncommon for aged men in a senile process to expose themselves in public. Certainly this is not desirable, and, indeed, can be frightening. However, unless the behavior is accompanied by other manifestations of severe senility, it is in itself not a reason to rush the aged man into a hospital.

By understanding different cultural implications of sexual behavior, the worker can avoid making the error that all so-called sexual deviations are pathological and harmful to the person and community. For example, not all small boys who sleep with their mothers have incestuous fantasies. Such a sleeping arrangement may follow a pattern within a family or in the wider culture, although it is not desirable for the boy's growth. Separating out cultural from pathological factors enables the worker to know how to deal with the specific situation—and to recognize, as an exaggerated example, that not all small boys who sleep with their mothers need placement or treatment.

When clues point to the fact that the sexual deviation is a perversion that affects the personal and family adjustment and, in many instances, threatens the community, the worker can make a referral to an appropriate source for treatment or supervision under controlled auspices. If treatment is not available, or if the person refuses treatment and is a threat to the community, the community must protect itself by placing the individual under custodial supervision or under some other legal form of authoritative supervision.

Apparent from the foregoing is the fact that physical as well as emotional illness can range from simple to highly complex problems. Physical and emotional illness frequently holds personal, familial, and social implications. But each physical or mental health problem has unique elements necessitating a differential approach by the social worker and strong community support that is reflected in the establishment and maintenance of a broad array of well-equipped community facilities offering diagnosis, care, and treatment.

PART FOUR

Requisites for Social Functioning

12

ESSENTIAL INGREDIENTS

PEOPLE ARE what they are by virtue of qualities impressed on them by nature and by habit. These qualities combine both to distinguish people from each other and to cause them to resemble each other. Each person carries the imprimatur of his heredity and of the successes or the failures with which his family met the life tasks in the successive stages of the cycle of family life. And each person has been influenced in his development by social, economic, and psychological conditions permeating the society of which he is part. These forces of endowment, of family, and of society interact and determine the manner and the competence with which the individual will fill his expected role in the conduct of developmental tasks of the family. These forces likewise determine how he will perform in all of his social roles through social interaction—biologically, psychologically, economically. The sum of his behavior in these several roles is the measurement of the quality of his social functioning.

The interactions of society and the family have been considered in earlier chapters: the impact of societal attitudes and environmental factors on the family's discharge of its primary socialization and economic functions, and the influence of these factors on the attainment by families of the socially accepted goals in our American society. Attention also was directed to the life tasks that are universally characteristic of the several stages of the cycle of family life and to some of the special tasks related to problems encountered by some families because the family is broken, or has problems with physical or mental illness, or because a member of the family must be placed outside the home for care.

What qualities are present in the individual family members that interact with societal elements and developmental factors to facilitate or hinder effective social functioning? That enable some people to perform satisfactorily in the face of crisis, or permit them to collapse before a modicum of stress?

The ingredients requisite for each person's capacity to adapt to changing circumstances, to cope with stress, and to function with a reasonable degree of competence in our society are legion. Among them are intellectual endowment, physical characteristics, the original strength of basic impulses (the life force in the person, that combination of energy and need driving him to want and to strive), the original strength of the ego (the organizing force in the person that perceives reality, protects the person against assault on the inner self and facilitates adaptation to change, integrates realistic demands, and acts appropriately in relation to what is perceived and integrated), the tendencies to physical health and illness. All of these interact with the family and society to shape the individual into the kind of person he is. This composite may be termed character or personality or identity; it is a vital force in determining the level of competence of the individual's social functioning.

The next four chapters focus on personality development, with particular emphasis on selected aspects basic to the social worker's understanding of people. The choice of only four out of many requisites for adequate social functioning—trust, self-esteem, identity, and communication—is not intended to imply that these are the only ones of importance. Rather, they have been singled out because the understanding and use of these in helping people in trouble with respect to social functioning are peculiarly in the province of the social worker. Trust and self-esteem are integral parts of the identity or personality. Identity or personality, used interchangeably here, is the total person with his strengths and limitations. Communication is the essence of human interaction and, therefore, of life, and is essential to identity formation and development. The fact that these special aspects have been selected for more intensive consideration in no way depreciates other necessary developmental ingredients, which are described in lesser detail.

CHARACTER FORMATION

Constitutional Factors

Indeed, certain constitutional factors significantly influence character development. People are constitutionally different from each other in such matters as predisposition to irritability or passivity and, therefore, in the way they react to life experiences. An active, demanding infant is likely to react more sharply to delay in being fed immediately upon feeling hunger than a constitutionally passive child who is content to wait. The first infant may develop a chronically irritable character if his needs are not met rapidly.

Physical Maturation

The rate of physical maturation also is an important factor shaping character. A baby cannot learn to talk, walk, or control elimination until mind and body have matured to the point where these things are possible for him. The older boy or girl cannot become a parent until sex organs mature. How a child walks or talks or develops sexual characteristics varies from individual to individual. Whether or not a particular rate or style of development is a problem depends upon how the development is viewed by the family, by the culture, and, therefore, by the child. If developmental rates differ among children in the same family and are accepted by the parents as desirable, or at least without concern, the character of each child will be molded accordingly. He will be reasonably comfortable with his difference if his parents are; he will be uneasy about his difference if his parents are. A child who cannot readily compete with others because he is smaller than the average for his age may have an aggressive chip-on-the-shoulder attitude as part of his character, or throughout life he may plead extenuating circumstances because his small stature prevents him from achieving what others do.

Childhood Illness and Defects

Congenital defects or early severe illness also contribute to character formation. Inevitably, character development is influenced by the fact of a child's blindness or that he has suffered a brain damage. If, in addition, the parents cannot master their feelings about the defect or illness sufficiently to permit the child's reasonable development, he will acquire fixed undesirable character attitudes and traits. For example, he may view himself as too damaged to take any or limited responsibility for his behavior, as having a "right" to have everything done for him and to expect the world to give to him unconditionally. At the other extreme are some parents who are so determined to deny the existence of the congenital defect that they demand from the child normal or equal competence with all others. The degree of strain such expectations place on the child may severely distort the shape of his character. His wish to please his parents makes him a person who is overly aggressive and competitive in ways that society finds unpleasant and difficult to cope with. Similarly, severe early illness affects character. Separation fears of a hospitalized child can become embedded in the character as phobias of various kinds. Undue dependency and clinging can become a way of life. Denial of the trauma caused by the illness can lead to an attitude that defies danger in situations where realistic caution is needed. Early illness, if chronic, can create a personality that is pervasively anxious and fearful about all aspects of living or that, in an attempt to control the fears, develops a constricted, inhibited or compulsive character trait.

The Family

Separate from these factors, although intimately interwoven with them as a major contributor to personality development, is the nuclear family. The family's manner of dealing with illness in childhood or with more or less serious congenital defects either nurtures potential strengths or interferes with the individual's normal growth and development. The kind of conscience a child develops, his ideas, his values, his psychosexual development—all of these are influenced by the way the family feels and acts about the life force in the child. The responses of the family to the child's growth impulses, which always exist, condition the child's ego development, that is, his internal ability to manage himself as a person as well as to manage himself in relation to the physical and social environment. As he grows, the model discernible to the child in the parents' relationship with each other as well as with the child and with the other children in the family conditions his identifications: it decrees the nature and quality of his relationship not only with his parents but also with others in his environment. His character development also is affected by cultural patterns unique to his own family and by the pattern unique to the larger culture to which the family belongs. The family's cultural trust or distrust, the family's ability to meet demands of the larger culture, society's approval of the family's culture, or society's relegation of the family's culture beyond the pale with resulting disadvantageousness and discrimination because of race, religion, poverty, location or other special factors—all or any combination of these either positively or negatively influence character development. In short, character is created by the dynamic interlocking of *all* of these factors, not just an occasional or isolated one.

In addition to the need for physical and economic security, an essential ingredient for social functioning is a family life that permits the individual to use his growth impulses to the maximum. Thus, the family needs to strike a balance between adequate stimulation toward growth and an inordinate amount of pressure; it needs to permit development of individual identity and healthy interdependence in the family; it needs to grant freedom to the individual to move away from the family to the outside world; it needs to encourage the establishment in this outside world of a good relationship in work and love.

Mutability

Character is shaped in the early years of life; however, it is not necessarily fixed into an unalterable mold. The impulse to grow, the forces in the family, life experiences in the larger environment, physical factors, societal conditions, all continue to affect and modify character. It is well known, for example, that a specific individual's intelligence quotient is not immutable, that an I.Q. can be markedly altered by a change in the environment that produces a reduction in stress along with good opportunities to learn. The intelligence has existed, but unfavorable life conditions have kept it dormant. All human beings want to better themselves even if they are so battered that they deny the wish. Given opportunities to fan the spark, noticeable changes can take place in those whose personalities otherwise are regarded as retarded, spineless, shiftless, hopeless, and so on.

Disadvantageousness

Oppressive poverty and scapegoating related to race, religion, class, geographic location, or other conditions contain deeply significant implications for character formation. Many times people caught in these disadvantaged situations present certain characteristic attitudes and traits by which their personality development is judged to be inferior; as a consequence, they *become* inferior. These traits frequently are expressed by excessive withdrawal, excessive anger, excessive physical aggression, mistrust and flouting of authority, suspicion of the world; often they are deemed to be inborn and irreversible. But they are the products of society and they are reversible if latent capacities are expanded.

Such expansion requires cognizance of the causes of the problem and application of a multi-pronged approach based both on understanding that excludes coercive efforts to alter the characterological attitudes, and on positive modification of the environment aimed at the removal of external stress and providing practical opportunities for competent social functioning. Achievement of the latter depends in large measure on the responsibility that society assumes for true acceptance of cultural differences so that people are not forced into disadvantageous positions. Should this occur, as it already has among several groups in our society today, provision must be made for an array of essential social welfare services as well as for education, health, employment, housing, and rehabilitation resources to be drawn upon in changing or modifying destructive forces in people. Such services and resources hold the means for effecting the positive changes in trust and self-esteem essential for identity and for the development of communication that channels dysfunctional aggressive expression into more thoughtful and controlled demonstration of feeling.

Normal Character

To understand what causes deviations in the personality and to acquire some guidelines for judging the nature of a deviation requires a baseline description of "normal character." A precise description is impractical, however, because the spectrum of normality is wide and comprises various components related to society, to the family, and to the individual in a changing world. One way to describe the normal person is this: his way of handling his life course is reasonable in relation to his reality, and his reality is reasonably congruent with that of other people in his culture. His ways of protecting or defending himself in everyday life and under special stress show flexibility and are adaptive to the particular life situations. He has effected reasonable solutions to developmental tasks. If under stress he regresses to less appropriate ways of behaving, the regression is temporary and enables him to mobilize himself to meet the crisis rationally. He is appropriately anxious in relation to stress or crisis, and his symptoms are transitional and appropriate to his age and his stage of development. Thus, stress might cause a two-year-old child to have nightmares which do not persist once the stress is relieved. A mother might experience severe headaches during a stressful period, but these are transitory and depart with the mastery of the stress. Because conflict is the essence of life and growth, the normal person for the most part handles conflict in a rational way and recognizes irrationality that may crop out. He thinks well of himself, but he also perceives the wishes and needs of others; his sense of his own identity enables him to accept differentness and individuality in others. In effect, the normal person has reasonable ability to love and to work, the two main tasks in life; his social functioning is competent.

If individuals are to develop satisfactorily along lines that encourage and enhance appropriate social functioning, their physical, emotional, and economic needs must be met during all stages of life. Every human being has a breaking point and it differs for each one. In any stage of life, undue stress, even if mastered, may exact too great a price to allow for continued sound development.

13

TRUST

M<small>R. JAY</small> made it clear to all and sundry that he trusted no one but himself. He did not trust the public welfare worker to understand that he had to be at home all the time because his wife was competent neither to do the housework nor to manage the children. He did not trust physicians because they could not cure him of a long-standing backache. He did not trust employers because they always took such advantage of him that he had to leave every job after a few months. Mr. Jay's basic and pervasive mistrust led to the family's dependence on public welfare for more than ten years during which no appreciable constructive changes occurred in the family's circumstances in spite of many and diverse efforts of agency personnel.

Mr. Jay is the extreme example of the way inability to trust can affect all aspects of an individual's and family's life, marriage, work, learning, and child rearing. In our complex society failure to trust in oneself and failure to have confidence in the integrity of others is productive of breakdown in the wide range of relationships and the wide range of communication required for adequate management of life tasks. There are many gradations in this very important aspect of life, from Mr. Jay's extreme distrust of anyone or anything, to the opposite extreme of persons so indiscriminately overtrusting that they cannot distinguish between what is trustworthy and what is dangerous. The continuum comprising healthy trust and healthy mistrust—collectively designated here as trust—is an essential ingredient for adequate self-management. Unhealthy trust or mistrust pose serious obstacles to competent social functioning.

THE MEANING OF TRUST

How do healthy or unhealthy trust and mistrust develop? How does this element influence people's management of life tasks? What are the implications for working with people who are known to social agencies because they cannot independently master life tasks? What are the origins of healthy trust and mistrust? How can failures or gaps in development of this personality ingredient be dealt with by social workers?

The Roots of Trust

The development of healthy trust and unhealthy mistrust, like other aspects of personality growth, is a psychosocial process that has its roots in the family and, therefore, in the culture in which the family lives. Ability to master trust and mistrust is basic to the ability to test, assess, and respond to reality; and in the ability to trust can be found, to a considerable extent, the foundations of healthy self-esteem. The factor of trust is molded by the earliest experiences in life; it is the first component of mental health development in life. It can be described as a fundamental attitude toward oneself and the world—an attitude that derives from the experiences in the family during the first year of life. Modes of behaving with others, feelings about oneself as a person who has *worth* or *worthlessness*, are the far-reaching results of trust. Cultural differences in families may be expressed in different styles of feeding, holding, or swaddling the young child. But the development of basic trust always depends on the quality of relationship to the child of the mother or mother's substitute, a quality that should combine sensitive care in meeting the child's needs with a firm sense of the mother's own competence and trust in herself. When a parent can function in this way with even a fair degree of consistency, the child can accept and tolerate permissions and prohibitions because he senses that they have meaning and are neither irrational nor random in nature. When the management of the child is conducted with a genuine self-trust on the part of the parent, conflicts that may arise from external influences or from the culture of the family need not lead to basic disturbances in the development of trust in the child. Thus discomfort can be caused by changing points of view about demand versus scheduled feedings or breast versus bottle nursing. But the discomfort will be transient and minimal in a mother who is attuned to the needs of the child and has confidence in herself.

People who are basically mistrustful because of early mismanagement by parents lacking the sense of self-trustworthiness often believe themselves to be "no good" or "left out of everything" or, like Mr. Jay, compelled to rely only on themselves. People who are overly trusting because the parents lacked self-confidence and placed no prohibitions on them, often cannot cope with the vicissitudes of life because they have not learned to wait, how to judge reality, how to handle inevitable frustrations.

Although pragmatically it has been validated that healthy trust stems from early life experiences, it would be an error to assume that the personaity of the mother is the sole index to this developmental phase. Other aspects in the life situation need to be taken into account. The state of the marriage, illness or death in the immediate family, loss of meaningful people in the extended family —any of these may interfere with the establishment of a good relationship between parents and child. It also is difficult to insure a consistent development of trust when parents are preoccupied with the adequacy of resources for meeting basic economic needs or when they are bombarded by difficulties accruing from their membership in a culturally disadvantaged minority group. It is a tribute to many families that in spite of insufficient economic assets and of social disadvantages, the ego capacity of self-trust is sufficiently well developed that they can establish and foster it in their children.

The Effects of Impaired Trust

The effects of this stage of life development are far-reaching. Although healthy trust is not the only factor in learning, it is a basic element. The child who develops a good fusion of trust and mistrust is actively receptive to learning. He trusts the teacher, but at the same time confidence in himself enables him to raise questions, to doubt, to sort out for himself the answers so that learning becomes an active, internalized process in which knowledge is absorbed productively. The child can take in learning, stop long enough to integrate it, and then take in more. He can share knowledge and, in the sharing, learn. His good attention span and his ability to listen actively make it possible for him to endure dullness or ineptness in a teacher—he learns to withstand frustration. The child who seriously mistrusts may be a passive surface learner, a poor learner because he is not genuinely receptive to learning. He is therefore easily distractible; his attention span is so poor he often resorts to disturbing behavior. He cannot tolerate the struggle involved in learning, cannot "hear" the teacher because he cannot trust her to give to him. The child who has his early needs met indiscriminately, fully, without well-managed prohibitions, often is a non-learner because he expects everything to be poured into him without exertion on his part. He is too receptive, too unquestioning. If he feels that the teacher is withholding, not willing to spoon-feed him, his lack of tolerance or frustration may be expressed by clowning, distraction of other children, or other disturbing behavior.

Learning has obvious relationship to choice of vocation, level of education, earning ability, ability to remain on a job or to leave a poor one, to be promoted in work. Healthy fusion of trust and mistrust has patent implications for the ability to effect good relationships in work, in marriage, and in child rearing. A prerequisite of healthy fusion is the ability to assess one's reality, to make responsible choices and decisions, to use the help of others with a minimum of ambivalence and a maximum of cooperation.

Characteristically, the person with basic mistrust will seek to hold himself at a distance in relationships while at the same time demanding immediate and unquestioning meeting of his needs. His perspective on reality will be skewed. He is suspicious and has a chip-on-the-shoulder attitude. Like Mr. Jay, he expects to be denied, rejected, and taken advantage of. In relationships he often "beats the other person to the gun" by fighting, leaving a job, or provoking an incident so that he can justify his anger at being denied. This is his way of rejecting *first*, thereby quelling his fear of being rejected.

The person who has been given "everything" without prohibition often will passively agree with suggestions or offerings. His reality assessment is poor; his judgment is distorted. He is passively demanding in relationships and shows irrational anger when denied. He makes little or no effort to work out solutions and will attempt to maneuver others into doing *for* him by his seemingly sweet reasonableness and compliance.

The Fusion of Trust and Mistrust

In essence, healthy fusion of trust and mistrust is evidenced in capacity to test reality, in the readiness to trust in others and the self, along with a readiness to challenge, to question, to arrive at valid decisions and choices. It is a major and basic ingredient in the development of appropriate self-esteem. It is marked by a minimum of unhealthy ambivalence in relationships, communication that is clear and direct, and healthy dependence and interdependence in the nuclear family as well as with others outside the family.

Certainly there are many gradations between the extremes of healthy fusion and basic mistrust. And basic mistrust may assume various forms. For example, the overtrusting person expects complete giving and mistrusts those who do not comply. The way in which a person approaches an agency for financial aid or assistance with some other personal or family problem provides clues to his capacity for trust, his potential for constructive use of agency services, and the quality of his working relationship with the social worker.

All people in our culture have ambivalence about seeking help. Self-esteem is threatened because of the premium placed by our society on self-management and economic independence as an index to social and mental health. Numerous studies in recent years have underscored the fact that most people do not seek the financial assistance until their situation is desperate. Likewise, there still is considerable reluctance to expose "weakness" and to ask for help for personal and family difficulties. Ambivalence will be expressed in a variety of ways according to basic personality traits, of which trust is a most significant one.

The person who is reality-oriented will try to manage as well as he can with whatever resources he has at his disposal; he will not wait to ask for help until he is at the rock-bottom desperation point. The person who trusts others and himself will present his request clearly and directly, although possibly with a tinge of embarrassment; he will make the facts known, and will understand why facts need to be given. He will see the worker, without distortion, as someone whose job it is to *know* so that he can *help*. Such a person will raise valid questions about procedures, about the information requested, and about available services. To ascertain that the agency is the right resource for his problem, he will ask about the qualifications of the agency and the worker. He will cooperate with procedures and plans that are valid and useful; he also will use his own initiative in working on his problem.

The seriously mistrusting person may demand assistance prematurely, or he may wait until he is very desperate because he does not believe that help actually will be forthcoming. If he has waited until he is at the desperation point, either he will demand help without providing explanations or information about his need or he will expect to be rescued without making any effort in his own behalf. He will view questions as an attack on himself, on his honesty, and on his competence. He will demand indiscriminately, as his right; he will want to be given at least as much if not more than anyone else gets; and, at the same time, he will be suspicious of offers of assistance. He will confuse the worker with all the others in his life experience; and he may try, often with success, to provoke the worker to react with anger and rejection. He may be submissive, giving inaccurate data because he is seeking to please the worker by presenting himself as a "good" client. Then he will feel hurt, thinking the questions are unwarranted. He will expect to get whatever he feels is his right without any investment on his part. He may view the worker as an all-feeding mother robin, poised to drop ever-ready food into his mouth.

These clues, in their strongest manifestations, are likely to appear in the initial or even the first few interviews, when tension is high and prevailing personality characteristics are apt to emerge more grossly than later. This requires that the worker be sensitive to the existence of these clues and their possible meanings. It requires also that the worker consciously maintain a high degree of self-control lest he reject or further enrage the applicant, or be seduced by the compliance of the mistrustful person. The worker needs to avoid permitting his reactions to obscure his responsibility for fact-gathering and understanding.

THE MANAGEMENT OF TRUST

It is not possible to undo the impairment in basic mistrust. But it is possible by a correct approach to nurture and develop some capacity for constructive trust in most people who are so impaired. Experience has demonstrated that people in trouble—whether they initiate the approach to the agency or whether the agency initiates the approach at the request of someone in the community —have some constructive longings and aspirations which can be capitalized on to begin the process of trust. It has been found that even the most socially disorganized families have wishes for better life possibilities for their children. Unless people can be helped to develop some sense of trust, they cannot involve themselves in working constructively on their problems in order to move in the direction of grasping these life possibilities. They may suffer someone else to take over the problem, or even enjoy this, but they will not be able to participate actively in the utilization of community resources; nor will they be able to turn their own personality resources to profitable account. If the attack on the family problem of the mistrustful person is to be effective, therefore, the development of trust must be the first step toward his involvement, for such involvement is fundamental to any resolution of problems.

Approaches

A differential approach is needed in work with different kinds of clients. To the person who has a well-developed fusion of trust and mistrust, the worker is often an important provider of knowledge. Knowledge may include information about the nature and use of available agency and community resources; it may include understanding about personal or family matters that are troubling with regard to the characteristic behavior of adolescents, for example, or some aspect of child rearing. It may include strengthening and supporting the person's capacity to mobilize his own resources when he is overwhelmed by a task such as might face the family temporarily immobilized because of the death of the breadwinner. This family might need financial assistance; it might need help, given by the active listening of the worker, to express and work through the various aspects of mourning. The mother might need to know the mourning needs of the children and to be helped with these, including understanding of how children use disturbing behavior to express their distress. Exploration by the worker of how crises have been managed in the past, and what in the day-to-day functioning shows intact areas and indicates individual and family coping ability, provides clues to the appropriate and selective use of techniques: active listening, reality discussion, conveying of knowledge, realistic suggestions and guidance and support of the surviving parent's own ability to perceive and cope with reality, and so on.

The approach is quite different in continuing work with a person who suffers from basic mistrust. If this is one whose deep mistrust is expressed in terms of undue suspiciousness, anger, expectation of denial and unrealistic demands, the first step is to get a "foothold" into the situation. Even the person who rejects the advances of the worker will rarely be unwilling to pour out complaints. The worker tries, by listening, to identify some current problem that is real, something needed and wanted, but also something that is not too threatening or anxiety-provoking to the shaky self-esteem, and something that the worker can quickly provide or help the family to procure.

Mrs. Langer delivered a barrage of needs when the worker went to the home and introduced himself as someone who wanted to help because he knew the family was in trouble with the community. Mrs. Langer attacked him and the community at the same time that she complained about having no money for clothing for the children, the terrible rat-infested apartment, a child who made her life miserable by bed-wetting. She wanted the school to "get off her back"; she wanted Mr. Langer to stop drinking.

Instilling Trust

Where to begin? One thing Mrs. Langer wanted and that could be achieved, was better housing. This not only was an outer reality need, it also was an inner reality need: it became clear that to Mrs. Langer, moving to better quarters meant becoming respectable, a rise in status and self-esteem. Housing also was the least threatening point at which to begin with Mrs. Langer. Her fierce protection of her children against the school would not permit that as a point of entry for working with her. Nor was the bed-wetting: she had implied that the worker would criticize her for this, and her sharp reaction toward the school indicated her readiness to react similarly to any semblance of criticism on the part of the worker. She could not tolerate Mr. Langer's drinking, but no "outsider" could help. Beginning with work on *one* need not only gave the worker a reason for returning, it also was the first step toward the possibility of trust and of involving Mrs. Langer in the process of working on other problems. To have started with more than one need might have been overwhelming to this disorganized chaotic woman and family; she could channel her energies into the encompassable goal—a need about which both Mr. and Mrs. Langer were positively united.

Mr. Jay did not want the worker to do anything. He fought the worker's coming because he knew consideration was being given to placing the children out of the home. He told the worker he would kill anyone who would try to remove his children, and he meant it. The worker said he could not guarantee against this possibility in the future, but what he had in mind was to see how he could help Mr. Jay with the children at home. Neighbors were complaining about the children rummaging in garbage cans for food, about snatching items in local stores. Mr. Jay, the cook in the family, contended that he gave the children plenty of food. The worker granted this but suggested that, as a man, perhaps Mr. Jay did not provide enough variety. Kids like change. Mr. Jay could acknowledge this point and it became the foothold: discussion of food, planning for health and variety, and cooking hints. At this point the worker did not challenge Mr. Jay's need to be the family cook. Nor did the worker use his knowledge about Mr. Jay's job difficulties, his refusal to accept medical aid for his back, his refusal to permit Mrs. Jay, who appeared to be quite ill, to have a medical and psychiatric examination. All these, though urgent, would so have threatened Mr. Jay and increased his suspiciousness that he would have denied the worker entry into the house.

In each of these cases with mistrustful people, the workers moved toward the solution of a problem before there was thorough understanding of the people and their problems. To wait to gain such understanding in the face of so little tolerance for delay or frustration would have made a foothold highly improbable. Concern often is expressed by social workers that the approach suggested in these cases would foster insatiable dependency needs. However, this is not likely to be a problem when the need is a real one, in both an outer and inner sense. When these needs mesh and are appropriately met, over a period of time the rise in self-esteem offsets undue dependency demands. Increased self-esteem frequently accompanies involvement, even if it is only minimal; and as a result of self-involvement, unwarranted dependency demands are likely to abate.

Small as they were, the gains in the beginning development of basic trust and the rise in self-esteem both of the Langers and the Jays were not achieved overnight. To establish a working relationship requires persistence, consistence in approach, and disciplined self-control on the part of the social worker. Mistrustful people will test, provoke, and set traps for the worker—sometimes in unpleasant ways —over quite a period of time. They will expect the worker to come to the home as planned, even if no family member is at home when the worker arrives. They may refuse to talk, or they may attack the worker verbally for fancied failures or his inability to provide something desired by the family. They may tell the worker not to come, and be enraged if he acts on this. They may agree to use a resource, fail to do so, and project the blame on the worker. Any negative reactions by the worker, especially in the early stages, are likely to be interpreted as rejection. The initial period of contact often requires frequent and prolonged home visiting, both not readily available to a worker with an exceedingly heavy case load. Whatever time is possible should be given regularly and consistently. Experience has shown that *frequency* of contact is not necessarily as significant as *regularity* and *consistency*, and keeping of promises with respect to the use of time. When trust and involvement in the working relationship have been established, greater use of telephone visiting and less frequent use of home visiting can be effective. Emphasis is placed on the importance of home visiting because experience indicates that such mistrustful people either will not come to an office, or will come only when they want something specifically. It is difficult to establish a working relationship under these conditions. Once such a relationship is established, the person may be able and willing to participate in working on his problem by coming to the office regularly.

Developing Trust

As the person is gratified by the worker's interest and active meeting of real needs, as trust is initiated and self-esteem begins to grow as a consequence of some even slight achievement, other problems can be worked upon also. The sequence of selecting problems to be worked on should always be from the less threatening to one a little more difficult for the person to face or handle. Many times it becomes possible either to work on more than one problem at a time, or for the worker to initiate discussion of matters the client does not bring up or of which he is not aware. This decision should be keyed to evidence of success and to increased tolerance for failure and frustration. When Mr. Jay saw improvement in his children's health and complaints about them decreased, he could move toward recognizing and accepting his wife's need for a full medical workup and treatment. Subsequently he was able to request a medical examination of his back. After much discussion he agreed, in the light of Mrs. Jay's serious disabilities, to experiment with the use of a homemaker while he underwent vocational testing. After the Langer family moved, Mrs. Langer asked the worker to intercede with the school. Later it became possible for her to talk without verbal abuse and screaming. The worker began to inject ideas about child rearing, which Mrs. Langer eagerly accepted. Much later, when the intensity of her attacks on Mr. Langer had lessened, his drinking diminished somewhat and he held jobs with steadily increasing regularity.

In the process of establishing a working relationship with socially and psychologically disorganized families like the Jays and Langers, it often is desirable and sometimes necessary for the worker to be the bridge from the family to the community. The Langers could not approach or deal with the public housing agency which they mistrusted. Mr. Jay's belligerence and suspiciousness probably would have destroyed the plans for medical examination had the worker not prepared him and the medical resource in advance as well as after the examinations. When trust, self-involvement, and self-esteem are somewhat developed, a new working goal can be set: helping the family to begin dealing directly and constructively with a community and its institutions such as schools, social agencies, and hospitals. As in the earlier working phase, this may require continued support from the worker, including sympathy and encouragement when efforts fail and frustration re-arouses hurt, anger, and attacking behavior. The worker must expect and accept misguided, inconsistent effort, failure, and back sliding. But the disappointments will be less intense and the worker can help the person by anticipating these possibilities in advance as, for example, preparing a man for not obtaining the job he is seeking. The basically mistrustful person rarely is introspective because, as has already been stated, he learned early in life to handle his feelings by his behavior. Sometimes, along with an increase in trust and self-esteem, it is possible to engage in helping people to examine the meaning of their behavior. Mrs. Langer did not reach this stage. Mr. Jay, because of the excellent intelligence and greater flexibility in his personality, gradually revealed doubts about his behavior on jobs; he was able to use help to work through a number of his problems. This would not have been possible without the earlier and basic work undertaken by the social worker.

It is far more difficult, although on the surface it appears to be easier, to develop healthy trust in the person whose basic mistrust is expressed through compliance and submission. Such people, who expect the unequivocal granting of whatever is required to meet all of their needs and who, therefore, have poor reality testing capacity, may act out through antisocial behavior when they are frustrated. They may fall easy prey to destructive advice or suggestion. They tend to entrap the worker by seemingly ready compliance, by expressing pleasure over advice, then frustrate the worker by failing to carry through, after offering apologies and manifold excuses. It is not easy to avoid these seductive entrapments.

The differential approach in this type of distrust is frequently through instituting external controls without *becoming* the control. Such mistrustful persons need an educational process in which reality is pointed out through helping them to consider alternatives to their behavior, by helping them to face the consequences of destructive behavior, and by later stimulating self-questioning and questioning of others. Direct advice should be used sparingly because, although they seek it, such people do not use it unless they are in serious danger to themselves or others.

Basic mistrust, of course, is not always as gross as in the Jay and Langer instances. The qualitative and quantitative differentials in the approaches that have been suggested provide a working base. The social worker should expect and accept some testing and questioning of himself and the agency from any person.

Regardless of the specific nature of trust and mistrust, the overall approach is the same: respect for self-esteem; alleviation of mistrust by honesty, consistency, and concern; as much provision and latitude for self-direction and self-autonomy as is consistent with a person's abilities and the agency's resources and procedures; working with an order of problem that is encompassable by the person. The goal is better self-management of life tasks, to whatever extent is realistically possible in the light of the individual's social and economic resources and personal capacities.

It would be an error to assume that social workers alone can eradicate the problems of mistrust. This requires changes in the broader economy and culture in which the disadvantaged find themselves. However, social workers can take an appropriate part in movement toward these changes out of their knowledge of common human needs. This is a major task for social workers but no more important than working directly with the individuals and families to develop basic trust. Without this personal ingredient, the provision of concrete social resources, no matter how rich, may not be usable by people who, for reasons of emotional deprivation that includes lack of ability to trust, are not truly accessible to constructive ways of meeting social needs.

14

SELF-ESTEEM

I GUESS I *wanted to show everybody and me, too, that I'm a man!* This was the explanation given the probation officer making the court-ordered presentence investigation of the "circumstances" that led to a twenty-one-year-old's actions during a flare-up in a racially tense neighborhood. Without any vocational skills, a drop-out from the tenth grade ("What good would it have been, man?"), he had held only occasional, always menial jobs ("Poor pay, man!"). Of his family—three younger siblings and his divorced mother whose income came from her work as a file clerk, with intermittent public assistance—he said only "With me gone, they'll have more bed room."

The real circumstances? Certainly one major circumstance in the complex that brought this young man to the point of pressing his finger on the trigger of a gun and killing a passing truck driver was the absence of an essential requisite for social functioning: self-esteem. A lack of self-esteem does not necessarily and inevitably lead to the extreme antisocial behavior illustrated above. It does, however, determine to a considerable degree the competence with which an individual performs in our society.

THE MEANING OF SELF-ESTEEM

Loss of Self-Esteem

Not all deficiencies in self-esteem result from basic lack of development; there also may be a temporary loss of self-esteem. A man who loses a job may need to ask for financial assistance; his sense of self-esteem may be regained when he finds a job and again becomes a breadwinner. Loss of self-esteem may be temporary when a mother's illness interferes with her capacity to care for her child and she has to relinquish the child-caring functions to a substitute for the duration of the illness.

Most people from time to time undergo some feeling of loss of self-esteem because they cannot comfortably or completely manage a particular situation, be it an incident at a social party, a disagreement on the job, or a child's defiance of the parent around a small or large issue. Many people who seek or are pushed to accept help with their problems sustain a loss of self-esteem. The concern of the social worker is with the many kinds of situations that range from the person who temporarily is overwhelmed by a minor or major crisis to which he responds by an immobilizing loss of self-esteem, to the person suffering from a basic lack of development of self-esteem so serious that it interferes with adequate personal and social functioning.

The Essential Components

It was pointed out previously that the capacity to trust is one basic developmental ingredient of self-esteem. A second ingredient is control. This element becomes of utmost importance when the child begins to explore his world on his own, that is, to walk and to talk. At the same time that this biological development is taking place, he usually is expected to begin to control his body elimination function. He is asked to learn to retain and to eliminate in an organized fashion. Thus commences a battle for autonomy in the child and between him and his parents. The child wants to do what he wants to do. If control by the mother over the child's exploration of his world and of his body functions is too rigid or too early to enable him to undertake control of himself gradually, he feels powerless; he will choose to give up making his efforts, or he will *pretend* that he is in control, that he needs no one to lean on, or he will fight control by stubbornness, willfulnesss, and anger. None of these choices permits him to develop an adequate sense of self-esteem: whatever control has been effected is not really *his* but has been externally imposed.

As Erik Erikson[1] puts it, from a sense of self-control without loss of self-esteem comes a lasting sense of autonomy and pride. The sense of self-control gained at the expense of self-esteem is accompanied by a lasting sense of self-doubt and shame. This persistent sense of shame may result in the kind of person who cannot and dares not achieve; it may be covered over by defiance which later leads to delinquency. The person who lacks self-esteem because he continually has doubts about himself may become an indecisive, constricted human being who is compulsive to the point where adequate functioning is not achieved.

Development of Self-Esteem

Learning and later work have much to do with the development of self-esteem in the early stage of life. The child who lacks self-esteem has so great a struggle over obeying or not obeying that it impairs his capacity to learn. He arouses in teachers feelings of anxiety, anger, helplessness. Learning involves a struggle between self-autonomy and acceptance of outside boundaries. Self-esteem means acceptance of himself and acceptance of others in terms of limits. The child who lacks self-esteem may submit and learn superficially, or he may fight against learning, or he may concentrate his learning in a constricted area and thereby deprive himself of a rich life experience.

The adult person who is beset by self-doubt, shame and, therefore, low self-esteem, may never realize his potentials in work. He may forever be quarreling with authority in a manner that causes him to lose job after job; or he may fail to advance vocationally because he is continually embroiled in fights against authority. The same holds true in love relationships. The central issue in many marital problems

[1] Erik H. Erikson, "Identity and the Life Cycle," *Psychological Issues* (New York: International Universities Press, 1959), p. 48.

becomes a question as to which marital partner is going to control the other, which one is going to win. Or there is the classic sado-masochistic marriage in which one partner submits to emotional beatings from the other, or one partner is continually degraded in order to bolster the shaky self-esteem of the other.

In addition to the tightrope of firmness and tolerance that parents need to use to develop self-esteem in this early period of life, social factors must be taken into account. Parents who are frustrated in their own lives, not only because of personal reasons but also because of restrictions that society places on them economically and socially, are not readily able to promote self-esteem in the child. If later, in school or at work, the person is regarded as socially inferior, this self-doubt and low self-esteem will be enhanced and he will either withdraw or act out in socially unacceptable ways.

Trust and self-control are two fundamental ingredients in the establishment of self-esteem. Often both are lacking or underdeveloped when people need help for one reason or another. The social worker's approach becomes an essential determinant as to whether the person needing help will be able to use the help productively or will refuse it or misuse it.

The Scott family was known in the community as a "no good" family. This appellation was applied not only to the Harold Scotts and their five children. It designated the entire Scott "clan," the extended family of sisters and brothers and their children as well as grandparents. The community viewed this clan as degenerate, defective, a continual expense because they contributed nothing in taxes; they just "took" because they were continually off and on public assistance. No one was sure who fathered which children in various of the family units; drinking, brawling, thieving were commonplace. The school isolated the children either by placing them in special classes or by expecting nothing from them in the usual classroom.

Although different family members expressed different points of view about life, the prevailing sentiment of the family was "what's the use, nothing good can happen to us." They attributed the success of others to "good luck and pull," never to work and effort. Any money they earned was best spent immediately, if not for necessities then for drink because otherwise someone would get the money away from them. The Scotts' low opinion of themselves was reflected by their unpainted, weed-grown, semi-rural community homes with sparse, inadequate, and dilapidated furnishings. The Scott men and some of the women worked at odd jobs that no one else in the community wanted; they had no wishes or thoughts about bettering themselves. The children dropped out of school as soon as possible and the community made no effort to alter this situation even though there was noncompliance with legal school attendance requirements.

What made the Scotts "no good"? All of the facts are not known but the piecing together of materials from social agencies and from family members discloses that the description was first applied to the present family's great-grandparents. They had migrated into the community from another part of the country in search of work. The first Negro family in the community, they were met with curiosity, reserve, and suspicion. At first the great-grandfather earned a living by odd jobs; he did relatively well and his family, although isolated, seemed content and thriving. When the great-grandmother became mentally ill, from unknown causes, the process of social breakdown began. The community offered neither resources for her care nor support to the family. The life of the family deteriorated economically and in other ways. They withdrew into deeper isolation, and the community drew away even further to avoid the children who had become troublesome. The children who reached adulthood found equally "shiftless" mates elsewhere and brought them into the community. The pattern of withdrawal, isolation, belligerent behavior, shiftlessness, and emotional and social anarchy became a fixed way of life. In the present generation the family units fought each other but also clung together. More Negro families had moved to the community but the Scotts were alienated from them also. The other Negro families held themselves aloof; to them the Scotts represented the worst of white people's ideas and fears about Negroes. The community saw the Scotts as being what they were because of inherited "bad blood," an irreversible condition.

THE MANAGEMENT
OF SELF-ESTEEM

Work with the Scott clan required a many-dimensional approach. Resources were available but had not been used by the Scott families. For example, many efforts had been made by the public assistance workers to find jobs for the men, but the men did not keep these. Some positive spark had to be found that could be fanned into a flame. The social worker selected the Harold Scotts as the target because at least he was the one who had fathered all the children in his family, and he seemed to have some, if uncertain, concern for them. He was asked if he would engage in rebuilding a shack used by his children for play so that they would have a place to which they could go instead of roaming the streets. If he would undertake to do this and find some others to help him, supplies would be provided. It is unlikely that Harold Scott would have agreed had his wife not pushed him: she was tired of being the one to face the barrage of community complaints about the children. She enlisted the help of another Scott wife who nagged her husband into helping Harold Scott. To the accompaniment of jeers and skepticism of other men in the clan, these two men began to work. The social worker aided with supplies and "know-how," but the two Scotts did the work. They needed constant encouragement to return to the task, but finally completed it. The pride of the two men and their wives in the finished product, which most of the Scott children began to use, was inordinate.

Thus were planted the seeds of self-esteem. These had to be nurtured in a variety of ways—not by piling on resources, but by opening channels for the family to trust and to use. The school was persuaded to test the children. Much to the community's surprise, the range of intelligence that existed in the rest of the community was found to exist also among the Scott children. This spurred the school to pay attention to the children, to begin a real process of education. A small play group was formed for the children of the mothers who worked. The immediate objective of this group was to relieve the mothers, but there also was intent to socialize the children. The mothers then were stimulated to meet with each other to discuss the children.

The two men who had worked on the shack wanted to maintain and embellish it. They drew several other men into projects connected with this goal. These projects required some money and, to procure it, the men gradually undertook to work more regularly. As they did, some of the drinking diminished; the belligerent behavior in the community became more controlled.

The first man in the Scott clan who had credit extended to him in the community was jubilant; this incontrovertible evidence that he was trustworthy and could trust served as a model for others. The public health nurse's entry onto the scene was geared to the beginning interest of the mother's group in the physical welfare of the children. Self-esteem rose as the families began to acquire some money and to fix up their own homes, and as the children showed some success in school. Over a span of seven years, major changes took place. Problems, of course, persisted, but on the whole the Scotts no longer were a burden to the community and had more than a foothold on the ladder of community respectability.

Evident from the Scott experience is the fact that personal break-down can come about because of social breakdown and, in turn, can contribute to further social breakdown to the point where both the participants as well as the community see the circular deterioration of behavior as irreversible. But the Scotts also demonstrated the fact that incompetent social behavior is reversible if resources are used in a manner that fosters and engages self-esteem. With the Scotts this required a carefully timed, coordinated utilization of an array of social resources. It also required involving people to work in behalf of themselves by providing them with opportunity to carry out a task of personal interest to them, but neither asking them to do too much for themselves before they were ready, nor doing the job for them. The task selected was not only of interest to them; they could realistically succeed with it. Moreover, it also was one that could lay the groundwork for social organization of more than one person or one family unit. In this instance, social organization was used to counter-act social breakdown, and social organization became the means for enhancing personal help.

Not all families need this approach, whether they be clans or single families, or nuclear families with extended families. Generally required, however, is the worker's awareness that all people in our society who need help suffer from some loss of self-esteem and have to be met by an empathetic approach. More specifically, those people who suffer either from temporary, though severe, loss of self-esteem or from a basic developmental problem in this regard, may present themselves as excessively belligerent, demanding, controlling, or overly compliant, or as completely indifferent. Inevitably such reactions provoke negative feelings in the worker and an inclination to respond in kind unless the worker bears in mind that such behavior by the family is a defensive facade to conceal hurt.

The worker also must keep in mind that self-esteem, like a flower, is easily crushed or damaged, and that the temptation to take over and handle a problem for the family who seem crushed and despairing should be avoided. Such an action would serve only to lower self-esteem. Some people merely need recognition of the blow to self-esteem to mobilize themselves. Others require the worker's patient awareness of the pain behind the behavior; verbalization may deepen the depression. Still others must have concrete resources to stimulate the latent wish for self-esteem. As the work with a person or family progresses, the worker should carefully time the phasing of tasks that are manageable and can aid in the nurture of the beginning self-esteem.

Implications of Culture

That there are specific cultural implications in self-esteem should be understood by the social worker. Loss of job does not carry the same implications for men in all cultural groups; for example, the type of job may be especially meaningful in some groups and not at all in others. A man in the middle years of his life who has lost an executive job may suffer a much greater blow to his self-esteem—and show this by depression or alcoholism—than the man who is accustomed to the vicissitudes of procuring and losing each one in a series of jobs requiring little skill. A family's specific behavior may reflect cultural differences about child rearing. For example, some cultures practice greater permissiveness than others with regard to control of body elimination, and the implications for loss of self-esteem may be vastly different in some than in others when a child wets after the age of three. It is well to remember that all people in relation to their group and individual identity need to "save face" in their own ways.

Implications of Age

Age and stage of development also carry particular implications for self-esteem. The adolescent is singularly vulnerable. One of the hallmarks of adolescents in their search for identity is an uncertain and shaky self-esteem. It is quite generally known how sensitive the adolescent is about presenting a "front." His state of biological, sexual, and social turmoil causes shifts in attitudes and feelings from day to day and from moment to moment. His uncertainty as to who he is makes him especially susceptible to any criticism related to loss of self-esteem. Consequently, the social worker's respect for the adolescent's feelings and thoughts, and for the defenses that guard his self-esteem, will enable the worker to proceed in such a way that the adolescent's self-esteem is not hurt and, therefore, he does not withdraw or act out as a way of bolstering his self-esteem.

Old age is another period of life when self-esteem is likely to be severely shaken. The losses that older people sustain in jobs, in retirement, in friends and relatives, make them feel useless and not needed. The loss of self-esteem frequently is related to depression in older people, to their need to dwell lingeringly over past events marking their successes, and to paranoid ideas about what others have done to them. The social worker's willingness to listen to stories of the past, to empathize with expressed and unexpressed feelings of loss, and to try to find ways to restore feelings of self-esteem, are significant factors in enabling older people to manage themselves better. Older people need to be needed, to feel useful if they are to maintain some of the sense of self-esteem requisite for preservation of their health and social functioning.

Implications for Identity

The development, nurturing, and preservation of appropriate self-esteem is a vital ingredient in the development of identity. Without it people cannot function adequately. Loss of self-esteem is a significant factor in personal and social breakdown. It can be developed, or its downward course reversed, if appropriate measures are undertaken through personal counseling and social organization. Assessment of the particular family's characteristics and circumstances offers the clues as to the appropriateness of the measures to be initiated, as well as their timing. Had the approach employed with the Scotts been available in his growing years to the family of the young man awaiting sentence for murder, would the tragedy have been averted that engulfed him and his family, and the victim and his family, and left an irreparable mark on the wider community?

15

IDENTITY

THE COHERENT sense of self, of one's total character or personality, is identity: what a person has been, what he is, and what he wants for himself. He is all of these things at all times in his life; and he is these things because the developmental period in his life coincided with certain points in our social and economic history. Today's adult who was a hungry child in the Oklahoma dust bowl during the Great Depression still carries with him memories of which he may be totally unaware: parental anguish as his parents sought to obtain food for survival, rootlessness as they moved across a suspicious "belt-tightened" nation angered by the drought and economic disaster that combined to spread distress. Such an adult may not know why he becomes frightened and anxious when he is hungry although he has plenty of money. But he may recall with bitterness the necessity to work in the fields beside his entire family so that together they might earn enough to eat, yet not enough so that he could go to school "like others" and prepare for a life of work that might have given him more than a weak toehold in a changing labor market with less and less need for men like him.

Today's adolescent whose father died in Korea bears the impact of an external conflict now pretty much a matter of history. And today's Negro child living in an area where there was a race riot will be accompanied throughout his life by feelings aroused in and around him by the struggles of today's crusade for civil rights.

THE MEANING OF IDENTITY

The person's self, then, is not only what he has been and is and will be as an individual in a family; it incorporates also what he has been and is and will be as a part of a social organization—the wider society. Thus his identity is bound up with group identity in the sense that his parents also were conditioned, as he is, by such factors as the standards of the class of which they were part and the characteristics and tradition of the culture from which they came. The social organization in which the person lives continues throughout life to impinge on the self.

The self, or identity, also can be viewed as the individual ways in which a person masters life experiences, that is, the use of the *ego* to synthesize experience. The ego may be defined as the organizing and governing mechanism in a person that controls the negotiations and conflicting ideas within himself and between him and his physical and social environment. The ego's functions are expressed by a person's perceptions, judgment, planning, and actions that are in accord with space-time (developmental tasks at different stages in life), and with the life plan (his wish and the social organization in which he lives).

In the words of Erik Erikson: "A conscious feeling of having a personal identity is based on two simultaneous observations; the immediate perception of one's self-sameness and continuity in time; and simultaneous perception of the fact that others recognize one's sameness and continuity."[1] Erikson further sees ego identity in its subjective aspect (that is, not conscious) as the awareness that there is a self-sameness and continuity to the ego's synthesizing methods to master life experience, and that these methods safeguard the same-

[1] Erik H. Erikson, "Identity and the Life Cycle," *Psychological Issues* (New York: International Universities Press, 1959).

ness and continuity of one's meaning for others. Thus the development of the self, or identity, is both conscious and unconscious; it contains the essential life forces (drives and instincts); the conscience and the ego, with the ego having a main function in synthesizing the life forces, and the conscience policing the internal needs in relation to the demands of outer reality. The development of the self, as was indicated previously, depends on a variety of factors that include, in addition to the individual and his family, the social organization in which he lives. The state of mind that a person *feels* and is *in* at any given time, is his sense of self at that time, but it always includes what he *was* and what *desires* he holds for the future. This is why so much emphasis is put in social work on understanding the "person-in-his-situation," that is, what he is now in relation to his current stress. It is why the worker will seek special data from the past that indicate how the person has handled stress or crises situations before and that help, therefore, to illuminate him as he is now and his characteristic ways of dealing with stress. It is why the worker will want to know the person's hopes and wishes for the future, for *hope* enables the person to struggle with his present dilemma. Without hope he can have no expectation that matters as they are will end or change, and without expectations of such kinds, he is bereft of incentive or motivation to act in a way that will produce change. The state of mind also depends on, and is related to, what is frustrated in the person by the social organization or what it offers him in the form of constructive and practical opportunities. This also is why social work is concerned with effecting those social changes that will influence the person's present and future positively.

The Import of Conflict

In the development of identity the state of mind always reflects a conflict in making choices: between what is right and good and what is wrong and bad; between the wish for personal gratification and the wish to please others; between the wish to live as one desires and acceding to the restrictions and demands of the social organization; between the wish to change the world in accordance with one's own heart's desire and the wish to conform to the world as it is. Such conflict—and the necessity to make choices to resolve it—is the essence of life. It promotes growth in identity; it enables people to master tasks unless personal problems in development or familial or social organization pressures so seriously intensify the conflict that growth becomes problematic and appropriate tasks cannot be mastered.

Because it is also natural to the human condition to wish to externalize conflict, that is, to be rid of the conflict by placing good and bad outside the person, individual identity becomes intertwined with group identity. Accordingly, a particular group by reason of race, religion, or class, becomes good or bad; certain occupations are good or bad; women and men are good or bad; particular appearance and dress are good or bad. The irrationality of this is not apparent to the individual. He is not necessarily aware that he has both a personal and a group identity. Many people are aware only that what is known and familiar is good, and what is different and alien is bad because the unknown threatens one's personal identity.

Correction of Distortion

This, too, has particular meaning for social work. In the broad sense, there is continual work to be done in social organization to enlarge the scope of group identity. The correction of misperceptions and distortions of personal identity enables the person to function better with himself and within the social organization in which he lives; the worker engaged in direct person-to-person preventive or rehabilitative work can aid in the development of personal identity by offering such corrections. People who are excluded, exploited, and suppressed come to believe that they are bad; they have no self-esteem, and they are distrustful of the world. Parental errors in child rearing may lead the child to believe he is bad or inadequate; he has great difficulty in meeting the demands of the world.

As part of *their* human condition, social workers possess biases that are inherent in their personal and group identity. To deny these, to shut them out of conscious awareness, leads to overreaction in work with people; the result is either under- or overidentification with the problems people present. Under- or overidentification on the part of the worker in the long run cannot be helpful; either stands in the way of aiding the person to examine his problem and to make choices and decisions freely and without the prejudiced influence of the worker.

Some consideration was given earlier to certain ingredients requisite for the formation of character: constitutional factors, heredity, physical conditions, trust, and self-esteem. There are, however, some other aspects of identity formation that warrant attention.

Each stage of development contains normal progressions that not only overlap in space and time but also contain the seeds for crisis; time and space (the world outside the individual's internal self) are on a continuum with flat, relatively quiescent periods punctuated by relatively high sharp points, the crises. Each stage of development, if normal, proceeds smoothly but has in it high points that also are normal. Each stage of development has in it conflicts that must be resolved; and, if the conflict is not to be overwhelming, there must be some defense against it.

The Use of Defenses

Such defenses, then, as denial, projection, repression, identification, and displacement also are part of identity; the use of them makes our character what it is. The fact that defenses exist is inescapable. How they are used in the service or disservice of mastering life experiences, and how they are used in a stress or crisis situation, is the concern of the social worker endeavoring to help people who are in trouble. Defenses need to be assessed in the light of whether they are appropriate to a given situation and whether the cost of using a particular defense is too high. For example, Timothy maintains that he is not in trouble because, after all, his school work is going well; at the same time, an uncontrollable facial tic is overt evidence that he is paying too high a price for the defensive denial or repression. On the other hand, the aged person may project his feeling of uselessness on the outside world. This is his way of defending himself against depression. Many people may not actually be defensive, but realistically angry at the world when the world refuses to permit them to express identity needs.

The worker needs to distinguish between a defense and a reality, and when the defense is appropriate or so inappropriate that it distorts the perception and thus interferes with social adjustment. Each person develops characterological defenses unique to him. Again, the fact that the defenses exist, or that one person uses more of one kind than another, is not significant unless the defenses interfere pervasively or seriously with mastery of required life tasks or unless they specifically interfere with performance of a current task.

The worker needs to know when to try to modify or alter a defense and when to leave it alone. This can be done only by testing how important the particular defense is to the person at a particular time and how flexible it is as the person begins to examine his problem. Mr. Jay, for example, was unable to tolerate any touching of his paranoid defense of believing all employers were against him until some growth in self-esteem took place.

Similarly, all people regress to earlier ways of doing things when they are under pressure or when a new task is imminent. Because his jealousy makes him feel insecure, it is common for a young child to begin soiling again when a sibling is born. If this behavior is temporary, it should not cause concern. It also is common for an adolescent to regress in cleanliness as he struggles with his unique maturational tasks. And in preparation for the serious task of marriage, lovers often will resort to playful behavior more characteristic of younger people. It is as though this play gives them a breathing spell in which to prepare for the new experience.

The Developmental Phases

Each stage in development of identity has its conflicts, its defenses, its regressions, its plateaus, and its crises. At each stage the healthy personality actively masters his environment, shows unity of personality, and perceives the world and himself correctly. Various tasks are in the ascendency at different times until the person as an adult is a whole person, a strong self. The proper rate of development in a proper sequence governs the development of identity. Each stage carries with it those aspects of ego functioning that are not defenses, but are inherited ego characteristics: motility, perception, memory, intelligence, and the ego's coordinating and integrating tendencies. Each stage also is influenced by outer realities, the culture or social organization in which the person lives. Thus it can be said that the self, the ego identity, develops along three main lines: inherited ego characteristics; influences of the instinctual drives; and influences of outer reality, which include the family and the outside world.

THE MANAGEMENT OF IDENTITY

The mastery of various tasks continues throughout life in the formation of identity. It is necessary for the child to master the task of sexual identity at each stage of development if he is to achieve adequate sexual functioning as an adult. The main emphasis in the early years of this task occurs in the fourth, fifth, and sixth years of life. During these years, if his parents provide the climate that facilitates his working on this task, he learns to identify with the parent of the same sex and to give up his infantile sexual interest in the parent of the opposite sex. The child then emerges clearly as a boy or girl; the identification is apparent to the child and to others. The child whose models are inadequate, however, may not achieve success in the task or he may only succeed partially. If, for example, his is a broken family in which the mother is the only constant figure in the home and there is no father model present—or he has a series of fathers—the child may develop an identity in which men are viewed as being irresponsible and uncaring and the women are the only carriers of love. It seems to him to be better, then, to be like a woman. This often is the basis for homosexual development. Or he may view the father's irresponsibility as freedom or license to behave as one wishes, and the mother as weak and to be despised. This reaction can be translated by the child into the uncontrolled aggression of the delinquent who believes he can do as he pleases. When to this is added, as is frequently the case, a social environment in which other children live in similar circumstances and in which additionally, poverty is a way of life, the child's distorted view of himself becomes reinforced. In other words, he becomes part of a group identity that influences personal identity in terms of masculinity and femininity. This is a basis for uncontrolled group violence in adolescent gangs.

The child who is exposed to inadequate models because parents are constantly at loggerheads or do not carry out the roles expected of them in our society—the strong masculine father and the loving, giving mother—gains a distorted view of himself. Depending on which parent he chose as his model for identification, he may see men as bullies, or as weak and ineffectual; he may see women only as loving, or he may see their love as weakness. He may be afraid to identify with his father and so identify with his mother as the sexual model; or he may reject his mother and equate sex and love with destructive aggression. If, in addition, outside forces reinforce these attitudes, as occurs when society denigrates the parents because of poverty or race or other such reasons, the problems of identity are compounded. Masculinity is then expressed in violence, personally and socially.

Children who do not master the tasks of identity and who suffer from mistrust and lack of self-control, or who achieve only partial mastery, are impaired in their capacity to work and, therefore, to learn. The social world is now larger: it includes the school and neighborhood. For the child troubled about his sexual and aggressive identifications, any creativity or capacity to learn may be taboo because in order to learn he must "look" with eyes psychologically open. He must be curious. Children exposed to serious conflict between the parents may have little energy for learning. Children who do not know their father or who are culturally disadvantaged tend to have little or no incentive to learn; they fail to develop curiosity and initiative. Children who retreat from conflict and fail to identify with either parent tend to become "as if" people: having no core personality of their own, they identify temporarily with any person or group; they will follow whoever seems strong at the moment. In a socially disorganized neighborhood or community it is these individuals as children and later as adults who are likely to get into trouble not as leaders, but as followers. The capacity to identify depends on achieving sufficient equilibrium between areas of conflict arising in the different phases of development; and failure of children to establish this balance results in personality defects or impairments. Thus the child who is afraid of the father may not be able to learn because he cannot risk the errors that almost inevitably are associated with trying. He cannot accept himself; he cannot accept others; he fights learning or withdraws from it. If unresolved conflicts from the earlier stages are added in this stage of development, the human being feels inferior. And he is inferior.

In Latency

Repetition and habit are powerful forces in life. The child who has not successfully mastered the early developmental phases encounters great difficulty in learning during the so-called latency years, the ages between six and twelve. If he feels inferior and the social organization reinforces this feeling, he has considerable trouble establishing habits for applying himself industriously to work; for him at this age, the work task is learning. Patterns of truancy, of school failure, of anger toward the outside world, of withdrawing into an internal world are established and may begin to take on rigidity.

In Adolescence

All the forces of identity become a battleground during adolescence. This is the time when every aspect of identity formation is heightened and acutely brought to the fore. The adolescent struggles with a multiplicity of identity aspects: sexual satisfaction; expression of hostility and aggression; the expression of love and securing of love; self-esteem and recognition; expressions of creativity. He is trying actively to establish his identity in terms of his place in society and the place of others in society; he is struggling to secure membership in a definite and stable human group; he is struggling with conflicts about what is morally right and wrong, about the "right" values and standards.

Ultimately, in order to know what to do with his life, he must examine alternatives and make choices, and then accept the consequences of his decisions in all of these areas. He plays different roles, trying each on for size as he makes different choices. His school performance may go up and down, or he may give school up altogether. His group identity with peers heavily influences his choices and behavior, as does the social organization in which he lives. A disorganized family life and a disorganized, deteriorated community will affect the range of his choices, his values, his moral perceptions of what is right or wrong. There was a time of almost unquestioning acceptance of the concept that everything goes back to the individual and family. This is now subject to considerable modification because of growing recognition of the concurrent impact of the outside world on identity formation, and that the time of adolescence is particularly vulnerable to external forces that shape character.

Identity conflicts are favorably resolved if the family, school, church, neighborhood, and community understand the conflicts and offer unobtrusive guidance and firmness and tolerance in reasonable doses. If a social worker is in the picture for any reason, this helping person needs to evaluate the nature of all the forces impinging on the adolescent and to plan a strategy that takes into consideration all of the forces converging on him—not only on the adolescent himself, but also his family, his school, his neighborhood, his groups. The social worker also has to offer unobtrusive guidance in helping the adolescent to examine the alternatives open to him and to make constructive decisions.

Some adolescents cannot be reached either individually or through the family because their own internal disorganization and that of the family is so great. Such adolescents tend to seek identity formation in the outside world. It then becomes necessary to try to reach them through their group identity, through the gangs to which they belong, and to try to find the groups and individuals in the community who can offer some better choices to these adolescents. Or it may be necessary to bring about massive modifications in the social organization—through economic changes, special education programs, group education for the adults in the community, and the like. There is no single correct or practical approach. The approach or approaches adopted must be based on an analysis of the constellation of forces that impinge on identity formation in a particular situation and may require a multidisciplined and multifaceted attack.

The older adolescent, the near-adult, struggles with further identity conflicts with respect to true self-autonomy: he desires it, and at the same time he fears it. He wishes to leave home to find forms of intimacy other than those available in his home. He struggles with questions about loving and working. Can he love, and is he lovable enough to commit himself to another? Can work become truly purposeful as a life choice? If the outcome of the conflict is favorable in the light of all the previously considered factors, he emerges as an adult who *can* work and love, who *can* identify with what is good in social organization and fight against what is not good, who *can* identify with a group or groups that give him a solid sense of belonging, who *can* respect the differences of others, and who *can* within the limits of his endowment and of the outside world behave spontaneously and creatively. He cannot function adequately or comfortably either personally or socially if his own personal identity conflicts are not resolved, if the social organization does not permit him to use himself constructively, or if he is in acute negative conflict with the outside world.

Throughout Life

The problems of identity are never fully and finally resolved. They must continue throughout life if growth is to continue and life tasks are to be mastered. Every person possesses many identities that cluster around the core personality. In marriage, for example, there are the roles or identities of husband, wife, breadwinner, housewife, parent of young children, parent of older children, middle-aged person struggling with separation from grown-up children, employer and employee, lover, friend, aged person. Every phase, each role and activity, carries identity conflicts that merge into each other even as they retain distinct characteristics.

The seeds for crises exist in every aspect and phase, depending on how vulnerable the person is because of his past life, his present circumstances, his view of the future, and the world around him. The occurrence of crises does not necessarily imply breakdown. A crisis may mobilize existing and latent ego strengths in the person or family, and it may mobilize a community to constructive action. The person who maintains some equilibrium, some balance in the struggle between conflict and adaptation, masters each phase of the identity struggle and moves on to further growth. The community that maintains some balance in its own identity conflicts between change and resistance to change provides a social organization that promotes good group identity for its citizens. In other words, a person must learn in the course of his life to commune properly with himself; he must learn to communicate with others in such a way that he hears, feels, and responds appropriately to others; the community must learn to communicate with him so that his identity is maintained and nurtured.

In a democratic, pluralistic society—where needs are diverse and choices, at least for the majority, are wide-ranging—openness of communication is essential for the establishment of personal and group identity. For identity can survive major conflicts, provided the supporting familial and societal framework of life is stable.

16

COMMUNICATION

LIFE HAS meaning and purpose only as people communicate with each other, no matter what the frequency, the form, and the manner of communication. Communication is the process by which the human being transmits his thoughts, ideas, wishes, feelings, beliefs, values, longings, and aspirations. And it is the process by which he learns another's thoughts, ideas, wishes, feelings, beliefs, values, longings, and aspirations.

Communication is much broader than speech or language, aural or verbal vocabulary. Speech (aural language) is a biological development that generally occurs in the second year of life. Language is the form that makes speech intelligible. Communication encompasses speech and language but is different because to communicate means to reach other people so that they can respond. Communication includes speech and language, but it does not necessarily require or depend on either. For example, people who are in the depths of psychological illness communicate something by the withdrawal itself as well as by the specific form the withdrawal takes. The mother learns to understand her child long before he speaks, although no one else can. The infant communicates his needs by crying, by smiling when he sees the mother, by the way in which he nestles or becomes rigid when he is picked up, by the cooing responses to the mother's voice.

THE MEANING OF COMMUNICATION

Its Form

Communication takes many forms. It is expressed through verbal language and sign language, through body posture movement, through facial expression; both verbal language and nonverbal convey feelings, attitudes, and a variety of shades of meaning. We communicate in order to make ourselves understood, to understand others, to have our needs met, and to meet the needs of others. In this sense healthy communication means emotional maturity. Communication that is lucid, direct, and sufficiently open to be readily and correctly understood by others, assumes the existence of a high degree of emotional maturity. Such expression means that the communicating individual has achieved basic trust in himself and others, has good control over his impulses, has a good sense of identity, and respects the identity of others. He can see himself as a worthwhile person even as he respects differences in others. In essence, communication is the dynamic by which the business of life is conducted through interaction with other people.

Its Cultural Characteristics

Communication possesses individual, family, and wider cultural characteristics. It is learned in the family culture and later is extended to include the outside world. The family culture not only is unique for each family. It is influenced by the larger culture in which the family exists, and by traditions accruing from the origins of the family. John Spiegel[1] describes the latter as "attitudes without

[1] John Spiegel, "The Resolution of Role Conflict within the Family," Harvard University (Mimeographed), 1957.

awareness." This is to say, each family has unique ways of communicating that derive from the nuclear family; these ways are built in from birth and are so completely taken for granted that they do not readily lend themselves to description by the individual. These built-in attitudes often contain the values, the standards, and the routine ways of behaving within the family that simply are accepted without the necessity for verbal communication in order to be understood. Family members who speak of being "tuned in" to each other often are referring to this kind of communication.

The stereotyping of individuals and families by their cultural origins is a popular pastime. The Italian family frequently is described as close and warm, its communication characterized by verbal volubility, use of meaningful facial expressions and lavish hand gestures. By contrast, the American Indian is stereotyped as communicating largely in nonverbal ways, with facial impassivity and expressive use of the body.

One of the prevailing stereotyping concepts today is that a "poverty of culture" deprives some families because of the unavailability of cultural resources, or disadvantages them through discrimination against them with regard to the accessibility and use of resources; families who are caught in the poverty of culture fail to develop necessary language communication. An example is the child who is bewildered when asked to go the the blackboard because "blackboard" is a word unknown to him. Although it is not possible to generalize that a poverty of culture is always related to a culture of poverty (manifest primarily as inadequate income), nevertheless there often is some association. Middle-class families do tend to have and to make use of resources that influence spoken and written language development. Therefore, at least at the level of verbal communication, they can function better in schools, jobs, and the community beyond the particular cultural enclave. In their study of the use of psychiatric facilities in New Haven, Connecticut, Hollingshead and Redlich[2] point out that people who do not have the ability to communicate in middle-class language do not fare well in psychiatric treatment because the psychiatrist is not attuned to paucity of verbal communication. Social workers have had much experience with clients who are initially difficult to reach because the differences in the worker's and the client's backgrounds have not given them either a common vocabulary or common life experiences, and so understanding by the one and trust by the other proceed slowly.

[2] August B. Hollingshead and Frederick C. Redlich, *Social Class and Mental Illness* (New York: Wiley, 1955).

Some people, regardless of economic class, do not possess language or verbal facility because they come from a family culture that does not prize this type of communication. Because the United States has a pluralistic culture, it is imperative in social work that cultural variations be understood if work with people is to be effective.

Essentially, modes of communication are learned in the family. Prevailing ways of expression include not only unique family culture features but also unique social and psychological aspects that influence communication development. Understanding of the psychological aspects of communication can be facilitated by some examination, albeit brief, about the way communication develops. Two primary ways will be delineated here: modes and levels.

Modes of Communication

Speech and written language are two main modes of communication. To acquire facility in speech and a range of language expression, the child needs stimulation in the home. Some families do not value intellectual pursuits *per se*. Language development in these families may be normal: the parents may promote verbalization as the main mode of communication and, from an early age, the children have the experience of hearing their parents talk to them and to each other. However, there is constriction in learning because the family places a greater premium on the child's conforming to school expectations than on the value of learning. These children do have a tendency to learn and to achieve good grades in order to please the parents. But there may be little excitement in the learning and little wish to acquire knowledge. The result is likely to be limited development of imagination, of creative fantasy, of capacity for abstract thought. In all probability, work patterns in later life will reflect the same constrictions even though there may be very good native endowment. In today's world, when work increasingly requires capacity for abstract thinking, lack of stimulation in early childhood may be a personal handicap and a loss to the economy of the nation.

This is an area of special concern for those in education and in social work. These are often stable families who are not known to social agencies. Although the primary task may be the school's, social work does have a function in involving these families in enrichment programs, perhaps through family life education groups, through work with parents in nursery school programs, or perhaps even earlier through the parents who bring their children to well-baby clinics. Similar consideration should be given to the stable families who are more oriented to action or motor communication, who highly prize physical development and skills, and who are relatively unconcerned about language development. Because these stable families represent personality development that is at a competent level of maturity, they may constitute a resource for a society that more and more needs people who are motivated to acquire knowledge for the increasingly complex tasks in today's world.

Some families lead lives socially and psychologically so chaotic that parents do not really relate to the children, do not stimulate them toward language communication, and the children, therefore, fail to learn proper communication. These parents rarely speak to their children; it is taken for granted that orders will be obeyed automatically, frequently on an adult basis. When such parents do speak, it is in a fashion generally characterized by screaming and cursing, and directions to children are indefinite or shouted. Punishment rarely is expressed verbally. The parental dearth of language skills many times is reflected in children who do not know the names of common or simple objects or colors, or who do not understand how to "tell" time.

Families like these often are described as "action oriented": their behavior is essentially impulsive and erratic, and comprises their essential mode of communication. Failure in language communication is manifest in severe delays in development. These children show excessive concreteness of thinking, very little capacity for abstract thought, and great difficulty in following directions when they are in a classroom. Learning impairment is serious to begin with and as the children show signs of failing they begin to shun learning. As time goes on and the failure to learn is compounded, it becomes a fixed way of life. They tend to be unable to contain motor behavior, their restlessness in class gets them into difficulties, and many drop out of school as soon as possible. Jobs for this group are scarce. These young people have no skills and they have limited potential for obtaining work that either requires or will develop abilities. And the probability is strong that the same pattern will be transmitted to the succeeding generation.

Social work, along with other disciplines, can offer much to interrupt this sorry chain. It is well established that the first year of a child's life is of utmost importance for the development of intelligence. This year, and probably the second also, is the crucial time for the development of the language function. The human speech sounds the baby hears act as environmental stimuli or "releases" for the human speech sounds he makes in response. Normally, of course, these stimuli surround the baby in his own home. But if he is in foster care of some kind—a foster family home or an institution—he may be less exposed to these releases. In most foster family homes speech sounds are readily available. The situation in most institutional settings, however, is quite different. Institutions with insufficient staff—adults who are available to talk to the babies— are especially lacking in this element so vital to the infant's development; the amount of talk tends to decrease in direct proportion to the amount of routine care provided.

The talk of mothers to their babies is an important contributor to the infants' development, and its early deprivation creates a lasting handicap not completely reversible by later learning. This has special significance for the social worker who, in relation to work with economically dependent families, is helping a mother to decide whether she should or should not work outside the home. What parent substitute will be available who will expose the children to speech sounds? How much energy and opportunity will the mother or the parent substitute have to talk with young children in the time beyond that absorbed by a job? Of course if the mother is not communicative in any event and seems unlikely to develop a communicating quality, the question may be a moot one. Nevertheless, it is a point often overlooked when very young children are in the home. It is a matter that also warrants some consideration when a mother, working or contemplating work outside the home, is arranging or rearranging supervision for her children during her absence; it is a matter that the social worker needs to take into account also when a placement plan is being developed.

Certainly, the provision of nursery schools for the child beyond infancy also is of the utmost importance, as are other special educational facilities for the early school years. Experience has shown, however, that many socially disorganized, language-poor families do not make use of nursery schools. The parents lack sufficient trust and the mothers are often too competitive with the children on a primitive, infantile level either to permit the children to be enrolled or, once enrolled, to permit them to attend school consistently. Direct work is needed with the parents to establish a foundation of some trust before the children can make effective use of nursery schools. The work with the parents should include active use of language by the worker. The worker should talk about everyday matters as well as about problems, doing this repetitively to encourage the use of vocabulary and to increase language facility. The worker also can be a liaison between the parents and nursery school to further language communication. It is later possible to establish parent groups led by nursery school teachers or social workers to further understanding of child-rearing practices as well as to relate the parents to a wider segment of the community and to the necessary language communication.

School social work is a necessity in the elementary and secondary schools and particularly for the noncommunicating type of family. The social worker has a variety of tasks to encompass: direct dealing with the parents to help them relate in proper ways to the school, aiding teachers to understand the child and family situation; interpretation to school boards of the needs of children and the resources required to meet the needs; community organization participation to effect necessary education changes in the light of child and family background and needs.

Levels of Communication

The majority of families in most communities as well as within cultural segments do possess adequate resources of speech and language communication, but oral or written communication is not the only mode for expression. Different forms of behavior are significant devices for communicating. As was stated previously, behavioral communication has cultural and social components; it also has significant psychological components: what is directly and easily observable, and what takes place at different levels of interaction.

All people communicate verbally and behaviorally on a number of levels: the manifest, the latent, and the unconscious. The manifest level refers to what is consciously said or expressed through a direct action of the body, a gesture, facial expression, silence, or other nonverbal means. The latent often is described as subconscious, or just below the level of consciousness. It adds the meaning and feeling to the manifest verbalization and behavior. The latent meaning and feeling may be in accord with the manifest content or they may be at serious variance, creating confusion or lack of understanding in the person who is asked to respond.

The unconscious level is not known to the communicating individual but heavily influences communication of manifest and latent content. The well-known slip of the tongue is the classic illustration of unconscious influence on meaning and verbalization. Unconscious communication is based on such personality development aspects as basic trust in the first year of life, self-control and self-autonomy in the second and third years, and the resolution of early sexual and other identity tasks in the fourth, fifth, and sixth years of life. The mastery of these tasks depends on the relationship or patterns of communication between parents and child, and parents to each other. The child who is adequately stimulated in a loving and trusting relationship with parents and at the same time exposed to reasonable permissions and reasonable frustrations and limits, develops patterns of communication in which unconscious expression and latent and manifest content are consonant with each other. All tie together in such a way that the child can communicate meaning and feeling directly and realistically, and can respond to others in a like fashion.

The child who has difficulty in any of these stages of development will have problems in communication. A failure in basic trust inhibits learning; it inhibits ability to understand, to make learning needs known, and to establish a give-and-take relationship. A failure in control patterns may constrict learning through inordinate compulsive attention to details, or through ritualistic features that bind imagination or creativeness. Or a high degree of intellectualization may evolve at the expense of feeling comprehension. Such phenomena may be accompanied by a stubborn need to do things in a certain way—to hold on to being "right"—that makes communication very difficult. A failure in identity tasks during the early school years frequently results in a failure to develop and exercise initiative. This is the stage of development in which children want to discover the world. They want to find out everything, to "see for themselves." But if finding out is taboo because they have not resolved the sexual and aggressive tasks, they also may not be able to learn to read because curiosity through seeing has been curtailed. Speech problems may occur, vocabulary building be diminished, and curiosity as a creative impulse be inhibited with resulting problems in communication.

Dr. Phyllis Greenacre[3] has pointed out that interference by psychological problems with speech development in the early years results in an undue reliance on the use of behavioral or motoric methods of communication. Speech in such instances does not become a channel for communication. It becomes a channel for attack, defense, projection, denial, and other mechanisms that may be destructive.

Failures to establish healthy, open communication within the family affect learning, work accomplishments, marriage, child rearing, and relationships with the outside world. The ideal communication pattern, as has already been indicated, is congruent in verbalization, meaning, and feeling on all levels. This is rarely achieved even in the most "normal" of families. It can become a serious problem when there is marked incongruence in communication or when congruence is destructive of personality development and family self-management.

[3] Phyllis Greenacre, *Trauma, Growth and Personality* (New York: Norton, 1952).

THE MANAGEMENT
OF COMMUNICATION

The several kinds of family constellations described in Chapter 4 utilize and respond to verbal and nonverbal modes and levels of communication somewhat differently.

The Adequate Family

It was stated previously that the adequate family generally has been able to function with reasonable competence in all aspects of life, but suddenly is overwhelmed by a crisis that leads to a need for some assistance in regaining the equilibrium that enables the family members again to exercise control over their life tasks. Communication may initially be difficult to establish if the family is immobilized by shock, for example, because of mourning. But with some support, communication becomes clear, direct, and oriented to the realistic demands of the situation. These families, once communication channels have been opened, are able to remobilize themselves and to resume mastery of their situation.

The intervention by the worker is at a minimal level, the family perceiving the worker to be a person whose objective is to assist them —a help their maturity permits them to utilize effectively. The worker's communication also can be direct, often providing knowledge about necessary social resources and supporting the family's ability to manage for itself. Some adequate families, for example, may experience temporary disorganization early in a mourning situation. Reactive depression is common; children may show unusual behavior that creates anxiety in the adult. Family treatment may be the device of choice to enable the whole family to mourn together, to permit expression by all of the members about their feelings of loss, anger, or depression. The worker is somewhat in the position of a moderator who encourages expression of feeling and helps the family to understand and handle unacceptable feelings and behavior.

The Chaotic Family

The chaotic family, as was illustrated earlier by the Burns family, often resorts to the use of speech and language to attack, provoke, deny, or project difficulties onto others. Messages may be congruent in the sense that meaning, feeling, and speech reflect the same thing, but the messages are irresponsible and dependent on the impulses of the moment so that there is neither an orderly nor a coherent process of communication. The main function of the social worker, after the development of some trust, is to endeavor to effect communication changes in the family through changes in role performance of the members. The worker, by active use of language, in effect offers a demonstration to the family members of how to talk to each other, and how to listen to what someone is saying. In working with the family as a group, the social worker explains and interprets to others the meaning of what is intended or actually being said by a family member. Such activity by the worker is indicated because this type of family is oriented to action and does not readily understand the connection between words and meanings and feelings.

In essence, the worker demonstrates that fighting and recrimination are not the only ways of communicating, and he teaches better ways. Discussion is focused on everyday matters in the present, for these families are not introspective; they live in the present, with few connections either to the past or to the future. The worker becomes a benign but firm parent figure to all, and repetitively shows that appropriate words can replace inappropriate words and behavior. The worker then moves to demonstrate how parents should behave as parents, what their responsibilities are, how children should behave in school and at home. Expectations regarding changes in communication have to be slowly geared to what the family can accomplish and to the realization that movement and changes are not only slow but frequently punctuated with regression.

In the case of the Burns family—where Mrs. Burns was in daily communication with her mother, who made decisions for Mr. and Mrs. Burns—the worker did not take over the grandmother's role, for this would have perpetuated a primary problem. And much of the work with this family was done in the home rather than in the social worker's office. For it was in the home that the parents would need to carry out their marital and parental functions, and the necessary learning could be expected to proceed more effectively in this setting. The worker discussed day-by-day events with the family, stimulated ideas among the family members about how to do things, encouraged any efforts that were made, discussed responsibilities for and with each member, praised evidences of responsibility. It was obvious that the family understood what was happening: six months later they invited the worker as the sole guest to a party to celebrate an achievement. Without Mrs. Burns' mother to help or advise, Mr. and Mrs. Burns had purchased new spreads and curtains for the bedroom. In a small way this was Independence Day.

The main feature of the help to the Burns family was work with all the family members together. Experience has shown that work with a chaotic family often is more effective when undertaken in this way. Because these families tend to be action-oriented rather than reflectively thoughtful, they are not inclined to understand communication that places a premium on the use of the intellect. When they can *see* what their behavior is like in an interactional process in the family, and when the worker can show them the nature and consequences of destructive behavior, they are much more likely to grasp the implications and to begin to work on the behavior. In many of these families (not the Burns, where the main problem had been one of infantilization of both parents by their families) whose emotional and social chaos is due to severe early deprivations, work with individual members may not be successful because they are too fearful of a one-to-one relationship they cannot trust; they want, yet fear, dependency gratification; the members may be too rivalrous with each other to permit any one person to be the focus of help. The fact that *all* are being asked to give something up in exchange for something different is a factor in mobilizing the family to work together on problems.

At the same time, the social worker needs to be alert to the possibility that in some of these families the stress is particularly felt by one member. The worker may need to provide supplementary nurturing of that member while working simultaneously with the family as a unit. Furthermore, in some situations the one member who is excessively preoccupied with himself and cannot in any way comprehend the needs of the others may require a period of attentive interest focused on him; that may of necessity be a forerunner to family treatment. This was the case with Mrs. Lee, who was so enraged over her husband's desertion that she could not respond in any way to the needs of her two small sons until her wounded self-esteem had been assuaged. Only then could she be interviewed with the children and helped to work on her serious emotional and physical neglect of them.

Clarification of role performance as expressed through better communication with an attending reduction in disorder, often is the goal that is achieved. To this end the worker uses himself as a model for clear and direct communication, a model that this type of family tends to incorporate as an ideal. For some families this is all that can be achieved—although it actually is a great deal. The achievement allows for order in the home and releases growth potential in the children. Some families can go beyond this and use help in establishing clearer identities for each family member. The Burns family needed knowledge about good child-rearing practices as well as support for their growth impulses. That they made excellent use of the work with them was evidenced by the fact that the children settled down and began to perform reasonably well in school; Mr. and Mrs. Burns matured in their relationship with her mother; and they behaved in appropriate ways as parents.

The Neurotic Family

A broad range of family communication patterns is manifest among the kinds of families generally designated as neurotic.[4] Out of the myriad neurotic communication patterns, only a few of the more common ones have been selected for presentation here. In the broadest sense, neurotic communication is characterized by misperception in communication: neurotic distortions or displacements and projections that becloud needs, wishes, and feelings. In some families, intellectualization is utilized as the chief mode of communication and produces discrepancy either between the use of the mind and the use of feelings in an effort to allay neurotic anxiety, or in ways that reflect fixed neurotic characterological attitudes. Communication often shows a basic capacity to perceive the needs of others as well as the reality of life situations, but there also is blunting of perception and distortion of reality in the particular areas that cause conflict and indicate the existence of neurotic problems. In contrast to the pervasive motor tendency in chaotic families, acting-out instead of talking and reflecting may be sporadic, occurring at particular points of stress or when the neurotic personality is under stress. Basic trust, self-autonomy, a sense of identity exist, although in variable degrees depending on the severity of the neurotic problem. In contrast with the character problems, the neurotic character or person with a clear neurosis recognizes that his irrational behavior or any symptoms he may feel are markedly different from "normal" modes of behavior. He may possess insight into the nature of his problem, but he is not necessarily able to use his knowledge of himself in his relationships and communication with others. He may have considerable verbal facility and use it appropriately or inappropriately as a defense against anxiety. Anxiety frequently is demonstrated in the use of speech as well as in body behavior. In painful areas the characteristic defense of repression interferes with clear and direct communication. Qualitative assessment of communication clues is required to understand the nature and depth of the neurotic difficulty. The range extends from the severe to the mild.

---

[4] For discussion of neurotic families, see Chapter 3.

Individuals and families vary greatly in the matter of neurotic be-havior. Some families manage a variety of life tasks very well until they encounter a maturational snag to which they are particularly vul-nerable either because the particular task rearouses old partially re-solved conflicts or because the task comes at a time when the family has other additional problems which make the task too difficult to encompass concurrently with confidence. Adolescence, for example, is a normal point of vulnerability for all families. Some families ex-hibit special communication vulnerability during this developmental phase because it rearouses old conflicts in the adolescent's parents. Some families are particularly vulnerable in this phase because the parents in the middle years are struggling with difficult vocational problems that in our society are not amenable to upward change; or they may be facing the problems of aging in their parents. The points of special vulnerability differ among families. Some become vulnerable because of their past life experience or on the arrival of first or later children, or when the children leave either for school or marriage, or when retirement is in the offing. Other families are vulnerable to anniversary memories such as when a family member reaches the age the parent was when he died. Some are particularly vulnerable to separations, whether these be occasioned because the husband travels in connection with his work or a child is preparing to enter kindergarten.

Decisions about treatment methodology, whether with family members together or with an individual, depend on the extent to which the neurotic communication reflects problems in the inter-personal functioning of the family, or the extent to which it reflects personal problems that may spill over in a family but which a family cannot work on until or unless individual difficulties are ameliorated or resolved.

Techniques for dealing with neurotic communication cover the whole range of available skills and will vary with the requirements of any given situation at any given time. They may include guidance or suggestion and advice, probably in small doses because these people cannot do what they so often know should be done. More common is the device of helping the person to think, to reflect on his prob-lems, to sort out reality from irrational feelings and thoughts and actions, to understand why he feels or behaves as he does, and oc-casionally to help him get to some of the roots of his problems. The same techniques are used as in family treatment but, in addition, work is directed toward intervening in confused family communica-tions by pointing out their existence and meanings and reasons for their existence, and by working with misconceptions and distortions that the family members may display toward each other. The worker serves as a person with whom the family or family members test and sort reality from irrational perceptions.

The Psychotic Family

A major feature of the nature of communication in the psychotic family has come to be called "double-bind communication." This refers to a pervasive use of messages within the family or to the sick member, messages that are on several levels at the same time and that are incongruent with each level. The Peters family referred to in Chapter 3 illustrates double-bind communication. Even as she protested that she wished Judy to be well again, the mother showed by the way she held Judy on her lap, caressed her in seductive, infantile ways, and cooed to her, that she wanted and needed Judy to be her sick baby. Mrs. Peters was not, of course, aware of this. Judy responded not to the verbal messages, but to the underlying real ones. If she grew up as one side of the mother wanted, would Judy lose the gratification gained from being the mother's baby? If she stayed a baby, could she really please the mother and the father who angrily pushed her to talk?

Individual work with Judy for a year and a half netted no results, nor did work with the parents. In a last effort, the worker decided to meet with the three members together. The child remained mute, but by her facial and body expressions, she communicated feelings of mixed despair and satisfaction when the parents battled and accused each other. The worker interpreted the child's communications to the parents and theirs to her. This helped the parents to begin to recognize how they were using the child and the necessity for focusing their attention on the marital conflict itself. The beginning break into the double-bind communication came three months later: as the family paused during a stroll to chat with a neighbor, Judy pulled them away, saying, "You're supposed to be with me today, not with someone else."

Individual work may be both necessary and effective in many instances where psychosis is present. There is, however, some evidence that while causal factors in schizophrenia range widely from organic to constitutional to unresolved symbiotic relationships between mother and child (as illustrated in the Peters case), this is in part an illness due to faulty communication in the family. It may well be that whether a patient is hospitalized or worked with in an outpatient clinic, or a voluntary or a public family agency, family treatment should be undertaken as the sole method, or in conjunction with help extended to the individual family member.

The Peters represented a somewhat extreme situation, but various kinds of social welfare agencies have many people described as "ambulatory schizophrenics." A major need among these is the establishment of communication with the sick individual and, increasingly, between him and his family. Families both fear and do not understand the offbeat or bizarre communication of the sick member; nor do they understand how they feed into this behavior. The worker's task is to help both the sick person and other family members to communicate, to the extent that they are able, their feelings of conflict, anger, fear. This can be accomplished by making them aware of inconsistencies and incongruences in communication as well as of double-bind messages and responses.

Hospitals are finding that discharges planned with patient and family together tend to be more effective and to last longer because conflicts can be verbalized and worked out more reasonably, fears reduced, and anxieties allayed about harming the patient or being harmed by him. When better communication between patient and family is established, the family can approach the patient as another family member rather than as a special outsider who must be approached via a path of eggshells. Experience has shown that when the social worker engages a patient and family together in a hospital setting, the patient tends to respond earlier and to require hospitalization for a shorter period.

It also has been demonstrated that work with the total family may be advisable in order to break into multiple double-bind communications and to help the family establish realistic ways of operating if it is a psychotic family, in which every member shows signs of the illness even though there is adaptive functioning in some areas of life. The George family had one hospitalized thirteen-year-old girl and three other children who, they feared, would tread a similar path. There were school complaints about daydreaming, underachievement, and difficult behavior. The Georges could be described as a psychotic family. Mr. George was preoccupied with his job as an executive and he performed well. At home he was completely withdrawn, spending his time with a stamp collection. Mrs. George's constant refrain was that she must be crazy because she had damaged her children and they hated her. Eleven-year-old Mike believed that every two years he would do something that would bring disaster to the family. Nine-year-old Mary began each interview with "My mother hates me. I'm no good, I'm lousy." Six-year-old Mark was withdrawn, with only one interest: How could he get to outer space? It took many months of working with this sick family unit, repeatedly using different illustrations they provided, to convey to them how each member accepted total responsibility for everything that went wrong, how every occurrence in life, big or small, was viewed as a major disaster, and how they fostered these ideas and feelings in each other. Some results gradually were observed. Mr. George began to come out of his shell; Mrs. George stopped saying she was crazy and began to behave as though she was not completely helpless; the school performance of the three children changed remarkably.

SPECIAL BARRIERS
TO COMMUNICATION

There are special barriers to open and adequate communication between family members and between the social worker and family members. Some of these barriers are erected by the fact of placement out of the home and the dynamics present in such situations. The separation of children from parents, with the associated injection of such nonfamily individuals as foster families or institutional personnel, creates conditions that vitally affect communication in a variety of contexts. These were discussed earlier with reference to placement tasks and to broken families. Likewise, the placement of adults—young, middle-aged, or elderly—poses characteristically difficult communication problems. These also were considered previously.

But barriers also may be present in other kinds of situations. The fact of difference in language orientation may impede communication, both because the family's first language may not be English and the social worker cannot speak the family's native tongue, or because —as is referred to elsewhere in this volume—the client's and the worker's life experiences and their framework of reference differ so that they can find common vocabulary and modes of expression only with difficulty. Both situations require patience and experimentation in order that the worker and family either may discover the words holding common meaning or find a reasonably competent interpreter whose presence does not inhibit the family's communication of intent and feeling. Social workers have to make a special effort to overcome such artificial hurdles which complicate the already complex problems in communication. Whether usual or special barriers to communication exist, it is the social worker's responsibility to know his own communication ways and his own communication biases if he is to understand and successfully work with communication problems in others.

PART FIVE

Helping Troubled Families

17

THE TASKS OF
THE SOCIAL WORKER

THE STORY is told of the woman in the middle
of the last century who felt that she had hit upon the solution to
the problem of alcoholism in the London slums. That the men drank,
she felt, was due neither to a love of drink nor to a love of convivi-
ality. The trouble lay with the women. The workingmen's wives were
notoriously poor cooks; the result was that their husbands' stomachs
were in deplorable condition so that they, poor fellows, could obtain temporary relief from the pangs of chronic indigestion only
through indulgence in alcohol. The wise woman from the upper
classes planned to organize cooking schools for these unfortunate
wives in order that they might learn to prepare meals that not only
would restore the gastric mucous membranes but also would so
delight the husbands that they would sit about the dinner table
until after the closing time of the pubs.

THE GOALS

This "lady bountiful," aware of a problem with implications of a broad nature for the community and at the same time laden with trouble for individual families, was undertaking to provide an answer to the problem—an answer consistent with the social and cultural attitudes of her time. For her, the world was divided into two easily identified groups. On the one hand were the fortunate ones who were called to their station by Providence; they knew exactly what should be done by them as well as by other people. On the other hand, there were the ignorant, deluded ones, also placed by an inscrutable Providence in their humble and unfortunate circumstances—perhaps in order that the chosen might exercise their wisdom upon them. This second group was pretty sure to do things wrong, and they necessarily had to depend on a kindly but firm control.

Today's social worker has only one thing in common with the lady bountiful of that former era: an interest in helping people to attain or maintain a good level of social functioning. The means used to achieve this over-all goal, the general circumstances that prevail, the resources available, and the motivations for helping—all of these differ so much from those of that earlier era that to refer to them in the same paragraph or context is inconcinnate! Different too is the knowledge about human behavior and how, in the light of this knowledge, people with problems can be helped so that the latter can be coped with in the fashion most effective for the troubled individual and acceptable to the community at large.

We know, for example, that without any doubt there are few things more difficult to achieve than to help other people and, at the same time, leave them free to manage their own affairs and live their own lives. We know that people cannot be coerced into changing their ways: persuasion and admonition may produce improvement, but such improvement is not likely to be lasting. To achieve long-time improvement necessitates entering into a relationship in which the person whose ways are troubling to him or to others will make some effort in his own behalf toward effecting the indicated change. In this connection we know also that people do only what they want to do, whether the wish lies close to or above the surface or is so far below that it is completely out of the person's consciousness.

And we know that whether or not the troubled person will use help—and with what success—depends on a variety of factors that differ with every individual and every family's circumstances: the marital and family equilibrium, the personality development of each family member, the environmental factors that impinge upon the family's life, their cultural and other values, and the interaction of all of these elements with and upon each other.

This kind of knowledge has given rise to recognition that there are different goals that today's society can hold with respect to different families and family members. One is to help the family members to make maximum use of their potentials for competent social functioning—to facilitate the self-realization or self-fulfillment consistent with personal, family, and societal goals and which precludes the likelihood that the individual will cope either inadequately or not at all with the crises and stresses inherent in life tasks. This is a preventive approach in the purest sense of the word, and it requires the availability of a multitude of community institutions and resources and a community climate of attitudes that singly and in combination permit the achievement of such self-realization: adequate schools, housing, vocational opportunities, goods, and services, that are equally available and readily accessible to all segments of the population so that the family's primary economic and socialization functions can be successfully fulfilled.

Another goal is to help those families already confronted with problems in personal and social functioning to master their troubles while these still are minor in form and effect—a goal attainable by a "nipping in the bud" process. The achievement of this goal likewise calls for the presence of a wide array of community resources as noted above, but with the addition of some others: social welfare programs, services, and agencies; health and mental health facilities; rehabilitation services of many kinds; agencies of various types concerned with meeting financial need, training and retraining and employment needs, counseling of many types—all with a primary focus on helping families and individuals to cope with a problem they already face, and to bring it under control so that it does not recur.

A third goal is to extend help to those families and individuals with complex or multiple problems, where breakdown in social functioning already is evident. The objective with some in this group may be treatment that enables them to master the problems as effectively as possible: they may be able to do so completely or partially, but their adjustments enable them to regain or maintain some competence in the conduct of the developmental tasks inherent in the several stages of the cycle of family life. The objective with others is to keep the total situation, already severely damaged, from deteriorating further. In effect, this calls for two aims. The immediate one is to maintain the status quo with the hope that a combination of circumstances and professional skills will make it possible to achieve the longer-range goal of improvement in the situation. If improvement cannot be expected to take place in the marital and family equilibrium, intervention should yield some positive results with respect to the children so that they, *as* children and later as adults, can function more adequately as heads of their own nuclear families and as members of the wider society.

MAJOR FUNCTIONS
OF SOCIAL WORKERS

There are many models for helping people who are or who may become troubled, some of these models calling for work in behalf of the community as a whole and the distressed person as part of the community, some calling for direct intervention through helping processes conducted directly with individuals and families or with individuals as part of other groups. Unlike the aforementioned lady bountiful, today's social workers function in three major respects in the field of social welfare.

Planning and Administration

The social worker may be a specialist in identifying existing social needs and anticipating those that are emerging in our dynamic society. In this aspect of social work, the social worker may design and develop social welfare programs on a national, regional, state, or local scale to meet or anticipate needs; he may be the primary initiator of programs and services or may work in conjunction with other specialists toward a common goal—specialists in housing, education, health, or law. He may function as an administrator of a particular program, directing its operation, innovating program ideas, and modifying others in the interests of constructive services to people.

He may, concurrently with or completely separate from his functions as an administrator, have responsibility for giving service to individuals and families directly if his agency is a small one; in a large agency he might also carry one or two cases at a time for direct service. By reason of his own direct service or his knowledge of the work of other staff members, he might note categories of problems and their impact on individual functioning, making these needs known to the agency board and using his understanding and skill thereby to shape and influence programs and services. As a uniquely informed citizen, the social worker can assist in formulating and influencing social policy and social welfare legislation. He may participate in studies that disclose need, then pave the way for indicated programs and services.

Thus, in a sense, every social welfare worker, because of his knowledge of human beings and their common needs, has an indirect and a direct responsibility for affecting public social policy, welfare issues, programs and services as well as a direct and indirect concern with individuals. The provision of programs and resources has to be geared to the common good; the common good in a democratic society, however, should always be based on the needs of the smallest but most potent unit in our culture: the family and its members.

Early Detection and Melioration

A second major function of social work is the early identification of situations with incipient or latent problems. In this connection case finding is becoming increasingly important and new programs and services have been emerging with a focus on the meeting of needs before serious problems develop. This function is being conducted in connection with homemaker services, family life education, nursery school and "Operation Headstart" programs, special projects of school social workers to alert teachers to needs of gifted, culturally disadvantaged children, and others. In the interests of detecting troubles in their earliest stages and preventing their maturation, social workers may function as organizers, interpreters, leaders of groups, case finders, trouble shooters (as in the case of detached street workers—"detached" from an office setting but not from the gangs with whom they endeavor to work), and so on. The social worker conducting these problem-detecting activities develops a variety of skills that are acquired from understanding human behavior. Each setting in which such activities are conducted requires special know-how for purposes of carrying out specific operations, but the basic knowledge and skills that are required are transferable among settings.

Treatment and Rehabilitation

The largest number of social welfare workers in public and voluntary agencies are engaged in work with individuals and families where breakdown has already occurred in the social functioning. Work with this group may be designated as "tertiary prevention," a term in wide use in the field of public health and which, when applied to social work, refers to direct intervention indicated in order to prevent further deterioration by removing obstacles to growth and to mastery of necessary life tasks. The success of such prevention often leads to improved, if not always completely competent, social functioning. The successful improvement or the successful maintenance of the status quo, if that is the immediate goal, is the consequence of social work treatment or rehabilitative activities carried out by the worker and the affected individual or family.

The problems that are the object of tertiary prevention are manifest, and they range in degree from mild to severe. The problems may either be caused by or contribute to the fact that the family does not have enough money to meet its basic needs. They may derive from social, emotional, or physical deprivation or from inadequate social and psychological family resources. They may reflect lack of knowledge about and lack of access to economic and social resources; they may be symptomatic of social deprivation arising from cultural differences; or they may be connected with physical problems of one or more family members that create social, economic, personal, and family problems.

Tertiary prevention is concerned with problems of interpersonal as well as intrapersonal conflict. The former include conflicts between the family and the outside world: difficulties in family life, such as marital discord, parent-child problems, family problems of aging, deviant behavior in a family member that creates problems for family management, difficulties of family members with school, work, and so on. The intrapersonal conflicts focus on problems that are within the person, though expressed in the family and in the outside world. These include difficulty in holding a job; deviant and perverse behavior that lands the person in trouble with legal institutions; personal unhappiness; dissatisfactions with oneself about masculinity and femininity; about fears related to achievement, and the like.

THE WORKER-CLIENT RELATIONSHIP

The Relationship Defined

The work with these problems is conducted by face-to-face contact with an individual, or with a nuclear family group (parents and their children), or with members of a nuclear family and members of a family of origin (family in which the parents grew up), or with groups of unrelated (peer groups) or related people (groups of marital pairs or of nuclear families). Substantial tertiary prevention activities are carried on in work with groups other than the family group, and the same knowledge about human behavior is required to engage constructively with nonfamily groups in the melioration of the problems of the members of the group. However, discussion in this chapter will in general be limited to the work directed toward treatment or rehabilitation of family members, individually or as part of the family group, and carried on by the worker who—in contrast to group or community organization workers—generally is designated as a caseworker.[1]

The social caseworker may carry total or major responsibility for the treatment or rehabilitation of the individual or family, or may collaborate with or have the assistance of another profession such as psychiatry, public health nursing, or psychology. The social worker may call on consultation services available within or outside the agency to deepen understanding or to provide him with a specific area of help in reference to a particular aspect of behavior or treatment or rehabilitation; or the worker may call upon community resources within the agency itself to provide the family directly with special kinds of services such as nutrition counseling, homemaker service, medical care, tutorial help, and legal aid.

Regardless of the resources that the social worker may utilize in the client's behalf—whether it be direct service, collaborative activity, or consultation—the social worker's relationship with the family and its members generally is a primary one. It may be as the helping person extending initial and continuing counseling service, or as the connector between the family and other community or agency resources required to meet the social needs of the family—as the catalyst making it possible for the troubled family to make effective use of a particular resource in the total effort directed toward improving social functioning.

Several basic features differentiate social casework with troubled families and family members from other kinds of social work and from other disciplines that deal with problems that are similar or, in some respects, identical. One is that social casework addresses itself

---

[1] Casework relationship is used here generically to describe the one-to-one or one-to-one family group, regardless of the setting (public or voluntary, family or children's services, medical or psychiatric or corrections facility, schools) and regardless of the position, title, or classification (social worker, public welfare or child welfare worker, probation or parole officer, counselor, school social worker, psychiatric social worker).

to the individual situation, whether it involves one person or a family unit. Another is that the social caseworker characteristically seeks to help people who are in trouble because they cannot manage difficulties of everyday living, or are in a state of crisis as individuals or as a family; their problems may be incipient or fully developed.

The social welfare worker with primary job responsibility as a caseworker works with individuals and families through the medium of a "casework relationship." It is in this relationship that troubled people and the worker together look at the existing problems and act toward developing or freeing the potential or existing resources or strengths within the person and family that may be instrumental in dealing with the problems. Both worker and clients bring something to the relationship between them which is oriented to a problem, a task too difficult for the person or family group to manage without professional help. The relationship is time-oriented in frequency and duration of interviews, and the span of time required to deal with the problem. It is disciplined in the sense that the worker uses his knowledge, values, feelings, and attitudes in the interests of the client and not in his own interests. It is empathic in the sense that the caseworker feels *with* the client rather than *for* him; at the same time the worker maintains enough distance from the client and his problems to assure that his perspective is retained so that the client is enabled to use his own capacity for self-help to the fullest. It is based on knowledge of human development and behavior, the common and special needs of people, and knowledge about resources appropriate to these needs. It is based on theories of methodology regarding how to mobilize and free energy in people so that they can deal with their problems more effectively. The worker-client relationship, then, is an integral part of methodology in work with individuals and families.

Factors Influencing Worker-Client Relationships

The ingredients in the worker-client relationship are necessarily different with different clients. Some people use the relationship reasonably and realistically: they are relatively adequate individuals who use the worker as a helping person who can assist them in solving their problems. Some people who have problems in one area of life but manage well in others may present different reactions in the course of their counseling relationship. They will view the worker objectively and neutrally in some respects, but with regard to the troubled area may develop special relationship features that appear as resistance to facing or working on the special problem.

Anger, projection, depressive reactions, sudden irrational demands on or feelings about the worker may emerge. These need to be recognized by the worker for what they are. Such irrational feelings are always a reaction to the situation, but for a variety of reasons they are discharged on the worker. Sometimes this is because the person does not dare discharge them directly on the family members; sometimes it is because this is the way the person behaves with all people; sometimes it is because the worker is an accepting target. In any event, they are brought from the person's past life situation and create problems because they are emotional and out of control. For example, Mrs. Elder lashed out at the probation officer who had reminded Mrs. Elder that she had agreed to try to control her demands that sixteen-year-old Tom ask his remarried father for items like a bicycle or an increased allowance. Mrs. Elder had acknowledged that the boy's disturbing behavior generally occurred after one of these nagging episodes and seemed connected with his fear of rebuff by the father (which the boy at no time tested) and his guilt and anxiety at "failing" his mother. Nevertheless, she continued to egg the boy on. "You just side with that man who left his own wife and child to fend for themselves!"

In other instances, an emotionally very deprived person may look to the caseworker to fulfill the role of a parent figure, a parent who is different from his own, a parent who is kind and giving but who helps to control and manage the destructive effects of the individual's anger about deprivation. When they establish some trust in the worker, such people tend to place on him the full force of their frustrations, anger, expectation of rejection, and their irrational demands. If the worker gives too much emotionally (for example, is *very* sympathetic and undemanding), these people become frightened of the closeness and either run away from the relationship or try to provoke the worker into rejecting them. If the worker is not giving enough, they may increase unreasonable demands or leave the interview situation because they are so hungry for affection. When they develop trust they may accept the worker as an ideal and endeavor to please by doing what they sense the worker wants them to do and in the way the worker seems to want them to do it.

Particular personality features also condition the special nature of the worker-client relationship. People who use intellectualization as a defense need to maintain distance in the relationship and resist encroachment by the worker into the emotional sphere. The person who has problems about authority and self-control will resist the worker who tries to get him to relax rigid controls or to exert more self-control. He will see the worker as too soft or too punitive. He tends to fight and argue in the relationship. The compliant person will too readily yield and may follow suggestions uncritically or respond to what he thinks the worker wants without really investing himself in thinking about and working on the problem.

The individual's stage of development also influences the nature of the relationship. The latency-age child, for example, may not readily establish a relationship with the social worker because this youngster still is largely dependent on his parents, sees them as the primary source of his gratifications and as the source for meeting his needs and helping him with his problems. The young and middle adolescent generally does not yet trust adults and does not readily admit to the need for help. He is wary of establishing a relationship. With the adolescent the worker must be scrupulously honest about what he represents, what he can and cannot do if he is to establish a working relationship. The adolescent who moves on to adulthood without having developed the requisite amount of trust not infrequently becomes delinquent; to establish a meaningful relationship with such an untrusting person usually is a hard and long task. He has had few experiences in which another person did something for and with him out of affection and kindness. To such a delinquent person the social worker represents the very social structure—probation, parole, training school, prison—that the community has devised to deal with just such untrusting ones who act out against society. The aged person often sees the younger worker as a child or an adult son or daughter at the same time that he feels helpless because he has a problem he cannot manage. In establishing a relationship with such a person, the worker needs to recognize both the sense of helplessness and the uneasiness about asking help of someone younger.

Cultural features play a part in the worker-client relationship. Not all cultures are attuned to the confiding of problems to "strangers," or to considering a relationship apart from the family or the immediate cultural group. Distance in the relationship will be based on these factors and not necessarily on personality features. Sometimes a worker who is part of the culture is better accepted because the troubled person feels he will be understood by this worker and is more comfortable in the relationship. Sometimes, however, this is a negative factor. The client may think that the worker of the same cultural orientation looks down on him or is ashamed of him because he is in trouble, that the worker is "harder" on him because he has tarnished the culture's image by his inadequacy or his trouble. The worker's self-awareness of how he feels about cultural differences and similarities is an important factor in establishing a relationship. Culturally deprived people, especially when this is connected with economic deprivation, are distrustful about establishing a relationship. They have learned not to trust offers of help. Some of the same considerations are relevant with regard to ethnic factors.

For the worker, the relationship is conditioned by his own life style, that is, his own personality and his characteristic ways of relating to people. It also is conditioned by an understanding of the client's needs, resources, and goals—and by the self-confidence, gained from this understanding, that he is a person who can be helpful to the troubled family or family member. By virtue of his role as a social worker and the stressful circumstances that bring the troubled individual to a social welfare agency, the worker is in a unique position of influence. Regardless of the experience and training he brings to his tasks—both of which, of course, add important dimensions to the quality of the relationship and its over-all effectiveness—and regardless, too, of how strong a person he is in his own right, the social worker is perceived by the client as healthy, strong, and influential, and therefore can be *expected* to be helpful. Inevitably, in relation to the factors that create the situation leading to the worker-client relationship, the worker is the stronger person and, accordingly, can be relied upon for help.

For the client, the relationship is conditioned by his greater or lesser awareness that to be a client means he must want something: something to be done *by* him or *for* him. This does not imply that it is necessary for a client to know at the outset specifically *what* he wants or how to go about realizing his wishes. Many people are not "motivated" to use help; nor do they know what is entailed in a worker-client relationship. They can, however, learn to want to do something or to have something done for them. They can learn to understand the helpful nature of the worker-client relationship if the worker is patient, persistent, and can find a point of common interest through which to bring to the client some hope that his problems might be mitigated or ameliorated. This was illustrated in the Scott case (Chapter 14). It also is demonstrated over and over in families dependent upon public assistance. Once steps have been taken by the worker to meet the family's objective needs (food, medical care, and so on) and the family begins to feel trust in the worker and in the agency, the family member's sense of self-esteem begins to rise (boosted by the feeling of being worthy of being trusted and, therefore, trusting) and attention can be directed toward work on problems that both result from and contribute to the family's financial dependence. They can look at the meaning of behavior that prevents a member from holding a job or pushes a father to desert. Increased understanding is generally accompanied by enhanced motivation—*knowing* what the problem is generally brings some hope that it can be handled. Enhanced motivations strengthen the client's interest in and use of the relationship with the worker.

The client's way of letting the worker know what he wants and his consequent use of the relationship is conditioned by the client's life style (personal, family, cultural), his current needs, and his unique way of participating, which likewise is related to his personality and his culture. The meshing of these attributes by the worker and the client is the essence of any social worker-client relationship.

The goals of social work also influence the functions and responsibilities of the worker. As was stated earlier, the broad goal is to help the individual or the individual family make the best resolution possible of everyday problems, taking into account the client's personal comfort and effectiveness and, at the same time, his influence on other people in his immediate circle. The scope of this goal includes dealing with problems that are either in an incipient or an overt state, the affected individuals experiencing difficulties in relation to themselves, in relation to others in the family, and in relation to the larger social world. Specifically, the goals are to strengthen latent or existing resources in the individual or family through the freeing and using of emotional and physical energy; to increase capacity and ability to deal with problems; and to expand resources in the environment with the aim of accelerating the desired increase in capacity and ability to deal with problems of everyday living and with problems of relationships with others in the environment.

But the achievement of these goals with any degree of success in given situations must be predicated upon some determination of what the client's own goals are—long-range or immediate goals, realistic or irrational goals—and to what extent the practical goals of the client are congruent with those of social work and of the wider community comprising the client and the social work profession and the social welfare agency. The successful outcome of the worker-client relationship is dependent also on what expectation, if any, and by what means, if any, the client foresees the attainment of his own goals—or, if such attainment is a dream that cannot possibly materialize, how flexible the client is with regard to substituting a more realistic and socially acceptable goal that *is* possible of achievement. This assessment of the individual's or family's goals must be geared to the available internal and external resources that can be mobilized in behalf of enabling the client to master the troubling problems.

RESOURCES

The potential and actual resources that the worker may employ for aiding a family or individual to cope effectively with problems assume many forms and have varying values. These have to be identified as early as possible in the worker-client relationship and continually reappraised during ongoing social work activities, taking into account that time and other circumstances inevitably produce some changes, cast certain qualities in new lights, and stimulate some resources and behaviors to new levels of effectiveness. It is in the personal and environmental strengths, no matter how faint they may appear, that hope lies for improvement in a particular situation; recognition and assessment only of weaknesses impede progress toward better social functioning.

What, then, are the resources to which the social worker directs his attention? Of primary importance are those within the individual or within the family group. These include proper trust in the self and others;[2] self-control; self-esteem;[3] identity;[4] ability to think, reflect, and perceive; ability to communicate;[5] ideals (aspirations and life goals); values; physical well-being; nurturing (affection, love, capacity to love, capacity to work);[6] social adaptation and internal resources that support the family's daily operation and that offer a climate in which individual and family can develop and meet life tasks. The client-worker relationship requires that the worker have an appreciation of the relative strength and weakness of these individual resources on a case-by-case basis if the individuals or families are to be helped to exploit their strengths for the purpose of increasing their ability to cope with crises and stress.

Environmental factors that may represent resources external to the family personalities and act as support for the client's inner resources also have an important role in helping troubled families. Progress in working with a family often is dependent on the worker's knowledge of environmental factors that undermine or reinforce the family's own resources and the appropriate use of environmental resources for supportive purposes. How this operates can be seen in the case of Mr. Fowler. After two years of unemployment and rebuff

[2] See Chapter 13.
[3] See Chapter 14.
[4] See Chapter 15.
[5] See Chapter 16.
[6] See Part Three.

after rebuff, he no longer bothered to follow up job referrals. What was the use? His lack of education, his lack of training or skill, his "ugly black face"—these factors were against him in any competition for the few unskilled jobs that appeared from time to time. His deepening depression, his refusal to leave the house, his growing reticence caused mounting anxiety in his wife. She, too, was beginning to display serious evidence of depression, neglecting the children and herself, withdrawing from her husband and relatives. The availability of a new resource, "preconditioning" under a Community Work and Training Program, failed to interest Mr. Fowler. The worker recognized that Mr. Fowler's self-esteem had been so battered that another rebuff would be intolerable. While it was unrealistic to believe that he would not be accepted for this training, it was clear that he could not trust himself or the worker enough to take the risk. Mr. Fowler reluctantly gave in to the public assistance worker's persistence and agreed to report to the assignment when the worker offered to drive him to the project office and wait while the placement interview was conducted. When he was assigned to a parkway repair project, Mr. Fowler was sure that he would find the job gone when he reported to the foreman. The worker took Mr. Fowler to his assignment the first morning, heard the foreman (an employee of the Parks Department supervising this training activity) tell him what was expected of him. Two days later the foreman urged Mr. Fowler to "slow down" for he would exhaust himself before the morning had passed, that the pace he had set for himself was physically impossible to maintain. Mr. Fowler replied, the foreman reported to the worker, "This is the first chance I've had to be a man for more than two years; I can't afford to spoil it!" He was hired as an employee of the Parks Department.

In some instances the major effort is directed toward enabling people to use available social or community resources in proper ways. Some people lack knowledge about resources; some are too fearful to use them; others cannot until some groundwork has been laid for their use. It is not uncommon, for example, to find that culturally deprived people not only do not know about resources, but their sense of alienation from the larger community deters them from using those of which they are aware. Until some trust is established, they do not begin to overcome their fear of the resources and their anticipation of rejection. The worker needs to pave the way both with these disadvantaged people and the resource. Some people are so emotionally deprived that they fail to use social resources or, when they do, antagonize the resource with what appear to be excessive demands. These individuals, too, anticipate rejection, provoke it, then retreat in anger and frustration. Experience has demonstrated that, until they feel accepted, understood, and valued by a worker, they either do not utilize available social services appropriately or at all, or they antagonize employers, landlords, or school personnel.

Accordingly, it is impossible to divorce the effective use of social resources from knowledge about and work with people. Knowledge and skill are equally required whether the work is focused on attainment of environmental modification or on adjustment of psychological problems. Both for "nipping in the bud" situations and tertiary prevention, the distinguishing characteristics of the knowledge used by social workers include understanding the person in his unique situation, with the emphasis on what is needed to help him with his problem. The main features are knowledge about human growth, development, and behavior; knowledge about interferences (biological, social, psychological, and cultural) that delay or distort growth; knowledge about tasks of working and loving that must be encompassed at all stages of life (trust, control, identity, sexualization, learning, working, marriage, child rearing, old age), and interferences with these tasks that stem from inner difficulties or external social difficulties; knowledge about social resources; knowledge about methods (interviewing techniques, the worker-client relationship, use of social resources) that will free and mobilize energy so that troubled people can manage their life tasks with whatever degree of success is permitted by the range of personality and environmental resources available to them.

THE SPECIFICS OF THE TASKS

The relationship between a particular worker and a particular client may begin at the point of application to the agency for help, and appropriate tasks may be initiated at that time.[7] The relationship may begin when an application or an intake worker transfers the case to a worker who either will engage in the exploratory process or continue with certain tasks in accordance with a treatment or rehabilitation plan initiated at an earlier stage of the client's contact with the agency. In an agency that observes geographic boundaries or other administrative factors that may cause transfer of a family's case from one worker to another, the tasks may be those started by the previous worker or they may be new ones, depending on the circumstances that precede or follow the transfer.

[7] See Chapter 18.

Independent of the point at which the relationship between a worker and a family is established, the worker needs to know—from his own assessment or that which preceded the transfer of responsibility for the family's case to him—about the family's own hopes, goals, needs, strengths. If he is the intake worker, his inquiry about the applicant's own goals and ideas for attaining them is an important step not only in the direction of enhancing the applicant's self-esteem in an essential way and not only because the answers offer the worker vital clues about the personality and potentials of the applicant; such an inquiry also often serves to start the thinking of the person who has been immobilized by his trouble or has not known how to proceed to deal with it. It goes without saying, of course, that raising the questions requires some exercise of caution: if the inquiry is couched in accusatory language or carries tones that are other than warm but matter-of-fact, the applicant may feel threatened and distrusted, thus adding complexity to the worker's task.

The worker who will be dealing with the client likewise needs to know the client's own hopes and goals. If these are not already contained in the agency's record, such an inquiry can be used by the worker as the device not only for learning things of importance to him but also for conveying to the client his interest in what the client has to say on this score so that they can work together toward a common, realistic, and acceptable goal. In any event, the tasks of the worker are specifically related to the needs and desires within a particular situation, and these needs and desires may alter with new or changing circumstances.

The Range of Tasks

The tasks of the social worker are undertaken in accordance with what needs to be done in behalf of the client or what enables the client to act in his own behalf. They are geared to what the client cannot do for himself because he lacks the resources, because he is experiencing personal difficulties, or because difficulties in his life situation stand in his way. The tasks are aimed primarily at helping the family or family members to cope with immediate trouble and to help in such a way that the family members achieve the maximum growth possible for them and learn how they can cope adequately with other problems that arise in the various stages of the family life cycle. Of course, there are certain situations that have limited, if any, potential for growth. These require chiefly what might be designated as a holding operation. In these, as for example instances of severe mental impairment, help may necessarily be restricted to providing for maintenance or custodial needs or a relationship for the purpose of protecting the individual family members or the community. The focus often is on enabling the relatives to cope with the problem caused by the impairment and, in general, to prevent the problem from becoming worse.

The range of tasks is broad and varied. A particular family situation may call for the performance of only one; it may require a number of tasks that are carried on either simultaneously or consecutively.

Communicating Knowledge

An important task of the social worker in most settings is conveying knowledge about social resources and how to use them, and about ways of doing things. For example, information may be given about health, child rearing, job management, or household management, because the client either may not possess the necessary information or because he entertains misperceptions that interfere with appropriate functioning or management. Advice and suggestion may be used directly or they may be offered indirectly by pointing out alternatives that expand the client's horizons yet leave him free to make choices.

Modeling and Mediating

The worker may communicate sound methods for achieving control over troubling situations by logical discussion of alternatives or by active demonstration or example. Mr. Jay learned about better ways of feeding his children through discussion of recipes and foods. The worker also showed him an easier and better way of cooking cereal by directing Mr. Jay while he was preparing breakfast. Mrs. Little was provided with a homemaker so that she might learn how to manage her large household of children. Worker, homemaker, and Mrs. Little met regularly to discuss specific tasks. When a worker showed Mrs. Page that she could control her four-year-old by picking him up and quieting him in the midst of a temper tantrum, Mrs. Page for the first time had a sense of hope that, with the worker's help, she could become able to handle the developmental tasks over a period of time.

It is not uncommon that the worker serves as a model without being aware of this contribution. Mrs. Jackson, who had been a recipient of public assistance for four years, was assigned to a work program under the community action provisions of the Economic Opportunity Act. She had never before been employed and faced this new phase of her life with considerable apprehension. Several months prior to the assignment, Mrs. Jackson's social worker had left the agency; Mrs. Jackson was not ready to trust the new "young thing." In an interview with the latter two months after Mrs. Jackson had begun to work, she confided in the "young thing" that her greatest fear had been not around how her children would handle her absence during the day, nor about how she would be met by the disadvantaged families she was to visit in the course of her work; she had worried about how to dress for the job. She had thought back over the several years of contact with different social workers, recalled the simplicity of the clothes they wore and the manner in which each greeted her when she opened her door to them; she adopted similar dress and similar modes of greeting.

The social worker often has the task of acting as an advocate for the client and as a liaison between the client, the neighborhood, and the wider community. Many troubled people cannot speak up in their own behalf either because they lack knowledge or because they are fearful. Mrs. Peters' complaints to the landlord about her rat-infested apartment were unavailing. Because Mrs. Peters could not do it, the worker undertook to handle the complaint with city authorities. The Klein family had succeeded in antagonizing school personnel so that they refused to talk with the parents about Sam's behavior that was so disturbing in the school setting. The worker served in a liaison capacity, interpreting the points of view of parents and school to each other so that Sam no longer had the sanction of his parents to behave as he wished, and the school stopped sending him home almost daily to an infuriated mother and father.

Mrs. Williams frequently was involved in violent quarrels with her husband over the poor quality of meat she bought for immoderately high prices. The worker learned that the neighborhood market where Mrs. Williams traded because she could defer payment when she was short of funds, and to which she now was considerably in debt, exploited her timidity and dependence, giving her poor cuts which she did not know how to refuse. The worker accompanied Mrs. Williams to the market, observed a transaction and intervened (as agreed in advance with Mrs. Williams). Gaining courage from this modeling experience, Mrs. Williams was able to react appropriately to the butcher's behavior—and to carry the new pattern into other areas of daily living.

By his clear, direct communication, the worker may show a client or family how misunderstanding may occur because of distortions in communication; how illogical or irrational ideas, feelings, and behavior interfere with a realistic perception of a problem; how to learn better ways of communicating within the family and with the outside world. The worker may help people to observe their own and others' behavior or to reflect on their ways of communicating. He may help the client to sort out realistic aspects of his problem. The worker may aid the client to perceive and think about connections between his feelings and his behavior, and connections between his feelings and behavior toward others within the family and in the outside world. And the worker may help the client to perceive connections between his present feelings and behavior and his past life experiences. In these ways the worker contributes to the development and increase in the person's perception and better use of himself.

The Barbers' primary mode of communication was through fighting among the family members and outside the family. One of the main areas of work with them was to reduce the fighting. The first step was to show them how it interfered with the good things they wanted for the family and for each family member. The next step was to help them see how failure to be direct and clear in communication led to misunderstandings, hurt feelings, and incorrect perceptions of reality. The third step was to substitute other action for the fighting by persuading them to pause and reflect before battling. They learned that not everything is black and white and that, for example, when Mrs. Barber told Jane, aged nine, not to damage a piece of furniture it did not necessarily mean that Mrs. Barber hated her. It was a simple, realistic request. Mrs. Barber learned that if she asked Jane not to do such a thing in a calm, decisive way instead of screaming and telling Jane that she was no good, the results would be better and calmer.

Mr. Jay gradually learned that if he were nudged in a store, this could be, and often was, accidental, that it did not mean the other person was deliberately trying to provoke him. As a consequence of repeated efforts of this kind on the part of the worker, Mr. Jay learned to manage himself better in a job. His increased understanding of himself and of his reality led to greater self-control.

Assigning Priorities

To give selective attention to current needs, range of vulnerabilities, and potential capacities of the person, generally requires that the worker assign priorities to the scope and timing of urgent tasks. There is increasing emphasis on understanding and working with the "here and now," the current problem of most concern to the person or the family. The worker attempts to identify which is most troubling among a multitude of problems that may be presented and which can be undertaken that are most likely to be responsive to efforts toward improvement. In effect, the worker first focuses on those problems or parts of problems that the client has tolerance for working on, that will offer the least threat to his or his family's equilibrium, and that will bring the earliest possible success or positive gratification. The selection, of course, differs with different people. Out of a welter of problems, the least threatening and most gratifying may run the gamut of family and social problems: housing, a child's enuresis, damaged self-esteem, or others. It has already been stated that all people are vulnerable to stress and problems in different ways, their vulnerabilities depending not only on past life experience but also on the current life situation. Also, people may be more or less vulnerable at different stages in life or to different kinds of problems. The assignment of a priority to a particular task should be related to these differences in vulnerability.

Mrs. Madden approached the juvenile probation agency five times in six years with a problem about her daughter who was obese, a poor learner, had no friends, and was "bound to get into trouble." In between she sought help from two child guidance clinics and three private psychiatrists. She could not use consistent help until the girl was fifteen, partly because Mrs. Madden had more empathy for an adolescent than a younger child and partly because her own feeling of low self-esteem diminished as she became successful in a job during the year preceding her last approach to the agency. She was now less vulnerable and she was more able to tolerate examination of the problem. This case illustrates the need to examine each situation in its current aspects and not to take for granted that previous failures to use help always mean that people will continue to be unable to use it.

Mr. Lynn could not face the fact of retirement from work. Suddenly his world had fallen apart. He had no use for "Golden Age" groups or recreation of any kind. Not for him were leisure-time activities. His health was good but he was immobilized by not working. Despite Mr. Lynn's urgency about work, the first matter to be approached was his feeling of worthlessness. The worker encouraged him to talk about his work and his past successes. She supported his feeling that he had been and was still a useful member of society. In this way, his feelings of depression lifted and he became less immobilized. To the worker's surprise, he managed to find part-time work that was gratifying and important to him. As he asked that old age assistance (supplementing social security benefits) be discontinued, he commented that the worker "showed me I'm still pretty good and I'm proving it!"

Both cases illustrate the importance of focus on the current distress with the selective use of past or historical data only as these are needed to illuminate the present problem. The trend in social work is to obtain historical material when it seems pertinent to current issues and not as a routine assembling of information that *might* hold answers to a problem. As work with a family proceeds, more data may be needed from some past phase of a person's life to shed light on a current matter; or such data may emerge spontaneously. A brief picture of employment history may suffice in one situation; in another there may be need for information about work attitudes in the man's family of origin. A full developmental history may be needed on a child who has never achieved in school; but search for a specific trauma or cause of onset may be more to the point with another child who has a sudden change in school performance.

Emphasis on the "here and now" also means early emphasis on understanding people's potentials for better self-management. What has the person tried? How has he met crises before and what does he want to do now? What steps does he think might be taken in this regard? This necessitates the client and worker exploring together what is needed now and what can be done about this need, in this way meshing the client's objectives and the worker's goals. Work proceeds from one objective to another in a sequential series of intermediate objectives rather than focusing on a far-off goal that is too remote to interest the client or which he may have neither the tolerance nor the capacity to pursue. The "here and now" emphasis also places time in a different relation in work with people.

Because the working goal is to free potential capacity and energy to work out one's own problems, there is no premium on long- or short-term work. As soon as an objective is reached and the client knows how to use his own energy to work on the problem, the social worker's task may be at an end. The client may return for help with the same problem or with a new one, but the intent for client and worker in the use of time is not necessarily to resolve a specific problem definitively but to set in motion ways of dealing with problems. For some people this is enough: it is as much as they can use at a given time. Other people may have a wish, a need, and the capacity to examine more than the one problem, and they will wish to do so. There appears to be no correlation between length of service and success in resolution of problems. Occasional interviews or telephone calls may serve one client well; others need long-term continuing and frequent contacts. Some people want and need help only in a crisis; others want and can use help in examining themselves and their problems at some length and in some depth. Each of these patterns has value.

Important tasks of the worker may involve instilling of values, aspirations, and goals appropriate for the client and consonant with the community's standards, and developing means for achieving such goals. In this area the worker helps to broaden the horizons of people's wants and needs by making known to them what can be achieved realistically. A school dropout may be encouraged to resume an educational activity through a work-study program; a family's work and educational goals may be stretched and developed; vocational retraining, better housing, inculcation of better social values—all have their place in work with people. His understanding of people's changing needs and desires enables the worker to take part in the development of needed new services in the agency and in the community. Such understanding facilitates his utilization of new models of approach to problem detection and melioration and his undertaking of newly emerging or refined methods for working with people—as, for example, family and group treatment.

The Commonality of Tasks

The tasks are common to all social workers whose methodology centers on the use of the client-worker relationship, and to various degrees they are performed in all settings: voluntary and public, family or children's agencies, medical or psychiatric facilities. One or another task may be highlighted more in one type of agency than another. Depending on the objectives and programs of a given social agency, special knowledge and skill may be necessary for the completion of different tasks. A worker in an agency whose primary function is the provision of financial assistance needs special knowledge and skill in understanding the meanings of money to different people, and the impact of these meanings upon an individual's behavior—including his management of money. A worker in a psychiatric hospital needs special knowledge about and skill in working with mentally ill people. The worker in a child-placing agency needs to know how to select and work with foster parents, how to match placement resource and child; a worker in a family agency that does not place children needs special knowledge and competence in family treatment.

In any setting, the worker needs to understand people and their needs, to identify those areas that are in his field of competence and those that require specialized attention, and to enlist the help of another specialist when this will serve the interests of the family and the community. In all settings, however, a beginning has to be made with the troubled person needing help. In general, too, recognition has to be accorded the fact that ours is a family-centered society. The following two chapters, therefore, single out the helping aspects of the application and intake process and the family approach to treatment and rehabilitation. Because of the frequency with which social workers in a variety of settings need to utilize knowledge about environmental (as contrasted to personal) resources and the techniques of money counseling, these two subjects are presented in separate chapters.

18

APPLICATION
AND INTAKE

IN MANY WAYS, the most crucial time for a troubled person is the point at which he asks for help. The request may be made of a friend, a relative, a social worker, a psychiatrist, a minister, or some other professional or nonprofessional source of help. It may be a request for advice: how to obtain vocational retraining; how to persuade a husband to return to the home or to protect the family against his return; how to convince sixteen-year-old Jimmy that he should give up his "bad companions" and return to school or how to make it clear to fifteen-year-old Essie that "she's heading for trouble." The request may be for tangible assistance in some form: a loan until payday, public assistance, treatment of a medical condition, child care. Or the request may be an announcement: "I just can't go on!" or "I'm at the end of my rope!" or "My husband (or wife, or child, or mother-in-law) goes out of his way to provoke me!" Irrespective of its superficial or pervasive nature, however, the request for help made especially to a social agency or to a member of any of the "helping" professions inevitably is an admission, no matter how it is masked, of inability to manage one's own life, or a particular aspect of it, at a particular point in time.

The request to a social welfare agency for help may be voluntary in the sense that the person to some extent has accepted the fact that he has a troubling problem and that he cannot cope with it alone; the request may be involuntary in the sense that it is presented not on his own initiative but because of community pressure—neighbors, the police, the school.

Whether the application for help is voluntary or involuntary, it is attended by a variety of feelings. The person may be angry, submissive, frightened, hopeful, belligerent, demanding, resentful. He may display a wide spectrum of emotions that shift and alter during the course of the interview, their form and intensity mirroring the ambivalence about asking for help that is always present to a greater or lesser degree. For example, one common aspect of ambivalence is shame, which may be manifested by an inability to provide necessary facts, or by antagonistic, provocative behavior, or by denial that there is a problem ("that teacher is just talking through his hat"). Ambivalence may be reflected in other ways. Thus, cultural life styles, as in the Mexican family in need of financial assistance, may compel the husband to push his wife to apply: Seeking aid is not consistent with masculinity and threatens his status as the family head, but supplication is appropriate to and consistent with a woman's role. Not only is the gamut of human feelings and behavior seen at intake; characteristically these emotions appear in heightened form.

The request for help is crucial also for the worker. How he feels, behaves, and responds to the verbal and the nonverbal behavior of the applicant may influence not only the course of the initial interview but also the immediate outcome of the request for help as well as how productive or unproductive the direction chosen for the giving of service is likely to be. The worker's exposure in this first meeting to the ambivalence and to the covert feelings of the applicant, particularly those that appear hostile, may bring to the surface the worker's own negative biases and attitudes, or his own frustrations or uneasiness engendered by knowledge that the agency's resources or limitations may not be adequate to solving the applicant's problems. As a consequence of his *feeling*, rather than *thinking*, the worker may be unable to "hear" the applicant out; he may use a routine, stereotyped approach to all people; he may reply to the request for help—or even anticipate the request itself—by setting forth immediately restrictions that may limit the agency's services to the applicant; or he may respond with impatience to demands. The worker's ambivalence or his failure to perceive *this* applicant and *his* trouble as different from other troubled persons may enhance the shame and anger the petitioner feels at having made the request; his frustration may lead him to retaliate with further hostility. If the request, however, is met with understanding and some warm interest in being of help to him, the applicant's guilt and shame will be somewhat allayed or channeled into mobilizing his abilities to take some action about his troubling situation. The worker generally will be much more able to establish a better working relationship with the client if the worker remains alert to the fact that it is not the *worker* against whom the barrage of negative feeling is directed, but the situation, and sometimes the client himself.

The level, mode, and quality of communication between the applicant and the social worker in the initial interview in large measure sets the tone of the relationship that can be expected during the entire intake process, with its focus on appraising the nature and extent of the person's needs and how (and where) they can best be met. It also sets the pattern for the quality and success of the continuing relationship of the applicant and the agency in the effort to find and implement appropriate and acceptable solutions to the family's problems.

DEFINITIONS

The term "intake" has two meanings. One is literally a "taking in" of applications and requests. In this context, intake serves as an index to the ebb and flow of social problems and needs in the community and to the extent to which the community's arrangements, tax-supported and voluntary, have resources and sanctions for meeting these needs. An economic recession or a curtailment of jobs in a certain sector of the total economy or of a community may bring an influx of applicants to a public assistance agency because the unemployment insurance benefits could not span the continued unemployment situation. An increased number of applications may be received by various agencies for help to families of deserting fathers, or families with parent-child relationship problems of specific types, or needy families moving from certain rural areas to urban centers, or abandoned children. The data gathered in intake about the concerns and needs that people from all walks of life bring to a social agency have special import for planning through central planning bodies, public and private, for the meeting of social needs by governmental and voluntary agency services.

The other meaning of "intake" is as a process for understanding the request the troubled person brings to the agency and for taking steps appropriate to helping him to deal with the problems for which he seeks help. This process is one in which the skill of the worker is utilized to understand the manifest as well as the underlying meaning of the request; to understand what problem or problems the request represents; to engage the person in talking about and looking at his problem; and to begin to consider with him the kind of help required, where it can be secured, and how to go about obtaining it. This is done by establishing a channel of communication between the worker and the applicant by sympathetic listening; by eliciting pertinent data through pertinent, nonthreatening questions; often by putting the silent uncomfortable person more at ease through asking him for factual "face sheet" data that he usually can readily provide; by encouraging the person to explain the request and his feelings about it; by asking him what solutions he may have in mind or what attempts he has made to handle the problem. Whatever the specifics used toward this end, the primary intent is to make it as easy as possible for the person to explain what the problem is that troubles him, and why it does. This process requires the worker to have a body of knowledge about his community and his agency, and about how human behavior more or less subtly indicates personal or social difficulty.

The achievement of a common understanding between the person and worker may result in service that is completed then and there; it may eventuate either in supplying the applicant with information about another resource in the community that may better serve him, or in referring him to such a resource. The decision they reach may be that service would be continued in this agency. Such continuation of service within the agency may be for the purpose of continuing to explore more specifically the question as to the kind of help needed or, if that already is clear, to embark on a program of joint effort to ameliorate or resolve the problem.

The two meanings of "intake" are not mutually exclusive. Each represents a facet of a community's responsibility and desire to serve people in trouble, and the two facets are interdependent. The range and the availability of social resources are the consequence of whatever and in what fashion social planning takes place in a community; such social planning—its excessiveness or limitation or even its nonexistence—seriously affects the operation and, hence, the intake philosophy, policies, and methods in a social welfare agency.

People go to social agencies with a wide variety of requests, problems, and needs. Some people select a particular agency because they know what that agency's function is—marriage counseling, public assistance, child placement. Some are referred for specific services because the referring source—a school, a minister, another agency—has knowledge about the agency's special functions, such as mental health agencies or old age assistance. Many go not knowing much about the agency and unclear about the help they seek or whether or not this agency is the appropriate one: the behavior of a child may lead the parent to ask that the child be "treated" when the trouble is really in the parents' marital discord; or a deserted mother may ask a voluntary family agency for some financial assistance until she can find a job, yet she is not really an employable person and should be applying instead for Aid to Families with Dependent Children. How the potential client is met initially and how the worker responds to his request depend not only on how the worker relates to the applicant as one human being with another, but also on his feelings about helping people and his point of view about the agency he represents; the agency's philosophy of intake is also a determinant.

Some agencies are concerned chiefly with the presenting request (the request as it is made, as "presented" by the client) and decide on the basis of the applicant's description of his problem whether or not he can be served by the agency within its defined function. To some agencies the important factor is not just the specific surface problem seen in the request, but also its attendant ramifications; on this basis they decide whether the problem is within their scope of service. Differing philosophies will affect the worker's approach to the troubled person. It is the authors' point of view, to which this chapter is addressed, that the focus of the intake process should be on understanding what the person is requesting; what it is that is troubling him—or the community; and how he hopes, with the agency's help, to help himself. This means that the initial approach must consider the request as it is made, or as it is identified by the applicant, whether or not he has "landed" in the right agency. The overt request may be a cover for the problem that is *really* the troubling one and that the applicant, for any of many reasons, cannot describe—it is too disquieting, he senses but cannot concretize or pinpoint it, he lacks the experience or the capacity. Thus, the aforementioned parent may ask a family agency for help with the "troublesome" child because it is too disturbing to disclose at once what the mother finds difficult to admit to herself; namely, the problem is in the marriage that is threatened with momentary collapse. A specific decision about service should be made, therefore, not just on the request for "treating" a child; nor should it be based on an immediate conclusion that the agency is or is not the suitable one or that the child should be referred at once to a children's clinic. The decision should derive from understanding about what the request *means*, and what the person wants to try to do about it. This implies the likelihood that the intake process may include more than a single interview, that in fact it will span the exploratory process from the point at which the request is received to the point when a decision is made that nothing further can be done by this agency, or a plan is initiated for continuing help in the agency undertaking the intake steps, or for referral elsewhere.

The importance of the social worker's alertness to the meaning of the request is not limited to certain kinds of agencies. Voluntary or public, family counseling or corrections, a medical or a school setting—in any of these the problem presented to the intake worker may be clearly what the applicant says it is, or it may be that what he *says* is his problem may be only a mechanism that is acceptable to him for making the approach to an agency with his request for help.

In many public and voluntary agencies, there is a division of responsibility between the application interview and the continuing intake exploration (with the worker who has the latter task either going on to work with the family in accordance with whatever plan is formulated, or transferring the case to a third person for extending the service). In such situations, the application interview generally is primarily for the purpose of obtaining specific data necessary for determining eligibility for the agency's services. This procedure may stem from administrative determinations *per se*, or it may relate to the fact that the form and content of the application may be legally determined, as in public assistance, or probation and other court-connected agencies. It is necessary that the application worker and the intake worker view the application as the first step of a continuous process and not as an isolated task. Otherwise, the first interview may be routine and leave the client with a sense of not being "heard" or understood. The continuing worker, if he thinks of the application interview as a routine for screening gross eligibility, may pay scant attention to the data already obtained and request that some or all of it be repeated, to the discomfort and, often, exasperation of the applicant.

The skill with which the administrative reasons for obtaining information in a separate application interview are integrated with the helping function of the worker varies considerably among workers.

The ability to effect such integration may be influenced by the agency climate: its procedural requirements, the amount of time that the worker may have to conduct each interview, and the agency policy regarding the use of seasoned or new workers in this assignment. For example, a public assistance agency with a heavy intake and limited choice among personnel who can be available to handle an influx of applicant requests may require answers to specific questions in order to initiate the giving of assistance—or, in the instance of continuing aid already initiated, specific answers may be required at legally-prescribed intervals to assure that there is no interruption in the provision of economic assistance to those who continue to be eligible. This kind of intake, or application, situation is illustrated by Mrs. Marshall.

Mrs. Marshall, a sprightly little Negro woman of fifty-five years, complained to the county official that she had been denied assistance for herself and three grandchildren for whom she had responsibility. The father of the children was dead, the mother confined to a mental hospital. Mrs. Marshall had tried to support the three children through her work as a domestic but was unable both to care for the children and to work full time. The official's inquiry revealed the fact that Mrs. Marshall had indeed been denied even emergency assistance pending the completion of an application for Aid to Families with Dependent Children. The reason for the denial was reported to be her possession of more than $3,000 in cash. Asked whether she had told the worker that she had $3,000 in cash, Mrs. Marshall replied "Certainly." Asked whether she had had this money, she said "Certainly not!" She explained that the public assistance interviewer had confronted her with a long list of questions printed on a form from which she had no time even to look up at Mrs. Marshall; she simply asked each one, barely waiting for an answer to the preceding question. When the worker asked if Mrs. Marshall had a savings account in any institution, Mrs. Marshall said no. When Mrs. Marshall was asked whether she had any savings on the outside, Mrs. Marshall said no. Then the worker said "How much money have you in the bank?" At this point Mrs. Marshall angrily replied "$3,000," then said to the official: "You know, if you ask a silly question you can only get a silly answer."

The routinized method of obtaining information defeats the purpose of the interview. If routine questions must be asked, the worker should explain the reason to the client so that the client can both become a party to the completion of the requirements affecting him and have an opportunity to be seen and heard as a *person* with a problem that has brought him to the agency to seek help. The routines

in interviewing may serve as a crutch to the worker who is not comfortable about facing problems that are distressing or facing the unhappiness of the person who is seeking help, whatever its form. The
worker must approach each interview and each person to be interviewed with awareness of the fact that *this* person being interviewed
is different in important ways from *all other* persons, that his problem is different from the problems of all other persons, and that,
while the problems may contain common elements, the approach to
the understanding of the problem and its ramifications must be
uniquely developed for this particular individual.

PURPOSES AND USES

The same general approach is indicated whether the applicant's first opportunity to identify what he views as the problem for
which he is asking help is with an application interviewer or with the
worker who will also undertake whatever exploratory aspects are indicated—including those that may be legal requirements such as
determination of place of residence, or financial resources (including
those that adult children may provide), or establishment of paternity,
or ability of a father to contribute to support, and so on. The nature
of the "presenting" problem (that is, presented by the client) may
indicate the advisability of giving some immediate help—economic
assistance or a medical referral, for example—without engaging in
extensive exploration first. Certainly, not all problems are hidden
ones and the reality basis of many is immediately observable. Clues
to the possibility that the presenting problem differs in some form
or degree from the real problems may be noted not only in *what* is
said, but *how* it is said—or not verbalized but communicated in nonverbal ways.

Mr. Keller complained that the state employment service personnel made no effort to help him locate work during the time he and
his family managed on unemployment insurance benefits. ("What
are those employment people doing to earn their money?") Now the
family had exhausted its financial resources and were in immediate
need until Mr. Keller could find and be paid on a job. ("A fellow can
only depend on himself!")

The worker had observed Mr. Keller's swaggering entrance into
the office, but also the drooped shoulders and the tenseness in the
face before Mr. Keller had realized the worker was looking at him.
Only as Mr. Keller was encouraged to describe what he thought were

obstacles to his employment did he disclose that his wife had had what he thought was "a nervous breakdown"; she had been talking about suicide, and for weeks he had been fearful about leaving her alone to do more than hurry to meet the "signing up" requirements for unemployment insurance and dash home again. He had not brought this problem anywhere before. ("A man should take care of his own.") Both financial assistance and help in understanding and using a mental health resource were given at once; the matter of Mr. Keller's re-entry into the labor force could be explored only after these other immediate pressures were eased—or shared.

Mr. Link asked the voluntary agency for money to enable him to visit his sick mother in another city. He was visibly upset, found it difficult to discuss the facts about his need for money, and wanted an immediate definite answer when he learned that the agency had funds that could be used for such a purpose. The worker explained that she needed to know why he wanted emergency help before she could know how to help him. His tension continued as he gradually revealed that he had come to this city as a student on a minimal scholarship basis, had selected this place because it was far from home. He felt he had been too "babied" by his mother. His father had telephoned the previous evening. The mother might need an operation, and Mr. Link wanted to be near her.

Mr. Link had come with a specific request for a concrete service. The worker accepted the request and began to explore it and the conditions that led Mr. Link to making it. One might wonder about the validity of this kind of exploration had the agency not had funds available to meet such a request. Does the worker have a "right" to involve the person, asking questions when he knows that his agency cannot directly meet the request? The same question might be raised about requests for money for basic needs in a public agency, or for homemaker service, camps, nursing homes, and so on—in short about any request for a service that may not be available in the agency the person has elected to consult. The same question is relevant to requests of other kinds, such as help with problems of marital discord, child placement, vocational or school difficulties, parent and child relationships. Is such exploration an invasion of the person's privacy when the requested service is itself not available in the agency? Is it better just to hear the request and send the applicant elsewhere? These questions apply to all agencies, public and voluntary, family, children's, psychiatric, medical, and others.

Implicit in the philosophy about intake is that both applicant and worker should understand the basis for the requested help and whether and how the request can be met; and, therefore, that no valid decision can be made to grant it, deny it, or refer the applicant elsewhere for the help he seeks until such understanding is reached. Exploration of this kind indicates respect: for the person's wish and ability to participate in examining the difficulty; for his right to use or reject help or a referral for help when he understands the range of alternatives open to him; for his responsibility to make decisions about his own destiny. The worker respects the person's right to decide what he wants or can tolerate, but that this can come about only when there is mutual sharing of knowledge based on the kind of exploration that leads the person to understand his problem as clearly as possible. In the Link case the worker, whether or not the agency had funds, could not offer the specific help needed in or outside the agency until she explored the request, the problem, and the need that were represented in the factual request.

SOME TECHNIQUES

It was noted above that the person seeking help of some type from a social agency for the first time often has little idea of what to expect. If he has been referred by a friend or a minister or the school or some other resource that has some knowledge about the agency, the troubled person may have some preconceived positive or negative ideas to add to the various feelings he may have about what kinds of people need and use social services. If the help he needs is to be sought from a public assistance agency or some other that is often the object of public criticisms, his feelings of guilt and anxiety, in particular, will compound his distress. He may initiate a contact with the agency, even complete the application interview, then fail to return—or he may return long after he had said he would and only after his situation has deteriorated.

The Exploration

The help is likely to be more constructive if sufficient consideration is given by the worker—and the agency—to the earliest contacts. For this reason the orderly sequence of the "how" of intake exploration is delineated here but with a cautionary reminder: The successful exploratory process requires a high degree of warmth and spontaneity in the interviews, with the worker alert to the clues the client presents, and direct or indirect application of these to determine the path of the exploration. No outline can be rigidly followed (as Mrs. Marshall demonstrated). However, an outline in the "back of one's head" helps the worker to take responsibility for directing the interview and intake process. Such direction helps the person to explain his situation, to expand or limit material, and to comprehend why certain facts are important to the understanding of his needs. This direction conveys to the person the sense that he is being heard with empathy and intelligently. It is the basis for the establishment of a working relationship, the medium through which the person and worker are enabled to work together on the problem.

How did the person come to the agency, through what source, and why did he come now? It is important to know what precipitated the present request: Was it something specific such as the loss of a job? A fight with a husband? A school suggesting or requiring it? From this the worker often learns what the current stress is, how the person feels about it, and how he feels about coming to the agency. What is the request, what has he tried to do about it himself, and how does he think the agency can help him? What, if anything, does he think it possible for him to try? Such questions often help the worker to begin to understand the kind of person the client is, how he handles crises, why this crisis is different from or similar to others in his life, what capacities he has for working toward a solution, how immobilized he is.

The social worker is interested in the current problem as the person sees it. If, for example, he lost his job, the worker will want to know the circumstances, the kind of job, the work history, the efforts and impediments related to obtaining another; his physical condition; how he feels about work and the jobs he has held; what his emotional state is; if he is realistic about his opportunities or overly anxious or depressed, and so on.

The worker notes the person's appearance and behavior as he gives face sheet and other facts. How well is he related to the facts of his request? What kind of feeling is shown as he talks about his problem and himself? How appropriate is his feeling about the problem? How defensive is he and does the defensiveness change as he becomes aware of the worker's interest and empathy? In this way the worker also is learning how much the person is motivated to work on his problem.

Again, since the worker's interest and concern are not only with the person as an individual but with him as a member of a family, the exploration also takes into account how the family affects and is affected by the problem. How do the family members feel about and react to the problem? How do they influence it? What are the family values: cultural, social, physiological, and economic, that bear on the problem? And what family interrelationships affect the problem and may well affect the outcome?

In raising such questions or in elaborating on them when spontaneous material is forthcoming, the worker keeps in mind that the client should know why these questions are pertinent to his request. The worker will pose questions that clarify but do not threaten the person's self-esteem or sensitive areas; otherwise, the person may withdraw or lash out because of fear, anger, or anxiety. Sensitive areas are noted, but they are not necessarily directly touched except as they might be essential for handling the specific request. Well-timed questions and comments elicit needed facts that often carry emotional implications, but no direct effort may be made this early to understand underlying feelings unless this measure is imperative for clarification of factual data. The questions that must be answered for purposes of some legal or quasi-legal organizations—such as public welfare or child welfare or probation or parole agencies—may expose deep troubled feelings: when this is so, the reasons for the questions, which may be mandated by law, should be interpreted by the worker. The questions and comments are often beneficial and healing, but since neither the worker nor the individual person can ordinarily make a decision this early about what help is needed and how and where it is to be provided (except financial, material, or certain other tangible aids), it is best not to stir or open up feelings that the worker may not be in a position to work with on a continuing basis.

In the first interview with Mr. Link, the worker asked if he had specific knowledge about his mother's condition. No, but he was sure it was serious. He had asked his father and had been told the problem was minor, but Mr. Link knew better. The father always minimized things. Could he reach his mother directly and discuss it with her? Mr. Link stopped for a moment, seemed greatly relieved. Yes, he could. He had been so worried he had not thought of that. He could believe her. Would he be granted a loan if she really needed him? The worker said she could not promise. They would have to discuss his financial situation and see whether this would be the answer. He might need some other kind of help. An appointment was made for the following day. The worker thought Mr. Link's anxiety was out of proportion to the facts and suspected troubling difficulties in his relations with his parents. However, no reference to these speculations was made to Mr. Link.

The outline suggested for intake at first sight may seem to be formidable. However, the immediate purposes of intake are to give the worker a picture of what the person wants in his request and the material that will illuminate this rather than knowledge of deeper aspects that may need to be gone into later. It should be kept in mind that the suggested outline is not mandatory; that in any given situation the nature of the exploration may be limited and that the worker has to select those areas that are most appropriate to the person's problem. As is evident in the interview with Mr. Link, the intake process may require more than one interview. It continues until the worker is reasonably certain that the agency has suitable service to offer and that the person wants and can use help. Concrete help may be given during this process to meet an emergency or facilitate exploration when there is a realistic need. Other members of the family may need to be included in the exploratory process. Additional clarifying information may be obtained from schools, medical sources, employers, and so on. Consultation may be needed with the supervisor or with others such as psychiatrists or legal personnel.

In the instance of Mr. Link's request, the worker asked questions that enabled Mr. Link to examine his situation with some perspective and to mobilize himself to take constructive action. These questions also tested Mr. Link's capacity to be realistic. His responses gave clues to personality strengths. Although the worker has to be alert to the presence of pathology and distortions, it is of the utmost importance that, from the beginning, evidences of strength be sought and tested. For example, there was indication of Mr. Link's hostility toward his father. This was noted for future reference, but no effort was made to elicit further evidence at this time lest Mr. Link be overwhelmed or diverted from the purpose of the interview.

In the beginning of the interview Mr. Link demanded an immediate direct answer. He resisted the worker's questions until he understood why they were necessary. Resistance to giving information is frequently encountered during intake; it is important to endeavor to understand the reasons for it. Is the resistance related to lack of knowledge about the agency and how it functions or to ambivalence about coming to the agency? Resistance is overcome often when the person knows the reasons for the worker's request for factual knowledge. Important, too, is the worker's sensitivity to evidences of resistance and to timing in handling this. With regard to resistance, as is true in the handling of anxiety, guilt, or hostility, the worker needs to be aware of feelings of his own that may affect his ability to obtain necessary information.

Mr. Link was given no promises—promises that perhaps could not be fulfilled. Nor was he told: "I need to know more about you." Such a comment often confuses and angers the client for he feels he already has explained his situation to the best of his ability. The worker, using the knowledge gained in the interview, shared with

Mr. Link something specific that would require further exploration if his call to his mother disclosed that he should go home: further exploration of his financial situation with focus on a loan as a possible way of helping him, and a promise to further examine other problems if this were to be indicated. Sometimes people fail to return to the agency when next steps or reasons for further consideration are not made explicit or are inadequately discussed. In such instances there is a failure to enlist the participation of the client and his motivation to use help is diluted or vanishes. Sometimes people who are under orders from a court or similar authority or who have compelling survival needs (for food or shelter, for example), return only to insure their freedom or survival, as the case may be. They do not respond to other "help" that may be proffered and which, from a long-range point of view, may be exceedingly important to their adequacy in social functioning. It also is not unknown for some people to jeopardize their freedom or to resort to impractical or antisocial means for meeting their survival needs rather than returning for "help."

Further examination of the interview with Mr. Link shows that while the worker listened carefully to spontaneous material, she took responsibility for guiding the interview to clarify the request and to open up new areas for his consideration. This is the way in which a worker-client relationship begins. As with Mr. Link, it permits shifts in attitude about the request that has been made and, again as with Mr. Link, often mobilizes the individual to begin to take steps that will clarify or resolve his difficulty. Because the primary use of the relationship in this early period is to understand the request and the problem and to engage the person in working on this problem, the worker does not probe into areas that might create difficulties in transferring the person to another worker for implementing a plan for helping him. Inappropriate probing often results in eliciting material that ties the person to the intake worker. In this sense, if the agency's practice is to transfer the case to another worker after intake exploration, it is advisable not to bring to the fore the kinds of feelings and confidences that may lead the person to resist transfer, or may cause him to withdraw from continuing service.

Mr. Link returned the following day. His anxiety had not abated. He had telephoned his mother and she had assured him that she was not seriously ill but would like to see him. When the worker commented that he still seemed worried, he blurted out his need to go home. It had been a mistake to leave home. Ever since he had come to the city he had been unable to concentrate on his studies. He was failing. Was this the first time he had been away? How had it been in the army? Mr. Link relaxed somewhat. He wondered why he was in such a panic now. He had done well in the army, had risen to sergeant. He had done well in school before. When he returned from the army he felt smothered by his mother, and had left home against her wishes. She had written him many reproachful letters. Maybe he should try to stay here. He would like to see if he could succeed. The worker wondered if, since he seemed troubled by his relationship to his mother, he would want to continue discussing this with another worker? He said that he would. At present he thought a loan was not the answer to his trouble.

Further exploration in this interview disclosed information about the school and army experiences pertinent to the problem; Mr. Link was able to think about his past experience as it related to his present difficulty. During this process, he became aware of the deeper meanings of his original request and, through this, became aware of the need for a different kind of help than he had originally envisioned. He was now ready to continue to work on a different but related problem to that which he had first presented; now, too, he could move on to another worker.

It was still not entirely clear what specific kind of help Mr. Link would need; a clearer understanding would emerge as Mr. Link and the new worker considered together the various implications of his current dilemma. Out of this would come a deeper understanding of Mr. Link as a person and what he needed, perhaps continued service in the agency, perhaps psychiatric treatment.

The skill of the worker in eliciting reality as well as psychological facts without undue exposure of feelings is of significance during intake. Too early involvement of the person's underlying feeling may precipitate withdrawal from contact. Similarly, exposing the central problem as the worker sees it when the person has little or no awareness of the problem in relation to his request may be bewildering, may give him a feeling of not being understood, and may result in his refusal to become involved with the agency in a meaningful way —or he may withdraw completely if he has a realistic choice.

At times a worker finds it difficult to bear the kind and amount of anxiety that an applicant displays. This is understandable; the applicant's overwhelming anxiety creates tension in the worker as well, and may result in a wish to provide quick relief. The attempt may then be made to reassure the person by universalizing his problem, by pointing out that a particular difficulty is not unique to him, and that there is no need to be so anxious. This can be a valid approach when used with discretion based on knowledge. The danger lies in offering wholesale reassurance too early and without basis in fact.

Mrs. Meyer was overwhelmed with guilt because she was a "bad mother." The fact that her husband had deserted and she was dependent on public assistance reinforced her self-depreciation. The further proof in her eyes was that George did well in kindergarten and was completely unmanageable at home. She seemed immobilized by anxiety over her inability to control the child. The worker assured her that the problem could not be so serious because George was adjusting in school. This well-meaning attempt at reassurance only confirmed Mrs. Meyer's worst fears that she was the culprit. It took several efforts to undo "false" reassurance. With another person such premature or unreal attempts to allay anxiety through reassurance might justify the person's belief that the problem is too insignificant to warrant efforts to correct it.

Mrs. Ross, on the other hand, had to be helped to become a little anxious in order to work on her problem. She protested when the public agency from which she was receiving financial assistance validly required that she go to work because her children no longer needed her at home all day. Mrs. Ross thought the request was unjust and she wanted "someone" to intercede. The worker suggested that perhaps Mrs. Ross would like to tell him about how she lived and why her children needed her. Gradually Mrs. Ross revealed the fear that if she went to work her children would be "forever on my back" as her husband was before he deserted the family. By the end of the interview Mrs. Ross had some concern about what her attitude might do to her children. She was ready to discuss this further.

It would have been understandable for the worker to align himself either with or against Mrs. Ross, to react positively or negatively to a mother's wish to stay home with her children. Had this happened, the true problem could not have emerged. The worker endeavored to help Mrs. Ross examine her situation to the best of her ability. Before she left this interview, Mrs. Ross asked how she would continue, how she would be helped. Out of this came a decision that the worker would continue to see Mrs. Ross to discuss her worries about taking a job. Mrs. Ross accepted responsibility for continued discussion with the worker. She was now anxious about the real problem instead of openly antagonistic and denying the existence of a problem by placing it upon the public agency's requirement.

Special Problems

The worker may be overwhelmed by aggressive or hostile behavior on the part of an applicant. Again, as part of his professional armament, the worker needs to control his own feelings if he is to understand the reasons and meanings of what often appears to be a personal attack on him. When the attack is directed toward the agency, the worker does not need to defend or repudiate the agency's limitations; he accepts the fact that his agency like all others has limitations and restrictions and that it also has resources that can be utilized. In other words, the worker must identify with the agency even while recognizing its weaknesses if he is to truly "hear" the troubled person. He can then correct misperceptions, explain limitations, and facilitate the utilization of whatever resources are available.

Often, to further understanding, other family members or people who affect the problem need to be drawn into exploration during intake. This may be time-consuming and difficult, but when it is indicated it may, in the long run, prove to be both economical and productive. A reluctant family member may refuse to come to the office and it may be advisable to carry the intake exploration to the locale of the home. Sensitivity to family values and culture is required to determine when and how other people are to be approached, whether via office or home interviews. When complaint by the community is involved and some affected family member refuses to come to the agency, it is necessary for the worker to approach the family, to be honest about the complaint, but also to try to find some entering wedge, some area of concern that is acceptable to the person and family and will permit them to participate in the intake exploration.

The applicant who does not understand the ways of an agency because of language or cultural differences must be reached in other ways. Mrs. Hernandez applied for public assistance. A letter was sent for the next appointment. When Mrs. Hernandez failed to keep the appointment, the application was cancelled. She applied again. Only then was it clear that she could not read English, was not accustomed to receiving letters, and had thrown the letter away. Similarly, Mr. Jasper did not keep his appointment for the specified time because in his rural background time had no significance. Until he was able to understand the importance of time to others, he would wander into the agency at different times and feel rejected when he was not seen because the worker was not available.

An applicant may not receive a good "hearing" if the worker is prejudiced by a previous record that shows poor use of the agency's help in the past. The record is important but it should not be used to bias the worker with respect to a new application. People do change; their life situations alter for better or worse, and attention should be paid to what the applicant is asking for now, what he has tried to do himself, what he wants, what he hopes the agency will do.

Of great concern to many workers is the silence which sometimes occurs during an interview. This may be present for a number of reasons. For example, the adolescent who is under a probation order or has some other kind of official relationship to the worker may use silence to emphasize his hostility toward the worker, toward the agency, toward the court that ordered him to have these contacts, toward the world in general. He protects himself against the expectations of others by silence. The worker who is able to accept the reason for such silence and be silent too without an undue degree of discomfort, generally will find that the adolescent becomes increasingly uncomfortable and makes some kind of comment: it may be a hostile one, it may be a direct attack on the worker, it may be a demand to know why he is there. The fact that he is able to resort to words, even angry words, is an important clue to the fact that his silence represents anxiety, even guilt. The presence of anxiety, as has been noted, is essential if the individual is to be motivated to use help. The venting of anger in words, uncomfortable as this may be for the worker, is nevertheless a positive sign in their relationship.

Some people use silence not as a symptom of hostility or resistance but because what they have to say is so disturbing to them that they have difficulty putting it into words, or they need to consider very carefully how to phrase what they have to say. In these instances hasty interruption of the silence by the worker may shut the client off because he is then unable to work out how or if he will voice the point that is troubling to him. A man, for example, may have some difficulty in describing to a woman worker a matter that involves sexual intimacy; a woman client may feel similar embarrassment with a male worker. Each may need considerable time to speak at all, or to speak in terms that are acceptable to their own cultural values as well as in keeping with the vocabulary they know to be familiar to the worker. Silence may be a necessary tool in some interviews for giving the client an opportunity to remobilize his forces before moving on from one point of difficulty to another. Caution must be exercised by workers in assessing the meaning of a silence and its most effective use.

Just as some persons use silence to defend themselves, others use a spate of words to protect themselves against exposure. There needs to be some assessment as to what motivates this verbosity. Is there a repetition of an idea? Is there a flow from one subject to another without any single one being adequately enlarged upon? Is the flow of words responsive to a question? Is the flow related directly to a question or is it peripheral, an avoidance of a direct answer?

Garrulity occurs for different reasons. Sometimes, in the aged person, it is a return to earlier years when the individual had full control of his faculties and his affairs, and he now needs to employ a barrage of words to convey both to himself and to the worker that he still is in control of his life. A child may bounce from one subject to another, not settling on anything, but talking constantly to keep the worker from saying something that might be disturbing to the child. The use of words as a defense, both by the very young and by the aged, may be a very healthy thing. The quality of words, the changes from subject to subject, or the preoccupation with a single idea require the worker's attention. The neurotic person may engage in a steady stream of talking, not only to describe anxiety but to use the words to reinforce the anxiety.

Verbosity, like silence, is an important clue to the worker about the behavior patterns of the person being interviewed—patterns that are good or faulty. If it is a healthy use of words, the flow is easily interrupted. A direct question, even if it has to be repeated, will elicit a direct response and help the individual to concentrate on the purpose of the question and the purpose of the interview.

The unhealthy flow of words does not lend itself to interruption so readily. If anxiety is very deep and is being expressed in this fashion, the worker may need to interrupt repeatedly, focusing each time on asking a question that can bring forth a response that the client feels competent to make. Something as simple, for example, as the age of a child, or the children's school grade levels, may serve to break the flow. The question must be simple, direct, and have some relevance to the total situation. It serves the same purpose as channeling deep anxiety into specific action so that the emotional energy that is being spent in anxiety can be used in constructive activity. In these instances some questions may be necessary which would elicit no more than yes or no answers.

The person who is unable to stay with a particular idea because it is painful, or because he just does not want to, often resorts to giving only a minimal answer to a question the worker thinks is necessary. In these kinds of situations it is important to so phrase the question that the answer cannot simply be a yes or no. It must be either "I don't know" or a response that contains specific content. Unless the person being interviewed can be engaged in answering questions more fully than through the simple yes or no, the worker cuts himself off from possible clues that could be picked up for elaboration, for clarification of the nature of the problem, or for assessing the kind of person who is asking for help and the kinds of ways that help can be provided. Similarly, the worker needs to avoid making a statement, then asking "Isn't this right?" The worker thus places the applicant in the position of agreeing either because he is a passively conforming person who does not like to disagree even if the information is wrong, or disagreeing because of resentment or hostility or some other device he uses for defending himself against having to change in some way that he suspects or knows is expected of him.

Despite a worker's best efforts, it is not always possible to engage people in working on their problems, whether these be gross or refined. Some people need to test themselves and agencies before they can settle down to working on a problem. Some can only permit themselves to come once or a few times if they have any choice—which generally is precluded when certain public agency services or court-ordered voluntary agency services are involved. Some want and obtain immediate relief from anxiety that may or may not be temporary. Some mobilize themselves to independent effort as a result of a single interview. Some require the worker to make persistent and consistent efforts to reach them.

Whether people return to the agency for help, whether they arrive at the "right" agency, whether they need persistent follow-up to be reached, the job of the worker at intake, while difficult, is clear. It is to attempt to understand the request, the person-in-his-situation, and the problem in order to make some tentative or final decision regarding what is needed, how and where the most effective services can be provided, and how to enable the person to make use of that service. The success of the intake process is pattern-setting for the troubled person; it is the precursor of the success with which the needy person will use the services of the agency toward resolution of his problems and regaining or attaining mastery over the factors interfering with his effective functioning. If he can come to trust the intake worker —and, thus, the agency—and if the application and exploration, with their concomitant services, can be handled with his self-esteem intact or enhanced, his potential for productive response to counseling will probably be realized.

19

CONTINUING WORK
WITH FAMILIES

TO HELP MAINTAIN *and strengthen family life*
. . . is a comparatively modern statement of public social policy,
long implied in our society but not made explicit until its relatively
recent incorporation in the Social Security Act more than twenty
years after the Act was enacted. This statement of public policy,
which now is a mandate for federally-aided public assistance programs, has long been an objective of voluntary as well as public social
welfare services.

METHODS AND GOALS

Over the years various approaches have been used to
achieve the objective: direct work with individual members of a fam-

ily group, provision of public funds to enable children to remain with their widowed mothers, work with the marital partners or work with one or both parents and a child, and others. Only in recent years, however, has there been a sharp focus of attention on the importance of the social worker—or *any* helping profession—working with the family as a group to strengthen the family. It is true that in earlier days social workers did conduct interviews with a family member in the presence of other family members. These, however, were not planned with a specific *family goal* objective. The benefits that accrued to the total family as a socially functioning unit were incidental to other objectives such as meeting survival needs, helping the breadwinner remain attached to the labor force, working with the personal difficulties of one member or with the marital pair, and so on. The family was approached more as an assembly of individual personalities than as a socially, emotionally, economically, and culturally interacting unit.

Expanding knowledge about human behavior and social systems has facilitated the development of new insights and new approaches to the helping of troubled families. For many years one prevalent method of reaching and helping people has been the one-to-one method. This method has frequently included involvement of the family in planning for an individual, and in dealing with crisis situations, though for the most part it has concentrated on one member or several members of the family. This continues to be an important and effective method of help, but learnings in the last several years have permitted enlargement of this framework of helping methodology. Variations have occurred and new ones continue to emerge with regard to reaching out to people who will not themselves seek help, in the use of group methods, in short- and long-term work, in a host of preventive programs—all of these modifying the conventional one-to-one method. Work with families is one of the many constructive concepts and methodologies included in the evolution of helping methods.

In any of the above methods of direct work with troubled people the goal is to help them to alleviate, to ameliorate, or to achieve mastery of their problems. This includes work on interfering feelings, actions, and attitudes so that the individuals can be freed to act constructively in their own behalf and to find their own identity and place *as* individuals within the family and in the wider society. A traditional function of social work has been to help people who have difficulties in social and personal adjustment, and social work long has recognized the inextricable intermeshing of social and personal factors having an impact on adjustment. From this intermeshing it follows that the part of social work that is concentrated on direct help to people in trouble is vitally concerned with their interpersonal relations within the family and in the larger world. Problems or satisfactions in interpersonal relations reflect conflicts or resolutions that are both intrapersonal (within the person) and interpersonal in his relationships to the family and the outside world. "No man is an island unto himself," and any problem, any form of helping inevitably involves interpersonal relationships: the person's needs and wishes, and those of the other people in his life.

In this sense, whether in a one-to-one relationship, or with family members together, or with a total family group, all work with people is interpersonal. It always touches on interpersonal relationships through helping people assess and use reality and through examining important life relationships, whether in the past or in the present, and whether the goal is alleviation, amelioration, or mastery of the problem. People's conflicts are expressed and experienced in their current life relationships, but they contain many remnants of the past. Individuals vary considerably in terms of how they deal with the remnants of the past, and these, therefore, may need to be understood in order to comprehend the impact of a particular remnant on a particular person's current mode and level of functioning. The major concern, however, is to understand why help is needed now. What set of circumstances, within and external to the person and the family, has upset the usual ways of managing so that the affected family members are unable to cope with problems in an accustomed way or in accordance with their potential capacities? What is needed to help? What will be the most effective helping devices? How can people be reached who do not voluntarily come to agencies or who, when they do come, are not necessarily able to make use of service?

The growing body of knowledge testifying to the fact that identity is achieved not in isolation and by self-autonomy but in the family interpersonal system has been a stimulant to work with families as a helping method. This method also has gained in importance as techniques in one-to-one treatment have been refined and it has become evident that no single method suffices to meet the needs of all people or to mitigate all problems. For example, it became markedly noticeable that, when work in relation to a marital problem focused upon work with one spouse, that one became better but the partner became worse; in some instances the marriage was threatened. Or the partner not in treatment resisted changes that inevitably must characterize successful treatment and undertook to sabotage the treatment, with the consequence that the spouse being worked with could not persist in treatment in the face of these efforts and prematurely discontinued seeing the worker. Similarly, work with an adolescent often was stalemated or interrupted because the destructive gratifications the adolescent was obtaining in his conflicts with his parents offset the gratification available in the helping process.

Despite the considerable success of the various methods for helping troubled families, enough dissatisfactions were present to encourage experimentation with work with families as a method of help. This method, now beyond the experimentation stage, draws heavily, as do other methods, on the concepts contained in Parts Two and Four of this volume, particularly the theories relative to the rules that govern the family, patterns of conflict and resolution, marital and family equilibrium, and the tasks of the individual and the family in various stages of the cycle of family life.

"WORK WITH FAMILIES" DEFINED

"Work with families" can be described as a method that deals with the family as a system of interpersonal relationships. It is different from work with other kinds of groups because the family group is not a group of individuals artificially brought together for a specific and time-limited purpose. The family exists on its own, each member of the family having a unique identity and, following the sessions with the worker, going back to living with others in intimacy. Understanding of group dynamics is useful in work with families. Application is limited, however, because parent-child family groups differ sharply from the peer groups in which group dynamics concepts are especially valuable. The conflicts in the family group are intermeshed in the home as well as in the sessions with the worker; between sessions they continue to reverberate in the home. The objective in work with this kind of group is directed toward increasing the competence of the family as a *whole* and, therefore, the competence of the individual. The focus remains on the *family*, its interactions and transactions.

The intent of work with families is to influence the family network system by relaxing, modifying, or breaking up the regressive or fixed equilibrium that is creating problems. For example, when a family is concerned about deviant behavior in a son and the behavior appears to be due to a seductive relationship with the mother, one usually finds a covert or overt disturbed marital relationship; a disturbed mother-daughter relationship in which the mother has not provided a good model for the girl; disturbed relationships of the father with the mother and daughter and other children in the family; poor identification of sons with the father, and so on. Family work attempts to influence the total network rather than to change only one element within it, such as the mother-son relationship. The efforts to influence the network focus on communication among the family members: there is direct intervention in the interpersonal arena with family members present, with the aim of changing the nature of communication among and between the family members,[1] thereby altering the destructive parts of family equilibrium.

Presently there are many different working definitions of family work. One states that the work must include the total family unit residing in a household, except for children under nine years of age; they are deemed too young to participate actively in the sessions.[2] Another stipulates the inclusion at all times of all family members except children under five years of age; this definition also allows several sessions with the parents alone at the beginning of the contacts.[3]

The working definition employed in this chapter is: family treatment is the process of planned intervention in an area of family dysfunctioning. Family treatment is centered upon the dynamic functioning of the family as a unit, and the primary technique utilized is some form of multiple-person interviewing. Shifts to other techniques (individual, conjoint, concurrent, combined, and total family interviews)[4] are related to the emergence of new diagnostic data or treatment developments and are undertaken in the context of the total family treatment goal. Because the goal of treatment requires focus on the family, some form of multiple interviewing remains the major treatment technique. This definition permits flexibility in work with families both in the exploratory treatment interviews and in planned treatment after a decision has been made as to what help is needed and who in the family should be included in direct work.

It should be noted that family treatment is pertinent in all types of social agencies—public, voluntary, hospitals, clinics; in all kinds of problems—marital, parent-child, unmarried mother, adoption, child or adult placement; and with all age ranges. The emphasis in different agency settings may vary, but the family approach is relevant to all.

---

[1] Refer to Chapter 16.

[2] John E. Bell, *Family Group Therapy*, Public Health Monograph #64 (Washington, D.C.: U.S. Government Printing Office, 1961).

[3] Virginia Satir, *Conjoint Therapy* (Palo Alto, Calif.: Science and Behavior Books, Inc., 1964).

[4] See Chapters 6 and 7 for treatment techniques.

Thus a patient in a hospital or clinic may be identified as in need of direct work with a social worker. It is valuable both to the family and to the patient if the worker, the family, and the patient undertake the necessary planning as is discussed in Chapter 8. In child placement work, natural and foster parents may need to be brought together for work in behalf of the child. In public and voluntary family agencies, scapegoating (problems acted out or focused on one family member) is commonplace and often cannot be intercepted without the family's involvement. The schizophrenic's illness often is part of a total family illness which has to be modified via changes in family equilibrium if changes are to be made in his condition. Planning for aged people may be ineffective unless the family concurs about the nature of the plan.

EXPLORATION AND EVALUATION

Decisions to determine who is to be worked with at a given time, and with what specific objectives, require preliminary exploration. This exploratory process can be described as exploratory treatment because much happens in the dynamic interchange between the worker and family members that sets the framework for the specific areas of treatment to be undertaken.

Identification of the family includes data about those who live in the household, their ages, relationships, work and school data. It includes the type of neighborhood, the kind of home lived in, the socioeconomic status, and outside relationships (organizations, religious affiliation, extended family). Much can be learned about a family from these usual "face sheet" data not only in terms of the content itself but also from the way in which the data are given. Feelings frequently emerge as this material is provided and these offer clues to how the person sees himself or the family perceives itself; how help is viewed; what areas are painful; where there are attempts to conceal material; where there is pride in achievement. Mrs. Byrd, for example, found it very difficult to provide data about her marriage and Mr. Byrd's desertion in relation to the ages of the children for the information pointed to the probability that the children had different fathers. She could, however, give school information readily and with pride. The worker's focus in obtaining the material on the areas in which Mrs. Byrd took pride made it possible for her to be comfortable enough to reveal more accurate information about the less successful parts of her life. Data about the kind of home often disclose a picture of the family's values, standards, and hopes for the future. The nature of religious affiliation may be a potentially helpful resource to be utilized with regard to a troubled person or family.

Presenting Problems

What is the reason for application or referral? Who suggested that an application be made? What is the problem that exists now? When did it first appear and under what circumstances? What has been tried already, and what does the family see as answers to the problem? Have the different family members ideas about how to handle the problem or about its solution? Understanding these ideas and feelings can be of the greatest significance in planning. Any member of a family can describe the problem only from his own viewpoint, his own feelings about being hurt, his own ideas about who is to "blame." Often in the process of seeing the family members together, a clearer picture emerges of the problem and clues how to begin working on the problem are evident.

Mr. and Mrs. Ames were exceedingly upset about the pregnancy of fifteen-year-old Sue. They could not understand how this could happen in their family, to their daughter. Ellen, seventeen, was adamant that Sue had to leave home so the disgrace could be hidden and that later she must give up the baby. Mr. and Mrs. Ames vacillated between anger and pity for Sue and in their vacillation tended to accept Ellen's solution. The younger children were frightened by the turmoil in the home, by the unaccustomed fighting of the parents. They sensed something was wrong. In a series of family sessions that included the parents, Ellen, Sue, and two younger children of thirteen and eleven, conflicting feelings were disclosed and examined. Ellen was both angry and jealous; angry because Sue had humiliated her and the family, jealous because the parents were partially sympathetic to Sue. Sue was frightened and ashamed. At first she thought she must leave home, and this also terrified her. The younger children were upset, but they also were relieved to discover the cause of the parents' battling. Painful though these family sessions were, feelings could come out directly and could be gradually modified. As a result, the parents became less immobilized and Ellen less adamant; they were able to undertake planning that was in the best interests of all.

The Ames case illustrates the fact that a hidden family secret in reality often is no secret to the family members, and that when the hidden fact can be exposed, it can be tackled in a more reasonable and rational way. This is not to say that certain specific events and feelings are not private. In an over-all sense, however, a family secret that disturbs all members is generally known at least in its broad outlines to all of the members; they are more disturbed by the efforts at secrecy than by the consequences of its disclosure.

The Clare family applied for help because of the school problem of ten-year-old Jerry, who was an underachiever. The parents seemed unduly upset. In the family interview, Mrs. Clare suddenly blurted out that Mr. Clare had been hospitalized for several years with a paranoid-schizophrenia diagnosis. Jerry, she said, did not know this; he thought his father had tuberculosis. Although the words had not been used in the home, Jerry did know and in the interview said so. The worker was able to assure the parents that observation did not indicate that Jerry was mentally ill. This had tremendous meaning for the family, all of whom had been living with the fear that Jerry's school failures were a sign of inherited illness.

The Ames case also exemplifies the fact that work with many families can be more effective when the whole family is mobilized to work together on a problem. No one feels singled out for blame or responsibility. At a particular time one member may be more distressed or more vulnerable than another. When the worker is seeing the family together and the members therefore have this help available to them, it is frequently possible for the less upset member to give support to the more disturbed one at a point of special vulnerability.

Not all family members may feel the need of help; some may resist it. Often, however, they can all be motivated to take some part in working on the problem even if the part is minimal. It is not uncommon, for example, for fathers to feel that a child's problem is between the mother and the child. If the worker can convince the father that his child needs his direct concern, he may continue to meet in the family session despite his belief that he had no part in the child's difficulty. It is common, in these circumstances, for the father to become more actively involved in working on the problem. A strong appeal to both parents in behalf of a child rarely fails. This is illustrated in the Grave case in which the situation appeared to be hopeless. Mr. and Mrs. Grave were locked in marital combat and little could be done to modify this. Mrs. Grave was the complete martyr; Mr. Grave was on parole, a long-time drug addict; John, at thirteen years of age, was in difficulty in school and with the juvenile court. The first approach in this case was an attempt to work with Mrs. Grave alone; there was a general idea that Mr. Grave was hopeless. When efforts to help her failed, consideration was given both to placement of John and to a divorce for Mrs. Grave. Both plans failed. The parents could neither give each other up nor let go of

John. The next step was to work with Mr. and Mrs. Grave together and with John separately. This was effective. Nothing could be done to alter the marital conflict or the drug addiction, but the fact that John felt his parents were both concerned about him and at least talking together about him enabled him to stay in treatment and to make use of it.

Intra-family Patterns

How the various family members interact with each other with regard to day-to-day responsibilities and to their respective developmental tasks has special import for appraisal of factors that impede or enhance the family members' impact upon each other and the family's social adequacy in self-management.

The division of responsibility in the home in relation to work, finances, discipline of the children, management of competition over tasks to be performed—each of these aspects may hold clues useful to understanding. How are responsibilities divided and handled? Who makes the decisions about these? What is the nature of activity in relation to responsibilities, that is, who does what and who shirks what? Do these responsibilities change appropriately as the family grows and develops?

Mrs. Clark worked. Mr. Clark was incapacitated because of multiple sclerosis. Mr. and Mrs. Clark were clear about their respective responsibilities—why they had to be as they were. Despite being bound to a wheelchair and having responsibility for household tasks, the father, and the mother, made it clear to the children that he was the head of the home and a strong male figure. Certainly the boys missed having a father who could participate in active games in or outside the home, but this could be adjusted to because Mr. and Mrs. Clark were unquestioning about division of responsibility. The problems in such a situation can occur when resentments over role reversal begin and mount, when the parents become competitive for the children, when the father withdraws or abdicates his responsibility, and when the mother discharges her resentment by overt or subtle depreciation of her husband to the children.

The patterns of identification constituted no problem in the Clark family but they do in many families where parents are not so unified in what the place of each is as a parent. It is advisable to explore these areas. What are the alignments and collusions in the home? Is each parent clear about his and the partner's place and responsibilities as parents? Do they operate satisfactorily as husband and wife, thereby establishing sound models for the children? Do they establish appropriate models of masculinity and femininity for the children? Here again flexibility is important. Children need different models in their development at different phases of growth. An adolescent boy should identify with his father and align himself with the male. Alignments and collusions are healthy, necessary, and related to phases of development. They become problematic when they are rigid and are used destructively to split the family. Parents who do not understand this can become upset, for example, when a five-year-old girl appears suddenly to become attached to her father and rejects the mother. Yet this is a necessary step in the child's development: she is learning to identify with both parents, not just the mother.

In troubled families the parents may foster unhealthy alignments and collusions. A mother, disillusioned in her husband, may foster a boy's contempt for his father and lead him to align himself against the father and all men, thus instilling feminine identification in the boy. Parents may speak of one child as belonging to the mother, another to the father; each side is then pitted against the other. Often the main work with families is to intercede in such unhealthy alliances and collusions so that growth can proceed.

The transmission of values plays a vital role in the development of the various family members, who are more susceptible at some phases than at others. What, then, are the moral, ethical, and religious values in the family? Are the values of the parents similar and constructive, or are they points of conflict between the parents? Do the children accept these values or rebel against them, appropriately or inappropriately? An adolescent questions his parents' values as part of the growth process, but if his development is healthy, he emerges into adulthood accepting them along with values of his own. If the family is dishonest, this corruption is transmitted to the child and becomes part of his personality. A family that indulgently laughs at a child's cheating makes him feel that this behavior is acceptable and right; he may resort to this kind of behavior, for example, as a way of ensuring that he remain in college. He places the blame for his cheating on pressures from the college to succeed instead of either accepting responsibility for his own work or dealing with these pressures in more constructive ways.

Patterns of growth and independence fashion personal development at various stages of the individual's life cycle and of the family's life cycle. How does the family regard and handle separateness and separation, dependence and independence and interdependence at these several stages? Can parents permit the child to assume responsibility for separateness appropriate to his age and abilities? Can they let him be dependent on them and yet foster self-management compatible with his ability? Each family has its own abilities and vulner-abilities in this area. Some families can permit proper separateness and independence when the child is five, but they have great difficulty when the child becomes an adolescent. The reverse may be true. There are innumerable variations on this theme in and among families. School phobias are illustrative of problems associated with the family's inability to permit separateness and separation. The conflict between the wish to have a child grow and the need to hold on to him as a child is indeed universal, and inappropriate resolution of this conflict often leads to immature development or distortions in personality formation. One of the grossest illustrations is the family in which symbiotic relationships (inability to permit *any* separate-ness) can lead to psychotic resolutions.

The handling of feelings in the family is an area particularly re-plete with clues to aid understanding of the coping abilities of the family members. For example, how does the family handle anxiety? Is it handled reasonably or through inappropriate behavior, depres-sion, hostility, physical illness, or withdrawal? How is love expressed? Is it tender, with proper giving and freedom of feeling, or it is ex-pressed through material giving or withholding instead of directly? How is sexuality handled? Is there a good sexual relationship between the parents or is sex used as a weapon to give or withhold? Can the parents deal with the sexual feelings of their children? Do they use the children seductively? Can the parents permit the children to de-velop their own sexuality?

The capacity for handling stress and crises is an important index to the potential for or actuality of adequate functioning. How do the family members manage the usual stresses of daily living? How do they handle crises or the unusual stresses? Every family has its own capacities and vulnerabilities to stress and crisis. For example, one family may be more vulnerable to financial stress than another. Simi-larly, illness affects families differently. Some families join forces and become a cohesive unit in a crisis; others become fragmented, or col-lapse. Some adapt to crisis situations and meet them adequately; others place the blame outside the family group or find a scapegoat in the family—or even line up against each other. Some families ap-pear to enjoy living in a constant state of crisis. This enables them to avoid looking at and working on problems. Indeed, such families often create crises.

The activities of the family offer meaningful clues to the quality and form of the intra-family patterns. What are the characteristic activities in the family and what is their frequency? How are deci-sions made and who does the planning for them? Similarly, what are the activities that father-mother, father-son, or mother-daughter engage in? Where do these activities take place, and who participates?

Individual Family Members

Each individual in the family should be known in terms of his personality dynamics and structure. Specific data are needed with regard to the child about whom a complaint has been expressed or who is himself troubled as well as troubling. What are the symptoms or the behavior that are complained about? In what areas does he function adequately? What is his intelligence? What is his feeling about himself and his family? What is his behavior at home, at work, in school, with peers? How is his health? What are his activities? If there are siblings, similar data should be obtained about them.

What are the father and mother like? What is their appearance? What are their feelings and behavior toward the one complained about and to others in the home? How do they see and feel about themselves? How do they function at home and outside? What specific history is needed to understand them? If others are living in the home, such as grandparents or other relatives, the same kinds of data should be provided about them.

Such data are comprehensive and significant but are not necessary in such detail for all situations. What *is* needed in *all* situations is understanding of what the current problem is, why the family is vulnerable at this time, what the major patterns of behavior are, and what the adaptive, coping capacities are. When these factors are understood, specific parts of the data enumerated above are used selectively for each family to deepen the understanding. It is not unusual that when a crisis has occurred requiring immediate action of some type, the worker is able to obtain only some clues to the above points rather than facts; he may be compelled to wait until the crisis has passed before he is in a position to acquire a clearer picture of the family actions and interactions.

Family Communication Patterns

The exploratory sessions will provide the worker with knowledge and understanding of how the family members communicate verbally and nonverbally, how they deal with each other with regard to sanctions and prohibitions, failures, and misunderstandings.[5] The worker can see whether the most prominent patterns of

[5] See Chapter 16.

conflict are resolved by characteristic aggression or delinquency (a family that handles conflicts by rebellion), or by intimidation (a family that withdraws in the face of conflict into passive ways), or by immature behavior (a family that cannot face up to tasks and regresses under stress), or by each member becoming concerned only with his own needs. Some families show communication patterns that can be described as unstable and unsatisfactory; that is, there is great confusion and lack of structure in role performance. Often communication shows pervasive hostility, lack of perception of others' needs, excessive intellectualization as a defense against closeness, or excessive behavioral action in the place of proper verbal communication. Other families have unstable but satisfactory communication. These are families that can communicate, but an acute crisis makes the communication pattern unstable. Still others have both stable and unsatisfactory communication. These families maintain a stable way of relating, but at the price of turning one member of the family into a scapegoat.

THE CONTINUING TREATMENT RELATIONSHIP

When the exploratory process has yielded sufficient data so that the worker can arrive at understanding the family, its components and their interaction, it is then possible to move with the family toward a common and specific goal of improved functioning of the family as a unit. Both Chapter 17 on the tasks of the worker and Chapter 6 presenting various forms of treatment with regard to problems in marriage are specifically applicable to continuing work with families. The state of marital equilibrium is basic to the family's functioning or dysfunctioning. How, then, the husband and wife interact with each other is of fundamental importance; the quality of their parenting, or fathering and mothering, emerges from the marital equilibrium and establishes the quality and form of the family equilibrium. It also affects the formulation and implementation of the rules that govern the family, the ways in which the family manages conflict and its resolution, and how these relate to the presenting[6] complaint.

The exploratory process also should make it possible for the worker to assess such aspects as whether the family presents a problem that

[6] See Chapter 18.

is essentially a transitional crisis related to a phase in family development; whether it is a crisis that is externally induced in an otherwise well-functioning family; whether it is a crisis in a family chronically under stress, and whether the family members can or cannot be worked with together. This assessment also figures prominently in the determination of the form of treatment that should be applied to a given family.

It should be remembered that as work proceeds with a family, new information emerges and changes occur in goals of work with the family as some objectives are achieved. Such modifications will point to shifts in techniques about who should be worked with in the family, and when, and on what problem.

In general, work with families is related to assets that are discernible in exploration. These assets may include the fact that the family conceives of itself as a family or wants to function better as a family; active interaction in the family; communication that shows at least minimal potential or capacity to perceive the needs of the family members; recognition by the family that it has a family problem; shifting instead of fixed alliances. The use made of the exploratory sessions in family interviews and the willingness of the family members to work together as a group or together with various family members—these likewise are assets of importance that determine when work with the family should be the helping method of choice.

20

MONEY COUNSELING

THE FUNCTION of a particular social welfare agency seemingly may have no relationship to services connected with problems of money, yet there are few agencies that are not exposed in one fashion or another to money problems of greater or lesser complexity in the lives of those they serve. For example, nine-year-old Jimmy dropped out of the "Wolverines" in which he had been an active participant almost since the probation officer had introduced him to the group services agency and he had agreed to "try out" the experience with peers who, like Jimmy, were on probation. The group worker and the probation officer discovered that Jimmy was known to the other Wolverines as a "cheapskate," and that this and more forceful derisive names followed Jimmy's failure to put into the kitty the weekly quarter the members had agreed on. Jimmy's father, in his effort to control Jimmy's behavior, has denied the boy any money; Jimmy has been so closely watched that he has had no recent opportunities to pilfer the amount required for the weekly tithe and has been unable to face the contempt of his fellow Wolverines over his failure to utilize their habitual method for providing themselves with what they think they require.

Mrs. Thomas complained to the family service agency that her husband expects her to manage on "nothing." He doles out sums to be used for specified purposes. How can she live a "normal" life and stay with a man who is so "bossy"? Mrs. Thomas has made no connection between the fact that her financial demands on her husband are almost as insatiable as her demands on him for attention and affection, and that in reality his modest earnings and limited energies preclude his meeting these demands.

Mrs. White, who with her four young children is receiving public assistance, has purchased a Christmas gift for her blind mother—a vibrator chair, its cost of $560 to be met by monthly payments of $29. The mother, who receives Aid to the Blind, has not used the chair; it frightens her. Mrs. White is impatient with her mother's fear ("She just doesn't want to take anything from *me!*"), and cannot accept the validity of the creditor's complaint that she is "deadbeating" him merely because she is three months behind in her payments, having made only the first two.

Mr. Hodkins, who had stopped working as a television repairman a year ago to care for his terminally ill wife, had exhausted all of his financial resources. Two weeks after her death, he applied to a public assistance agency to help him with his "desperate need." He did not know where to turn in his bereft state and was immobilized by the traumatic experience of nursing his painfully dying wife. He saw his need as financial, and his self-esteem was at a particularly low ebb because he was unable to deal with something "so basic as money for food."

The child guidance clinic was surprised when Mrs. Jackson failed to bring her youngster in for the scheduled interview. She had been so anxious to have help with the serious behavior the boy was displaying and with which the clinic staff thought they could be helpful. Mrs. Jackson had made no response when she was told in the initial interview the amount of the fee she would be expected to pay for the boy's treatments; it was a modest sum, not out of keeping with the family's income and level of living. A follow-up research interview some months later disclosed that Mrs. Jackson had been fearful about asking her husband, the child's stepfather, for the money; he would "merely say the boy was not his responsibility!"

ASPECTS OF MONEY PROBLEMS

As in other kinds of situations discussed in earlier chapters, troubled people may express their distress in money terms. The financial problems may actually be basic as, for example, insufficient funds as a consequence of the death of a breadwinner or the loss of a job for reasons beyond the control of the individual; a serious crisis may have exhausted the financial resources of the family and created additional acute need—an accident or an illness or destruction of the family home by fire. And as in other kinds of situations where the adequate family is able to regroup its energies and resources to handle the crisis or stress with a reasonable degree of efficiency before moving on to appropriate mastery of the respective life tasks, so it is with adequate families whose financial need arises from external factors.

The adequate family may require some financial help from a voluntary or public agency as a temporary measure either for the family's maintenance or for the resolution of the unexpected debt; or they may need counseling about measures for consolidating debts in order to be able to encompass the various old and new obligations within the family's usual pattern of income and expenditures. The family may need long-term assistance as, for example, in the instance of the wife and children of a man who has become permanently disabled or is hospitalized or otherwise institutionalized.

In essence, the characteristic ways in which people respond to stress are evident also in the way they handle stressful financial problems, and these characteristic modes of functioning contain vital clues to the family's capacity and readiness to deal with stress-provoking situations that may or may not have a direct—or even indirect—connection with problems of money.

The personality factors present in a particular family will in large measure dictate the ways in which the family members handle money generally. If their attitudes about money and their values with regard to it are distorted, these attitudes will compound financial problems that may appear to emerge, essentially, out of an environmental crisis situation. Thus, Mrs. White, whose unresolved dependency needs were evident in her purchase of the vibrator chair, could not understand why the creditor's reality and hers were not congruent.

The effect of the combination of environmental factors, societal attitudes, and personality, always interdependent and interacting, is most clearly demonstrated in matters related to the receipt and use of money. Not only are there wide variations with regard to the nature and extent of environmental stress and individual capacities to deal with such stress, but also with regard to what constitutes need or aspiration. For example, one family may believe that television is an absolute necessity because of its educational and recreational value in presenting travelogues, lectures, and so on. Another may consider television necessary because it keeps the children occupied and "out of mother's hair." And still another may maintain that television is more an "idiot box" than a "culture box" and decline to permit its distracting presence in the family's home. These views may have no relationship to the family's ability to pay for television, as may be indicated by the fact that more than 90 per cent of American families have at least one television yet the income of a fifth of the American population is below the poverty line. The general community itself looks on television ownership with mixed reactions: in many places it is utilized as a device for hurricane or storm warnings, or for the transmission of school lessons; in others, recipients of public assistance who have television in their homes may be regarded with suspicion—do they have undisclosed financial resources? Do they misuse the assistance grant by diverting funds from necessities to items for unnecessary gratification? Are the grants just too generous?

Some less controversial items than television may also be considered necessary by some and not by others. A mother of five children may be perfectly willing to use some of her limited income for installment payments on an automatic washing machine, but her crowded dwelling may have no space for one or she may live in an area lacking electric power or gas facilities needed for operating a machine. Another mother of five children, with comparable family income, may elect to use a commercial laundry rather than invest the equivalent money plus "energy and time" in a home washer.

The social worker in any of a variety of agencies dedicated to helping troubled families can enhance his understanding of the family's general behavior, the interaction of the members with each other and with the community and their values and standards, through his awareness of the family's financial needs and aspirations, their realistic or unrealistic management of money, the attitudes family members express about money—its receipt and handling—and how they use money to manage the crises and stresses.

THE MEANINGS OF MONEY

Money has special meanings and is utilized in different and characteristic ways in various phases of the several stages of the cycle of family life. Each phase has attitudes and needs for money peculiar to the particular phase and stage. These attitudes and needs nevertheless are closely related to the attitudes and feelings about money in either the preceding or the subsequent stages of the cycle of family life, and they are markedly influenced by both environmental factors and societal attitudes.

Cultural Contradictions

Closely associated with the work ethic and the Puritan emphasis on the virtue of thrift and careful apportionment of one's personal financial affairs as evidence of independence is the concept that maturity is measured by an individual's capacity to procure and to manage income. While moral value is placed on the earning and husbanding of money, and while the person with adequate financial resources is regarded with esteem, it is not at all uncommon to hear money referred to as "filthy lucre" or that "money is the root of all evil" (although Mark Twain maintained that the *lack* of money is the root of all evil). On the one hand it is pointed out that "the best things in life are free," yet money is required to meet the necessities of life. The "almighty dollar" is sneeringly accorded omnipotence. The person who is deeply in debt arouses condescending commiseration or scorn, yet there is widespread advocacy of healthy support for the American economy either by putting money into circulation to stimulate production of goods and services, or by investing in a fashion that defeats inflation.

In themselves, these contradictions about money tend to foster ambivalence as well as attitudes of insecurity or guilt, the former about not having enough and the latter in seeming to place more emphasis on material than other values. There likewise is a tendency in our culture to judge people in money terms. The financially dependent person often is viewed as inadequate; the person who is independent financially, although he may be disturbed, hostile, unpleasant, not infrequently is regarded as "mature" and "successful."

Money in the Family Life Cycle

The earning of money and the management of money are societal criteria of adulthood and maturity. The essence of personal independence and self-sufficiency for the individual lies in his capacity to meet his own needs and those of persons dependent on him, and to meet these needs through his own resources. His sense of worth and self-respect receives nourishment from the fact that he earns and that the wages represented by his work are his to spend and manage as he wishes. His ability to provide for himself and to manage his resources is evidence of judgment: he thus establishes priorities, makes choices, defers planfully and constructively the gratification of current desires in the interest of future attainments.

Children in middle-class families are brought up with the idea that they will earn, that they will manage their earnings, that they will make sound choices, that they will plan for the future and manage their resources so that their wishes ultimately can be fulfilled. This is in contrast to the situation that prevails in lower-income-level families, particularly where education has been limited and opportunities for personal enrichment have been circumscribed. The very fact of limited income is a strong factor in keeping the family, including the children, focused on the immediate present. Income must be used to keep body and soul together. Planning for a future generally means a future right at hand, in full sight. There is a close relationship between the availability of income to meet current needs, the ability to deal with spatial and time factors (discussed in Chapter 5), and the ability to apportion the available funds in order to provide for the present (expenditures) and for the future (savings). The middle-class family, even though its funds may be limited, can think ahead to a future in which children may be going to college, in which funds will be needed to provide for such education. The lower-class family, however, is more inclined to lack aspirations of this kind because there appears to be little realistic opportunity to deal with the economics of such education. The consequence is that planning for future education rarely takes place.

The meanings of money vary not only with the different stages of the cycle of family life and with the personality structure of the individual but also with the family's cultural background. To the child in a family surrounded by poverty, money may have an unreal quality. He may *feel* that it carries power, but he may not *know* this from the actual experience of having money to spend. In some ways the current families of poverty, particularly in Appalachian regions or some village enclaves in the Southwest, resemble peasant families in the days of Robin Hood. Many of the latter saw no money through their entire lifetimes. They knew about it only through songs and stories and because of their awareness that the lords—and often the sheriff—could spend their wealth as a means of asserting their power.

In middle-class families too, money may take on a mythical quality, not because it is not seen often, but because they have it to use and have it for the asking. For children, then, in any kind of family, whether poor or not, money may appear to have no reality. If they are to use it constructively as a means to an end and not as an end in itself, they and their parents require help in identifying the nature of their attitude about and use of money. The importance of money counseling lies not only in helping the family in its handling of money but also in the fact that, as they learn to organize and plan around the use of *money*, they learn also to organize and plan with respect to *other* aspects of their living. Money counseling, then, serves an important purpose in its own right as well as in the capacity of a tool in aiding families to improve their social competence in a variety of areas.

Attitudes about and the use of money in many respects are governed by the way the developmental tasks have been handled in the cycle of family life. The family shapes the individual's attitudes as he grows from infancy through childhood and adolescence and emerges into an adult world with adult responsibilities. How the marital partners feel about money and how they handle it, individually and together, contribute not only to the quality of their marriage and their relationship to each other but also to the attitudes their children acquire about this necessary tool of life.

Chapter 6 described the implications of the fact that each member of the marital team brings separate life experiences and developmental patterns to the marriage. These different experiences and developmental patterns may include divergent attitudes about money. Money, often offered as the reason for marital discord or dissolution, is frequently a symptom of deeper problems. Either or both spouses may find themselves overwhelmed when troubles with or about money are added to developmental or environmental problems. It might be concerning quite ordinary expenditures that quarrels flare up and that the marriage is tested. Early in marriage an agreement needs to be reached about how the couple's income and resources are to be allotted, who will take responsibility for which aspect of management, and which responsibilities will be shared. Thus, a balance is reached in the division of responsibility (and, often, between income and outgo), and a pattern is set for the future. The attainment of a proper balance in the management process may be determined by a variety of factors.

Quarrels and complaints may be related to the amount of the family's income. The family may use income size as a measure of the husband's adequacy as a person and as a provider. Discord may be related to extravagant spending by a husband who is trying to keep his wife in a shaky marriage, or by a wife who is reacting to a dominating husband. He may indeed appear to be controlling. This may derive from a cultural pattern which dictates that certain financial responsibilities and management are solely the husband's. It may be a cover for insecurity stemming from a temporary loss of self-esteem due to stress, or from developmental failure to acquire an appropriate level of self-esteem. Or he may feel a need to control either because the wife cannot exercise self-discipline or because he has an emotional need to do so. Like Mrs. Thomas, the wife may make undue demands because she has a need to test her husband's love. Or she may have a need to be the one who controls, or she may have social aspirations which he may or may not share, or, sharing them, nevertheless feels he cannot finance.

Problems with money may center around other conflicts. A man who works at a job he hates but continues to hold because he needs the money he thus earns may direct considerable hostility toward the wife; correctly or irrationally he may see her as the cause of his having to spend his days and energies in a job he dislikes. Troubles may arise because of a wife's attitude toward housekeeping tasks. She may resist compliance with any expectations about her household management, or she may be compulsive in performing her household functions. In either instance, her failure to achieve an appropriate balance relates in large measure to the outcome of her developmental conflicts. She may see herself as a drudge; she may be slovenly or careless; she may be unwilling to carry on household management activities in order to show her husband that she does not need to be compliant. Any of these reactions may lead her to demand household appliances or services which the couple may or may not be able to afford; the demands—as well as her attitudes about and manner of operating the household—may lead to strained relationships.

Not uncommon is the expenditure by either marital partner of limited income for purposes that are satisfying to the individual but not to the couple. This form of self-gratification may be connected with the failure of the spending partner to receive from the spouse the affection or attention or even the respect he feels appropriate. Such spending may originate in unsuccessful resolution of dependency conflicts in early childhood. It is generally acknowledged that alcoholism, gambling, some narcotic addiction, and much mishandling of family money are the consequences of faulty personality formation.

To the social worker, the way a couple handles money, singly or together, offers an important clue to the way they handle other aspects of their lives together. If they are planful and thoughtful about the management of their income, no matter how limited or how generous, there is likelihood that they manage other aspects of living similarly. But if their behavior with regard to money is faulty —not because they have not *learned* to manage money or because they lack the intellectual endowment with which to manage it—the social worker may be able to help the couple bring problems of money management under control and, often thereby, other problems as well. The importance of the social worker's help in assisting the troubled couple to deal with a reasonable degree of effectiveness with matters centering around the management of money lies not only in the immediate practicality of such success for the family. It also has particular significance for the development of personality of the children.

Throughout the children's growing-up years, the central objective is the resolution of the conflicts related to developmental tasks and, consequently, development of the individual's ability to recognize and meet, according to his judgment, more and more of the needs that earlier had to be identified, evaluated, and satisfied by others. All through the process of development the individual is trained to take responsibility for determining his needs, evaluating them in relation to the amount of money he has, choosing how these needs are to be met. This self-management is taught from early childhood and becomes habitual in adult life.

Inevitably, the individual's own attitudes about the having and earning of money are the products of his growing-up experiences, the economic and social situation of his family, the social organization of which he and the family are a part, the feelings and attitudes of the family members about money and social status, and the way the presence or absence of money—or its bestowing on or withholding from him—is handled. He may come to equate money with security or love or achievement, and its absence with deprivation—physical and emotional—and, often, with discrimination.

The infant, completely dependent on parents or parent substitutes for sustenance and survival, may suffer serious privation in the poverty-stricken family: if his physical needs are not met, if he is hungry and cold, he feels unloved and insecure. The infant who is malnourished because parents are without sufficient funds to provide him with appropriate nourishment may also be emotionally malnourished, experiencing a deep affectional starvation which begins early in his life to influence his total experience in human relationships. Such a child often is a poor learner in school, the one who cannot arrive at the school on time, who cannot make connections between the present and the future. How can he trust the future he cannot see, when he cannot trust the present in which he *is*?

This child often becomes the adult who cannot understand that an employer may wish him to be on the job at a specified time each day. He is the child who often becomes the adult unable to manage credit devices: he cannot think ahead in terms of blocks of time punctuated by installment payments.

Actual physical deprivation may cause the child to view money as a source of power for gratification of needs or desires. The physical deprivation may be compounded by parental neglect—or the deprivation may be emotional and not physical and thus lead the child to see money and power and affection as one. The child in a family that is financially comfortable sometimes sees little of a socially busy mother or a mother gainfully employed; the time she spends with him is impatient and hurried, unaffectionate and reluctant. But she is generous with material things, if not with herself. Or the child's father may spend untold hours in his business or in personal activities that exclude the child almost completely from his presence, but he lavishes gifts and money on the youngster. This child may be physically well-nurtured, but his perception of the meaning and value of money may closely resemble the physically deprived child's.

The child in the family having problems because of lack of money may sense and share the parental anxiety, but the absence of money is evident, and he does not usually confuse this financial insecurity with his relationship to his parents. If, however, communication between parents and children is faulty, this clarity does not obtain and this child may grow into an adult who seeks affection through material acquisitions or by "throwing his weight around" as a device for commanding loyalty which he equates with affection.

Should the family be fatherless, with the mother carrying the family's economic function as well as the full socialization responsibility that ordinarily would be shared by the marital partner, the combined economic and emotional deprivation may have intergenerational effects like those portrayed in O'Neill's *Long Day's Journey into Night* where a childhood stunted by lack of material and affectional necessities shapes James Tyrone into a rich but miserly auto-crat, with devastating implications for his wife, who is unable to free herself from narcotic addiction; for his older son, who becomes a dypsomaniac; and for the other son, who is afflicted with tuberculosis. Tyrone's mother, struggling to support her children, gave them little; James and his wife also fall far short in the discharge of their socialization functions; there is every promise of similar failure in their sons.

Sometimes parents have money troubles which they are able to conceal from the children, who then are unable to understand why needs and wishes are denied. This denial of material items—and lack of communication between parents and child—is translated by the child into refusal of money; to him, therefore, money becomes a symbol of affection or rejection.

Money may be used as a substitute for love or as a device for manipulation and control or as a tool for punishment. Children quickly become aware that they can obtain a special kind of love and admiration from their parents once the children learn how to earn money, to bring it home, and to spend it appropriately. Accordingly, they learn also that money is a source of power, that it increases their ability to become independent, and that it can be used to buy some people or to withhold from others. They readily become aware that, aside from its real value as money, it is useful in relationships. As was discussed in Chapter 9, this is especially true when there is a stepchild in the home or when parents are separated; it also is a common tool for pitting one's own parent against a foster parent.

The adolescent with his sharply increased expenses for social and personal obligations commonly expresses healthy conflict about dependence and independence through money. If the family is financially comfortable, the adolescent will be critical: the parents are profligate, or not as generous with him as he thinks they might be. He may be extremely critical and depreciating of parental financial failures, and any merits they have may be obscured from his vision as a consequence. If the family is dependent upon public assistance, the youth may bitterly direct some of this otherwise normal rebellion against the public assistance agency, which appears to him to be a symbol of a hostile and restrictive society. If the father is in the home, although clearly physically or mentally incapacitated or desperately trying to find work in a labor economy that has passed him by, the adolescent will be scornful about his father's inadequacy as a human being; after all, the father does not work and earn and support the family.

The adolescent in a family dependent upon an agency for income maintenance frequently demands more money than the parents or the agency provide, and he wants no one to try to control the use of of it. The demands may be expressions of frustrated emotional needs; often they bear no resemblance to his reality needs. It is not unusual for public assistance or other money-giving agencies to have ceilings, prescribed by either law or agency policy, on the amount of the grant available to needy families. The ceiling may have little or no relationship to the actual economic needs of the family. It is not unusual for the adolescent in such a family to be particularly demanding of the parents or parent, knowing that the limited grant often is insufficient for even minimum adequate maintenance.

These situations become even more complex if the adolescent is a school drop-out and the state law governing public assistance requires that only older children in school be included in the family grant. Such an adolescent drop-out is faced with alternatives which may be unacceptable either to him or to a thinking society. He must remain with the family, sharing too-limited money that is not intended for his use and he thereby creates hardship for the balance of the family. He may resort to antisocial behavior, like stealing, in order to provide himself with some tangible means to justify remaining in the home. Or he may leave home to fend for himself, although he is unprepared vocationally, and often developmentally, to obtain and hold work.

It is not uncommon for the adolescent, poor or not, to spend money defiantly, neglecting to buy what the surrounding adults consider important items, but generally making purchases that are in keeping with peer standards. In the family with limited income this constitutes a special problem. The family may recognize that adolescents characteristically vacillate between outright penury and extravagant spending. The family may understand and accept the necessity for the adolescent to find a way through this kind of spending experience to a more responsible resolution of his maturation process. The family also may understand the importance to him of having an opportunity to make choices and reach decisions in the management of money while the amounts still are small. They may accept the value of trial-and-error learning—so important a part of identity formation—but they may feel they lack the financial resources to permit such experience which would save him, as an adult, from trial and error with larger sums of money.

The adolescent who is successful in obtaining work, or who receives contributions from an absent father or a remarried parent who is not in the home, tends to be possessive about these funds. Regardless of the family's financial circumstances, the adolescent is inclined to retain this money as evidence of his independence and his ability to manage himself. If he is expected to surrender some or all of his earnings or the contributions from the absent parent, a considerable degree of hostility toward the parents or society may develop.

This feeling of hostility will be exaggerated or constricted or masked or open, depending upon how he has been able to meet developmental tasks in identity formation. His relationships with the family members may be provocative and antagonistic. There may be impairment of his gratification in being able to earn or to contribute because he feels *compelled* to relinquish his earnings. This giving up of his earnings before he feels ready to assume responsibility for dependents not infrequently will cause him to feel that he is still considered to be a child, that controls are imposed externally; his self-esteem will be impaired. In such situations, the social worker can play an important part in helping the adolescent and the parents to understand each other's reality needs, to help the parents understand the developmental struggle in which the adolescent is engaged, and to help the adolescent begin to take pride in the fact not only that he is earning but that he is accorded respect because he is fulfilling an adult function.

The way adolescents view and use money can offer the social worker important clues to the adolescent's developmental maturation and indicate areas in which he may have difficulty as an adult. Neurotic uses of money by adolescents may take several forms, in each of which the social worker will detect signs of danger.

The big spender is the youth who is always at the center in the school canteen or the candy store, ready to treat everybody from seemingly inexhaustible funds and trying to buy friendships he does not know how to acquire otherwise.

The borrower is the child who is always borrowing lunch money, snack money, pencils, or paper—from teachers or from younger students. He grows angry when he is denied or does not receive the response he seeks in his unsuccessful bid for attention and affection of which he feels deprived elsewhere.

The hoarder grasps to himself or hides whatever material possessions he has. He is unable to part with money and always wants to add more to it. For him money is tangible and incontrovertible evidence that he is strong (and in being strong, is different from his weak or generally absent father). It is through money that his sense of self-esteem appears to be nurtured. If the hoarder was given the money, for example, by a divorced father, whose giving was motivated by affection, the adolescent has a strong need to cling to this money as a symbol of the love and care which he may or may not really be receiving.

The pilferer is the adolescent who sneaks money from the teacher's purse or from purses or pockets left unguarded in school dressing rooms. The consequent attention may mean that he is recognized as a person or that he has found a way of striking at the adult close to him; he is "getting even" with those he feels have discriminated against him.

The cost pricer is the adolescent—usually a girl, but sometimes a boy—who has a need to know the precise cost of a classmate's purse or wallet or shoes in order to acquire something that is better. This demonstration of "superiority" is designed to enhance limited self-esteem.

The bright drop-out offers still another form of adolescent neurotic handling of money. He is the intelligent student who announces that he must leave school in order to work either to maintain himself or to contribute to the family's support. In actuality, there may be no economic pressures upon him or his family, but he sees in this excuse one that is acceptable in a society that holds the work ethic dear and respects acceptance of adult responsibilities in those who are not yet adult. He may use what appears to be a socially accepted reason to cover his failure in school, his inability to maintain at least comfortable relationships with others, and to withdraw from a situation which contains stress. This manner of responding to a stressful situation reflects inability to identify rational alternatives and to arrive at an appropriate decision for which the adolescent can accept the consequences. The key to this rationalizing behavior lies in faulty development of trust, self-esteem, and identity.

Money has particular meanings for elderly persons, the seeds of these meanings having been planted in earlier stages of development. Diminishing physical capacities, often emphasized by the death of contemporaries, frequently lead to fears about the future and "security." Especially if, as a child, he suffered physical or emotional deprivation, the elderly person believes his security is measured by money at hand, and he will live frugally, hoarding his means. Refusal to spend *now* is a denial that the end of his life is approaching. There is an anxious clinging to savings and insurance policies; there is a reluctance to spend all of even a minimally adequate income, although he may experience physical suffering. These dynamics hold some explanation of the kinds of situations often reported in the press where, on the death of an elderly person who was thought to be starving, it is discovered that his quarters contain substantial sums of cash or many bank books.

Old dependency conflicts are stirred up in elderly persons. The aged person may become demanding and hostile in an effort to prove to himself that he is still of value to society, and this value takes the tangible form of money. His adult children may be impatient, not understanding the real reasons for requests that seem excessive. The social worker has to be aware of the reason for the frequent requests for "extras" for which the worker can observe no actual need. Such elderly persons respond positively to opportunities to talk about the days when they were in their prime. Such opportunities to talk often quickly replace the unrealistic requests for material help.

Increased dependency and lowered self-esteem may lead to guilt and depression so that the elderly person deprives himself rather than ask for help. He thus avoids manifesting that his status as a contributing member of society is reduced. A last vestige of independence, and symbolic of his capacity and ability still to control his own affairs, is the elderly person's handling of his income, no matter how small it may be. This accounts for the fact that many recipients of old age assistance who truly do not have enough resources to maintain health at a reasonably adequate level fail to share with the social worker their problems: they cannot afford to abuse their self-esteem by admitting to the reality of difficulty in managing even with an insufficient amount of funds.

The broken family characteristically is headed by a woman, and the absence of the father in itself—especially if he is living—creates a multitude of problems which complicate attitudes within the family about money and the uses to which it is put. As has already been mentioned, breadwinning, in our society, generally is delegated to the father, and the responsibility for planning and decision-making about family living and child rearing and discipline, to a greater or lesser degree, depending on the cultural, ethnic, and social class factors, also generally involves the father. The absence of the father profoundly alters the traditional roles, responsibilities, and relationships of the remaining family members. Strong feelings of hurt, anger, frustration, fear, anxiety, and guilt are produced. Some of these deep feelings may be displaced onto money.

The mother who fails to make an adequate adjustment to the father's absence may express her disturbance by spending on luxuries to gratify her own emotional needs or to "make up" to the children for the father's absence and her seeming inadequacy. She may spend recklessly as an expression of despair and resentment; or she may gamble or spend recklessly on alcohol. As was discussed in Chapter 9, money often is the device used by the parent to create strain and tension in the new family of the ex-spouse and to compete for the affection and loyalty of the children by the size and the frequency of material gifts made to them.

The unmarried mother is faced with all the money problems of any mother without a husband, but in addition, she must deal with the complex of feelings related to her unwed parenthood. To her, money may mean compensation for social disgrace; it may spell security for herself and her child; it may be an instrument for punishing the alleged father—through demands legally or otherwise instigated. Overindulgence of the child may serve the mother as a weapon for self-punishment, for handling her guilt feelings about the child's status, or her rejection of the child. Or overindulgence may serve to demonstrate to foster parents, to herself, to others, that she is adequate as a mother.

THE MANAGEMENT OF MONEY

Setting the Goals

A determination of the nature and extent of counseling with regard to problems of money that are troublesome to the family members or to others in the community should be made on the basis of the problem brought by the troubled family or family member to the agency and of the goals that are realistic with regard to the particular family and its total situation—including internal as well as external factors. There must be, for example, an assessment of the emotional readiness and the intellectual capacity of the family members to examine their money problems realistically, whether causal or symptomatic. The help that the social worker gives depends in large measure on this readiness and capacity and, therefore, on the level of the family members' self-esteem and trust. Problems around money do not lend themselves to resolution unless the person experiencing money troubles can trust himself and those involved with him to examine honestly why they use money in whatever fashion they do and, understanding this, to plan ways of altering the habitual and troubling methods of using money. Jimmy's father, for example, will not be ready to deal with Jimmy's antisocial behavior until the father can see how the absence of a personal allowance expresses to Jimmy his distrust of the boy and how this serves as a tool for control of the boy. The likelihood is that the father's failure to trust will contribute to Jimmy's fulfillment of his father's expectations that he will resort to theft.

Mrs. Thomas has to gain some trust in her husband's love for her and his readiness to give her all that he can afford—or has to give—before she can undertake to develop with him a realistic plan for management of household finances, a plan based on their *mutual* trust. Jimmy's father and Mrs. Thomas may have, in the opinion of the worker, the potential for understanding their ways of using money and for utilization of this potential.

The worker's assessment might indicate that Mrs. White offers a poor prospect for modification of behavior, that she has a limited tolerance for frustration, and that external controls may need to be established in order that she may manage the grant well enough to meet her family's basic survival needs. This might have to be undertaken without any effort being made to interpret to her the meaning of her pattern of purchasing. Approaches may have to be at a concrete level, with the concomitant recognition of the probability that her characteristic way of handling tasks other than the spending of money is impulsive, thoughtless, and largely self-gratifying. On the other hand, Mrs. White's installment purchases may increase because of a lack of knowledge about wiser ways of making purchases. She may respond, then, to suggestions of ways to handle her installment payments more effectively. In other words, the goal for working with a Mrs. White may be a limited one and focus on the day-to-day dealings with financial matters in order to keep indebtedness at a realistic level.

Mr. Hodkins has demonstrated considerable ability to handle his affairs in the past, including the crisis of his wife's illness and death. Is his "desperate need" really for financial help, or is this the expression of his grief over his recent bereavement? If his realistic sorrow is acknowledged, manifest strengths recognized, and he is helped to decide what his next step should be—how to take it and being encouraged in so doing—will he mobilize himself to regain mastery of his situation?

Had the worker wondered out loud why Mrs. Jackson made no reply to the information about fees, might Mrs. Jackson have shared her uneasiness about the child's stepfather's role in the family's problems and had access to some help in how to consider appropriate approaches to deal with her situation so that the child could be involved in the necessary treatment?

A family may be confronted with problems around money because of the behavior of an individual member who may gamble, drink, or become heavily involved in debt. These generally are problems that stem from impairment in development, as was discussed in previous parts of this volume. The dynamics for these kinds of behavior are similar. When expressed through excessive spending— in cash or use of credit arrangements—the family may face not only emotional and economic distress but also legal problems. Some people have a need always to be in debt, for example, and to have "power" over creditors as a device to compensate for a sense of inadequacy. Such people may have sufficient money to pay the creditor, but decline to do so on various pretexts—or on none at all. They have a need to be in control or to "get even with the world" in much the same way as Mr. Townsend (referred to in Chapter 10) who declined to pay for his board and care unless the operator of the foster home repeatedly requested payment. Such situations require the same approach as those in which the manifestations of problems are not in money terms. What has been stated in earlier chapters with regard to requisites for social functioning at a competent level is equally applicable, of course, in instances where money matters are either the symptom or the cause of problems in a family.[1]

Toward Solvency

Many families become involved in excessive debt because they have not learned how to manage their financial affairs effectively, or because they have not wanted to until confronted with a critical situation. The failure to learn may originate in developmental factors, or it may be the consequence of lack of experience—as is frequently true with young couples who have had no opportunity before marriage to earn, save, and spend. Their parents did everything for them. Now, on their own for the first time, they make the mistakes they should have experienced on a smaller scale in their growing-up years. And their inexperience is often compounded because the money management pattern of their parents has not served well either for the parents or their children.

Regardless of the reason for the money management problems—inexperience, personality difficulty, stressful differences between income and expenditures, there are certain procedures with which the social worker should be familiar and which he should be prepared to utilize differentially in accordance with the understanding he has of the family, their common goals, and the steps possible—in the view of the family as well as of the worker—to achieve these goals. The worker's help may be in the form of giving information. The worker may help the family to understand their own or community behavior with regard to money management. It may be necessary for the worker to assist in detailed review of the family's financial management in order to help the members to gain partial or complete mastery of the money troubles. It then may be possible for the worker to aid the family in applying *these* learnings to the conduct of other life tasks.

The Design

Both to permit better use of the money available to it and to deal with problems of overexpenditure (whether crises or not) require that the family engage in some planning—what may appear to be some hard fiscal labor. According to Robert Benchley, "The

[1] For full discussion of the meanings of money and counseling goals and techniques, refer to Frances Lomas Feldman, *The Family in a Money World* (New York: Family Service Association of America, 1957).

advantage of keeping family accounts is clear. If you do not keep them you are uneasily aware of the fact that you are spending more than you are earning. If you do keep them you *know* it." This *knowing* is an important key to solvency.

There are almost as many kinds of feelings about planning or designing an expenditure plan—commonly called a budget—as there are meanings of money. Some people fail to budget because they do not know how and they are sure that the use of such a device would be as constricting as a strait jacket. Some do not develop a budget plan because they think they have so little money it is pointless to work out a systematic way of spending it. Some do not like what they believe to be the "discipline" of keeping track of figures; they tend to claim they are poor at arithmetic.

Regardless of the reason that is offered, most families need to have some kind of device for keeping an acceptable relationship between their income and its outgo. The device does not always have to be written down; nor does it always have to be in connection with a complicated organizing structure like some of the available "budget books." The family that has the same income year after year and the same basic expenditures quickly learns how much is required for ongoing expenses and how much is left from this income for other items without the necessity for reducing this to writing on a regular basis. A periodic assessment to see whether any changes have been occurring—because perhaps the cost of living generally has gone up or family interests (in levels of education, or living standards, or forms of recreation) and, therefore, needs have changed, or because children are older—can help them decide whether or not to alter their spending and saving plan in a fashion consistent with these changes.

Most families, however, do need to follow some system for knowing, in light of just how much income they have, what the most effective ways are for spending and saving in order to meet current needs and to plan for future desires. Particularly the dependent family or the family with a low income or the family with higher income but rigid obligations should have some kind of design for managing their income because these families have the least prospect of flexibility in the use of money; they need a design to insure that they can see where the money is going and change its direction if this is indicated.

There are many families, however, who cannot carry out this task. In particular, many families in low-economic groups are not amenable to budget planning. This is not to say that they lack the intelligence, especially since budgeting can be a very simple matter. Rather, the obstacle is of a different order. It has already been noted that characteristically low-income families live only for the present and do not plan ahead. Budgeting *is* planning ahead. Likewise, low-income families often have difficulty with time, and time concepts are essential in *any* kind of budget planning—the mere word "planning" implies time into the future.

The Steps

There are specific steps that workers can take in helping families to deal with the matter of time and of planning into the future. For example, the family having difficulty in an urban center —or, for that matter, elsewhere—in setting aside from its income funds needed for future payments of rent or utilities or other obligations, can be helped with a system as simple as a series of envelopes, labeled by item and month (or week) for easy identification, in which specified sums can be placed for later expenditure. This is a device that is useful for many children in planning ahead.

A family, however, with the ability to do so, can be helped to develop a plan based on its individual needs, desires, and circumstances that will serve both to keep the family reasonably solvent and to master the task of the family's financial management. Such a plan commonly involves four steps.

The first step is a determination of the *total* amount of *income* received by the family, either in toto or by individual family members. This determination of income should separate the *regular* and reliable income from the *sporadic* or occasional sums that find their way to the family. Income from wages, from child support payments, from investments of various kinds might fall under fixed income. Overtime payments, however, or the child support payment that is not received with any degree of regularity, or the casual contribution from a relative or from some other source, needs to be viewed separately from the income that is relatively reliable. The worker who is engaged in counseling with a family regarding money matters generally will find it more expedient to project this kind of income over a year's period. The family, however, for whom it is difficult to think that far ahead, may need to confine itself to considering income only for the current week or current month. In considering this income, attention should be directed to income that is actually available in light of deductions that are mandatory (taxes or union dues, for example) and voluntary (charitable deductions or some group insurance).

The second step is to consider the identification and listing of *fixed obligations* incurred by the family, and to project these also, if possible, over a period of a year, noting them month by month. Thus the cost of shelter, which generally is a fixed amount, can be shown for each month of the year. The insurance premium that is paid only quarterly will appear at the appropriate intervals. The purchase of an automobile license once a year will appear at the specified due point. Installment debt obligations, which may be of varying or decreasing amounts, can be shown in relation to the other fixed obligations. Such a projection of the fixed obligations over a period of a year—those to which the person is legally obligated or which must be met without any exercise of judgment on the part of the family—enables the worker and the family to observe the points in time when the obligations reach peaks. These points in time constitute crisis periods in money management for most people, unless they have in some way succeeded in putting aside what will be required to meet these periodic obligations. These peaks also serve to show the relationship of credit purchases to income. The family obtains a visual perspective whereby it may be possible to become aware, not infrequently for the first time, that they are committing what may be a disproportionate amount of income to installment purchases or other credit arrangements, and to note a pattern of heaviest demand on income at certain points for which no special preparation has been made.

This second step also examines the fixed obligations in relation to regular income in order to ascertain what balance remains for *day-to-day living* and for protection of future income (savings, insurance, and so on). If day-by-day expenses for food, utilities, transportation, recreation, and other needs require more than the difference remaining between the fixed obligations and the regular income, the fixed obligations should be scrutinized to determine which can be modified or over what period of time they can be liquidated. This kind of scrutiny also is likely to uncover ways in which consolidation of some payments can ease the financial pressure; or this scrutiny may even indicate when an item that has been purchased should be relinquished. (Care, however, must be exercised to be sure that the relinquishment of the item does in fact relieve the family of the obligation to pay for it. In many states, despite the return of the merchandise, the purchaser is obligated to finish paying for it or to pay the difference between what he still owes and what a new buyer may pay the creditor for the returned item.)

The third step is an examination of what the family requires for meeting its daily needs. These *day-to-day expenditures* for most families offer the only opportunity for flexibility—to spend more money for food or recreation if income goes up, or to reduce the amount that is spent for groceries, clothing, or other items as income is curtailed. Included in this group of items should be *everything* on which money is spent and which the family can remember. It should be noted that a working wife may have additional costs of which she is not particularly aware, yet which constitute a drain on family income: baby-sitting services, coffee breaks, contributions to collections in the office for baby showers and other events which do not ordinarily affect male employees to the same degree.

The identification of the day-to-day expenditures generally is a little more difficult in some respects than the identification of items that can be categorized as fixed obligations. If the family being counseled does not know or cannot recall how much is spent for what (and a newly married couple will have no experience as a couple on this score), it is advisable for them to keep an honest record for a period of at least several weeks or a month so that they can use this information as a point of departure. The setting down of *all* of these items does several things. It brings to conscious awareness the multitude of items on which money is spent and those which may have less importance to the family members than others. It brings to conscious awareness what might seem to be disproportionate spending or unnecessary spending for one item as against another. It brings to conscious awareness the possibility that the family really cannot account reasonably for where some of its money goes.

Keeping of this kind of record calls upon inner resources that are present in varying degrees in different individuals. Joint consideration of the collected information reveals important clues to the worker as to what approach to use in helping the family to deal with its problems, of which money may be only one. For example, the marital partners who do not really trust each other will have greater difficulty in keeping a record of expenditures. A family in which one parent needs to be very controlling may find that the recording of daily expenditures serves as a weapon for the overly controlling person. The individual whose self-esteem may have suffered considerable damage may be unable to face an annotation of expenditures which appear to him to be critical of him as a person with reasonable competence in managing his affairs. The matter-of-fact, nonjudgmental approach of the worker is essential in enabling families troubled by money matters to begin to look realistically and directly at a source of trouble, to be able to concretize what otherwise is only a nebulous anxiety. Once concretized, it can be attacked and steps initiated toward mastery.

It is essential, too, for the worker to bear in mind that it is impossible for most people, especially in a large family, to remember all of the details of how money has been spent. This may be for reasons of personality, but it also may be that there is no need to remember all of them. Furthermore, one has to look with special care at the situation where such minute detail is recalled and recorded. Does this point to possible rigidity and compulsivity in personality structure? What are the implications of this kind of situation for modification of the troubling behavior?

The fourth step—often the hardest to really face—is to subtract from the fixed income the amount of fixed obligations to reveal the amount of money that a family has *available* for its everyday expenditures, and then to subtract from the figure remaining the amount *expended* for day-to-day purposes. Any balance left after the fixed obligations have been deducted discloses two things. One is that there may be insufficient money for meeting the daily obligations without resorting to drawing on any reserves that may exist, or borrowing. Consequently a re-examination and a reassignment of fixed obligations to be met would be in order. The other consequence may be that more money is left than a family had anticipated, indicating either that some items among their several expenditures remain unaccounted for or that they had more available for other uses than they had been aware of. If a family is to be solvent—meeting adequately its present obligations and also providing for future needs and aspirations—this step should provide some indication of what balance actually exists or what adjustments should be made in order to permit the possibility of some savings—savings for emergencies as well as for fulfillment of future wishes.

This four-step approach, followed in greater or lesser detail, is basic to considering with a family the nature of its money difficulties. If the problem, for any reason that may have occurred, is primarily related to excessive debts, a major assessment is in order to ascertain which of the obligations can be rearranged in order to facilitate their handling within the current income and without further indebtedness. For example, in addition to the $29 that Mrs. White was supposed to pay for the vibrator chair, she also owed $11 a month for the purchase of an automatic washing machine, $14 a month on a loan of $250 to be used as a down payment on the purchase of a used automobile, and $58 a month for car payments. She also was paying $16 a month for an electric refrigerator. Her income totaled $262 a month, of which $184 was in the form of social insurance benefits. (Mr. White had died two years before.) By the time the monthly obligations were paid—when they were—Mrs. White had only $134 left to feed herself and her four children, to pay rent (which came to $125 a month), to meet the cost of utilities and anything else that might occur during the month. As she looked at the listing of expenses to which she was obligated, she decided that as long as she was not employed she did not need the car. She was not willing, however, to take any action about the vibrator chair, or about the bronze-tone refrigerator which she thought was aesthetically important to her although another kind of refrigerator involving less money would have served the daily needs of the family.

It was evident that some of these obligations were scheduled to continue for at least a year—some were commitments for as long as five years. An important decision that Mrs. White would have to make, especially as her income was unlikely to be increased, was to consider which of these items she could do without (like the car) and which she needed to retain for any reason. Essential, too, was the decision regarding how she would approach the creditors in order to clarify directly with them the unlikelihood that she could meet these payments with regularity, and to consider the kind of proposal she could offer each of the creditors.

Only as Mrs. White becomes able to make practical choices among the items and realistic decisions concerning what she is ready to do about bringing her situation under control will she be able to move to a point of having sufficient funds available each month to meet the basic food and shelter costs. Furthermore, the experience of determining how she can approach the resolution of a present financial problem is essential to her learning to think about what is valid to purchase and in what way. With the worker's encouragement, often with the support of specific suggestions, Mrs. White was able to return the car without the necessity of continuing payments on it; she was able to exchange her refrigerator for one less expensive and thereby to reduce the monthly payments. She also looked around to find less costly housing, and she worked out a plan whereby her blind mother who lived next door could comfortably move into the White household and share the rent with Mrs. White.

When Mrs. White felt ready to do so, family conferences were held which included her mother. Mrs. White was astonished to discover her mother's distrust of the vibrator chair and her resentment of the fact that Mrs. White had purchased it without asking her mother what she would like. The air was filled with hostility as Mrs. White expressed her resentment that her mother did not appreciate the sacrifices Mrs. White was making in her behalf, and the mother angrily said she could "take care of herself." Mrs. White became aware of the fact that she had not truly emancipated herself from her mother, that she was more concerned with her relationship with her mother than she was with her relationship with her own children; she was amazed to discover that her perceptive mother was uneasy about Mrs. White's attention to her while neglecting her own children.

Significant in this kind of situation is the learning experience to the family that obtains from the necessity of examining the practicality of their financial position and taking steps to handle the several aspects of it. Mrs. White was able to determine the relative values to her of the various items being bought and to mobilize her courage and energy to consider directly with the creditors her financial situation: to tell them that she was dependent upon income maintenance programs and to engage their help. The plan that was developed resulted in the resale of the vibrator chair by the mother with minimum loss to Mrs. White; the car was returned, and the company which had sold her the appliances rewrote the contract to spread the payments in small amounts over a longer period of time without substantially adding to the total cost. Her success in resolving various aspects of the financial problem raised her self-esteem to the point where she decided she could begin to work out plans for the supervision of her growing children and begin to examine possibilities of training for some kind of job.

The four steps delineated above are equally practical in application to the family with considerable income and the family with too little, to the family maintaining a high level of living and to the family barely able to subsist. While the steps are the same, however, the wide differences in capacity, behavior, and other circumstances, including major functions of the agency, will govern just how the steps are followed in each instance, if at all. They will be differentially used in a situation like the Whites' or the McCormicks' (Chapter 3) or the Burns' (Chapter 16). They will be differently used in helping married couples to emancipate themselves from the domineering or controlling parents of either of the marital partners; they will be differently used in helping a family with adolescents (or younger children) determine whether it is or is not realistic to think that a personal allowance *can* be made to the child or that the older child *can* begin to receive an allotment of family income that will enable him to plan and execute the purchasing of his clothes or other essential items (or not essential, but which the family elects to provide).

In many situations, particularly among families receiving public assistance or some other income maintenance service, help to the family is not in the form of *how* to manage. The provision of money for the meeting of survival needs—and, hopefully, a little more— may be *the* way of providing the family with the help required. Other help of a tangible nature also may be given: medical care, an appliance of some kind, an educational plan. But the family may be able to manage its income adequately, even skillfully. There is no doubt of the fact that many mothers dependent upon Aid to Families with Dependent Children, for example, use the grant with great resourcefulness—and manage well, as do many families whose earnings are at an equally low level.

Some families may have periodic need for additional help because their ongoing income simply provides for no flexibility to meet the occasional special need, regardless of whether the family was planful or not in anticipating the need. Each special occasion consequently becomes a crisis and is handled accordingly. The counseling with such families may be around anticipating special needs when possible and examining the potentials of resources for meeting these or, if none can be developed, helping them to compromise so they can manage within that reality with minimum damage to self-esteem. Of importance in this difficult task is the goal of enabling the family with such limited means not just to apportion the funds to meet survival needs, but to encourage the consideration of the use of the funds as a step toward independence: examining alternatives, whatever they may be, is a process that not infrequently offers some hope and expectation of change that can *lead* to change and increased self-reliance.

MONEY AS A COUNSELING TOOL

It bears reiteration that, throughout life, money is a powerful motivating force: for the individual, the family, and society. It attains importance of some kinds in early childhood; it continues to influence behavior throughout life because of what it actually can do as well as what it symbolizes. It is necessary to satisfy physical needs; it often is used to satisfy emotional needs.

It motivates people to go into business for themselves, or to seek advancement in their jobs, or to procure education that will enable them to obtain the kind of work that will permit them both to maintain themselves and their dependents comfortably and, at the same time, to engage in work that has satisfaction for its own sake. Whether money is deliberately used in work with families as a motivator for change, for instilling aspirations, for achieving competence in social functioning, or whether money is used simply to meet survival needs, or whether there is neither direct nor indirect attention to the place of money in the family's functioning—the family's attitudes and behavior with regard to money contain valuable clues for effective work with the family. However, when money is used as a tool for direct help or for enhancing the worker's—and often the family's—understanding, it must be employed with care and sophistication so that it does not become a device for control rather than a facilitator for self-management and competence in social functioning.

21

USING SOCIAL RESOURCES

THE TROUBLES a family brings to a given social agency not infrequently require that the social worker augment or complement his own skill by the use of special resources, within the agency or in the community, in the amelioration of the family's problem or some aspect of it. Or the worker may find that the help the family needs can more appropriately be offered by another resource in the community. In the latter instance, the social worker may then accept responsibility for connecting the family and the resource by giving information to the family, or he may decide on the basis of assessment of the particular situation to make the referral directly. In the former, the worker may refer the family for the required service or he may initiate the contact alone or with the family, depending on the use it is anticipated will be made of the resource, and how—

if at all—the worker will continue with the family and with the social resource now being involved.

The social resources available to a social worker are of several kinds. They may be in the form of agency or non-agency resources in the community (a psychiatrist in private practice, for example); they may be in the form of services located within the worker's own agency, such as foster home finding or legal aid or work training or placement; they also may be in the form of consultative services of specialists in social work or another profession (home economist, group work consultant, or psychologist, for example) that are located either within the worker's own agency or elsewhere in the community.

Still another resource is available many times to social workers although often it is not regarded in terms of its utilization as a tool in the rendering of service to a family. This is the structure of the agency, with its congeries of policies and regulations which may be used in behalf of the family or brought into direct play in working with the family.

It is not the intent of this chapter to delineate all of the kinds of social resources that may be available to the worker engaged in helping a family or family member to master a particular problem or task. However, as an illustrative rather than as a comprehensive presentation, this chapter will direct some attention to the general use of community social resources, the use of group services as a tool in helping families, and the ways in which agency structure and policy may be constructively employed in providing the troubled family with help.

COMMUNITY SOCIAL RESOURCES

Family problems often are so complex in their nature and scope that the helping services of the social worker can be most effective when an array of resources is available to the worker for use in meeting particular needs or particular aspects of needs of troubled families. A family agency, whether voluntary or public, may have within it resources to provide for vocational training or retraining to assist in the resolution of debt problems, to assess and resolve legal aspects of family problems, and so on. Very often, however, if such services exist at all in the community, they are located outside the structure of the given agency; their use can be arranged only by a direct request from the family or, in many instances, by a referral directly from the social worker. The nature and timing of the utilization of social resources necessarily must be related to the total plan for work with a particular family. This plan, as earlier chapters have discussed, will have been developed on the basis of knowledge about the family's problem, the circumstances that have contributed to it, the ways in which the family has dealt with this and similar problems in the past, and the potential of the family members for mastering the present problems. The goals, which lead to the consideration that community resources be used, will have been formulated in terms of whether the expectation is that behavior and environmental factors can be modified over a period of time, or the stress of the immediate problem be relieved, or whether the situation can be kept from deteriorating.

The utilization of social resources is closely related to the process of establishing trust, maintaining or enhancing self-esteem, and assuring that channels of communication to and from the family are unclogged. Thus, the family member who turns to a social agency for help may feel rejected and his self-esteem reduced by the way the worker handles the matter of drawing upon other resources or referring the client elsewhere for help. If communication is lucid and direct, the family member will be clear about the purpose of the referral, the limitations of one organization in responding to a particular problem, and the opportunities present. He will be able to make a transfer without a sense that his problem is hopeless, or that he is, or that the agency is incapable of dealing with a problem like his.

The adequate person will be able to accept referral and take the steps necessary to follow through for the use of this resource. But even the adequate person may be immobilized temporarily by a crisis and unable to do anything except what the worker tells him. Unless the social worker then makes a direct contact with the resource and arranges the manner in which the family and the resource will come together, the likelihood is small that the person overwhelmed by crisis will follow through.

In some instances the immobilization and its associated anxiety are so great that the worker may find it advisable—if agency policy and time permit—to accompany the client to the appropriate resource, supporting him in this step, helping him to retain or gain a sense of trust in the worker's interest in him, and keeping his self-esteem at a level high enough to permit him to take action appropriate to his particular needs. Once such an adequate but temporarily immobilized person has made contact with the other agency, he generally is competent to follow through by himself with whatever action seems necessary.

The person who is a member of a chaotic family or a neurotic family may be unable to act independently upon a suggestion for the use of a particular community resource. Either the person is so disorganized that he is unable to focus on the reason for the use of the resource, or his speech and language are impaired to the extent that he cannot grasp the importance of the use of the resource. A worker may find that it is necessary to work out the arrangements for the referral and repeatedly propose the referral until the idea has become so familiar that the individual is then able, with help from the worker, to go to the resource.

This kind of reaction is not limited to special kinds of services such as those of a mental health clinic, although certainly it is more prevalent with respect to these. It appears also with regard to the use of other kinds of medical resources or the use of a legal aid facility, or referrals for employment assessment, training, or placement. Sometimes the failure of the person to follow through is caused by apprehension of which he may or may not be aware about what these facilities will offer. Sometimes his self-esteem has been so battered that he cannot face the necessity of asking for something, whatever it is, from still another community resource. It becomes a worker's responsibility to sort out situations in which the person is able to act on his own with only the suggestion from the worker, from those where more direct or even compelling action on the part of the social worker is indicated.

Special problems arise with reference to the use of psychiatric services. The mental problems, which may or may not be a part of the trouble that has brought the family to the agency's attention, not infrequently are related to shame, fear and, often, lack of understanding. As also was noted in the chapter on physical and emotional illness, many families tend to hide or in some way disguise the fact of emotional disturbance on the part of a family member. Therefore, they cannot bring themselves to utilize the services that are available to them. It is not uncommon in such instances to have the disturbed member actually reach a crisis state—a threat of suicide or a psychotic breakdown or some other overt form of deep disturbance—before the family can mobilize itself to use the help of the appropriate resource. It is exceedingly hard for many families to identify behavioral symptoms even in a bizarre form as mental disturbance; they are sure that the symptoms will pass. It is difficult for many families to take seriously, although a little anxiety may be provoked, the threat of a family member to commit suicide. They are familiar with the popular but often erroneous idea that the person who threatens suicide is not apt to carry out this threat. And there are many families who, largely because of cultural patterns, are very tolerant of the most bizarre kinds of behavior and accept the idea of hospitalization for a mentally ill member only at the point where a commitment by the court has been ordered because the patient is a hazard either to himself or to the community.

Reluctance does not extend only to the use of mental clinics and other psychiatric facilities. A father may think it "entirely unnecessary" for his child to participate in a group activity under the auspices of a social group work agency. The importance to youngsters of learning to interact with their peers on a healthy basis is not easy for all parents to grasp. If there are siblings the parents not infrequently say "there are plenty of kids at home." They see the group activity available in a specialized agency only as "fun" and they are not inclined to reward obstreperous or otherwise difficult children by providing them with what appears to be a purely recreational experience. Such parents sometimes reluctantly do accede to the suggestion but feel quite certain that it will be to no avail, and their acquiescence carries a note of humoring the worker. Of course the child, too, may be reluctant to accept a referral to a group work agency: if he is withdrawn he will be threatened by having to be with others. If his behavior has been acting-out and bordering on delinquent activity, he will resist the possibility of having to conform to the patterns within a group.

In considering, then, who should be referred to what kind of a resource, the worker needs to be clear about what the purpose will be with reference to a specific individual or family, how this service can be integrated into the total treatment of the total family, and the meaning of the obstacles that family members set up to avoid following through on a referral to a community resource. If the referral is to be at all effective, there must be an understanding on the part of the worker and the family and the community resource as to what the nature of their continuing relationship will be around the use of this resource. Will certain parts of the family treatment be assumed by the resource? For example, will the personnel in a mental health clinic carry full responsibility for the person who is seen as a primary patient, or should the referring worker continue with some part of the work with that person or his family? On what basis should the division of responsibility for work with the various members of the family and interpretation to each of the work of the other be decided? The issue really becomes one of whether the personnel in the agency will be working as a team or separately and what the responsibility of each will be in the total approach to the family.

When Resources are Lacking

The resources to be called on within a given community vary considerably from community to community. The social worker will seek to learn what his particular community has to offer, as well as what resources are not available. As was indicated in Chapter 17, the worker may undertake the task of developing a resource to meet a need of a particular family with whom he is working—and the success in one instance may lead to the development of a formal or informal service. Thus, in one small town with limited facilities for day care for children, it became apparent to the worker that Mrs. Griffith's endurance had reached the breaking point. Unless some systematic means could be devised to give her an hour or two each day to withdraw from overwhelming demands related to the constant physical and emotional requirements attendant upon the supervision of a seriously chronically ill child as well as three other young ones, there was every likelihood she would collapse and the consequent problems would be even more gigantic to handle than the current ones. With Mrs. Griffith's consent, the worker approached a church group (the Griffith family itself had no church ties), shared with them the nature of Mrs. Griffith's ordeal, and helped them reach and implement an enthusiastic decision to develop a relay system for relieving Mrs. Griffith for two hours daily—even if she used these only to sit somewhere alone. The positive effects of this help were immeasurable both to the mother and the whole family: for the eighteen months the child lived, this service was provided; its value lay not only in the respite it gave the mother, but also in her enhanced ability to continue to shoulder her responsibilities because "they cared" about her.

But many times even the most resourceful social worker is unable to locate community resources, formal or informal, to help a family with a specific problem. The problem may center around the severe mental retardation of a family member, or physical disability so handicapping that no presently known means can yield further help to the disabled person or his family. When resources simply cannot be found, the worker's task is to help the family to accept the reality of the situation and to work out even those plans that may be largely inadequate. At the same time, the worker should endeavor to help the family recognize logically *and* emotionally that the lack of resources is not the family's failure, that difficult as the situation may be, the family will somehow manage. The family may resent what appears to be the worker's failure to help, and may react with hostility to a "pollyanna" attitude. Nevertheless, it is not at all uncommon that this communicated expectation that the family *will* be able to carry the burden even if they cannot expect ultimately to master or alter the problem, helps to keep the family from sinking into immobilizing hopelessness and gives them some courage with which to continue with their difficult task.

The Range of Resources

Many important kinds of social resources are lacking in many communities. Not all, for example, have any or enough homemaker services or the wide array of facilities that are helpful in the care and development of children: foster family day care, child care centers for the well child or the one who is ill or suffers from some special physical or mental condition, group services of various kinds, and so on. Not all have legal aid services, or services that offer help in debt counseling in order to assist an insolvent or financially-troubled family to bring under control its financial management. Voluntary and public facilities for out-patient or in-patient care of the emotionally disturbed or mentally retarded or physically ill adult or child may be in short supply. Educational opportunities for the physically or mentally handicapped or for persons seriously culturally or socially disadvantaged may be limited or nonexistent. Not all communities have school social work, or "head start" programs, or visiting nurses services, or arrangements for vocational counseling. Not all have voluntary agencies with family counseling services or services to children.

Certain resources, however, are fairly generally accessible, and others are available to most communities, no matter how remote or small or isolated they may be. For example, public assistance is available in every state to the aged, blind, and families with children who meet the eligibility requirements established in the state for the federally aided programs (federal legislation makes mandatory the extension of such programs, when adopted by a state, *throughout* the state), and nearly all states also have federally supported aid to disabled persons. Likewise, Old-age, Survivors, and Disability Insurance is available to people everywhere. Similarly, certain medical programs are universally available, such as the medical provisions for the elderly, per the Social Security Act; and other medical programs (Title XIX of the Social Security Act) are present in most states.

Most areas also have public child welfare services available and these may include adoptions, foster care, protective services, and others. Some voluntary agencies reach most parts of the nation through regional arrangements if no local service is available. And almost every locality contains employment services (although the range of these services may vary considerably within a particular area and among states) under public auspices.

Work Training and Placement

One kind of resource that has been increasingly available during this decade is the resource, generally public, but sometimes voluntary, that has been focused on work training and placement. As Chapter 2 stated, a dominant value in our American culture is the work ethic and the expectation that adults will maintain themselves through their own work efforts, thus demonstrating their maturity and strength and independence. However, many people who turn to public or voluntary social welfare agencies for help, and many who live on marginal incomes without public assistance supplements, encounter considerable difficulty in obtaining or holding work consistent with their physical and emotional needs and their vocational capabilities. Others appear to lack motivation to work. The social worker in a voluntary or a public setting frequently is faced with tasks that include helping a family member to prepare to enter the labor force or to acquire skills and education that will enable him to remain productively attached to the labor force. Often a preliminary goal has to be attained: the stimulation of an unmotivated person either to prepare for or to procure and hold gainful employment.

Some of the conditions obtaining from our rapidly changing economic and industrial situation and that have an impact on people with limited skills or opportunities or motivations have already been discussed. What resources can the social worker call upon in dealing with the problems that are related to work or to its absence? Regardless of the capacity or motivation of the individual to be self-supporting, recognition must be given to the fact that certain minimal educational and vocational achievements are necessary preludes to productive attachment to the labor force, that lack of opportunities because of disadvantages associated with limited education or skill or race or geography or age are strong factors that separately or in the aggregate may contribute to a quality of hopelessness that countervails efforts toward employment. In addition, if those work opportunities that do exist lead only to work that the individual views as degrading because the low level of pay will not maintain him or his family, or is demeaning to self-esteem, there is reduced likelihood that the individual will reach out to grasp training opportunities that prepare him for assuming a role as an independent self-supporting provider for the family. The immediate and long-range vocational goals may be attained only by successive—and successful—small steps, and by selective examination and utilization of the increasing number and variety of work training and experience programs being established in communities throughout the nation. Such work training activities range from efforts to develop or conserve work habits and attitudes (including, sometimes, basic literacy courses) to improving or conserving existing skills or developing new ones. They may be administered under the auspices of a public employment service (like the Manpower Training and Development Act) or a public welfare agency (like those administered in accordance with Title V of the Economic Opportunity Act) or as an activity of some other organization or group with public funding like that under the Economic Opportunity Act or a private foundation.

GROUP SERVICES AS A HELPING RESOURCE

Groups and Developmental Tasks

Public assistance agencies, family service agencies, various children's services more and more are using group services in conjunction with the one-to-one and one-to-one-family relationship that has characterized such agencies in the past. The use of group services has particular significance in light of the fact that every person not only is a member of a family group but also is a part of the neighborhood, of the wider community in society; there are few parts of an individual's life which do not require interaction in some form or degree with others in a group. The child who is one of several in a family gains some experience in interaction with others from his life within the family, but he also becomes part of a group in school. He later becomes part of a group on a job. He may or may not be part of a group in a church or some unit with a social objective. Many children whose socialization in the home has been faulty, for any of many reasons discussed in earlier chapters, require an experience in a particular kind of group setting in order to learn how to interact with nonfamily members as a prelude to their more effective functioning as members of the broader society. The group may offer not only specific learning; it may serve also as a device for the control and modification of unsuccessful behavior.

One reason for organizing groups is to personalize social living and to make it comprehensible and acceptable. The child whose personality formation has not prepared him to participate fully in the wider community often can be helped by a small group experience that brings a smaller segment of the wider society into his experience and provides him with a stepping stone to the larger world. The fact that children need to have some kind of group experience is evident in many ways. Certainly it is common for the young child to create imaginary persons with whom he interacts in play: Indians, cowboys, assorted friends. If the child, growing older, continues to cling to these imaginary companions because he is not really separating reality from fantasy, this behavior may become a matter of concern. A group experience for such a person in that situation is not necessarily an appropriate answer. But the younger child who appropriately creates playmates tends to benefit by being exposed to real life peers with whom he is not the sole controlling person and with whom he learns to give as well as to take.

The older child, and the adolescent particularly, is commonly drawn to his peers and governed by the group behavior of his peers. But the urge to belong with others in an organized social group develops very strongly during the latency period, usually about six to twelve years of age, and continues through life. This is the age in which children want to start groups or have a gang. The idea of strength in numbers is appealing to them, but this also is an age when the children want to begin to escape from adult control and the adventure of moving beyond the family circle is enticing. These early attempts at organization of groups tend to fail unless they are organized and supported by adults. The self-centered nature of the interests of these younger children is still too strong for them to find a reasonable balance in give-and-take relationships, and very few children in this age group develop real leadership qualities. Some do, of course, but many display aggressive behavior that is not really leadership but a psychological form of bullying that serves as an outlet for a feeling of insufficient self-esteem and a failure in the development of self-trust. This kind of aggression evidences a bravado that is designed to assure the youngster that maybe he has something after all: note how others listen or obey or get out of the way. Significantly, youngsters in this age group tend to give their clubs or gangs names that imply aggression: "Wolf Pack" or "Indians" or "Lions." But these groups are organized to be strong and therefore they need a strong name; they usually aim to be masculine, and therefore they need a masculine name. The young child knows a great deal about being offensive, but he needs to learn how to be defensive and this is an experience he can productively obtain in a group activity.

By adolescence young people lean toward group activity, but there is a marked difference from their earlier kinds of participation. Now there are leaders and followers; the roles in the groups shift errati-cally. While some individuals may be described as "late bloomers," the patterns for functioning are fairly well set for individual per-sonalities. The nature of the pattern varies considerably with the strengths and the weaknesses and the personality formation of the adolescent and, consequently, group experience that is selected for specific purposes to meet the needs of specific adolescents must be carefully identified in relation to the development of the par-ticular adolescent. Care needs to be exercised so that the adolescent is not placed in a group situation where his already limited self-esteem will be further reduced, or where his trust cannot be main-tained at an appropriate level.

The nature of the group experience in adolescence can have a sharp impact on adult socialization. The values subscribed to by an adolescent group can effectively be used in helping some young people to begin to be emancipated from the family, to begin to as-sume responsibilities independent of the family responsibilities, to begin to feel their way as individuals separate from, yet part of, the family group. Often the values learned by the adolescent in a group are contrary to those that are present in his family. If the values in the family are distorted—or there are no standards—the group expe-rience may reinforce the inadequate models provided by the family. The adolescent may find himself in a group of peers whose families, like his own, are disorganized, chaotic, or follow cultural patterns not consistent with or acceptable in a predominantly middle-class society. Or his rebellion against parents—for whatever reason this may exist over and above the normal drive toward independence—may lead him to join a group holding values and ideas diametrically opposed to those taught in his nuclear family.

The social worker's task may be to involve the adolescent, who has been exposed to either of such situations, in a group that will permit or encourage the modification of the standards he has been acquiring or following or, at the very least, will make clear to him that his persistence in adhering to unacceptable patterns of behavior is contrary to the views of the majority in the group. His need to conform to the patterns of his peers can serve as a strong lever in altering the course of his behavior. If the attitudes in his peer group are antagonistic to those he holds and if there is no balancing inter-vention by a social worker or other person skilled in group dynamics and group leadership, his negative behavior may defensively become deeply entrenched. The peer group culture has a stronger influence on the personality development of the adolescent and young adult than almost any other social force. Because of this factor and because the peer group offers the adolescent an opportunity to express revolt against parents, against society, against specific kinds of authority, and to share the responsibility with his peers for his uninhibited expression of aggression, adolescents tend to seek out groups whose members have similar needs for behavioral expression. This is one of the motivating elements and social workers, reaching out to gangs with the objective of helping the majority to alter attitudes, know that the conversion of one will lead to the conversion of the others.

In old age once again there is a reversal in the balance of dependency and independency needs. Group activity may serve a vital role in enabling the older person to continue to feel connected with the world in which he sees his contemporaries becoming chronically ill or dying. The nuclear family no longer has much of a place for this older person, and some of the satisfactions earlier provided through direct family experiences no longer are as available. The older person frequently finds the stimulation of mutually interested companionship highly important and a factor that reduces the prospect of despair and depression. For some elderly persons an organized group activity as such does not suffice and a group living arrangement is desirable. For some who prefer a greater degree of isolation, a group living arrangement is dispiriting. The appropriateness of a group care living arrangement must be determined, as Chapters 8 and 10 have noted, on the basis of a variety of factors, including how interested in social activities the individual older person had been in earlier periods of his life, how ready he has been in the past to enter into a relationship that involves considerable give and take, and so on.

THE WORKER'S USE OF GROUPS AS A HELPING DEVICE

It is necessary for the social worker in any agency to recognize the importance and meaning of group life to individual and family functioning and to know something about its behavior at any age. And it is important, when a particular situation indicates the advisability, to be able to draw upon the community's social resources to make available to a given family or family member the advantages of participation in a selected group activity. The group services may be offered directly by the worker who is helping the family with other kinds of services. For example, an older adolescent boy facing the prospect of going out for the first time to find a job may be uneasy about how to approach this task. Other boys known to the worker may feel similarly, whether they express this or not. It is possible for the worker, and particularly one who is in a public assistance agency, to bring together boys with this common problem and provide them with the opportunity to form a group with a focus on how to approach an employer. The common interest clearly felt by the several members of the group serves as a binding force and enables the group, once it has become a cohesive unit, to move to other problems in which the respective members are interested. The joint approach of the boys to a reality situation which they find troubling in one way or another enables each to gain some courage as well as ideas from others, to recognize that the problems he faces are not unique to him and that he has the same prospects as the others to resolve the problems satisfactorily.

The social worker whose work focus does not include direct work with groups nevertheless may call upon group service resources that exist either within the same agency or a group services agency in the community. The worker whose experience is limited in the use of groups may find it advisable to use consultation available either inside or outside the agency in order to decide the kind of group that has most to offer a particular family or family member in the light of the goals established in resolving the family's problems. Three major kinds of groups are available.

The Educational Group

The educational group is organized primarily for the purpose of transmitting knowledge as in the example just offered with regard to the boys about to start job-hunting. Such groups formed for the purposes of education are of two kinds; both are related primarily to the level of sophistication of the participants. Thus a group of mothers who are recipients of Aid to Families with Dependent Children may benefit from group activities in which some basic information is transmitted to them, such as household management, child-rearing practices, or nutrition. They organize around a specific time-limited interest of current importance in their daily lives. The objective of the group is to bring information at a level and in a form that is comprehensible in light of education, communication levels, living arrangements (do they have hot water? is cooking done inside? on what kind of stove?). But there is a correlative objective: to enable these mothers, through social interaction with each other, to increase the level of their communication, to have an opportunity to increase their self-esteem—requisites for improved social competence.

Educational groups formed for the purpose of transmitting knowledge may also be created for persons who have a common interest in learning about a specific kind of information—for example, family life education. Such groups, which commonly are formed by family agencies, often voluntary, occasionally public, rely on a more sophisticated mode of communication than do the groups referred to earlier. The former type of group generally is problem-oriented; the latter sometimes is, but more generally the participants are in search of information. The social worker who undertakes to establish either kind of group may take responsibility for the conduct of the group and for bringing in specialists to provide particular kinds of knowledge, or he may serve in the capacity of a discussion leader, with the group members sharing ideas and reacting to information.

Counseling Groups

Of a different order are the group counseling units, which are of three kinds. One is designed to provide a socialization experience, that is, to provide a specific type of experience to persons with a particular kind of need. For example, a group of fatherless boys who need to have a masculine model may be brought together in a group not only because of the need for male identification but also because these particular boys have difficulty with one-to-one relationships. Similarly, mothers without husbands may join together not only for the interaction values that the group provides but because in the group each mother feels that she is not alone with problems unique to her and she can share with other mothers problems and devices related to rearing children in fatherless homes. The growing pattern of "parents without partners" groups focuses on this kind of socialization need.

A second group counseling form of organization is designed to alter behavior, attitudes, and feelings of the people within the group. The content of these group sessions tends to be focused not on a common special problem like fatherless families but rather on life experiences that appear threatening or dangerous and which require group support and reaction to keep under appropriate control. Such group counseling is carried on in a wide range of agencies, public and voluntary, sometimes by the worker who is working with a particular family having a member involved in the group, sometimes by another staff person within the same agency; and sometimes the group activity is conducted in an external setting. A hospital for the mentally ill may have groups of patients engaged in group counseling sessions; adolescents who have been unable to resolve some of the tasks of adolescence may participate in a peer group; or persons with a unique illness may come together to consider the impact on themselves and their families of their illness.

A third kind of group counseling unit is formed for the purpose of members giving aid and support to each other. Probably the best known is Alcoholics Anonymous, but there are other groups whose members have special problems and respond to group support and counseling. There is, for example, Recovery, Inc., in which patients, formerly mentally ill, meet together for their common and individual support in facing a community that greets formerly mentally ill persons with apprehension. Or there is a group of men, for example, who have been involved in training following surgery for cancer of the larynx, who will benefit from an opportunity to interact with others facing the same problems in learning new modes of communication, making new adjustments to living in our society, as well as in their family and vocational settings. These often are designated as "self-help" groups.

Group counseling units sometimes are formed on the initiative of the families. This is true particularly of the kinds that are designed to offer a socialization experience and to alter behavior, attitudes, and feelings. Some family social workers also take initiative in the formation of the latter kind of group but more often these are units that have been created under the auspices of an organization with a specific related function. The esophageal groups generally are established under the aegis of cancer societies, for example. The family's social worker may participate in the meetings of such groups when it seems advisable in the interests of encouraging the participation of an individual family member. Or the social worker may be instrumental in enlisting the aid of a particular special-interest organization in establishing a specialized group which can then be used as a resource by the person in need of its help.

The "Gang"

The third category of groups has elements markedly different from the other two. These are the groups already established and generally containing adolescents and young adults who have exhibited antisocial behavior in some fashion. These groups are approached by the neighborhood worker who endeavors to become associated with a particular group, to be accepted by the members with the hope of achieving some modification of social behavior. Characteristically, the social worker goes "where the action is." A family social worker may be aware that a member of a particular family unit is involved in such a group. The service of the family worker generally is related to conferring from time to time with the neighborhood worker in order that each will be aware of developing crises or special clues about behavior that have come to light and have an impact on the individual or the family, and that the goals for the members of the group are not inconsistent with those for the family. Certainly the goals will not be identical because the immediate objectives in reaching the members of such neighborhood gangs vary in many respects with the objectives of helping a family to acquire social competence. However, the goals with respect to the members of the group and the family need to be examined together to be sure that the work proceeding with one is not impairing the work that is proceeding with the other.

A social worker may wish to use other kinds of group activities as a social resource—group activities that are under the auspices of an existing social welfare agency but are not problem-related in any fashion. Thus the group facilities that exist in recreation departments or group activities available through YM or YWCA's offer resources for normal interaction of individuals with their peers.

AGENCY STRUCTURE AND POLICY AS A HELPING RESOURCE

The Public Assistance Agency

It is not unusual to find that in many communities the traditional abhorrence of dependency in our culture and the societal attitudes that swirl about the funding and policy-making aspects of public assistance deter people who are in financial straits from applying for the assistance for which they possibly are eligible. Sometimes such people find their way to other agencies or helping sources—a minister, for example—who are not in a position themselves to help the needy family and who undertake to refer the family to the appropriate public welfare agency. Because of lack of understanding of the objectives and administration of such a public organization, or because of the personal feelings of the referring person about official agencies (and attitudes about authority and limits), those making the referral often do so reluctantly and communicate this to the applicant, deliberately or unintentionally. There may be a reality factor to the reluctance if the particular public agency is one that even in our "enlightened" times gives inadequate or adequate assistance in a restrictive or punitive fashion. But conveying to the troubled applicant a mood of hostility creates an additional barrier to be hurdled by the needy person who has no recourse but to request the aid. The referring agency or individual, in these kinds of situations, can help the applicant to face the reality of his situation and to take the action necessary if he is to handle his pressing needs. In addition to informing the applicant about eligibility factors he might need to be prepared to understand, the referring agency (and staff), if it is able to base its concern about negative public agency operation on facts, should not abrogate the responsibility for taking appropriate measures to strengthen the position of the public assistance agency as a *positive* community resource to help troubled families.

Sometimes reluctance to make a referral to the public assistance agency grows out of a "protective" attitude toward the needy family by the referring source. One of the objectives in helping troubled families and individuals is to remain in contact with reality while they deal with the stressful problem; avoiding the use of a vital community agency to "protect" the family (assuming that this reaction does not derive from an assessment of facts in a given situation that may give valid rise to the question of referral) in actuality does the family a serious disservice in many ways, including delay that might add to the economic distress and encouraging a "looking away" from reality.

Legal Requirements

This wish to protect the family from what might prove to be a painful experience may arise with regard to a specific policy, such as the Uniform Reciprocal Support Act, and the uneasiness about the application of the procedures related to this Act may be shared equally by the public assistance agency personnel. Both the referring source and the public agency personnel need to examine such policies from the standpoint not just of their restrictive or negative aspects, but to identify the circumstances under which such a policy might actually serve as an important positive resource in the family's interest (in much the same way that we seek to find whatever might potentially be a strength in the seriously disturbed client!). The Uniform Reciprocal Support Act offers a pertinent example.

This requirement specifies that public assistance agencies notify the appropriate law enforcement officials when Aid to Families with Dependent Children is sought for children deserted or abandoned by a parent. The legislation represents our society's effort to deal with the gigantic problem of nonsupport from absent fathers and to insist that absent fathers assume and retain financial responsibility for the care of their children rather than relying on the community to do this. In many places, the procedures for implementation of this law make demands on a family that may be emotionally difficult, or even devastating, to meet. The woman who is fearful that the absent father will renew a pattern of beating either her or the children if he is reinvolved with the family, or the woman who knows that the psychotic behavior of the father has a detrimental effect on the children or herself, may find it very hard to muster the courage to follow the legal steps required. There is no doubt that the indiscriminate application and implementation of the provisions of this mandatory legislation may have an undesirable impact on members of the absent father's family. But there are some circumstances under which, unwilling as the mother may be to permit the contact, the results to children are sufficiently beneficial in the long run to justify some insistence on compliance. For example, the mother who is separated or divorced from the children's father may declare that she will have nothing to do with him, that he has no interest in her or the children, that he does not love the children, and that he has therefore "no right" to be in communication with them. This kind of mother often conveys to the children how abused she has been by the father, that he has no affection for them, that they are better off if they are not exposed to his wicked and rejecting ways. The effect on the self-esteem of a child who believes that he is not worthy of his father's interest and affection was noted in the chapter on broken families. The young child who constantly hears that his father does not care for him ("he never sends him a penny!") has particular trouble in separating money and affection. The required contact with the father sometimes serves to mitigate some of the young child's hurt, if the father then does make some contribution; even though the child may be aware that the money was given involuntarily, the *fact* remains that it *was* given. For some children, this *fact* has special positive meaning.

There also are many situations in which anger and inability or failure to communicate with each other prolong the father's absence. The necessity for compliance with the legal requirement has not infrequently served as a device for restoring communication between the father and the family, with temporary or long-term positive results.

There is other meaning to the child's development in an enforced continuing relationship reflected through the giving of support money even if the father remains estranged. The father's absence generally deprives the child of an adequate parental model, but the fact that there is continuity in financial contributions leads to some recognition on the part of the child that there are certain responsibilities that fathers are expected to assume and fulfill; one is providing for the family.

The law may require it, but there is reason to believe that it is fruitless for the social worker to endeavor to reach a father whose desertion of the family is not recent. The extended absence of the deserting father counterindicates the likelihood that he would be willing or able to carry any responsibility for the child's socialization. The same dynamics that led to the father's desertion probably will be present in his failure to give financial or other support to his children. In contrast is the separation which was preceded by some discussion, no matter how violent, with the mother. The fact that the father *plans* the separation to some extent with the mother is a clue to a greater readiness to feel some concern about the children and his relationship to them. Divorce or legal separation is a more responsible way than desertion for handling differences. If there has been some form of legal or understood agreement between the parents, this implies a continuing responsibility for and interest in the family members. In such instances, the mandate in the legislation may serve as a social resource of great value.

The implications, then, of the Reciprocal Uniform Support Act for contributing to the development of personality formation in children are several. There is need for the social worker and the mother to consider together what benefits will accrue to children if efforts to reach the father are pursued. This involves knowing something about the circumstances which led to his departure, whether it was sudden, whether there were warnings, whether it was discussed in advance. It involves deciding which has the more positive impact on children: some contribution and therefore connection with the father who may *seem* loving, whether he is or not, or a complete break with this important figure in the children's life.

Agency Assistance As a Motivator

It is not uncommon in an agency, voluntary or public, for the worker to observe behavior on the part of the adults that is inimical to the welfare of the children but to feel at a loss about how to intercede in the children's behalf if the parent seems unresponsive to any rational consideration of the impact of this behavior on the development of the children. At the risk of using material services as an entering wedge that might result only in superficial conformity in order to continue receiving the financial or other tangible help, it is possible to utilize such concrete services as a device for breaking a cycle of inappropriate behavior. The assistance the agency has available thus can be a social resource serving as a motivator. This can be illustrated by the case of the Kovacs family. Mr. Kovacs had come to the United States with his wife and two daughters as displaced persons after four years of displaced persons' camp life. He had considerable difficulty in making an adjustment to independent living in the urban center where he was located by the sponsoring agency. Years of living by his wits in order to survive, followed by years of complete and forced dependency, had contributed to the formation of an attitude of expectation that *somehow* his needs would be met either by some supernatural being (to which he attributed his survival during the war years) or human beings (who had assumed responsibility for him first while he was a camp resident and then for bringing him out of the camp to a new country).

The worker had focused on the strengths that had been evidenced by the fact of Mr. Kovacs' survival under extremely unfavorable circumstances and had helped him to channel these into again becoming a self-supporting, relatively independent person. From time to time he turned to the agency because of a crisis and expected that no question would be raised about why he did not handle the crisis himself, even though it might be minor and easily encompassable by him. When Mrs. Kovacs died of cancer after being bedfast for two years of constant need for intensive nursing care, Mr. Kovacs threatened to leave his work in order to care for the two daughters, now sixteen and eighteen years of age, and a two-year-old daughter. He thought the three girls needed his constant supervision. In order to enable Mr. Kovacs to retain as much self-dependence as was possible for him, it was thought that a homemaker should not be placed by the agency in the home, that it would be preferable for Mr. Kovacs to employ a housekeeper, with the agency supplementing his earnings sufficiently to pay the difference between what Mr. Kovacs could afford and the actual cost of the housekeeper. This plan was acceptable to the father and was put into effect. It soon became apparent that Mr. Kovacs relied on his two older girls to replace the mother and wife. Lisa, the older girl, had wanted to become a nurse, but Mr. Kovacs could not spare her from the household responsibilities. Sixteen-year-old Martha became illegitimately pregnant (see Chapter 9). The two-year-old was running completely wild, was out of control because Mr. Kovacs would not permit the housekeeper—a woman in her seventies—to exercise any kind of control over the child. The family's situation deteriorated steadily.

It was clear that Mr. Kovacs could not be reached in terms of what was good and important for his daughters, that he was preoccupied with his own needs and wishes, and those of his children were secondary. Efforts to counsel with him were met with indifferent silences. Finally the worker reached a decision: it was essential for Lisa's own life that the plan for nurses' training she had so desired but abandoned be reinstated; it was essential that Martha be protected from acting-out again as a consequence of the tensions and expectations in the household. Two-year-old Bess needed help in channeling her emotional and her physical energies. The worker announced to Mr. Kovacs that the wages of the housekeeper would no longer be subsidized by the agency. Because of the needs of the three children, however, the agency would provide a homemaker, but with the conditions that Lisa would be allowed to go to school and Martha, too, could undertake a specified school program. The girls would need to be freed of carrying so much responsibility for Bess and for their father. It would be the homemaker's task to maintain the household, serve as a buffer between the older girls and the father to the extent this was needed, and provide the youngest child with the kind of care essential to her. Mr. Kovacs was given no alternative between accepting the homemaker and having the agency discontinue any subsidy for the inadequate housekeeper he had employed. The worker recognized that, left to his own devices, Mr. Kovacs could employ only the same kind of housekeeper he already had: he had evidenced his "willingness" to employ a housekeeper, but she had to be completely under his control, which was possible only when he could select someone elderly, passive, almost infirm, with little prospect of finding other work. Faced with the ultimatum from the agency, Mr. Kovacs acquiesced, but only after both Lisa and Martha had threatened to leave home, with Martha announcing it would not be hard to be "a street walker." In this instance, the concrete service of the agency was used authoritatively in the interests of protecting the children, for the likelihood was remote that Mr. Kovacs would alter his own attitudes and behavior patterns, but new vistas could be opened for his three daughters.

The Kovacs family and the decision concerning conditions of aid has its counterpart in public assistance agencies also. The question has long been debated whether nonfinancial help can be effectively utilized by the person who is dependent on the same agency for his survival. The question has its roots in days when public assistance administrations were commonly restrictive, their emphasis on determining *ineligibility* and, when someone was found to be eligible, giving him no more than actually was essential for survival. It was assumed that any change in the recipient's behavior would be superficial only and would be a response to a need to *appear* to meet the worker's expectations of change in order to assure that the economic assistance would not be reduced or otherwise jeopardized. It was assumed also that people who were in need of economic assistance by and large could function effectively in our society if the single need for money for maintenance were met; furthermore, it was unjust to "impose" social services on an economically needy person. In times when public assistance case loads have chiefly comprised families whose primary need was due to loss of income through circumstances beyond their control, such as changing economic conditions or the death or permanent disability of the breadwinner, there was greater validity for the concern. But now many families in need of economic assistance for such reasons are covered by the social insurance provisions; as a consequence, the proportion has risen of public welfare families with severe social or psychological problems that are either the result of, or the contributor to, the need for economic help. A substantial number of these families are distrustful, as was described in Chapter 13.

Cultural, social, economic, and psychological factors have combined in some to stifle personality development necessary for reasonably effective social functioning in our society. Experience in recent years has demonstrated repeatedly that many of these families are part of a "culture of poverty" and their personalities are characterized by lack of trust, by low self-esteem, by hopelessness which precludes their thinking ahead in any kind of a planful way toward a different or better or more satisfying way of life. Experience also has demonstrated that the mere fact of persistent, unobtrusive interest on the part of the social worker can create a climate which is somewhat favorable for the development of some trust and some self-esteem.

If the social worker meets a critical need of the family at the point that it arises and without condemnation or judgmental reactions even if the crisis was of the family's own making, the deprived family begins increasingly to turn to the worker for emotional support and with some expectation that perhaps, after all, with the worker's help something can be done to deal with otherwise overwhelming problems. Such a relationship is long in the making and requires much persistence on the part of the worker before the essential quality of trust begins to appear. The fact of proximity and accessibility of the worker can be instrumental in opening the doors to work with the family around problems that are not necessarily related to the economic situation of the family. The illustration of the Scott family (Chapter 14) indicates how the long-term contacts, which are first around financial assistance and then move to other levels of meeting social need, can lead to a modification of behavior and result in effective participation in the community's life.

Recent experience of public welfare departments in locating of-

fices near or in a public housing project have disclosed the value of
the continuous accessibility of the worker to the troubled family and
the impact of the worker's warm interest on the family's incentive to
mobilize its energies in the direction of more effective functioning.
For example, Mrs. Adams told the research interviewer who was
engaged in identifying the positive and negative factors involved in
this kind of physical accessibility of the worker, that the fact that the
worker asked about her children, wanted to know how they were
getting along in school, and invited the children themselves to visit
the office to chat with him, caused her to feel very anxious and suspicious of his motives. Was he trying to see whether she was a good
mother? Was he trying to see whether her children were good? But
after a number of months in which she would pass him on the side-
walk and he would speak pleasantly to her, identify each of her children by name, and the children began to stop by the office to say
"hello," she realized that his interest was sincere, that he wanted her
children to have advantages that she may not have had. It was six
months before she could bring herself to ask him whether he thought
her fourteen-year-old boy could get an education and to what it
might lead.

Mrs. Adams had been "unreachable" in three years of dependence
upon public assistance. She had been polite when a worker called on
her, she had reported to the district office as required, she had filled
in numerous forms and answered various questions; but she had always maintained a strong reserve, never volunteering a word that was
not absolutely necessary, never seeing the worker as a person, and
expecting that the worker did not see her as a person. "Now," she
said, "somebody worries about me." The prognosis for Mrs. Adams
and her children has been considerably improved, not because the
worker took any carefully defined action toward altering her behavior
and that of the children, but because she felt that he saw her as a
human being. After Mrs. Adams became able to talk with the worker
about her children, she was able to approach him about what had
gone wrong in her marriage, to tell him she planned to remarry. How
could she handle herself so that this new marriage would not terminate by desertion of the husband? A referral for family counseling to
a specialist in this area proved successful.

Mrs. Adams was ready to begin a new life, her ability to deal
adequately with the new—and the old—tasks enhanced because a
worker moved patiently within the agency structure until Mrs. Adams
could see in it a resource to be trusted, and a social resource for utilization in gaining mastery of her problems in living.

SUGGESTED READINGS

PART ONE
The Family in a Changing World

Allport, Gordon W., *The Nature of Prejudice*, Doubleday, New York, 1958.

De Jesus, Carolina, *Child of the Dark*, Dutton, New York, 1962.

De Schweinitz, Karl, *People and Process in Social Security*, American Council on Education, Washington, D.C., 1948.

Feldman, Frances Lomas, *The Family in a Money World*, Family Service Association of America, New York, 1957.

Galbraith, John K., *The Affluent Society*, Houghton Mifflin, Boston, 1958.

Goffman, Erving, *Asylums*, Doubleday, New York, 1961.

Harrington, Michael, *The Other America*, Macmillan, New York, 1962.

Parsons, Talcott, and Robert F. Bales, *Family, Socialization and Interaction Process*, The Free Press, New York, 1955.

Schorr, Alvin, *Filial Responsibility in America*, U.S. Government Printing Office, Washington, D.C., 1960.

Towle, Charlotte, *Common Human Needs*, National Association of Social Workers, New York, 1952.

Weller, Jack E., *Yesterday's People*, University of Kentucky Press, Lexington, 1965.

Wilensky, Harold L., and Charles N. Lebaux, *Industrial Society and Social Welfare*, The Free Press, New York, 1965.

PART TWO

Developmental Tasks in the Cycle of Family Life

Agee, James, *A Death in the Family*, McDowell, Obolensky, New York, 1957.

Beck, Dorothy Fahs, "Marital Conflict: The Course and Treatment as Seen by Caseworkers," *Social Casework*, XLVII (4), April 1966.

Birren, James E., *Handbook of Aging and the Individual: Psychological and Biological Aspects*, University of Chicago Press, Chicago, 1959.

Cary, Joyce, *Charley Is My Darling*, M. Joseph Ltd., London, 1951.

Fraiberg, Selma, *The Magic Years*, Scribner's, New York, 1959.

Hartwell, Elizabeth E., "The Disadvantaged Elderly," *Social Work Papers*, Vol. 11 (F. Feldman, ed.), University of Southern California, Los Angeles, 1964.

Hemingway, Ernest, *The Old Man and the Sea*, Scribner's, New York, 1952.

Josselyn, Irene M., *The Adolescent and His World*, Family Service Association of America, New York, 1952.

Josselyn, Irene M., *Psychosocial Development of Children*, Family Service Association of America, New York, 1948.

Lewis, Oscar, *Five Families; Mexican Case Studies in the Culture of Poverty*, Random House, New York, 1959.

O'Neill, Eugene, *Long Day's Journey Into Night*, Yale University Press, New Haven, 1955.

Roth, Henry, *Call It Sleep*, Avon Books, New York, 1964.

Salinger, J. D., *Catcher in the Rye*, Little, Brown, Boston, 1951.

Scherz, Frances H., "Considerations for Involving Children in Treatment," *Social Casework*, XXXIX, (2-3), February-March 1958.

Scherz, Frances H., "Family Interaction: Some Problems and Implications for Casework," *Ego-Oriented Casework* (H. J. Parad and R. Miller, eds.), Family Service Association of America, New York, 1963.

PART THREE

Special Problems in the Cycle of Family Life

Clark, Margaret, *Health in the Mexican-American Culture*, University of California Press, Berkeley, 1959.

Richardson, Henry B., *Patients Have Families*, The Commonwealth Fund, New York, 1945.
Simon, Ann W., *Stepchild in the Family*, Odyssey Press, New York, 1964.
Vincent, Clark, *Unmarried Mothers*, The Free Press, New York, 1961.
Young, Leontine R., *Out of Wedlock*, McGraw-Hill, New York, 1954.

PART FOUR
Requisites for Social Functioning

Ellison, Ralph, *The Invisible Man*, Random House, New York, 1952.
Erikson, Erik, *Childhood and Society*, Norton, New York, 1950.
Erikson, Erik H., "Identity and the Life Cycle," *Psychological Issues*, Vol. I, No. 1, International Universities Press, New York, 1959.
Godden, Rumer, *China Court*, Viking, New York, 1961.
Green, Hannah, *I Never Promised You a Rose Garden*, Holt, Rinehart and Winston, New York, 1964.
Greenacre, Phyllis, *Trauma, Growth, and Personality*, Norton, New York, 1952.
Hansberry, Lorraine, *Raisin in the Sun*, Random House, New York, 1959.
Kaufman, Bel, *Up the Down Staircase*, Avon Books, New York, 1964.
Levin, Meyer, *Compulsion*, Simon and Schuster, New York, 1959.
Parad, Howard J., and Roger Miller, *Ego-Oriented Casework*, Family Service Association of America, New York, 1964.
Pettigrew, Thomas F., *A Profile of the Negro American*, Van Nostrand, Princeton, New Jersey, 1964.
Riesman, David, *The Lonely Crowd*, Yale University Press, New Haven, 1950.
Rubin, Theodore Isaac, *Jordi; David & Lisa*, Ballantine Books, New York, 1962.
Tolstoy, Leo, *Anna Karenina*, Oxford Press, London, 1919.
Wheeler, Keith, *Peaceable Lane*, Simon and Schuster, New York, 1960.
Wheelis, Allen, *The Quest for Identity*, Norton, New York, 1958.
Wilson, S. J., *Hurray For Me*, Crown, New York, 1964.

PART FIVE
Helping Troubled Families

Ackerman, Nathan W., *The Psychodynamics of Family Life*, Basic Books, New York, 1958.
Feldman, Frances Lomas, *The Family in a Money World*, Family Service Association of America, New York, 1957.
Fenton, Norman, and Kermit T. Wiltsie, *Group Methods in the Public Welfare Program*, Pacific Books, Palo Alto, California, 1963.

Garrett, Annette, *Interviewing: Its Principles and Methods*, Family Service Association of America, New York, 1943.

Green, Bernard, ed., *Psychotherapies of Marital Disharmony*, Grove Press, New York, 1965.

Hamilton, Gordon, *Theory and Practice of Social Casework*, Columbia University Press, New York, 1959.

Hollis, Florence, *Casework: A Psychosocial Therapy*, Random House, New York, 1964.

Kaufman, Irving, and Beatrice Simcox Reiner, *Character Disorders in Parents of Delinquents*, Family Service Association of America, New York, 1959.

Perlman, Helen Harris, *Social Casework*, University of Chicago Press, Chicago, 1957.

Rogawski, Alexander, "The Unique Opportunities of Public Assistance Workers to Help Families in Crisis," in *Family Mental Health Papers*, Mental Health Development Commission, Los Angeles, 1964.

Rubin, Theodore Isaac, *Sweet Daddy*, Ballantine Books, New York, 1963.

Scherz, Frances H., "Multiple Client Interviewing-Treatment Implications," *Social Casework*, XLIII (3), March 1962.

Scherz, Frances H., "Family Treatments Concepts," *Social Casework*, XLVII (4), April 1966.

Scherz, Frances H., "Exploring the Use of Family Interviews in Diagnosis," *Social Casework*, XLV (4), April 1964.

Selby, Lola, "Social Work and Crisis Theory," *Social Work Papers* (F. Feldman, ed.), Vol. 10, University of Southern California, Los Angeles, 1963.

Towle, Charlotte, *Common Human Needs*, National Association of Social Workers, New York, 1952.

Weisberg, Miriam, "Joint Interviewing with Marital Partners," *Social Casework*, XLV (4), April 1964.

INDEX